No. 1424
$19.95

CONSTRUCTING TABLES AND CHAIRS... WITH 55 PROJECTS

BY PERCY W. BLANDFORD

TAB BOOKS Inc.
BLUE RIDGE SUMMIT, PA. 17214

Other TAB books by the author:

No.   894 *Do-It-Yourselfer's Guide to Furniture Repair & Refinishing*

No.   937 *Modern Sailmaking*

No. 1044 *The Woodturner's Bible*

No. 1179 *The Practical Handbook of Blacksmithing & Metalworking*

No. 1188 *66 Children's Furniture Projects*

No. 1237 *Practical Knots & Ropework*

No. 1247 *The Master Handbook of Fine Woodworking Techniques & Projects*

No. 1257 *The Master Handbook of Sheetmetalwork . . . with projects*

No. 1312 *The GIANT Book of Wooden Toys*

No. 1365 *The Complete Handbook of Drafting*

No. 1454 *Constructing Outdoor Furniture, with 99 Projects*

No. 1504 *53 Space-Saving, Built-In Furniture Projects*

No. 1574 *The Illustrated Handbook of Woodworking Joints*

No. 1634 *Rigging Sail*

FIRST EDITION

SECOND PRINTING

Printed in the United States of America

Library of Congress Cataloging in Publication Data

Blandford, Percy W.
    Constructing tables and chairs . . . with 55 projects.

    Includes index.
    1. Tables.   2. Chairs.   I. Title.
TT197.5.T3B58   684.1'3   82-5692
ISBN 0-8306-2424-4   AACR2
ISBN 0-8306-1424-9 (pbk.)

Cover illustration by Keith Snow.

Contents

Introduction

Tables and chairs are the most used and most wanted pieces of furniture. These items are both attractive and functional.

Once man had acquired tools and the skill to use them, he started making furniture from wood. His early efforts developed from rather crude pieces to the beautiful chairs and tables by Chippendale and his contemporaries. Alongside these specimens of advanced cabinetwork were the more functional items described as "cottage" or "farmhouse" furniture. These items were produced by skilled woodworkers who did not have the artistic skills nor the financial backing to do more than cater to ordinary people's needs. These pieces of furniture are the prototypes of handmade furniture today.

The basic table pattern has a flat top and a leg at each corner. The seat is a flat top supported on legs, possibly with a back added. These basic concepts are subject to many interpretations, and much of this book considers variations on the theme. The seat may be at a convenient height, but its means of support can be dealt with in different ways. Chairs may be rigid, or they can fold. Tables may vary in size with the use of flaps and extensions. From the examples given in this book, an ingenious craftsman can design his own furniture.

Much furniture today is produced in quantity in factories. Some designs are quite attractive, but they are produced to suit quantity production. They may be adaptations of tables and chairs that were once hand made, but construction and some design points have been altered to suit production methods. An individual craftsman wanting to make furniture should not imitate mass-produced items. Some of the furniture may provide ideas, but remember that you have the facilities and ability to do things that the machine cannot.

It is worthwhile looking at tables and chairs that were produced before the Industrial Revolution. Some of the work of early immigrant craftsmen is particularly interesting. Obviously, some of it is crude and not worth considering, but the better examples of Colonial furniture can be examined. Similarly, there are comparable pieces of furniture made in Europe at about the same and earlier times. Do not necessarily make slavish copies, but see how the craftsmen did their work, particularly how they made their joints. Incorporate the ideas in tables and chairs that you make.

We are living in a machine age. Therefore, it makes sense to use mechanical aids, even in a small shop. There is no virtue in sawing wood to size by hand, nor for doing the first planing by hand, when a machine will reduce the labor. You may not want to employ machine-made joints where a hand-cut joint may be more appropriate. Plywood has made possible large panels of stable wood. Unless you are trying to reproduce an antique, there is nothing wrong with using plywood or other prepared material that is appropriate to modern needs.

There are materials lists for the projects described in this book, but little guidance on the choice of woods. Local supplies vary, and you may want to match existing furniture. Nearly all furniture should be made of durable hardwoods and given a protective finish that shows the grain. Softwood may be fine for basic things, and paint can be used on children's tables and chairs. This is not a book on how to make hammer-and-nail things or projects where rapid construction is the main virtue.

There are working drawings for all of the projects, usually in the three views of two elevations and a plan, which are the only ways of showing dimensions to scale. There are also accompanying pictorial and other views. The original drawings were made to scale, but in reducing to fit the book there may be slight variations. Sizes that are not immediately obvious can be found by comparing with something on the same view that is dimensioned. All sizes given are in inches unless otherwise marked. Where a view is symmetrical and only part of it is given, the centerline is shown by the draftsman's method of long and short dashes.

You should familiarize yourself with the contents of the first four chapters. To avoid too much repetition, some of the information that is needed for many projects is only given in those early chapters. Similarly, if the project chosen comes late in a chapter, it is advisable to skim through earlier projects in the same chapter to pick up points that may be of use in the later work. All relevant information, though, is given with each project, assuming that you have a knowledge of basic cabinetwork.

All the information you need to make anything described is given in this book. If you want to know more about a particular facet of furniture making, you may find my books useful.

If you want to learn more about tool handling, the making of joints, and woodworking in general, the book for you is *The Woodworker's Bible* (TAB book No. 860). *The Master Handbook of Fine Woodworking Techniques & Projects* (TAB book No. 1247) tells how to make quality furniture. If you want to delve further into the making of upholstered chairs, consult *The Upholsterer's Bible* (TAB book No. 1004). For the many methods of finishing wood, read *Do-It-Yourselfer's Guide to Furniture Repair & Re-Finishing* (TAB book No. 894). *The Woodturner's Bible* (TAB book No. 1044) explains the use of a lathe and the many things that can be made with it. If your need is furniture for children, get a copy of *66 Children's Furniture Projects* (TAB book No. 1188). *How to Make Early American and Colonial Furniture* (TAB book No. 1114) is another useful book.

I hope you will find this book helpful and that you will enjoy making furniture. May your tables and chairs be things of which you can be proud.

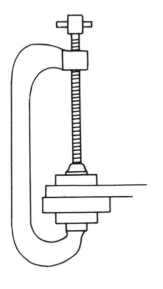

Chapter 1

Furniture Making Tools and Techniques

An important consideration when planning tables and chairs is attitude. The craft of cabinetmaking is one of the more skilled woodworking activities. You have to approach the work rather differently from house carpentry or outdoor woodwork, where the standards are not as high. There is very little hammer-and-nail work in the construction of good furniture, and you have to adopt a more painstaking and patient approach when the parts you make need a high degree of precision in their sizes and the cutting of joints. You have to aim at a greater degree of craftsmanship. Although skill is valuable, much can be accomplished with care and a slower approach. This may not be the economical way for anyone hoping to earn a living, but time is something of which an amateur has plenty. Some of the finest examples of modern furniture have been produced by amateurs, but they have been labors of love.

While you cannot make tables and chairs without tools, the number of tools you need may not be great. Obviously, a large collection of tools will be valuable, but good work can be done with a basic kit. Advertisers would have us believe that every shop should contain their products—particularly expensive machines. As with hand tools, a large range of power tools may be

valuable. Our craftsmen ancestors of not so long ago produced the finest work entirely with hand tools, sometimes aided by a few simple machines.

If you are starting from scratch and want to make tables, chairs, or other furniture of good quality, your first needs are the basic hand tools. An electric drill may be an early power tool buy, but your available money will be better spent on good hand tools than on more costly power tools. The basic tools that have stood the test of time are generally more useful than newer items for which special claims are made.

There are generally no tool bargains. Good ones are fine investments. You may get good used ones cheaply from a retired craftsman, but price is usually a good guide to quality when buying new tools. There are many established companies in the tool trade. They have a reputation to maintain, so their catalogs can be regarded as guides to excellent tools. Very cheap imported tools are not worth having. If they are cutting tools, the steel used may not be capable of taking and keeping a good edge.

BENCHES

You cannot make furniture without a rigid and substantial surface on which to work. Usually this takes the form of a *bench,* but for occasional use there may be a plank of heavy section that can be attached temporarily to a table or mounted on trestles. There may be a vise permanently attached to it, or you can use one that clamps on. If you can find the space for a complete bench, good work is much easier to achieve.

Many excellent benches are imported from Europe. The benches are usually made of *beech,* which is a good working surface that wears for a long time, due to its hardness and closeness of grain. The benches have one or more vises and usually other holding devices, along with storage drawers or cupboards. Such a bench is attractive. Its cost may not be justified, though, while you still have a limited amount of money to spend on tools.

A simpler bench can be made at little cost. You have to provide a working surface stout enough to withstand the loads imposed in planing, cutting, and assembling joints, and similar work. A heavy table is needed. The front part of the tabletop should be heavy and hard. The front piece should be possibly 12 inches wide, more than 2 inches thick, and be a close-grained hardwood. Although hardwood may be attractive for the rest of the bench, you can use softwood salvaged from some other structure.

Height should be about 30 inches, but you can tailor the bench height to your own height. Support a board temporarily and plane a piece of wood on it. Experiment to find a comfortable working height. It is better to err on the low side; you can keep up the effort longer than you would on a high surface. There is an advantage in length. Even if you never make anything longer than 48 inches, sometimes you will want to prepare long strips before cutting them into several parts. If there is a space limitation, you can manage with a bench 36 inches long, but twice that is better. Attaching a bench to a wall insures rigidity, but there are advantages in a freestanding bench which lets you go all round the thing you are assembling. If the bench is built-in, it should be more than 24 inches wide. A freestanding bench can be narrower.

When you make a bench, get firm joints and brace everything, so nothing can be formed out of shape under working loads. A simple construction is shown in Fig. 1-1. The leg assemblies can be halved and bolted or screwed (Fig. 1-1A). The top parts rest on the assemblies and are screwed down, with plugs over the screws (Fig. 1-1B).

The thinner board at the center acts as a well for tools in use. The board can be loose, so it can be knocked out. Clamps can be put through to hold wood you are working on or to pull assemblies together. Both sides should be hardwood for a freestanding bench. If the bench is attached to a wall, the rear board can be softwood. The top working surfaces must be true and level with each other.

Under the front top board is an *apron.* The apron supports the top under load and may have holes in it to take pegs which will support long work held in the vise (Fig. 1-1C). Make sure it is square to the top surface. You can put a shelf on the leg rails or completely enclose the lower part with doors or drawers. Any additional construction of this sort helps to stiffen the whole assembly.

The *vise* is an important part. There are wooden ones, but a parallel-action metal one fitted with wooden jaws is accurate and rigid at all opening positions. Fit it through a hole in the apron at a height that allows the metal jaws to be sunk and covered with wood. The inner piece is level with the bench edge (Fig. 1-1D). If you are right-handed, mount the vise towards the left-hand end.

Another thing you need is a *bench stop.* For planing and other actions, you need to work on wood with a motion that tries to push it along the bench, and this has to be resisted. The simplest stop is a piece of wood across the bench (Fig. 1-1E). You can buy adjustable stops to let in or through the bench top, but a simple adjustable one goes through the leg. It can be a piece about 1½ inches wide and 1 inch thick, but sizes are not critical. Friction will hold it, and adjustment is by hammering up or down (Fig. 1-1F). Such an arrangement may wear loose, and you can provide locking with a bolt and butterfly nut through a slot (Fig. 1-1G).

When you put down a plane, it should go on its side, so the cutting edge is not on the bench. You can put a strip across the tool well (Fig. 1-1H), and the plane will slope over that with its cutting edge clear. You may drill holes in the bench top for attaching holdfasts, but do not have any metal on the surface. After long use, you may want to true the top by planing all over.

Besides the bench itself, you will want a lower support. This is usually a trestle or a pair of them. Height may be about 20 inches, and the top is about 30 inches long. You can sit on the trestle to hold down the wood on which you are working. One knee will hold wood while sawing it. Two trestles will hold a full sheet of plywood while you are marking it out or cutting it.

The usual trestle has splayed legs (Fig. 1-2A). There are metal pieces available for joining on the legs, or you can let them into the top and brace them under it (Fig. 1-2B). Draw a side and end view full-size to get the lengths and angles of the legs. You can sit on a trestle for work at the bench like fretsawing, but in most shops an old wood-topped chair without its back can be used as a seat or another trestle.

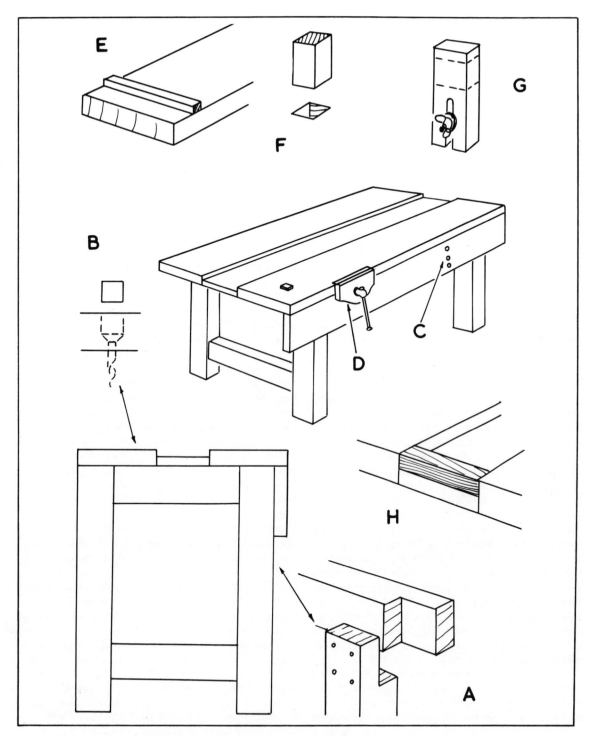

Fig. 1-1. Your bench is an important item, and you can make it yourself.

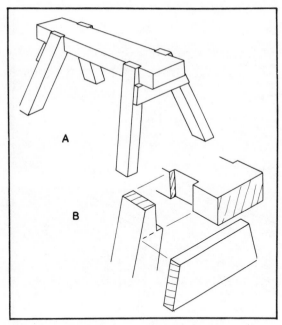

Fig. 1-2. A trestle gives firm support at a lower level than a bench.

SAWS AND SAWING

Much work on the bench is done with a *backsaw,* preferably about 12 inches long, with 16 teeth per inch. Even if you have a power saw, hand sawing is required in the making of tables and chairs. These handsaws may be *tenon saws* or *dovetail saws.* Those names are misleading, though as the saws are general-purpose bench saws.

Sawing on the bench is best done with *bench hooks,* preferably two that match, although for small pieces you work on one. Regard them as disposable. Chopping or cutting that may damage the bench top can be done on them. Replace them after much damage. A simple form has pieces doweled together (Fig. 1-3A). If you prefer to use screws, sink and plug over the heads. If the crossbars are cut short, the saw going through damages the hook instead of dropping onto the bench (Fig. 1-3B). The cut-back may only be at the right, if you are right-handed, but there are occasions when cuts will have to be at the other side. Make the length of a hook enough to go about the full width of your bench's front board (Fig. 1-3C).

When a saw cut is wanted exactly at the line, and with the minimum of raggedness of grain, mark with a knife instead of a pencil. This happens frequently at the shoulder of a tenon or the end that will take dowels. If you then pare on the waste side of the line, that makes a groove (Fig. 1-3D) which will guide the saw.

Other saws that you will need are a *panel saw,* maybe 24 inches long with 8 teeth per inch, for cuts greater than can be made with the backsaw, and a saw for curves. A *jigsaw* attachment for the electric drill, or a separate powered jigsaw, may cut all your curves, or you can do hand cutting with a *coping saw.* If you hope to make many items of furniture, particularly if they are to be for sale, a powered *band saw* is a desirable tool that will make straight and curved cuts through quite thick wood.

MARKING OUT

Furniture parts have to be marked and assembled accurately, or discrepancies can often be very obvious in the finished work. Have a straight steel rule, preferably 24 inches long. Besides measuring, it is a straightedge for testing surfaces and edges. For greater measurements, an expanding tape rule is a good choice. Folding rules may be traditional, but they have been superseded for cabinetwork.

You need at least one *try square* for testing squareness. If you only have one, it should be with a 12-inch blade (Fig. 1-4A). It is useful to have a smaller one, but a *combination square* will serve that purpose and others (Fig. 1-4B). Practice holding the stock of the square against the edge of a piece of wood with the thumb of one hand, while fingers press it and the blade down on the wood. If you test wood for squareness of section, always look toward a light so you can see clearly under the blade.

There is a sequence of preparing wood that should be followed whether you do it all by hand or have the help of a jointer. First, get one of the broad surfaces flat and true. Test with a straightedge in the length, across and diagonally. That is the *face side,* and there is a traditional mark to put on it (Fig. 1-4C). Next, get the *face edge* straight and square with the face side. When that is true, put its mark meeting the other (Fig. 1-4D). If it is a long piece of wood, put the marks elsewhere as well if you wish.

All other measuring of width and thickness should be done from the two face surfaces. If the wood is to go through the table saw, it is a face surface to be downward and the other against the fence. You need a *marking gauge* for hand marking to width and thickness (Fig. 1-4E). Basically it is a sliding head that can be locked on a stem, with a spur that projects. You set the spur at the right distance from the head and push the gauge along the work, tilted forward (Fig. 1-4F). Keep the head against a face surface and scratch the width parallel to it. Do this on both sides of the wood, and then plane down to the lines before gauging and planing the other way.

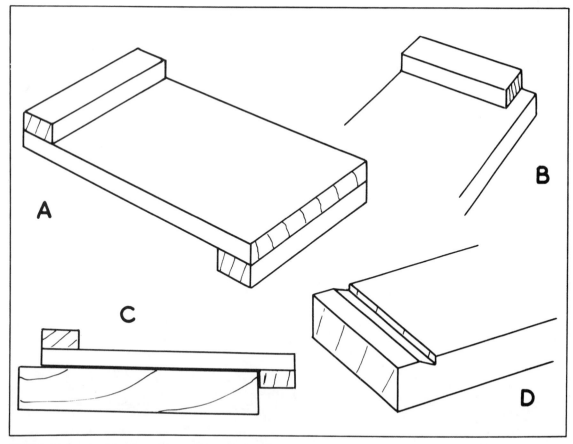

Fig. 1-3. A bench hook holds work for sawing on the bench.

Further marking of the wood is done with the square against a face surface and by measuring from one. When you come to assemble the work, all face surfaces of adjoining parts come in the same plane. By doing that, usually on the outside, you get faces level and any slight errors of size on the other side, where they are less important.

Not all marks and cuts in furniture are at right angles. For the other angles you need an *adjustable bevel* (Fig. 1-4G), which can be set and locked where needed. Use it like a try square with a pencil or knife.

PLANES AND CHISELS

Your cutting or *edge tools* are important parts of your kit. If all your wood is machine-planed, you may be able to have just a *smoothing plane,* such as the Stanley or Record 4 or 4½. You almost certainly need a plane with a longer sole, such as a *jack* or *trying plane,* for getting edges

straight, particularly when two have to be glued together. Wooden planes may still be obtainable, but for general use it is better to have steel planes. Another useful and inexpensive plane is a *block plane.* It is about 7 inches long and can be used in one hand for many smaller cuts, particularly across the grain.

Before you get very far into the making of tables and chairs, you will need to cut *rabbets* (Fig. 1-5A) and *grooves* (Fig. 1-5B). Some jointers can be set to make rabbets. It is possible to set a table saw to make cuts both ways and produce rabbets. The alternative is a hand *rabbet plane.* There are several ways to make grooves. You can cut several passes with a circular saw. You can mount a wobble saw in place of the ordinary blade and make a groove. The hand tool is a *plow plane,* which has blades of many widths to suit the grooves needed. A plow plane will also cut small rabbets.

Chisels are end-cutting knives. As you progress in furniture making, you will accumulate chisels. The

5

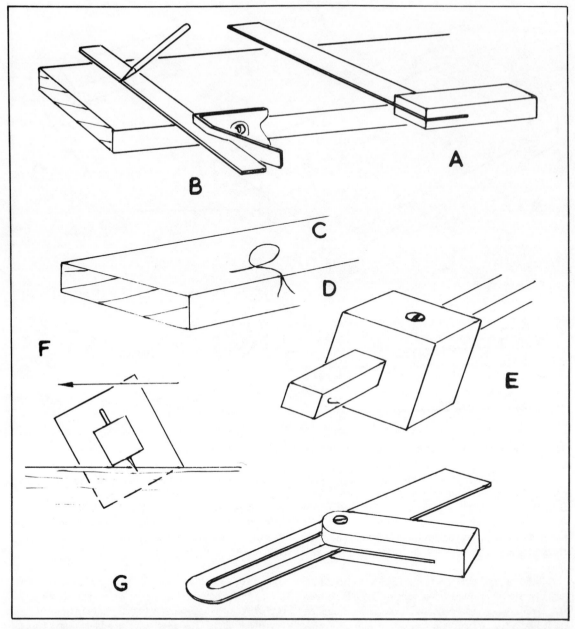

Fig. 1-4. Square lines (A and B) are important. Face surfaces are marked (C and D). A marking gauge scratches lines parallel to an edge (E and F). An adjustable bevel (G) can be set to any angle.

general-purpose ones are called *firmer chisels* (Fig. 1-6A). Get them bevel-edged (Fig. 1-6B). These chisels will cut into angles less than right angles and do all that a square-edged chisel will. At first you can get ½-inch and 1-inch widths, but you can buy more as you need them.

Firmer chisel handles can be hit with a mallet, which is less likely to damage them than a hammer. Longer, thinner *paring chisels* are not meant to be hit, but their greater reach has uses in cabinetry. *Gouges* are chisels curved in cross section.

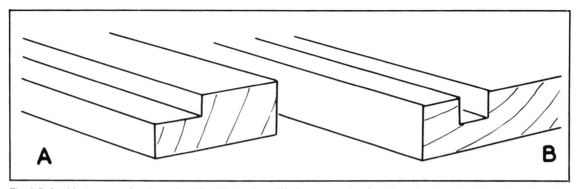

Fig. 1-5. A rabbet, on an edge, is made with a fillister plane (A). A groove, away from the edge, is made with a plow plane (B).

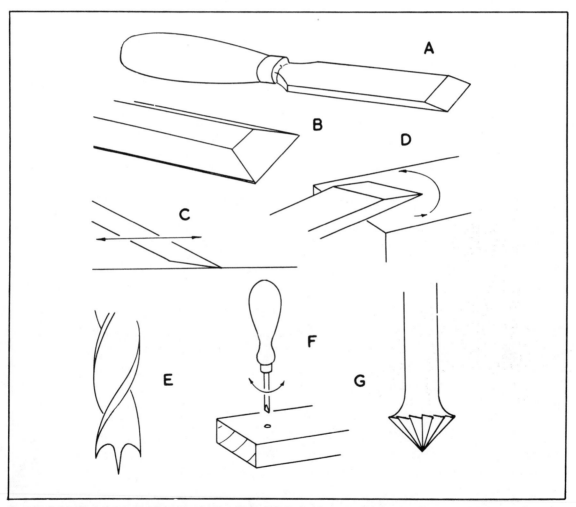

Fig. 1-6. A chisel may have square or bevel edges (A and B). Both sides are rubbed on an oilstone for sharpening (C and D). Drill bit, bradawl, and countersink (E, F, and G) deal with holes.

Obviously, edge tools have to be sharpened. You should have a coarse and a fine *oilstone.* They may be called *whetstones,* but to many people that implies the use of water. You should use a fine oil, such as light lubricating oil or even kerosene. For plane blades and chisels, get stones about 2 inches wide, 8 inches long, and 1 inch thick. The coarser one can be Indian or Carborundum manufactured grit. The fine one may be similar, or you can get Washita or Arkansas natural stone. Mount each stone in a wood box or hollowed block and provide a cover.

Sharpening is done on one side with the bevel downward (Fig. 1-6C). Move all over the stone to avoid uneven wear on it. Continue until you can feel a roughness on the flat side. That is the *wire edge* that has been rubbed from a keen edge. Remove it by rubbing flat on the stone (Fig. 1-6D) with a circular motion. For touching up an edge, you may only need to use the fine stone. If you first use the coarse stone, wipe the tool clean before moving to the fine one, so no coarse grit is transferred.

Sharpen frequently. A common fault of a beginner is to work with blunt tools.

DRILLS AND DRILLING

The general-purpose drilling tool for furniture making is a *brace,* with drills of many sizes that fit in its chuck. Even if you have an *electric drill,* there are situations where only the brace is suitable. Unfortunately, you need a separate drill bit for each size hole. There are expanding and adjustable bits, but they only have limited applications. For small holes to take nails or screws, metalworking twist drills that fit the electric drill or a hand-operated *wheel brace* are the best choices, up to about ¼-inch diameter. They need not be the high-speed steel drills for metal, but can be the cheaper carbon steel *jobber's drills.* Above ¼ inch there are woodworking drills intended for an electric drill. Get the twist drill versions (Fig. 1-6E), rather than the spade type, which will wander in the wood if used for deep holes.

There are many types of woodworking bits to use in a brace, mostly going upward in 1/16-inch steps from ¼-inch diameter. For most purposes your best buy is those bits with twisted flutes, a screw center, and two cutting spurs. Irwin is a well-known make of this type. Other bits without the twists are only suitable for shallow holes. These bits can be the choice for large sizes, say more than 1¼ inches, which do not usually have to be taken very deep.

A cabinetmaker favors the traditional *bradawl* for small screw or nail holes. Its chisel-shaped end (Fig. 1-6F) is entered first across the grain; then it is moved about one-fourth circle each way as it is pressed in. The advantage over a drill is that it does not remove wood. Instead the severed fibers are pushed back, and they will cling better to a screw as it is entered. Bradawls are easy to make in diameters up to ⅛ inch.

You need one or more countersink bits. They hollow the top of a hole to take a screwhead. The traditional cabinetry type is a snail countersink, which uses a single cutting edge, but today you are more likely to get the rose type with many cutters (Fig. 1-6G). There are versions to fit an electric drill chuck, but countersinking is better done slowly. The type to fit a brace chuck is a better choice.

FASTENINGS

A cabinetmaker has little use for nails. Assembly is usually via fitted and glued joints. If a nail is chosen, it is likely to be an *oval brad.* An oval brad goes in with its narrow way across the grain, and there is less risk of splitting. You have some use for *pins,* which is the general name for fine nails with small heads. They can be punched below the surface, then covered with stopping on an exposed surface. For this work you need a few *nail punches* of different diameters (Fig. 1-7A). A hollowed end is supposed to reduce the risk of slipping off a nailhead. Although you can buy punches cheaply, you can make them by filing or grinding pieces of steel rod or thick nail. Nails are sold by weight and graded by length and type. The system of grading nails by *penny* sizes is not applicable to the types used for furniture.

The household *hammer* may serve your cabinetmaking needs. It is the flat face that matters. Avoid a chipped one. A 12-ounce hammer will do for general work, but you can come down to 4 ounces for driving pins. A cross-peen hammer has a narrow crossed part opposite the main face, and that has some uses in restricted places. You also

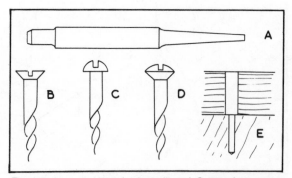

Fig. 1-7. A punch (A) sinks the nailhead. Screws have many heads (B, C, and D). Clearance and pilot holes are needed for screwing (E).

need a mallet to use instead of a hammer on chisels or for hitting wood. There are special cabinetmaking mallets, but any mallet of reasonable weight will do. For assembly, you can put scrap wood on the work and hit it with a hammer.

Ordinary screws have flat heads (Fig. 1-7B), but there are some places in furniture where it is better to have round heads (Fig. 1-7C). Raised or oval head ones may be needed for attaching metal parts (Fig. 1-7D). The length of a screw is from the surface of the wood, and within each length there are several gauge sizes. Common sizes are: ½ inch by 4 gauge, ¾ inch by 6 gauge, 1 inch by 8 gauge, and 1½ inches by 10 gauge. Screws are made in many metals. The common steel screws are suitable for many places in furniture, but a cabinetmaker prefers brass which cannot rust. Oak, in particular, will attack steel and cause rust.

The ordinary slotted screwheads are all you need. Phillips and other star-shaped slots are really intended for quantity production. You can use them, but they need special drivers. Holes for screws should always be carefully drilled, with a clearance hole in the top piece and a tapping hole in the bottom part. The screwing action pulls the top piece tight on the lower part (Fig. 1-7E). If the screw has to cut its way into the top part, it will not pull it downward. A screwhead may pull itself into some woods, while others may need only partial countersinking to help pulling in. Make a test before countersinking holes.

You need screwdrivers of many width ends to suit different screws. At first it is best to buy plain screwdrivers. The number of screws in any particular piece of furniture is not usually great, so the labor of driving is not much. Ratchet and pump-action screwdrivers can come later if you feel you need them. If you use Phillips-head screws, there will have to be at least three different sized drivers to suit them. It is possible to get screwdriver bits to fit a brace. If you use large screws, a brace makes tight driving easier. In some situations there may not be enough space for a normal screwdriver, so you may have to buy a few special short ones.

JOINTS

In general carpentry much of the work involves putting one piece of wood on top of another and attaching them with nails or screws. A cabinetmaker will always cut joints to fit parts together if that is possible. Occasionally he uses nails or screws, but many pieces of furniture are without metal fastenings.

Modern glues have made joints even stronger. There are many synthetic glues that are considerably stronger, and most of them are water-resistant. Some traditional joints that relied on interlocking parts are not so important, as glue will now keep less complicated joints together. Most of the available glues are suitable for furniture. Read the descriptions. The glue should be described as for wood only. If the glue is suitable for paper and other materials, it is not intended for furniture. If a glue is described as suitable for boatbuilding, it has a high resistance to moisture. Such glues are also mechanically strong. If a glue is in two parts, observe the directions, particularly the timing, if you want to get the best results. There are a few glues with a rather strong color. That may not matter with dark woods, but a dark glue line on lighter colored wood is not acceptable.

Although modern glues are stronger than the traditional ones, they need surfaces that fit closely. Some may be described as gap filling, but that only means very slight gaps. There is little strength in a thick piece of hard glue. Strength comes from a close fit and penetration of the glue into the wood pores. If you need to fill a space due to a mistake in cutting a joint, mix sawdust with the glue and press it in. The glue will then bond to the sawdust and the wood surfaces. Otherwise, it crazes with many fine cracks and loses its strength.

A simple joint is the *half lap*. If two rails have to cross level, half is cut out of each (Fig. 1-8A). If one is thicker than the other, very little is cut out of the thin one, and the other is cut to match. A half lap can be used at a corner. It is not the best choice for the corner of a frame, but if it is stiffening behind plywood, there can be a lap at the corner (Fig. 1-8B) and intermediately.

For a frame another corner joint is a *bridle* (Fig. 1-8C), with the parts usually one-third the total thickness. A similar joint is sometimes used at a corner of a boxlike assembly, and that is a *comb joint* (Fig. 1-8D). It is cut with a jig on a powered machine and is not a traditional cabinetmaking joint.

Mortise and Tenon Joint

The joint used more than any other in traditional cabinetmaking is the *mortise and tenon*. The mortise is a hole, and a tenon is the tongue cut to fit into it. Between two parts of the same thickness, a through mortise and tenon joint has the tenon one-third the thickness of the wood (Fig. 1-9A). A stopped or stub mortise and tenon joint does not go right through (Fig. 1-9B). A through joint may be tightened with wedges outside the tenon (Fig. 1-9C), or a central wedge is driven into a saw cut (Fig. 1-9D). It is possible to wedge a stopped joint by foxtail wedging. Two wedges are put in saw cuts. As the joint is

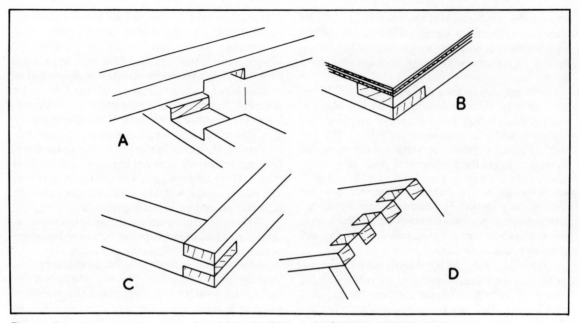

Fig. 1-8. Parts are lapped at crossings (A and B) or fitted into each other at corners (C and D).

drawn tight, they press on the bottom of the mortise and spread the tenon (Fig. 1-9E).

If a tenon comes at a corner or end, it may be cut back (Fig. 1-9F), or a haunch is stronger (Fig. 1-9G). If you do not want that to show, the haunch can be tapered (Fig. 1-9H). A problem comes with deep parts. Having a tenon too deep may weaken the part with the mortise by cutting away too much of it. The tenon may be in two, with a shallower dividing piece (Fig. 1-9J). The idea can be carried onto any number of tenons on a wide board.

In furniture, rails may have to join legs or other uprights in two or more directions. It is often possible to bring them in at different levels, so the tenons do not meet (Fig. 1-10A). If they have to come at the same level, it is sometimes possible to bring them toward the outside of the leg, so tenons can be long enough without interfering with each other.

In many constructions the rails have to be at the same level, so the only way of dealing with them is to miter the meeting ends. Be careful that the miters do not meet before the shoulders of the tenoned parts have come tight on the surface (Fig. 1-10B).

If the part with the tenon is fairly thin in relation to the other part, it can be barefaced, so there is a shoulder at only one side (Fig. 1-10C). One advantage is in the ease of pulling the joint tight. If you have the usual two shoulders and do not cut them exactly level, with each other,

one will pull tight while the other side shows a gap. In any case, when the tenoned part is much thinner than the other, make the tenon more than one-third the thickness of the wood for greater strength.

Dovetail Joint

The other traditional cabinetmaking joint is the *dovetail*. The dovetail may be hidden, but it is sometimes left exposed because of its attractiveness. The shape of the cut obviously resists pulling apart in one direction. Some craftsmen have particular preferences for the tail angles, but if you settle for one in seven, that is about right (Fig. 1-11A). You make a little bent metal template or set an adjustable bevel to the angle. Some old-time cabinetmakers were proud of their ability to make the pins between the tails extremely narrow (Fig. 1-11B). It is better to make them a little wider. It is possible to cut dovetails by machine or with an attachment for an electric drill. The result shows the pins and tails the same width (Fig. 1-11C). Such joints are perfectly good ones, but if you want to show your skill at cutting dovetails by hand, avoid this spacing and keep the pins narrower.

The width to make the tails is a matter of planning to suit the width of the wood. As a rough guide, the width of a tail should not be more than twice the thickness of the wood. The pin width should be about one-third of that, but

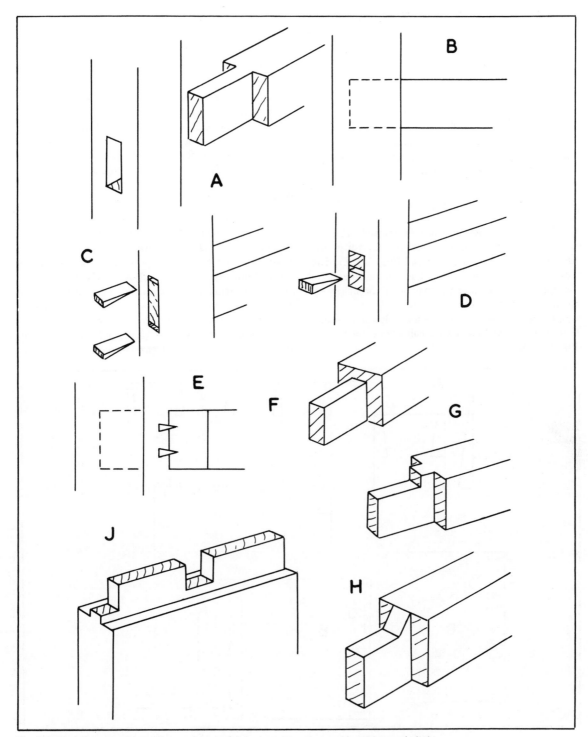

Fig. 1-9. Variations on the mortise and tenon joint are commonly used in tables and chairs.

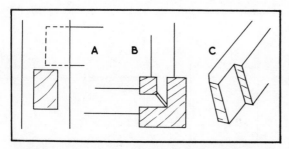

Fig. 1-10. Rails into legs may be at different levels (A) or mitered (B). Narrow strips can have barefaced tenons (C).

you will have to adjust sizes as you space the divisions to suit the width of wood (Fig. 1-11D).

The simplest dovetail joint goes through. This occurs at many corners, but for places like drawer fronts, the dovetail joint has to be stopped (Fig. 1-11E). The distance to cut back depends on the total thickness. Do not make that too thin, or you may break through when chopping out the sockets. For a drawer front, you may want to include a plowed groove for a plywood bottom. That can be hidden by arranging half a tail at the bottom (Fig. 1-11F).

There are many other versions of the dovetail joint. It can be used to strengthen a half lap joint (Fig. 1-12A). You can even dovetail it both ways (Fig. 1-12B). It is actually stronger than the other version.

Besides the stopped dovetail, which shows the joint formation on one surface, you can make it hidden by stopping in the other direction as well (Fig. 1-12C). The joint still shows the overlapping edge. Even that can be hidden by making a mitered dovetail joint, where there is a mitered part outside the joint both ways (Fig. 1-12D). This is certainly not an easy joint to cut.

Dowels

The old-time cabinetmaker made his *dowels* in short lengths as he needed them. He did not use them in so many applications as we do today. Modern doweled joints have come about mainly because they adapt easily to quantity production. A doweled joint can be made almost completely without handwork, but mortise and tenon joints do not lend themselves so well to machine work.

There are many applications in furniture construction where dowels make an acceptable alternative to mortise and tenon joints. At least two dowels in a joint are

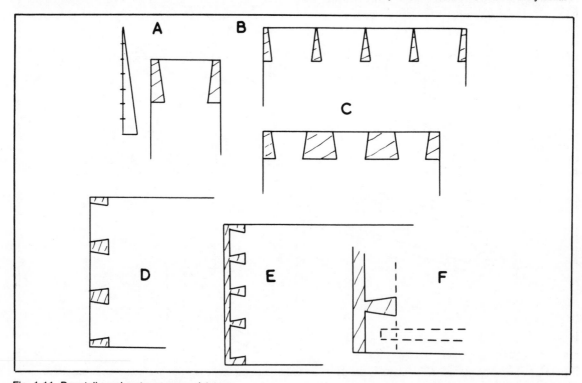

Fig. 1-11. Dovetails make strong corner joints.

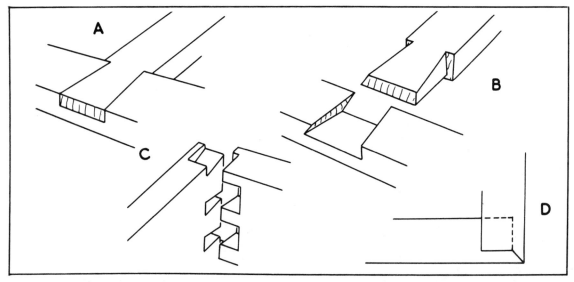

Fig. 1-12. Dovetails may combine with lap joints (A and B). They can be stopped (C) or secret (D).

needed to prevent twisting, and they should be of a size that will give a surface glue area comparable with the tenons they replace. The dowel diameter and the number of dowels should be chosen to suit the joint. As a rough guide, the dowel diameters should be approaching two-thirds of the thickness of the thinner wood. There should be not much more than their diameter between them. The depth to take them is not critical, but normally they should penetrate at least twice their diameter (Fig. 1-13A).

If you cut dowels from a long rod, eliminate any roughness at the ends by beveling all round. The holes drilled should match the dowels. A dowel coated with glue acts like a piston, and you must arrange for air to escape. Otherwise, the wood may burst. Some prepared

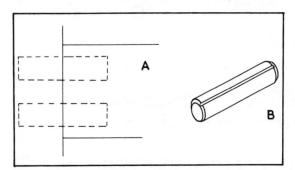

Fig. 1-13. Dowels should have a good penetration and may be grooved to release air.

dowels have spiral grooves, but with your cut ones a saw cut along the dowel will serve the same purpose (Fig. 1-13B).

CLAMPS AND CLAMPING

It is no use cutting joints accurately if they are not then pulled tight when you glue them. A variety of *clamps* are worth having. If you make much furniture, you may feel you never have enough. There are ways of improvising and reducing the need for clamps, but there is no alternative to owning several.

For anything within their capacity, C-clamps are good. Some large ones may not close to as small gaps as some small ones, but you can always use *packing blocks* (Fig. 1-14A). These are advisable in any case to spread the pressure and avoid damage to the wood surface. For small parts you can put weights on top instead of clamping, while the glue sets.

You need *bar clamps* for longer distances. They may be heads to fit on the edge of a board or on a tube, or long clamps with their own bars. Pull directly over a joint (Fig. 1-14B). If you find an assembly is out of square, slightly angling the pull may correct it (Fig. 1-14C).

Some of this type of clamping can be done with the aid of wedges. A block on a stiff board can have a wedge driven in (Fig. 1-14D). A better arrangement uses folding wedges. Have two identical wedges and drive them in opposite directions to get a parallel thrust (Fig. 1-14E).

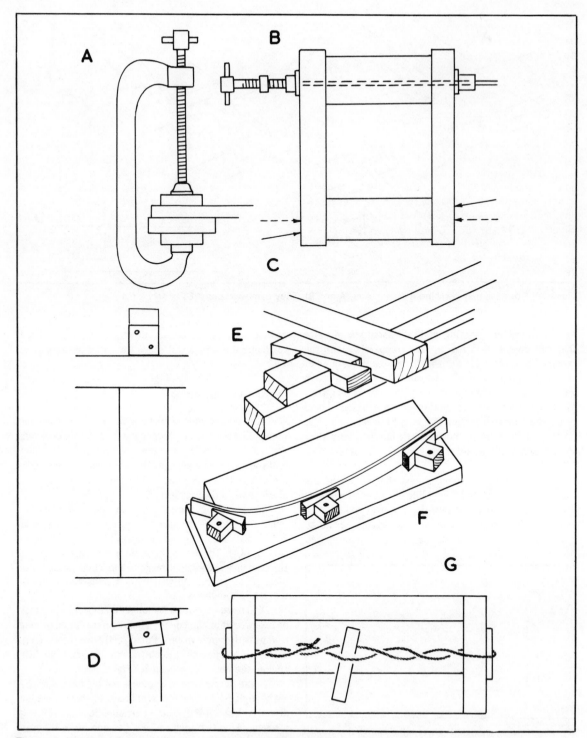

Fig. 1-14. Joints may be pulled together with clamps, wedges, or rope.

Wedges can be used if you want to bend wood, possibly laminated, around a former (Fig. 1-14F). The base needs to be quite stout, as the local loads are considerable.

Another way of pulling parts of a frame together uses rope as a *Spanish windlass*. Put one or more turns around over scrap wood. Know the ends together. Use a strip of wood and twist the rope to put on pressure. Wedge the strip against something (Fig. 1-14G). If there is nothing within reach, tie it to the rope.

If you cannot spare a clamp to stay there until the glue has set, it is often possible to drive a nail into the joint from inside where it will not show. Remove the clamp to use elsewhere. The nail prevents the joint from loosening during the setting time of the glue (Fig. 1-15A). Similarly in larger joints, a hole can be drilled from an inner surface and a dowel put far enough in to hold the tenon, without being visible on the outer surface. If a tenoned joint is wedged, the action of driving the wedges will probably be enough to hold the joint after the clamp has been removed.

There is a traditional way of tightening a tenoned joint, possibly in a position where clamping may be impossible or difficult. Drill across the mortise for a dowel. Drill a similar hole in the tenon, but position it a short distance nearer the shoulder, so when the joint is assembled it does not line up with the other hole (Fig. 1-15B). Taper the end of the dowel slightly and drive it through, so it pulls the tenon tighter into its mortise.

SYMMETRY

A piece of furniture must look right. If legs are supposed to be upright, they should look so from all directions. If corners are supposed to be square, there must be no doubt about it in the viewer's eyes. If opposite sides slope, they must match so as to make a pair. That is *symmetry*. There are a few examples of symmetrical furniture, but then the unusual shape is obviously intentional.

Right angles can be checked with a try square as far as that will go. If you have a 12-inch square and the corner is 36 inches across, a slight error at 12 inches becomes a more pronounced one at 36 inches. If you have a frame that should have square corners, the way to check accuracy is to measure diagonals. You can use a tape rule, but there is always the risk of misreading a graduation one way. It is better to use a strip of wood and pencil its edge (Fig. 1-16A).

The shape does not have to be square for this method. If taper is meant to be the same both sides, as in a chair seat, diagonals should still be the same (Fig. 1-16B) when you have the correct symmetrical shape.

For anything like a four-legged table frame, it is always best to assemble opposite sides first. Check their squareness by measuring diagonals, then see that they match by putting one over the other (Fig. 1-16C). You also have to watch for twist with this sort of assembly. Sight across opposite sides (Fig. 1-16D). They should be parallel in your view line. If not, force them to the other way slightly, so they spring back true before the glue sets. If you have to do this, check diagonals again in case you have altered squareness.

With the glue set in the joints of opposite sides, you can assemble the parts the second way without the risk of the first two sides distorting. You now have more checking to get the shapes right. With the clamps on, check diagonals on both sides in the new direction (Fig. 1-16E). Check squareness by measuring diagonals at the top (Fig. 1-16F). Also check twist by sighting across the legs in the new direction at both sides and by sighting across the top rails. If the legs are the same length and the assembly is standing on a flat surface, the whole thing should be true, but there is one more test. Stand back as far as you can and sight through the assembly from several directions. It is possible for all the surface panels to be apparently

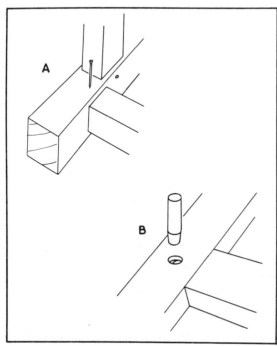

Fig. 1-15. Mortise and tenon joints may be held with nails or pulled together with pegs.

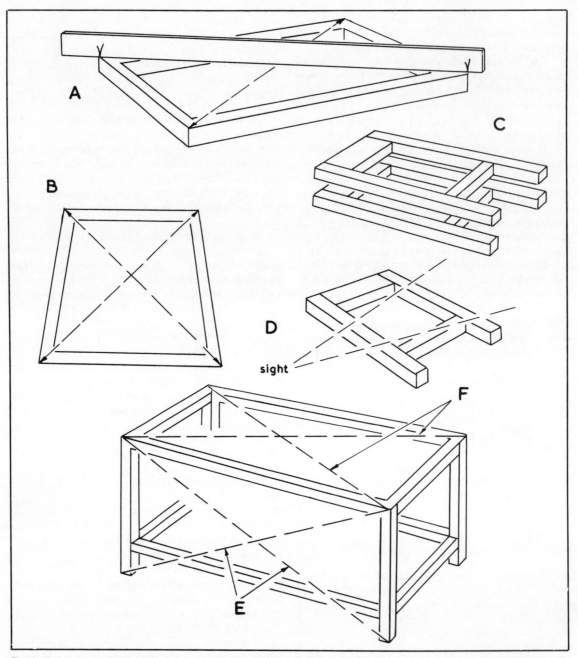

Fig. 1-16. Accuracy of assemblies is best checked by measuring diagonals. Matching parts should be checked against each other. Twist can be checked by sighting across surfaces.

square; yet there is an overall twist. As you look through the assembly, check that all legs are parallel as you view them. They almost certainly will be, but there may have to be slight correction. Finally, if there is any doubt about trueness, put a board over all four top rails and a weight on that while the glue sets.

16

Chapter 2

Basic Table Construction

When primitive man found something to sit on, he then needed a surface on which to prepare and eat meals. As he learned to use tools, he devised various tables. The methods of construction varied. We still use all sorts of table structures developed from the ideas of those early furniture makers. The obvious need is a flat working surface supported at a convenient height. It is in the arrangement of supports that there are the greatest differences, although tabletops can be of many shapes. There are many ways of making a table so the top can be reduced in area by folding or other means.

In early homes there was often a need for a table that could be taken down and be stowed away, possibly with its parts flat against a wall. The simplest table was made of a few flat boards that could be rested on anything convenient. The supports developed into folding trestles (Fig. 2-1A). Such tables were convenient for people like the pioneers moving westward, and they are still useful where extra tables are needed occasionally. The tables must be stored compactly, as in a meeting room used for many purposes. A further development was a takedown table, with the parts wedged or otherwise held together, so the completed table looked substantial. It could be disassembled into its component parts. Such tables and chairs were not necessarily crude. There are surviving

examples of attractive contemporary furniture used in the captain's quarters of fighting sailing ships. The pieces could be taken apart and stored when the ship was stripped for action.

There have been some designs with removable wedges and other devices in only part of the table structure. If the whole table cannot be taken apart, it does not seem logical to do this. The only exception may be where the wedges are used for decoration or for tightening if the wood shrinks. Some furniture that originated in Germany has prominent wedges in the underframing, but in this case the wedges are decorative and a feature of this particular style.

TABLE DESIGNS

The basic table is one with four legs arranged upright at each corner (Fig. 2-1B). A problem with four legs is the difficulty of making them stand level on an uneven floor. Three legs will always stand firmly, whatever the state of the surface, so some tables are made with three legs or with three feet projecting from a central pedestal. Three legs under a four-sided top will not look right, so the top may be hexagonal (Fig. 2-1C) or round (Fig. 2-1D). There are many attractive round tables with pedestal supports.

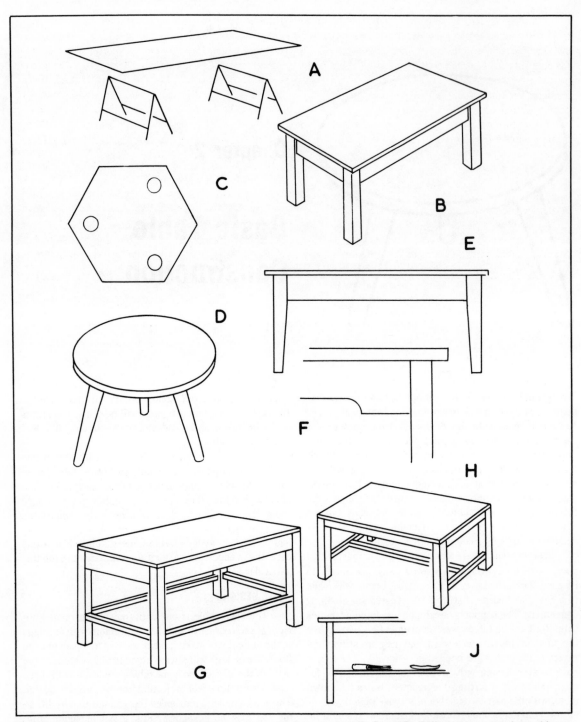

Fig. 2-1. Tables developed from trestles (A) through those with legs attached (B, C, and D). Stiffening can come from wide top rails (E and F) or lower rails as well (G, H, and J).

Four legs under a tabletop have to be braced, or the table will soon become shaky or even collapse. One way of bracing is to have deep rails at the top (Fig. 2-1E). It is the depth at each joint that provides stiffness. The central part of a rail may be reduced in depth (Fig. 2-1F), either for decoration or to provide clearance for the legs of a person sitting on a chair. Another method of bracing permits shallower rails under the top, but stiffness comes from rails lower down. They can be all round (Fig. 2-1G), or there is more clearance if lengthwise stiffness comes from a central rail (Fig. 2-1H). There are many variations on this, and rail arrangements are decorative features of many tables. A shelf attached to the legs, either directly or attached to rails, provides stiffening (Fig. 2-1J).

In another arrangement support comes from a pedestal at each end. Historically this probably followed the use of folding trestles, and the construction is some-times referred to as a trestle table, but that is not strictly correct. In one form there are four legs joined into sub-stantial cross members at top and bottom (Fig. 2-2A). A flat bottom will rock on an uneven floor, so shape it or put blocks under the ends to serve as feet (Fig. 2-2B).

There can be strong single pedestals at each end decorated by shaping, carving, or turning (Fig. 2-2C). The pedestals are joined by rails. There can be one deep piece at the center of the top or two pieces arranged further out. A bottom rail often has its section horizontal (Fig. 2-2E), but it provides better resistance to the rock-ing of joints if it is upright (Fig. 2-2F).

A different approach to table leg arrangements is to have them crossed at each end, making what is some-times called a sawbuck table, which is similar to an arrangement used to support logs being sawed by hand (Fig. 2-3A). In a rigid table there is a rail at the leg

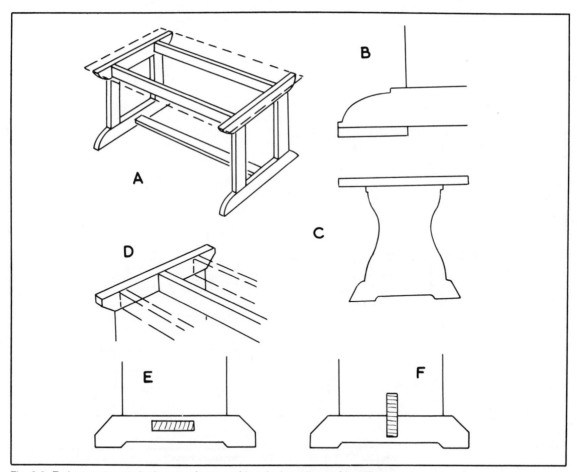

Fig. 2-2. End supports may be in many forms and lengthwise rails provide stiffness.

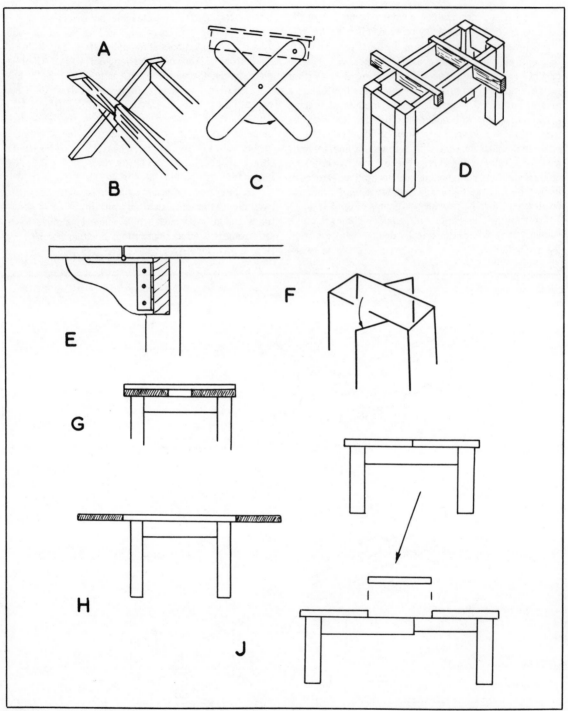

Fig. 2-3. Crossed legs (A and B) may also fold (C). Tabletops can have extensions supported in many ways (D, E, and F), or tops can extend with sliding (G and H) or removable pieces (J).

crossing and usually others joining the tops of the legs (Fig. 2-3B). The formation is also used to make a folding table. The legs pivot on a bolt at their crossings. The top is hinged to one pair of legs in such a way that the legs fold over each other, and the top folds against them (Fig. 2-3C).

FOLDING TABLES

It is convenient to be able to alter the size of a tabletop. If it is a dining table, it can then accommodate fewer or many diners. A side table can take up minimum space, but then be extended when needed. Usually part of the tabletop swings down when not required. This may be at opposite ends, although more often at the sides. Usually the drop flaps are at both sides to give a minimum area with them down—an intermediate size with one up and the maximum size with both flaps up.

Bars sliding through the rails under the central fixed part of the top may extend to hold up a flap (Fig. 2-3D). There can be hinged brackets (Fig. 2-3E). For a very wide flap, neither of these arrangements will hold the flap absolutely level. There is a risk of pressure on top tipping the table. For a broad flap, it is better for there to be a leg to the floor near its edge. This is arranged in a gateleg table (Fig. 2-3F), where a braced leg swings out like a gate. Such a table usually has quite a narrow central top, with most of the total area in the flaps.

Another way to nearly double the area is seen in a "draw-leaf" table. The closed top is square with a double thickness. The supporting framework is also square and rigid. It is not altered when the table is extended. The underpart of the top is in two sections on slides (Fig. 2-3G). They are arranged so they can be slid outwards far enough for the original top to fit between them (Fig. 2-3H); the extending flaps are supported by the slides.

Another arrangement has the framework arranged in two parts with rails sliding within each other. If the two parts of the table are pulled open, a loose section can be dropped in (Fig. 2-3J). Stiffness is provided by the sliding rails. In some substantial traditional tables, as many as three sections can be put in to more than double the total top area, but that arrangement requires skillful fitting of the rail parts.

DRAWERS

Drawers are fitted to many types of tables. A dining or kitchen table may have drawers at the ends or sides for *cutlery*. A desk table may have drawers under the top for writing materials, or the ends of the table can be blocks of drawers reaching to the floor.

A problem is arranging drawers is the allowance of clearance for anyone sitting and needing clearance for the knees. This means a drawer has to be shallower than may be desired. Another problem is the ease of sliding the drawer. A drawer which is wide in relation to its back-to-front depth may tend to stick due to wobbling as it is pulled (Fig. 2-4A). This can be eased by having two drawers in the same width (Fig. 2-4B). A drawer that is deeper than it is wide will slide more easily, so end drawers have better movements (Fig. 2-4C) than side drawers. If a table has broad flaps and a narrow central part, seating is then around the flaps. A table can have drawers of any depth in the ends of the center part (Fig. 2-4D).

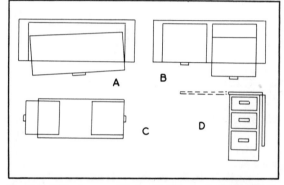

Fig. 2-4. Wide drawers (A) do not slide as easily as narrow ones (B and C), which can be stacked (D).

There are drawer slides obtainable that can be incorporated into table drawers, but it is more common to fit the drawer into wooden guides in the traditional way. Details of construction are given with actual examples later in the book, but the broad considerations are given here.

The drawer front and its rails should be the same depth as the rails at the sides of it (Fig. 2-5A). Some rigidity in the structure across the width of the drawer will be provided by the solid rail behind the drawer, but the narrow rails above and below the drawer front should be as stiff as possible and firmly jointed at their ends (Fig. 2-5B).

There have to be drawer runners that support and guide the drawer, so the side rails have their thicknesses made up to the inside of the leg, and other pieces are used for the drawer to rest on (Fig. 2-5C). The side pieces should be high enough to prevent the drawer from wobbling, and the runners underneath should extend wider than the edges of the drawer. Above the drawer at each

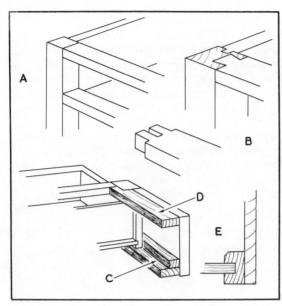

Fig. 2-5. Drawers need special rails with guides to control sliding.

side are kickers, which are strips the same thickness as the rail above the drawer front (Fig. 2-5D). They are there to prevent the drawer tipping downward as it is pulled out.

Details of drawer construction are given in later examples, but the sides have to slide easily. Most wear on the drawer comes on the undersides of the sides, and this area can be increased (Fig. 2-5E). The bottom of the drawer is always raised. The sides provide the bearing surfaces.

PLAIN TABLE

Although there are many table designs, there are certain details of construction that occur in many of them. The construction of a very basic plain table will illustrate these details. If they are understood, more advanced construction will be more easily appreciated. A plain table does not have to be ugly. There is a beauty in proportions. Avoid squareness if possible. An oblong or rectangle always looks more attractive than a square. The size in one direction somewhere between 1¼ and 1¾ the size the other way will look right. This applies to all directions from which a table is viewed, not just the size of its top. Suppose it is to be a table for use with a chair. The top has to be about 30 or 32 inches above the floor. It would then look good if it is 42 inches or more long and 20 inches wide. To clear a sitter's knees at least 24 inches

are needed, which means rails must not come more than 6 inches below the surface of the top.

If it is a coffee table, a side table, or some type other than one for use with a chair, there are not these limitations of size. Similar considerations should be given to proportions.

The example shown can serve as a kitchen table, although in good hardwood and attractively finished, it can be used in any room. Traditionally such a table was called a *tavern table*. Sizes are easily altered. Anyone inexperienced in making tables may find the production of one of these tables in any convenient size as a good introduction to the work (Fig. 2-6A).

We can make much stronger tables than our ancestors with modern glues. If joints are carefully cut and fitted, glue will provide ample strength. There should be no need for screws or nails. This table is without lower rails and depends on the deep top rails for stiffness.

The legs (Fig. 2-6B) are square and parallel to below the rail joints. Mark them all together (Fig. 2-6C). Do not cut off the excess length at the top until after the parts are joined. This protects the end of the wood and resists breaking out when the joints are being cut. Leave tapering the legs until after the joints have been cut; the wood will rest more firmly on the bench. Mark all round each leg. Use a knife against the square where cuts have to come, but otherwise use pencil.

JOINTS

The traditional way of joining the rails to the legs is with mortise and tenon joints having two parts in the depth (Fig. 2-6D). For a smaller table the tenoned parts could be *barefaced,* meaning that there is a shoulder only on the outside (Fig. 2-6E). This makes close fitting easier, as you do not have the problem of cutting two shoulders exactly opposite. Tenons should be between one-third and one-half the thickness of the rail.

The modern alternative is to use dowels (Fig. 2-6F). The number and thickness depend on the size of the wood, but there should be at least three dowels in the rail depth. Consider the glue area provided. It should be about the same as that of traditional tenons. Mortise and tenon joints are stronger and considered the more craftsmanlike method. If the section of the leg does not permit a good depth of tenon or dowel penetration without the tenons or dowels meeting each way, miter the ends. Allow a little clearance inside, so shoulders will pull tight.

Get the leg tapers even. With a suitable fence on a table saw, it is possible to remove most of the waste so

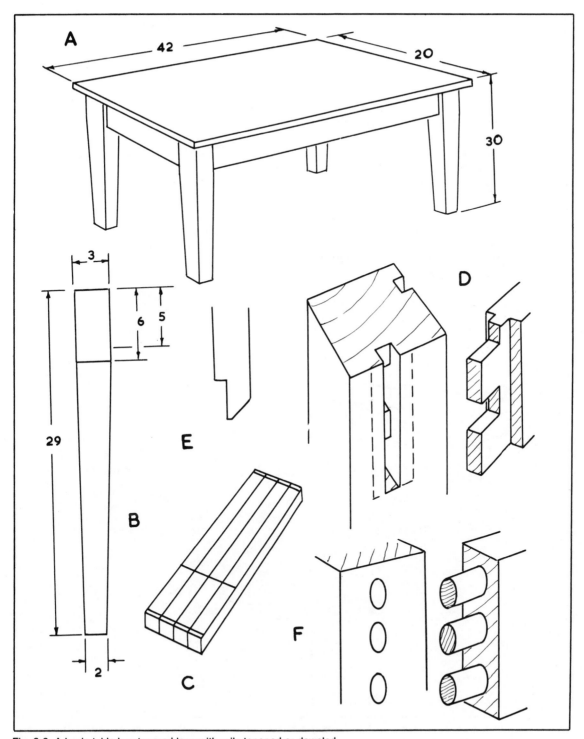

Fig. 2-6. A basic table has tapered legs with rails tenoned or doweled.

there is little to plane. Otherwise, taper by hand planing. Mark both surfaces for opposite sides and plane them, then mark the taper the other way and plane it.

ASSEMBLY

A finished table must be square in all directions. Any discrepancy becomes very obvious to a viewer, so care is needed to square the parts during every stage of assembly. Assemble the framework in two stages. Join a pair of legs with their rail and then the opposite pair to match them. Let the glue in these joints set before linking the opposite assemblies. Usually the first assemblies are the longer way. Pull the joints tight with clamps. If the clamps

have to be removed before the glue has set, dowels or nails can be driven from the inner surfaces of the legs into tenons or dowels (Fig. 2-7A).

The best way to check squareness is to measure diagonals, as the usual try square does not extend far enough. A piece of wood with pecked marks (Fig. 2-7B) is better than using a rule or measuring tape. Check that the assembly is not twisted, either by seeing that it rests flat on a true surface or by sighting one leg across the other. With one side known to be correct, check the second assembly by putting it in the correct relation over the first. The assemblies can be forced to the correct shapes while the glue is still soft. If the mortises or dowel holes

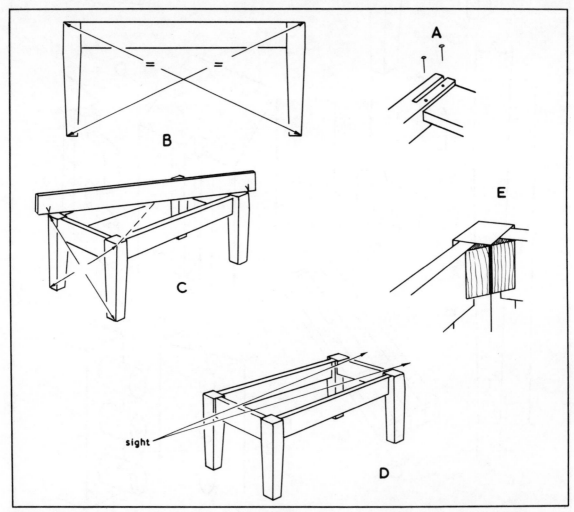

Fig. 2-7. Opposite sides are squared (A), then the assembly is checked for squareness (B and C), as well as twist (D). Corners may be strengthened with glued blocks (E).

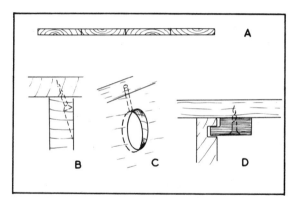

Fig. 2-8. Alternating grain reduces warping (A). Pocket screws (B and C) or buttons (D) hold the top to rails.

meet in the legs, make sure there is no surplus glue that will interfere with assembly. Wipe or scrape it out.

Add the rails the other way. At this stage you have to check diagonals across both ends, then diagonals across the top, while the table is standing on a true surface (Fig. 2-7C). Sight across the rails and legs in both directions to see that there is no twist (Fig. 2-7D). It is possible to get all parts true when checked diagonally, yet still have them twisted in relation to each other. Leave the assembly for the glue to set. If there is any tendency for the framework to twist or lift off the floor, put boards across the top to support weights while the glue sets.

Further strength in the corners can be provided by triangular fillets glued between legs and rails (Fig. 2-7E). These are almost as deep as the rails. Glue alone should be sufficient, although pins may be driven to prevent slipping. Level the tops of the legs with the rails. The whole surface should present a flat area to take the top. It can be tested by inverting on a flat piece of stout plywood or particle board.

TABLETOPS

The top can be a piece of veneered particle board or thick plywood, suitably edged, or it can be made up of several boards glued together. Any tendency to warp can be minimized if boards have their end grain opposite ways, as far as that can be arranged (Fig. 2-8A). Allow a good overhang all round. A greater overhang in the length looks better than making it greater in the width.

Edges can be left square. They can be rounded or molded. Shaping the edges or elaborately molding them is inappropriate for this type of table. Round the corners if the table is to stand in the body of a room. Even for a side table, the apparently square corners should be slightly rounded.

It is not good practice to attach the top to the framework with fastenings driven downward. It is better to leave the top surface free of marks. One way is to use *pocket screws*. The screw goes diagonally upward through the rail into the top, and pockets have to be cut with a gouge and chisel at intervals to let the screws in (Fig. 2-8B). A simple way of making a pocket is to use a large diameter bit in a brace. Enter it at right angles to the line the screw will take (Fig. 2-8C).

Fixing a top rigidly makes no allowance for the expansion and contraction of a wide top made of solid boards. Plywood and particle board do not suffer from this trouble, but solid wood can absorb and release enough moisture from the atmosphere to make an appreciable difference in the total width—enough to cause cracking or other trouble if the attachments are rigid.

One way of dealing with this is to use *buttons*. They engage with grooves plowed on the insides of the rails before assembly. Buttons are screwed at intervals around the underside of the top with their extensions free to move in the grooves (Fig. 2-8D).

Chapter 3

Basic Chair Construction

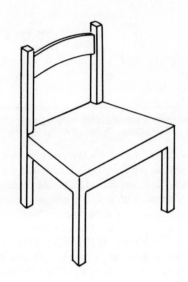

When early man changed from sitting on a rock to making furniture, he devised seats based on his anatomy. When be bent his knees, his thighs were supported at a height that allowed his feet to still touch the ground. He discovered that having an ample area to sit on was more comfortable than a small or narrow seat. He went on to add backs and arms to the seat, so he could relax. Those early seats were hard, and the idea of built-in padding did not come until much later. Instead, any softening was by skins draped over the stools and chairs.

Modern thought has to follow similar reasoning. A chair that does not conform to the shape of a person sitting on it will be uncomfortable and impractical. Making a chair to the wrong sizes is a waste of effort. Over the centuries the average person has got taller, and much of this development has come in the last century or so. If you visit an old building, you will find that the clearance under doorways is less than we would allow today.

Furniture today tends to be larger than some earlier examples. There is a difference between what we need and some of the classic designs of Chippendale and his contemporaries. We need an inch or so more on heights and areas. A modern lounge chair that we find comfortable would be too big for one of those ancestors, who would sit in it much as a child does in an adult chair today.

SIZES

We are not all the same size, so most furniture has to be made to average sizes. There are small chairs and high chairs to suit young children. Once a child has reached the age where he can attend to his own needs, though, he is expected to manage with standard adult furniture, even if it does not fit. One advantage of making your own furniture is that you can arrange the sizes to suit the user. If there is someone much bigger or smaller than the average size, a chair can be made to suit. The chair will provide much more convenience and comfort.

Most people when sitting upright are comfortable with a seat height between 15 and 19 inches. This is the height of their thighs. If the seat is hard, that is the chair height. If there is upholstery, allowance has to be made for compression. The usual height is 17 or 18 inches. The seat area is also important, particularly if there is a back. The width may be about 18 inches at the front, but from back to front is about 16 inches. The back of the seat is then narrower than the front on some chairs (Fig. 3-1A). There are several variations, but they take into account the posture of the sitter. Allow for a sitter bringing the chair to a table. The working height of a modern table is about 30 inches. A seat about 18 inches high allows for feeding and normal table uses for an average person. For

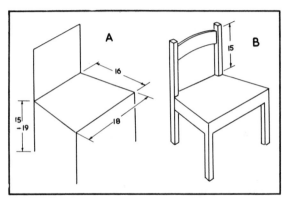

Fig. 3-1. Chairs have to be proportioned to suit an average person.

typing and some types of work, the chair needs to be several inches higher. For some purposes, there may be a need for a chair that brings the user's hands to about the same height they would be if he was doing the same thing standing.

If a chair is to be used for relaxing, it is usually lower and with a seat tilted back. Its back and front depth is greater to allow for the legs being angled forward rather than straight down. Such a seat usually includes thick upholstery, so the working sizes are those taken up under compression.

Much early seating was without backs—benches or stools. There are still uses for these seats. Lower versions suit children and may also serve as footrests. Benches and stools at normal height can be used at a table, and they may stow under the table more compactly than a chair with a back. If space is limited, two people can sit on a bench that takes up much less room than two normal chairs. A chairmaker producing seating for the home will usually find it worthwhile, including a few stools or benches. For the beginning woodworker, they are easier to make than most chairs.

Chair backs vary tremendously, mainly because they are used as decorative features. For practical purposes, support is needed in the curve of the back, and this is about 15 inches above the seat (Fig. 3-1B). Many chairs have backs continuing much higher. It is unusual today to take them to head height, but there are examples of chairs by the great furniture makers of past centuries where a high back is more of a decorative feature than an aid to comfort. There is a case for going higher than the small of the back, and many modern chairs have backs up to 24 inches above the seat.

A problem is the shape of the human body. If you sit on a flat, hard surface, your weight is concentrated on a few square inches under your hip bones. You will become uncomfortable after a short time. This is seen in the way an audience becomes restless after a short time on hard chairs when listening to a speaker, no matter how interesting he may be. One way of spreading the area of contact is to curve the seat front to back (Fig. 3-2A). If the curves are carefully designed, the thighs, as well as the hip bones, take the load. The sitter regards the seat as more comfortable.

A better shape is a compound curve, with the wood hollowed to be more like the shape of the sitter. This is seen in the seats of Windsor chairs (Fig. 3-2B). The effect is to spread the area of contact even more so, and the sitter regards it as a further step in comfort. With plastics that can be molded, it is possible to make seats that conform even closer to the body shape.

UPHOLSTERY

The average user will say that padding softens a seat. It does, but the padding gets pushed into shape to match the body sitting on it and settles to a degree of compression that conforms to a large area of contact. The larger the area of contact, the less is the actual weight on any particular spot. With padding there is movement when the sitter alters his or her posture, so the shape of support still conforms to the new position. Any rigid body support, such as the carved wood seat or the molded *polystyrene* shape, can only give the maximum comfort at one body position.

The value of upholstery has been known for a long time. Primitive man used loose skins as padding, but Romans and early Egyptians have left pictures of upholstered seats. One type is a slung piece of leather (Fig. 3-2C) which is still seen, although canvas is more common.

A further step is the interweaving of fabric pieces within a four-sided frame (Fig. 3-2D), giving a two-directional flexibility and a little more comfort. This is seen today in the weaving of rush, cord, and other ropelike materials to give a decorative pattern and some flexibility in a seat.

Upholstery in the more usual form has developed from loose cushions to built-in padding. Early upholsterers used materials such as straw, feathers, *kapok*, and anything that would compress and regain something like its original shape after release. More recent upholstery has included springs with wool covering. Flexibility of support was provided by interwoven webbing, similar to the strips described in the last paragraph. Coil springs were sewed above this webbing, with elaborate stringing

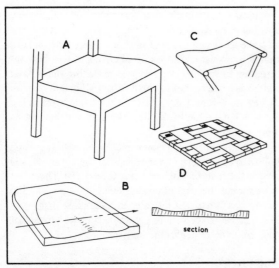

Fig. 3-2. Shaping or springing a seat with flexible supports adds to comfort.

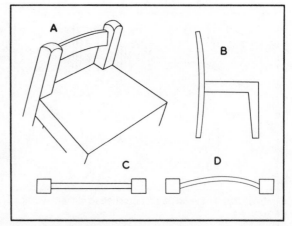

Fig. 3-3. Back rails may slope or the whole back can slope, with curves across for comfort.

and further layers of cloth and wool beneath the final cloth covering. That type of upholstery may still be found and new work may be done in that way, but for most purposes today it is simpler and satisfactory to use rubber or plastic foam. You will find that foam padding will serve all your needs.

Foam padding may go directly on a hard surface, or it can be given a flexible support. Interwoven webbing may be all that is needed, but for some lounge chairs rubber webbing is better. There are springs that can be put across in the same way. Examples of these applications are given in later chapters.

CHAIR BACKS

Some chair backs are upright, but the natural posture of a sitter does not conform to a vertical back. If the rear legs continue up vertically only as high as the small of the sitter's back, a curved cross member at a slight angle to vertical may be comfotable enough (Fig. 3-3A). It is more common for the rear legs to curve or be angled (Fig. 3-3B). Straight cross members suffer from the same problem as a flat seat; the area of contact is small and therefore uncomfortable (Fig. 3-3C). Curving across lets more of the person's back touch the wood (Fig. 3-3D).

On chairs such as the popular *ladderback* type, there are many cross members. The amount of curve in each piece may be different, as the maker tried to get these parts of the chair to fit as closely as possible to the parts of the sitter's back. Top and bottom curved pieces in

many chairs may be joined by vertical pieces. They are also curved in the most figure-shaped chair.

If the chair is to be given arms, there is scope for a considerable amount of shaping. It is important that the arms come at the right height and with the correct amount of flare for comfort. The top of the arms should be about 10 or 12 inches above the seat and be far enough apart not to restrict the sitter's body. Usually they flare outward toward the front and extend a short distance ahead of the seat. Examples are described later.

RIGIDITY

A problem with chair design comes from a sitter's tendency to want to move the chair about with his or her weight on the seat, and for some people to tilt the chair onto its rear pair of legs. If the only thing required was a support for a person sitting still, the only strength requirement would be in an up and down direction (Fig. 3-4A). If the seat is tilted under load, the thrust comes from the front of the seat toward the bottoms of the back legs (Fig. 3-4B). In an extreme case collapse occurs as the joints give way (Fig. 3-4C). The greatest strength built into a chair is to resist this load. There is less risk of a sitter tilting the chair sideways, but there must be strength that way. Attempting to slide a chair while sitting on it puts multiple strains on its structure.

The best resistance to collapse due to tilting comes from a solid side instead of corner legs (Fig. 3-4D). Some chairs are made that way, but for most situations owners expect their chairs to be on corner legs. If a chair is made with top rails only, resistance to tilting is due to the diagonal loads within the joints and rails (Fig. 3-4E). The

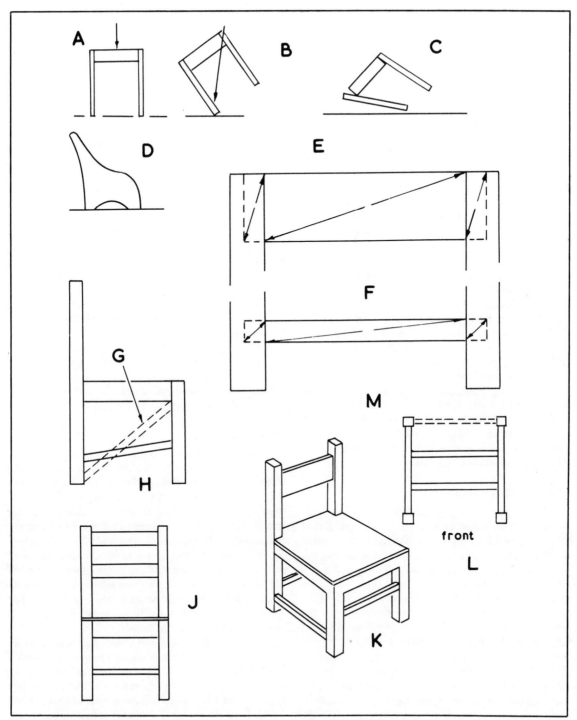

Fig. 3-4. Rails and legs have to be designed to resist loads in many directions. Rails have to be positioned to give leg clearance as well as stiffness.

deeper the rail, the better its resistance to tilting loads. A lower rail provides a backup resistance with its own diagonals (Fig. 3-4F). Some chairs have two lower rails, and these all aid in resisting tilting loads. Angling a lower rail provides strength. Ideally, it goes from the bottom of the back leg to the top rail (Fig. 3-4G). This is not aesthetically very pleasing, so chairs are not made that way. Some chairs have side rails angled upward slightly to gain some extra strengthening (Fig. 3-4H).

Strain crosswise may be expected to be less. The chair back provides some support in that direction, as parts in the back resist any tendency to collapse across (Fig. 3-4J). There is another problem in the location of crosswise lower rails, as the sitter may expect to be able to swing his or her legs back between the front chair legs. Sometimes a front rail is kept high for clearance (Fig. 3-4K), but it is more common to arrange these rails between side rails instead of between the front legs (Fig. 3-4L). Sometimes there is a rear rail, or maybe two, between the rear legs, but more often that rail also joins the side rails (Fig. 3-4M).

Obviously, satisfactory joints are important to the rigidity requirements of a chair. There has to be as much glue area as possible between side grain surfaces. End grain does not take glue well and will not contribute much to strength. Coupled with this requirement is the need to avoid weakening either part of any joint. It is of no use providing a joint with considerable glue area, if one or both of the wood parts are so cut away that they may collapse under an angular load. Joints have to be a compromise between glue needs and the retention of strength in the fibers of the wood.

MORTISE AND TENON JOINTS

To get the maximum resistance to tilting loads, joints should be as deep as possible. A tenon only part of the rail's depth (Fig. 3-5A) will effectively be reducing the tilting strength to a rail of the tenon's depth. For the lower rails and any other shallow ones, the depth of a tenon should be the same as the rail (Fig. 3-5B). If a mortise and tenon joint is made between two parts of the same thickness, often the tenon is made one-third of the wood's thickness (Fig. 3-5C). A chair rail usually goes into a thicker leg. In that case the joint will be stronger if the tenon is more than one-third the thickness of the rail (Fig. 3-5D). The thickness depends on circumstances, as two very thick tenons meeting at the same level in a leg may take out so much wood from the leg as to weaken it. Again, you have to compromise; a ½-inch thick tenon on a ¾-inch rail is about right.

For a deeper rail, it is better for the strength of the leg to divide the tenon into two parts, so there is solid wood in the leg between the tenons (Fig. 3-5E). Where a top rail goes into a rear leg that continues upward to make the chair back, that is the joint to use. It has to be modified for a front leg. If the top of the leg will not show, the tenon can be haunched so as to leave solid wood at the top of the leg (Fig. 3-5F). If the top of the leg comes above the rail level, you may be able to use the same joint as at the back. If not, or the top of the leg shows, cut down the tenon, but no more than is necessary to leave a little solid wood at the top of the leg. In this sort of work, it is best to leave some excess wood on the leg until after the joint has been cut, then trim off to avoid breaking out when chopping the joint.

The distance to take tenons into the mortises in the legs must also be a compromise. Tenons at the same level can go deeper if the rails are toward the outsides of the legs than if they are further in (Fig. 3-5G). It is common to go far enough in for the ends to have open miters (Fig. 3-5H), but that depth is not always needed. Solid wood left there provides strength in the leg. Long tenons are normally preferable. Sometimes it helps to have the tenons off-center in the rails, even to the extent of being barefaced, with no shoulder on one side (Fig. 3-5J). Such a joint is as strong as a central tenon. It is actually easier to pull tight and neat, because there is only one shoulder to bring close to the surface.

DOWEL JOINTS

Many chair parts are doweled and are satisfactory. There is a similar problem to tenoning in the need to get ample glue area without weakening the wood. There should never be less than two dowels, and that is difficult to arrange in the narrow lower rails. Small dowels may be arranged diagonally on a square end (Fig. 3-6A). In upper rails there may be room for three dowels. Their diameter should be more than half the thickness of the rail. There is no limit to the distance they can go into the end grain of the rail, but there are similar limits to those of the tenons in a leg. Miters may still be advisable (Fig. 3-6B). The distance into the rail should be between two and three times the diameter of the dowel.

The resistance to collapse when a chair is tilted back can be regarded as the diagonal of a tenon, so in a full-depth joint it is as great as possible (Fig. 3-6C). In a doweled joint the spacing of the dowels cannot go to the edges of the rails, so the diagonal becomes less (Fig. 3-6D). Strength in that direction is proportionately reduced. Dowels can hold a chair together in normal use and

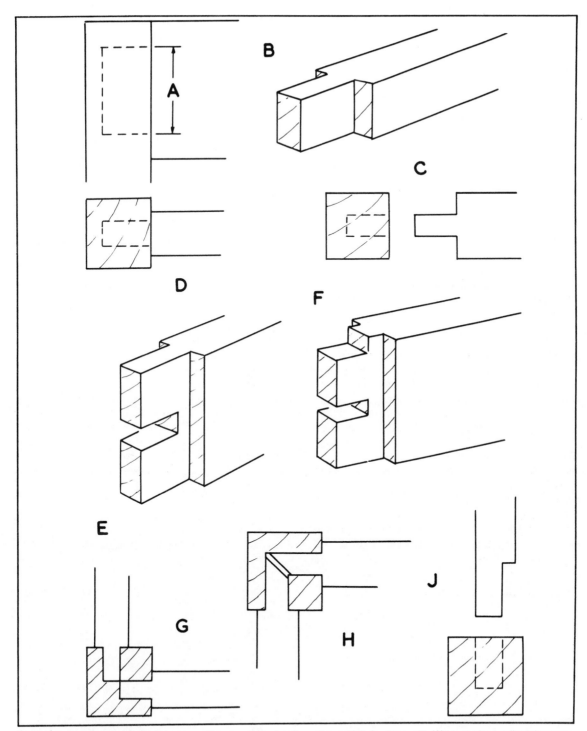

Fig. 3-5. Tenons into legs have to be correctly proportioned and may be multiple for deep rails. Within the legs, rails at the same level may meet or be mitered.

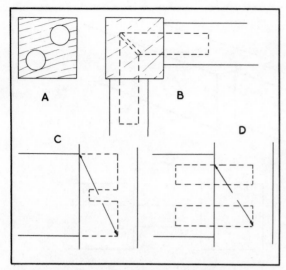

Fig. 3-6. Dowels may be arranged diagonally and mitered in the leg. Strength due to diagonals is less with dowels than tenons.

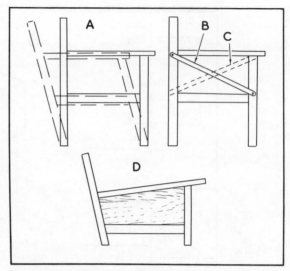

Fig. 3-8. Framed chairs may distort (A), but bracing (B and C) or panels (D) will resist this distortion.

are often employed. A close fitting doweled joint will often be stronger than one where the mortise and tenon joints have been inexpertly cut, so there are gaps filled with glue. Properly cut mortise and tenon joints are the cabinetmaker's way of joining chair parts.

In some types of chairs it is possible to arrange brackets at the corners that will be hidden by the seat. This is particularly so if the seat is arranged to lift out. A fixed solid seat obviously contributes to the strength of the chair, but some other form of bracing is worthwhile where the seat is separate. A solid wood bracket can be arranged at each corner (Fig. 3-7A). Cut it with the grain going diagonally. Either cut around the leg or cut to clear it (Fig. 3-7B). Join with glue and screws; angling the screws inward will pull the surfaces tight (Fig. 3-7C). Metal angle brackets are sometimes used for the same purpose.

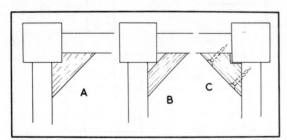

Fig. 3-7. Chair corners may have brackets or fillets fitted close (A) or cut round legs (B and C).

The considerations of rigidity just described are particularly applicable to dining chairs, but they should be kept in mind when considering other chair forms. It is always advisable to triangulate where possible. For instance, if part of a chair has squared corners, the strength depends on the sizes of joints. Failure comes when they can resist no more (Fig. 3-8A). If a diagonal brace is provided (Fig. 3-8B), that takes most of the strain and relieves the joints of much of their load. As shown, it is in tension. Another brace in the other direction (Fig. 3-8C) will resist strain the other way. Tension in a light strut is a better way of taking a load than trusting it to resist compression without bending.

In a lounge chair with arms, more strength is provided than may be realized by putting panels in the sides (Fig. 3-8D). You then have resistance to loads due to tilting by the diagonals within the panel.

In a fully upholstered chair, nearly all of the wooden framing will be hidden. Usually the feet and sometimes the ends of the arms are exposed in the finished chair. The hidden parts have to be strong enough, and care is needed in the joints. They do not always have the finish that is given where the woodwork shows, but adequate strength under all probable loads is important, particularly as the parts are hidden and a repair to the structure involves extensive disassembly. Some mass-produced, fully upholstered furniture has very poor inside woodwork. The craftsman should be able to do much better work.

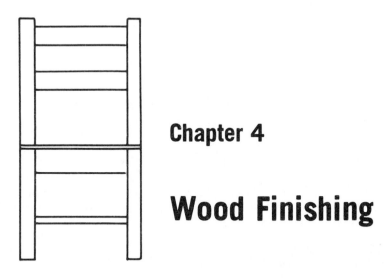

Chapter 4

Wood Finishing

The workmanship you put into a table or chair may be excellent, with everything to size and the joints perfect. If you do not give the work a good finish, though, the whole effect will be spoiled. There are some woods that can be left without any surface treatment, but there must be something applied to the surfaces of home furniture to allow for wear and protection and to enhance appearance. The woods that can be left untreated are those with natural oils which may have uses on boats or outdoors, but they are unsuitable for furniture.

The quality of an applied finish depends largely on the way the wood has been prepared. The first steps in finishing come in the accurate shaping and smoothing of the wood. You have to consider the final appearance at all stages. It is no use thinking, for instance, that ragged grain due to planing the wrong way can be put right at the finishing stage. This sort of damage is better attended to while you have the table or chair in pieces. You also need to be careful as you progress through construction. Do not handle the wood in a way that may produce dents. If you use clamps, put smooth scraps of wood under the jaws. If you have to hammer parts together, put scrap wood over the work to spread the effect of the blow and prevent damage. At the same time, think of the other side

of the work, and make sure that it is not damaged by resting on nails or any other uneven part of the bench top.

Keep your tools sharp. Using a blunt plane or chisel will cause poor surfaces or edges. Sharp tools produce better surfaces that will need less treatment. It is always better to cut than to abrade. There is a use for sanding, but it should be a final treatment on a surface already brought to a good state by work with cutting tools.

Much of your wood will be machine-planed. Buying the wood already planed or preparing it with your own jointer saves a lot of hard handwork and gets surfaces true, but it is unwise to leave a machine-planed surface as an exposed part of a piece of furniture. The action of machine-planing leaves ridges across the grain. If the machine-planing has been done carefully, these ridges are minute. There is a risk that they may show through the finish applied later. The cutters are at varying stages of bluntness. The pounding of rotating cutters that are not perfectly sharp tends to compress the surface fibers. Applying a liquid surface treatment may raise the fibers and give you trouble in getting the result you want. Such a surface may also cause trouble in gluing, as the *case-hardened* surface does not allow glue to penetrate properly.

For furniture, machine-planed surfaces should then be hand planed. This need only be a light cut, but it removes the machine plane marks and exposes a layer that has not been compressed. An alternative to a plane for some parts is a scraper, preferably the traditional cabinet scraper that removes very fine shavings. A cabinet scraper is useful when you are dealing with wild grain that does not answer to the plane whatever way it is used. A scraper can be used in any direction over a rough surface and will leave it as smooth as any tool can.

Excess glue can interfere with a finish. It prevents stain from soaking in evenly and may affect the appearance of any liquid finish put over it. If the glue used is a type that is soluble in water before it sets, wipe off any surplus around a joint with a damp cloth. Do not make it excessively wet. Be careful not to smear glue over other parts and leave it. If the glue has to be dealt with after it has set, you may be able to chip it away with a chisel or scrape it off. Be careful not to scrape away wood fibers as well, particularly across the grain, as the difference in surface texture may make a variation in the final finish.

Consider which surfaces are better dealt with before assembly. It is easier to scrape and sand a piece of wood loose on the bench than it is to try to give it a good surface when it is attached to other parts. There will be some parts better left until after assembly. If you expect to have to take off a few shavings to bring surfaces level after assembly, smoothing them beforehand may be a waste of time. It is usually best to deal with inner surfaces of main structural parts before they are put together. Rails and similar things may be cleaned all round before assembly.

If plywood will appear on the outside, examine the surface veneers. They may have been sanded during manufacture, but looking across towards the light may show irregularities. There is not much thickness to deal with, so you cannot remove much wood. A scraper can be used carefully on any parts that need attention. Even if you have plywood bought with a surface veneer to match the solid wood, check it carefully and do whatever is necessary to get a smooth surface before building it into a table or chair.

SANDING

You may have uses for a power sander, but that is not the tool a craftsman uses instead of a plane and scraper. In quality furniture construction, sanding is only a final process that should not take much effort or time.

Sanding is a carry-over from earlier days, when the abrasive used was sand glued to paper. This was followed by powdered glass, which is still obtainable and makes a good abrasive for wood. A cheaper grit is *flint*, which wears quickly and soon clogs with dust. *Garnet* is a good paper for general sanding of wood. It cuts well, does not clog easily, and has a reasonably long life. There are other manufactured grits, some of which are more suitable for plastics and metal than wood. Grits may be intended for power sanding. Be careful that the abrasive paper you get can be used on wood.

Silicone carbide paper is mainly for metal and plastic. One version of it is described as "wet-and-dry," meaning that it can be used with water. That keeps dust down. It works on very hard surfaces and may be needed if you apply a modern hard synthetic finish and want to smooth it between coats.

Nearly all abrasive paper available today has the grit held to the backing paper or cloth with waterproof adhesive. If you have doubts about the adhesive's waterproofness, warm the paper before use to drive off moisture and leave the glue stronger. A cloth backing will last longer than paper, but for most work the cheaper paper is satisfactory. Cloth is valuable if you are dealing with awkward shapes or want to sand a turning in a lathe.

Grits

Abrasive paper is available with grits of many sizes. In the past there have been many ways of indicating the grit size. Your supplier may call abrasives intended for use on bare wood *cabinet* papers, while those intended for rubbing down the applied finish are *finishing* papers. The modern way of indicating grit is by a number—the higher the number, the finer the grit. The roughest you are likely to need after planing is 60 grit. The finest you are likely to use directly on wood is 180 grit. There are others between in wide steps including 80, 100, 120, and 150. For light rubbing of finish coats, the numbers continue getting finer to 400 grit, which is further than you will probably go.

Other methods of grading grits have almost fallen from use. You should ask your supplier for a comparison with the grit numbers if what he has is marked differently. Paper for hand sanding is in sheets about 9 inches by 11 inches. If folded and used freehand, it may not last long. It is better to tear it into four pieces and wrap it round a block of wood thick enough to grip, and with a face about 3 inches by 5 inches. You can buy cork blocks or wood sanding blocks faced with hard rubber.

Techniques

Hand sanding a properly planed surface need not be very arduous. You can use an electric orbital or oscillating sander, which gives a surface treatment comparable with hand sanding. Do not use a belt sander or a disc sander for finishing.

On a flat surface, sand with the paper around a flat block and normally work with the grain. If you suspect slight unevenness due to plane marks, you can sand diagonally, but it is important to follow with further sanding along the grain. Scratches across the grain that may not show at this stage may become obvious if left to be brought up by the applied finish.

Do not start sanding before you have done all planing. Particles of grit embedded in the wood may blunt a plane cutter. You may be able to get the finish you want with only one grade of abrasive. If you want to follow one grit with a finer one, be careful that there are no particles of the coarser grit left to be picked up with the finer paper. They will travel with the fine grit and cause scoring of the wood's surface. Use a soft brush to clear the surface before changing to the finer grade. A *tack rag* can be wiped over the surface to pick up grit.

If you have to sand moldings, you may manage with the abrasive paper folded and used freehand, or it can be wrapped around a piece of wood that approximates to the molding section. Turned work is sanded in the lathe, but the action is across the grain. If the final sanding is with fine paper and you are sure that all the marks made by coarser grits are removed, it is unlikely that cross-grain scratches will mar the final effect. If there are long parts of the turning without beads or other shaping, it will help if you rub lengthwise with fine abrasive paper after the work has been removed from the lathe.

Steel Wool

Steel wool is an alternative to abrasive paper. Do not use the type sold for domestic scouring. For use on wood, steel wool comes in grades from 000 (finest) to 3 (coarsest). You will not need steel wool coarser than grade 1; 00 or 000 are the grades to use for finishing wood. Steel wool may be more suitable than abrasive paper for shaped parts. Some woods can be discolored by the use of steel wool. Make sure you remove all particles, as they can rust and affect appearance if left embedded in the grain. A damp cloth should lift out steel particles.

There is a tendency with some woods for short fibers to bend over instead of being removed by sanding. They may rise when the finish is applied and cause roughness. This should not be a problem with most of the furniture woods. If you want to make sure you have removed any of these fibers, moisten the surface with a damp cloth to raise them, then allow for drying. Further sanding should remove any offending fibers.

STOPPINGS

Wood is a natural material, and that accounts for much of its beauty. Wood is not of uniform texture, and you may have to deal with a flaw or blemish in an otherwise perfect surface. There is also the need to obscure or fill damage you have done yourself, such as a sunk nailhead or a joint that does not fit closely. You should plan construction so any natural *shakes* (cracks) in the surface come where they will not show, but you may still have some to deal with on an exposed surface.

Materials for filling cracks and holes are collectively called *stoppings*, although they may be referred to as fillers, which is a name better kept for the more liquid compounds used to fill the pores of grain before applying a finish. In some cases the mixtures are the same, but of different consistencies.

You can buy prepared stoppings or mix your own. The stopping should be as inconspicuous as possible in the finished work. This means that it should finish the same color as the wood. Some stoppings are supplied in different colors. Others are a neutral color and will accept stain. If the wood is to be stained, it is better to use a colored stopping after staining. If the stopping accepts stain, it may absorb the stain differently from the surrounding wood and finish a different shade. You may have to experiment with a new stopping.

Stick shellac or plastic stoppings (sometimes called *beaumontage*) are good for covering sunken nailheads or small cracks. The stoppings do not take stain, so they must be bought colored and used after staining the wood. Older workers used oil putty (a mixture of whiting and linseed oil), but it is not recommended. Oil putty takes a long time to set. The oil absorbs into surrounding wood, causing discoloration.

Plastic water putty is effective. It comes as a powder and is mixed with water to form a thick paste. Then it can be pressed into cracks or holes with a putty knife, screwdriver, or chisel. Any excess should be cleaned off quickly, because it sets rapidly. Do not mix more than you need at one time, as it cannot be softened again with water. Sand the area after stopping. Make sure there are no stray bits of putty left in the grain, as they may affect the appearance of the finish. Wood compound is the name of another stopping paste used in the same way as wood putty, but it takes longer to set.

Wood plastic (plastic wood) is a thick paste in cans or tubes, and it is the nearest thing to wood in its characteristics. It can be pressed into holes, with a little left above the surface, then sanded level. It does not contract as it dries. If you have to repair slight damage, such as a piece splintered off a molding, it is possible to build up with wood plastic. Bring it to shape with tools and by sanding. It is the only stopping compound strong enough to allow this work.

Glue should not be regarded as a stopping. It does its job by uniting surfaces that fit fairly closely. There is little strength in the glue itself, so it cannot be expected to fill a gap and hold the parts securely. When most glues have fully set, a thick deposit will craze—become a network of tiny cracks—and that is where the weakness is.

If you want to fill a gap and provide strength, as may happen in a badly fitting joint, it is possible to use a mixture of glue and sawdust. Then the glue bonds to the sawdust and does not craze. Mix sawdust from the wood you are using to quite a thick paste and press it into the gap. This mixture will not take stain.

If you intend to paint the furniture, the color of the stopping does not matter, but you still need to get surfaces level. If you use a resinous softwood, there is a risk of resin coming through paint long after it has been applied, particularly from end grain or from the vicinity of knots. There has to be a barrier over these places before starting painting. This can be shellac in alcohol, such as shellac varnish or French polish.

FILLERS

You can go ahead with applying a finish on many woods without any preparation after sanding, but woods with more open grain are better filled. Any wood under a microscope will show a mass of pores. If the pores are very small, they will fill with the finishing material, which will dry smooth. If the pores are large, the dried finish will show dents over them. There may also be lengthwise tiny natural cracks at intervals along the grain. If they are large enough to be seen, as in most oaks, the wood requires filling if you are to get a smooth finish. Most of the hardwoods used in furniture benefit from the application of a filler. These are broadly divided into *paste fillers* for open-grained woods and *liquid fillers* for close-grained woods.

Fillers can be bought already prepared. Some fillers can be used before staining, but others may resist stain penetration. It is better to stain before filling. Obviously the filler color must match the stained wood. In most newer fillers the material is a finely ground crystal called *silex,* or it may be some other fine powder. This is formed into a paste with linseed oil or other binder, then it can be thinned for a more liquid filler.

Prepared fillers come in many wood colors. In choosing a filler, let it be slightly darker than the stain, because fillers tend to dry lighter. If paste fillers are being mixed, prepare enough for the whole job in one mix. Make sure that there are no streaks or unmixed powder in a batch. It is difficult to get exactly the same color again in a new mix.

Spread paste filler evenly and thoroughly. Leave it long enough for the surface to dull, then rub over with a piece of coarse cloth across the grain to force the filler in. Change to a soft cloth and wipe along the grain until all excess filler has been removed. Do not rub too hard, or you may lift out the filler. You have to get filler everywhere, but be careful of leaving any on the surface, particularly in shaped parts or corners. In awkward places you can use a short-haired stiff brush. If excess filler becomes too hard to wipe off, it can be softened with *benzene.* Leave a filled surface for a day before applying anything over it.

Liquid fillers for close-grained woods are similar to the pastes but thinned. You can convert most pastes by thinning with turpentine or benzene. Brush it on and wipe it smooth when the surface has dulled. Shellac can be used as a liquid filler. Apply it and sand it lightly, then repeat. Shellac may be white or orange, and the latter can be used over any darker stains. If the final finish will be varnish, a thinned first coat of it will act as its own filler. Do not use varnish for this purpose if the finish is to be by another method.

Woods which have grain open enough to need paste fillers include oak, ash, chestnut, elm, and teak. At the other extreme, woods that need no filler include aspen, cypress, ebony, gaboon, magnolia, and most of the spruce and pine families. In between are many woods that are better with medium and liquid fillers. Some of these are butternut, mahogany, rosewood, walnut, beech, birch, maple, and sycamore.

STAINS

Many woods are quite attractive with a clear finish over their natural color. There are many woods that are stained to what has been accepted as their natural furniture color. The brownness of oak and walnut may be intensified. Mahogany usually has its redness intensified. Generally, it is good practice to make more of the existing color than to try to change it. It is wrong, for instance, to try to get a red effect on a brown wood. It is also wrong to try to make one wood look like another by staining it, unless you have something made of different woods that all have to be brought to the same color. If you know woods, you will see from the grain pattern that the wood below the stain is different from what you wanted it to simulate. Plywood panels may have to be stained to match surrounding wood. Stain may give an inferior wood an appearance of quality. If what you are making has to match other furniture in a room, you will have to choose wood and stain it to suit.

Stain should color wood without obscuring its appearance. The details of grain should show through. Stain penetrates the surface layers of the wood. Paints and other surface finishes have little penetration, and they obscure the grain. They can be built up to completely hide the base material, which might be wood in combination with metal.

Stain should color the wood evenly. The ease with which this is done depends on the solvent, as will be seen in the following details. A quick-drying stain has some uses, but it may be difficult to get into the wood evenly. A slow-drying stain is easier to apply evenly, but too long a drying time is inconvenient.

Stains consist of pigment to provide the color in a solvent. Different solvents have different penetrating qualities. A good range of colors is obtainable with each type of solvent, and it is the choice of solvent that mainly concerns the finisher.

Oil Stains

This type of stain is popular and has a light oil solvent such as benzene, naphtha, or turpentine. Ready-made stains are obtainable in all quantities and in colors usually described by the name of the wood on which they are intended to be used. The actual colors include a variety of browns, reds, yellows, and oranges, as well as deep black.

Oil stains penetrate quickly. Brush them on plentifully along the grain. Get the whole surface covered quickly and evenly. The intensity of the stain depends on how long it is given to penetrate. Use a cloth to wipe off surplus stain when you judge the color to be right. It will finish lighter as it dries and is covered with a clear finish. Oil stain is very tolerant. It will usually dry evenly, despite rather erratic brushing and wiping.

With all stains it is usually best to do the least important parts first, leaving the most prominent part (usually the top) until last. Move the work about, so the surface you are working on is usually horizontal, or nearly so. Work in a cross light, so you can see how the staining is progressing.

End grain will soak up more stain than the other surfaces and finish much darker. Quick wiping of the end grain will minimize this, but even then you may not reduce darkening very much. A better way is to partially seal the end grain. Put on a coat of thin shellac. Let it soak

in and dry before staining. Be careful not to get shellac on any adjoining side grain.

Although oil stain appears to dry rapidly, leave the work at least a day before applying a finish over it. The solvents are flammable, so take the obvious precautions while working. Destroy rags used for wiping.

Water Stains

Water stains are cheap and easy to use. They come as powders to mix with water. The supplier will indicate proportions, but you can vary the intensity of the color by using different strengths. Dissolving is in hot water. The cold stain can be bottled and kept almost indefinitely. You can mix powders for special effects. Concentrated stain can be kept and diluted when needed, but make sure of a consistent color by diluting sufficiently for a job at one time.

Water stain may not penetrate quite as much as an oil stain, but it is adequate. Drying time depends on temperature and humidity. One problem is the way water may raise the grain. It is advisable to wet wood with clear water first. Allow this to dry. Sand the surface smooth before applying the stain.

Use plenty of stain and apply it with a brush along the grain. For an even coverage, it is easier to apply two coats of a lighter color than to use one of a dark stain. Do all staining of a piece of furniture fairly quickly. It is not common to wipe stain with a cloth, but excess stain in corners can be lifted with the edge of a dry cloth or a dry brush.

Spirit Stains

A large range of colored pigments can be dissolved in *spirit* (alcohol). These include all the wood colors as well as blue, green, and yellow, which may be needed for special effects. You can buy powders which dissolve easily. Concentrated mixtures can be stored and thinned for use.

Penetration is quick and not always very deep. Drying is almost instantaneous. Thus, spirit stains cannot be put on smoothly over a large area. Use the brush rapidly. Keep the brush moving with sweeps. Refill as needed and follow a wet edge rather than a dry one. An exception is spraying, where a more even effect can be obtained.

Spirit stain is not the choice for the first staining of furniture because of the difficulty of applying it smoothly. Spirit stain has uses on molding where the narrow parts are unlikely to finish unevenly, and it is useful for touching up. You can use spirit stain over other stains, and it will penetrate some finishes to correct color on a damaged part.

Other Stains

There are other solvents, but oil and water are best for furniture. So-called pigmented oil stain is really thinned paint and is not to be chosen for furniture. Penetration is slight, and you are really applying translucent paint.

Some finishes are sold as varnish stains. These are varnishes with stain pigment added. They are not generally advisable for good quality furniture. The idea is to apply coloring as well as gloss at the same time, but the stain is in the finish and does not enter the wood. In later wear, any rubbing away of the gloss finish also removes the color, which would not happen if the stain had been applied as a separate first treatment.

There are chemical ways of altering the color of wood. *Permanganate* of potash crystals can be dissolved in water. When used as a stain, this turns most woods a medium brown color. The mixture is safe to handle and use.

Oak and chestnut can be given a deep brown color with ammonia. Traditionally, the wood was inside a cabinet where strong ammonia was allowed to evaporate. The resulting *fumed oak* is considered to be of a rich quality that cannot be reproduced any other way. More dilute ammonia can be brushed on in a well-ventilated place. Other woods cannot be treated.

VARNISHES

There was a time when furniture makers considered *varnish* as unsuitable for their products. They preferred one of the rubbed finishes, but modern synthetic varnishes are a different quality. Most are waterproof and with a good heat resistance. They can be applied to give a smooth hard surface. Usually the final surface has a high gloss, but it is possible to get varnishes with little or no gloss. Besides the use of varnish throughout, it is possible to build up with varnish, which is then sanded. Another treatment is used for the outer surface.

There are many varnishes. Household varnish may be described as quick drying. Some of the best varnishes are made for boats, but they are equally suitable for furniture. Varnish may be thought of as paint without color. Many varnishes actually have a slightly golden yellow shade, although that is not apparent over most woods or stains.

Traditional varnishes made from natural lacs required several precautions to be observed in their appli-cation. Synthetic varnishes are much more tolerant. A varnished surface becomes dustproof in about two hours, but the work area should be as dustfree as possible. The wood surface should be cleaned of dust. Vacuum cleaning is better than moving dust about with a brush. Be careful of drafts.

Varnish is affected by temperature. Varnish gets sluggish at less than 65°F. It may be too liquid at more than 85°F. Have the wood warm and stand the varnish can in warm water in cold conditions.

Use a clean soft brush. Do not use it for anything besides varnish. Do not stir modern varnish. Stirring causes tiny air bubbles that break on the wood surface and cause blemishes. Flow varnish on, with little attempt to brush it out. Brush with the grain. Work back toward the part already done and lift the brush as you go over its edge. Do not go back over a surface for another smoothing, as that may lift the varnish. You cannot put the surface right until sanding for the next coat.

A first coat may be thinned using the solvent recommended by the makers. Other coats are full strength. A very small amount of thinning will do. Never use shellac as a filler under varnish. When the first coat is dry, rub it down lightly with paper of a fine grit, such as 300 or 400. Clean off dust before the next coat. Three coats may give a worthwhile finish, but you can go on to four or five. Make sure each coat is absolutely dry before rubbing down and applying the next coat. Read the maker's instructions. With some synthetics there is a maximum, as well as a minimum, time between coats.

SHELLAC

Shellac has been used as a wood finish for a long time. Much older furniture was finished by French polishing, which is one method of applying shellac. Shellac dissolves readily in denatured alcohol (methyl alcohol, methylated spirits). It can be bought in liquid form in varying concentrations. Normal shellac is a golden color. If a clearer type is needed, there is a bleached shellac, but that does not keep very long.

Except for filling the grain, brushed shellac does not have much use on furniture. It does not wear very well and can be damaged with moisture and heat. In effect it is then a rather inferior varnish.

Traditional French polishing is a way of applying shellac to build up a surface with a smooth even gloss. It was one of the best ways of getting this effect in the days of the quality furniture makers a century or so ago. Shellac applied in this way suffers from the same problems of dampness and heat as brushed shellacs. Many old pianos show how a rich finish can be obtained by French polishing.

For modern furniture that gets normal usage, French polishing is not recommended. If you want to use the process, instructions are given in my book *Do-it-Yourselfer's Guide to Furniture Repair & Refinishing* (Tab Books No. 894).

SPRAY FINISHES

Spraying is the finishing process of most mass-produced furniture. The maker of individual pieces may prefer to avoid it. The usual finish applied with a spray gun is *lacquer,* which is formulated to give a quick finish that is highly resilient. If the wood requires sealing or filling, there is a suitable lacquer. Although most final lacquers produce a high gloss, there are flat and less glossy finishes.

Spraying puts the finish on without the risk of brush marks, but there can be flaws due to putting on too much at one place. Practice is needed to deal with furniture evenly.

Although actual spraying does not take long, there is a considerable amount of time used up in preparation and cleaning afterward. This is very little different for a one-off job or for working all day on a large number of items. That is one reason why spraying is more suitable for mass production.

If you want to use spray finish, you should familiarize yourself with the spray gun and its equipment. Practice with suitable lacquers, so you can get the desired effect before starting on the actual furniture you have made.

OIL AND WAX POLISHES

Some of the furniture that has survived for hundreds of years still has a fine polish. Age has enhanced its patina and sheen. Such beauty is the result of expert craftsmanship and either *wax* or *oil polishes.*

Oil is probably the older of the two polishes. Oil polish takes a long time to apply, although it produces beautiful results. Many oils can be used, but the most common is linseed oil. For the original method, oil is spread on, then polished by vigorous rubbing with cloth. Since most of the oil applied is rubbed off, and only a thin film is left in the pores of the wood, the building up of a sheen takes many applications at long intervals. Warming the oil by standing its container in hot water aids penetration.

Polishing at each stage may be started with a coarse cloth. Rubbing has to be hard and kept up for as much as 20 minutes. You can use a stiff brush instead of a cloth. Cloth wrapped around a brick can be used on a flat surface. It is the heat developed by friction that causes the polish, so there is some benefit in using a power polisher.

Using those traditional methods is time-consuming. One way of speeding results is to add a little varnish and turpentine to the linseed oil. One or two early applications of this mixture may be brushed on, but later applications should be friction-polished with a cloth.

Oil polishes can be bought. They contain other ingredients to hasten the production of a good finish.

Wax also has a long history. The finish it produces lasts longer than oil. There are many kinds of wax used for polishing, but *beeswax* produced by the honeybee is most popular. Turpentine is used with most waxes to make a paste or liquid polish. *Carnauba wax* is hard and is made into a polish with turpentine and other waxes like ceresin or paraffin.

Dissolving waxes to make your own polish can take some time, and it may be better to buy prepared waxes. Usually the wax is used in its natural color, but it can be darkened with oil stain.

As with oil, using wax directly on bare wood can be a lengthy process to build up a good finish. Where oil tends to sink into the grain, wax tends to build up a surface film. Wax can be applied over other finishes. This makes it suitable for much individually made furniture, where the maker wants to give it a different finish from mass-produced items.

You can treat your new wood with shellac, lacquer, or varnish sufficiently to seal the wood and make a coat over the surface. Rub that down with sandpaper, steel wool, or a mild abrasive powder such as pumice on a damp cloth. Remove any dust from that work.

Wax has to be applied all over the surface. You may need a brush in corners or moldings, but application is mainly with a cloth. Get the wax on without any attempt, at first, to polish it. Leave it for 10 minutes or so. Rub it briskly with another cloth. Polish first in all directions, then along the grain. If it is a hard wax polish, the first rubbing will need considerable friction. A stiff brush or cloth around a brick will help. Do all of the first polishing by hand, but you can use power polishing later.

You do not have to go all over the surface at one time with wax polishing. You can concentrate on part of it. When you have done other parts, a final all-over polish will get an even effect.

Wax polish can be used to follow an existing finish when the furniture has been in use for some time. Prepared furniture polishes contain wax. Some modern versions require very little rubbing, and there are spray finishes that leave a good surface without rubbing.

PAINTS AND PAINTING

Most furniture is finished by one of the methods already described. Painting is unusual, except that it may be the choice for a child's room or for special effect. Although paint will obscure the wood grain, it is important that you get a good finish to the wood surface. Paint will not necessarily hide bad workmanship or a surface with blemishes.

Like varnish, there has been something of a revolution in paint production. Products of some makers are not compatible with those of other makers. The choice and sequence of paint coats are not always the same.

If the wood is very open-grained, filling as for other finishes is advisable, but otherwise the paint can be expected to bridge pores and finish level. In a normal system the first coat is a primer. Its purpose is to soak into the grain to provide a grip and a base for further coats. The recommended primer is not always the same color as later coats. Primer is followed by an undercoat. This is a flat finish paint that has a color compatible with the final coat. In some systems the primer is thinned undercoat. Apply a second undercoat if the first layer does not appear to cover very well. It may be rubbed down to provide a smooth base for the topcoat. Read the directions for the topcoat. Like many synthetic varnishes, it may not have to be stirred and applied with the minimum of brushing out. Usually it is inadvisable to apply more than one layer of topcoat paint. If you need to build up, do it at the undercoat stage.

Chapter 5

Simple Seats

Man's first seats were stools and forms, and these are simple to make. There are none of the compound angles and curves that occur in more advanced chairs. Simple seats have a place in the home today, so they are always worth making.

For newcomers to chair making, stools and forms are useful introductory projects. Some of the simplest chairs are really stools with backs added. They provide the next step to stoolmaking.

Although the more basic seats have hard tops, man's first attempts at providing comfort included the interweaving of various materials, before he came to full upholstery. The modern version is often described as *rush seating,* but the materials used today are mostly modern alternatives to rush. The woodwork to carry this sort of seating is quite simple. The methods of working the seats are not as complicated as a view of the finished product may suggest. By following the instructions with the examples, you can make attractive seats with your first attempt. If you can make the wood parts, you should certainly experience no difficulty in making the seating.

In this basic seating you have some straight edges to work from and square angles for getting shapes symmetrical. As you progress, symmetry has to be obtained by

working about centerlines. Some of these examples lead you in that direction, while producing attractive seats of simple form. Even if your interest is mainly in more advanced seating, you will benefit by making simpler things first, or at least by reading and understanding the instructions.

FORM

Not so very long ago only the head of the household had a chair. The rest of the family sat on forms, benches, or stools. A *form* is still useful as an extra seat. If made of hardwood and given a good finish, it may be used indoors when extra seating is needed. If made of more utilitarian wood and nailed together, a form can make a garden seat. The sizes shown (Fig. 5-1) provide a seat at a suitable height for use at a table, and the length is sufficient for three children or moderately-sized adults.

Prepare the wood to size. Be careful that the long parts are without twist. Sighting along them from an end will show if they are flat. Prepare the two sides so they match.

The important detail is the slope of a leg. Draw one end of the form full-size (Fig. 5-2A). Notice that the extremity of the leg comes vertically under the end of the

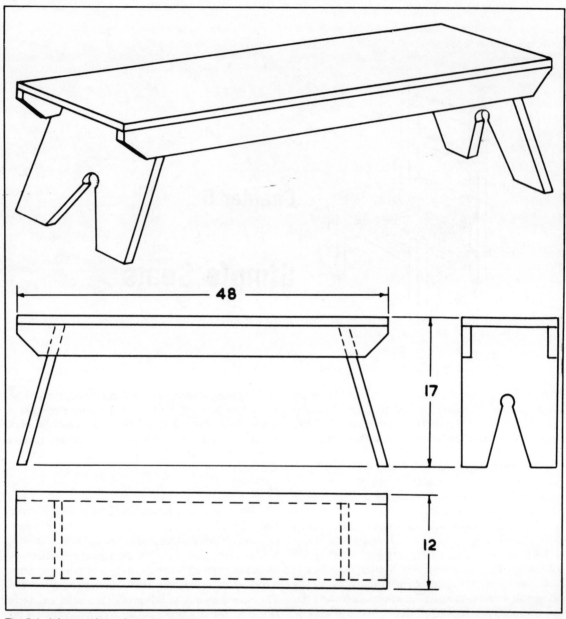

Fig. 5-1. A form makes a long strong seat.

top. There is then no risk of anyone sitting on the end causing the form to tip. Set an adjustable bevel to the angle the leg makes. Cut the ends of both legs to it. The feet are formed by drilling a hole and cutting into it (Fig. 5-2B). Trim the edges of the cut straight and take off any sharpness.

In the simplest construction the legs may be cut to fit completely round the sides, but that puts considerable load on the nails or screws. The form may still be acceptable for use outdoors if long screws are driven into drilled holes. It is better workmanship, though, to notch the sides. Do not take too much out of the sides—¼ inch is enough (Fig. 5-2C). Make the widths of the notches only just enough to take the thickness of the legs, so the parts have to be forced together for greatest strength.

For a simple form, nail the parts together, but even then it is worthwhile using glue—a waterproof type if the form is to be used outdoors. For a better construction there can be dowels into the top (Fig. 5-3A), or screws may be driven through counterbored holes down into the sides and legs (Fig. 5-3B). The heads are covered with wood plugs. Fasten through the sides into the legs. Plugs

of contrasting color provide a decorative effect.

Trim the top level with the sides if necessary. Take off all sharpness and round the corners. The form will be lifted by putting hands underneath, so make sure there are no rough edges or projecting lumps of glue.

Materials List for Form

1 top	12×48×⅞
2 rails	4×48×⅞
2 legs	12×18×⅞

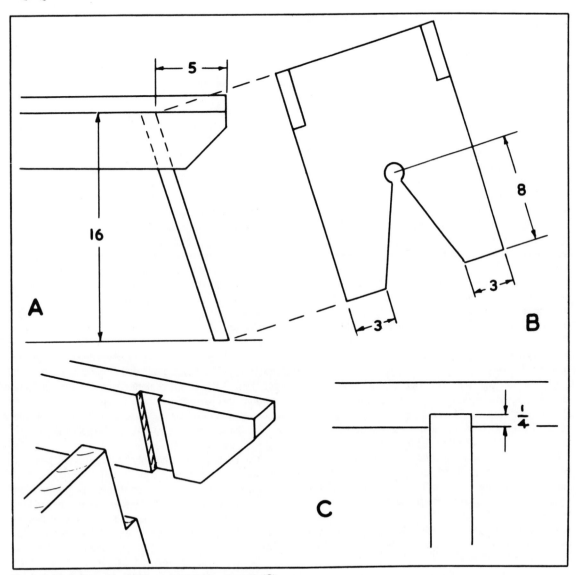

Fig. 5-2. Angled legs (A and B) are notched for strength (C).

43

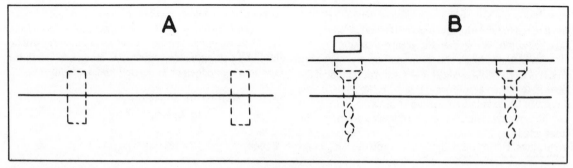

Fig. 5-3. The form top can be doweled or held with counterbored screws.

TALL STOOL

A seat at a height greater than the ordinary chair has many uses. The tall *stool* can be used at a bar, but it can also be used in situations where you usually stand, yet need to rest occasionally. Most woodworking activity has to be done while standing, but you can conserve your energy when marking out, checking a drawing, or doing something else that does not require standing, although you want to use your arms at the same height. There are many times when a woman appreciates a high seat—working in the kitchen, laying out dress patterns, and doing other activities where she needs to reach further over a table than is possible with a normal chair. A tall stool may be needed when a child must be seated higher than in an ordinary chair if he is to take his place at the meal table.

The stool described here (Fig. 5-4) is straightforward and of the simplest form possible, yet it is good looking and comfortable. The lower rails at alternate heights act as rests for legs of different lengths, and by staggering them in this way their ends can make stronger joints than would be possible if they were all at the same level.

Mark out the four legs together (Fig. 5-5A). Be careful to pair the markings for the lower rails to allow for the different heights. The joints shown are mortise and tenon. Dowels are unsatisfactory for rails of small section, although they can be used for the top rails.

Mark all the rails together to get the lengths between the shoulders the same (Fig. 5-5B). Mark the shoulder lines with a knife rather than with a pencil for greater accuracy, particularly if the cuts will be made with a handsaw. Gauge the thicknesses of the tenons to match the widths of the mortises. If a mortise gauge with two points is used, the same setting between the points can be used for all parts.

Cut the tenons. Drill out some of the waste in each mortise and chop them to shape. Make sure each mortise goes slightly deeper than the tenon will reach, so the shoulders will pull tight.

Leave a little extra wood at the top of the legs until after the framework has been assembled. Bevel the bottoms of the legs. The stool can be completed without any decoration, but it is possible to do some decorative chamfering all round each leg or just on the outer corners. The simplest is done with a round plane or a chisel used bevel-downward. Mark the limits of each hollow and scoop out, judging the widths by eye (Fig. 5-5C). A traditional way to decorate is by wagon beveling (Fig. 5-5D), so named from its use on the woodwork of many horse-driven farm wagons. This can be further embellished with other nicks (Fig. 5-5E). If done all round, the decoration should be confined to the space between the top rails and the other rails. If only on the outer corners, the decoration can go most of the leg's length.

Assemble a pair of opposite sides first. Check squareness and that they match each other. If suitable clamps are available, use them. Otherwise, it is possible to hammer the joints tight, with scrap wood to spread the blow (Fig. 5-5F). Drive a thin nail into the inside of each joint (Fig. 5-5G) to prevent movement while the glue sets. Join the opposite assemblies with the rails the other way—again checking squareness in the side view and that the shape is correct from above. Be sure that all four legs are level on a flat surface.

The best base for the upholstered top is a piece of plywood. Cut it to shape and take off all sharp edges. Drill some holes that will allow air to pass as the cushion compresses and relaxes. As the wood top will be hidden, there is no need for attachments from below. It can be glued and screwed downward on the framework (Fig. 5-5H).

Cut a piece of plastic foam or some foam rubber slightly bigger than the plywood top. Bevel around its lower edges with a sharp knife for about half the thickness (Fig. 5-6A), so the covering will pull it to a neat curve (Fig. 5-6B). The material chosen for the top depends on where the stool is to be used. For shop use, it should be a tough plastic-coated fabric or imitation leather. Something similar may suit other situations. If a woven cloth is to be used to match other room furniture, first cover the foam with light plain cloth. Follow this with the outer cloth. The foam will be pulled to a more uniform shape.

Plastic-coated fabric can be pulled underneath and tacked directly (Fig. 5-6C). Loosely woven cloth should be turned under to prevent fraying (Fig. 5-6D). Start on

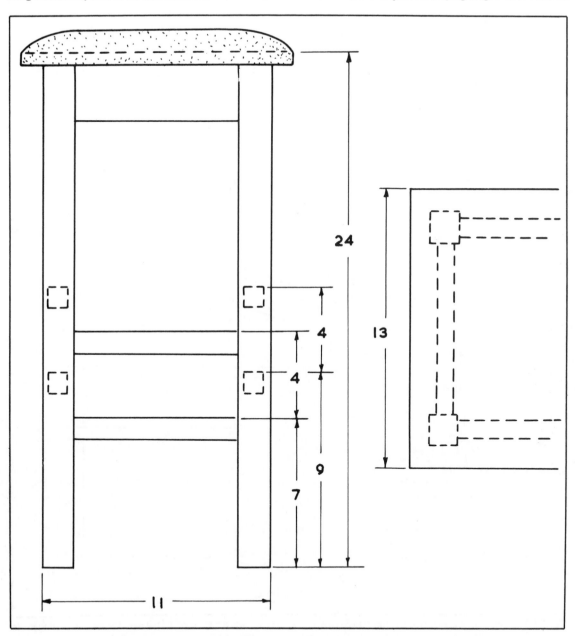

Fig. 5-4. A tall stool is stiffened with double lower rails.

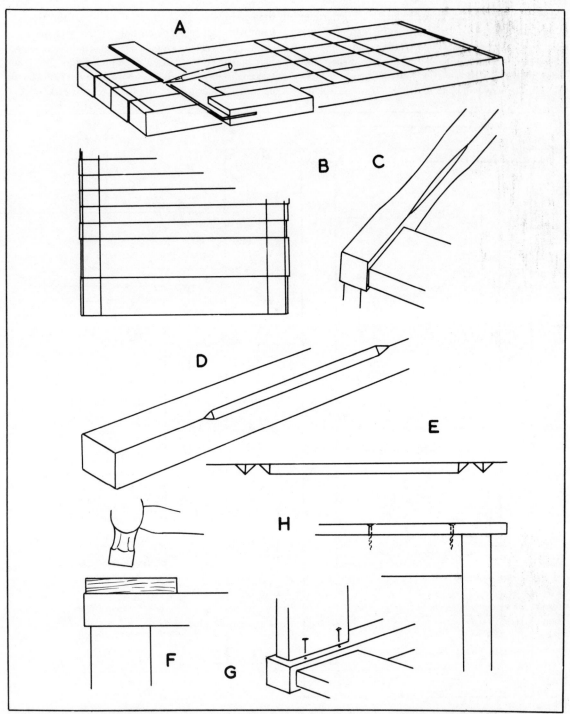

Fig. 5-5. Mark legs (A) and rails (B) together. There can be bevel decoration (C, D, and E). Use a pad when hammering joints (F). Nails clamp joints while glue sets (G), and the top may be screwed down (H).

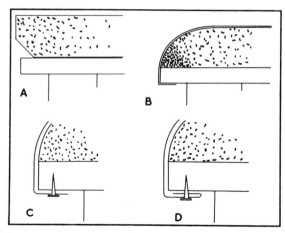

Fig. 5-6. Foam padding is pulled to shape by the covering.

opposite sides. Pull down the foam and tack it under the plywood. Do this the other way as well, then start working from these central tacks toward the corners. The spacing between tacks depends on the material, but about 1½-inch spacing should suit. If the effect is not even the first time, lift some tacks and reposition them. At the corners neatly fold the surplus material and pull it under for tacking. If the plywood corner has been rounded, the folds can be spaced evenly. Use the same folding arrangement at each corner.

Materials List for Tall Stool

1 top	13×13×½ plywood
4 legs	1½×25×1½
4 top rails	2½×11×⅞
8 lower rails	⅞×11×⅞

CHILD'S LOW CHAIR

The smallest child in a family likes to have a chair that has been scaled to suit his or her size. He or she will grow and not need it very long. Unless there are other children coming along or you can pass the chair to another family, the chair need only be made for a short life. Simple construction and cheap materials are what you want. This chair (Fig. 5-7A) is intended for a very young child, although it can be scaled up for a bigger one. There is a good spread of feet, so tipping is less likely. The back support is all that is needed. The chair is intended to be used without padding. If you want to fit cushions, increase sizes by an inch or so.

The two sides are ½-inch plywood. Mark them out, including the positions of the other parts (Fig. 5-7B). Cut

carefully and round all edges, including those below, as the owner will almost certainly turn the chair over.

There are two ways of making the seat and back from plywood. You can use solid wood, but that tends to make the chair heavy. Thin plywood can be framed round to make up the thickness to about 1 inch (Fig. 5-7C). The chair looks better if these parts are doubled with thickening pieces between to make up the same thickness (Fig. 5-7D). Carry the crosswise pieces through, so the other strips come between them.

The seat is given a slight taper (Fig. 5-7E). After stiffening, round the front edge and take off the sharpness from the rear edges.

Check the width of the back against the seat's rear edge. The back is shown with a curved top (Fig. 5-7F). Either stiffen behind with a wider strip or use two narrow ones. Round the top in section and take off sharpness from the bottom edges.

It may be satisfactory to nail the chair parts together, but if the chair comes apart in use the nails can be dangerous. It is better to glue and screw from outside. Three 8-gauge by 1¼-inch screws in each position should be adequate.

Check over the finished chair for roughness, splintered edges, or anything else that may hurt a child. A brightly painted finish will be the usual choice.

Materials List for Child's Low Chair

2 sides	14×14×½ plywood
1 seat	6×9×¼ plywood
1 back	7×8×¼ plywood
stiffening from	1×36×¾

PEASANT CHAIR

Many European countries have chairs that are really made of fairly thick slab seats on four legs, with a back added. They are particularly common in Germany, Austria, and Switzerland. Immigrants brought these designs with them, and chairs of this type may be welcomed by families who can trace their ancestry back to those parts of Europe.

Thick seats and backs are characteristic of the chair type. The wood needs to be fairly thick to get sufficient strength into the back joint. There can be a lot of leverage on the back by a sitter. This has to be resisted by the joint, as there are no other parts to share the load. With thinner wood, there is a risk of breaking.

The example shown (Fig. 5-8) is based on a traditional form. Sizes may be varied to suit available mate-

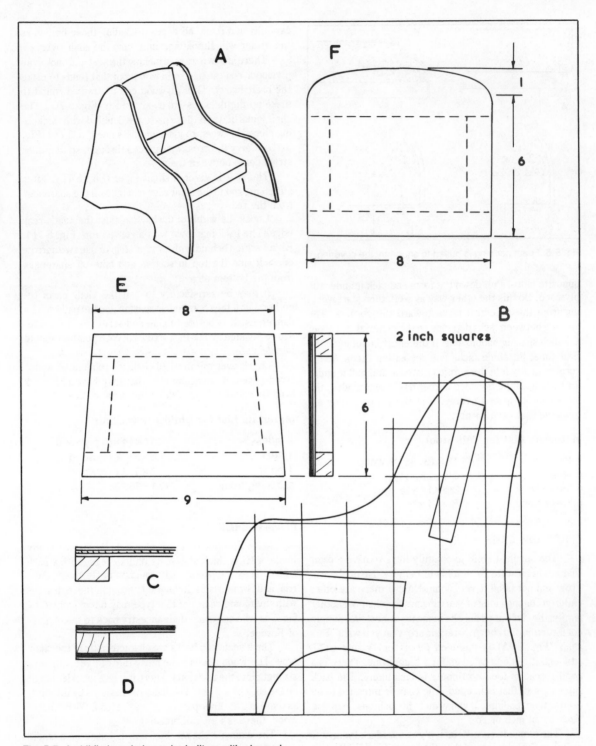

A

F

1

6

8

E

8

6

9

2 inch squares

B

C

D

Fig. 5-7. A child's low chair can be built up with plywood.

Fig. 5-8. A peasant chair follows a European traditional pattern.

and use it for marking the appropriate parts of the joint. Remember to allow for this slope when cutting the tenons. Do not go too far with saw cuts, as they will show in the finished chair. Make the tenons too long, so they can be trimmed after assembly.

With the joints cut, finish shaping the outlines of the seat and back. The seat edge can be left square, but its appearance can be lightened by beveling all round underneath and then rounding (Fig. 5-10E). If the involved curves of the back are too much for your equipment, or you prefer something simpler, the back can be made with a very similar outline to the seat, being wider at the top.

The front legs slope outward at about 10° to vertical and the back ones 20° to vertical. In some original chairs the legs are plain turnings, with enough left at the top to pass through holes drilled in the seat. Holes should be 1 inch or larger. Use an adjustable bevel or a template as a guide while drilling (Fig. 5-10F). Drill another hole in a piece of scrap wood for testing the legs as you turn them. If the bottoms of the legs are turned rounded (Fig. 5-10G), you will not have to cut angles across them, providing you get them all set at the same depth in the seat.

Make a saw cut across each leg before assembly. Drive the leg in so this is at right angles to the seat grain. After cutting off the surplus wood, drive a wedge into the cut (Fig. 5-11A). If the wedge was driven in line with the grain of the seat, there would be a risk of splitting.

The legs can be square, preferably tapered toward the bottom (Fig. 5-11B). The corners can be planed off to make an octagonal section (Fig. 5-11C). These legs have to be attached to the seat with mortise and tenon joints, with the shoulders and mortises cut at the slope checked with the adjustable bevel (Fig. 5-11D). Do not make the tenons too thin. They should also be made too long for trimming after fitting, but make a saw cut for wedging. Arrange that diagonally so the wedge will be across the chair grain (Fig. 5-11E).

The wedged ends of the legs may provide a traditional attractive appearance, but some of these chairs were made with the legs not carried through. There is plenty of thickness to provide strength if they are stopped. Whether the round ends of turned legs or tenons on square ones, the joints can be tightened by foxtail wedging (Fig. 5-11F). The small wedge hits the bottom of the mortise and is forced into the saw cut to expand the wood as the joint is finally driven tight.

Remove sharp edges from the seat before assembly. It needs no treatment except for the usual sanding. The back is also basically square-edged, whatever its outline.

rials (Fig. 5-9). Boards can be glued to make up the width, but the thicknesses should not be reduced much below 1½ inches. Mark out the seat (Fig. 5-10A). Prepare the wood for the back and mark that out. The shape can be scaled up on a pattern of squares about the centerline (Fig. 5-10B). It is easier to cut the joint before shaping the parts.

The joint is a form of multiple mortise and tenon (Fig. 5-10C). Strength is needed in the direction of the grain in both parts. Keep the parts narrow—certainly not wider than squares. Avoid wide tenons. They are weaker and more likely to break out the grain at the back of the seat. The angle between the seat and back should be about 100° (Fig. 5-10D). Set an adjustable bevel to this

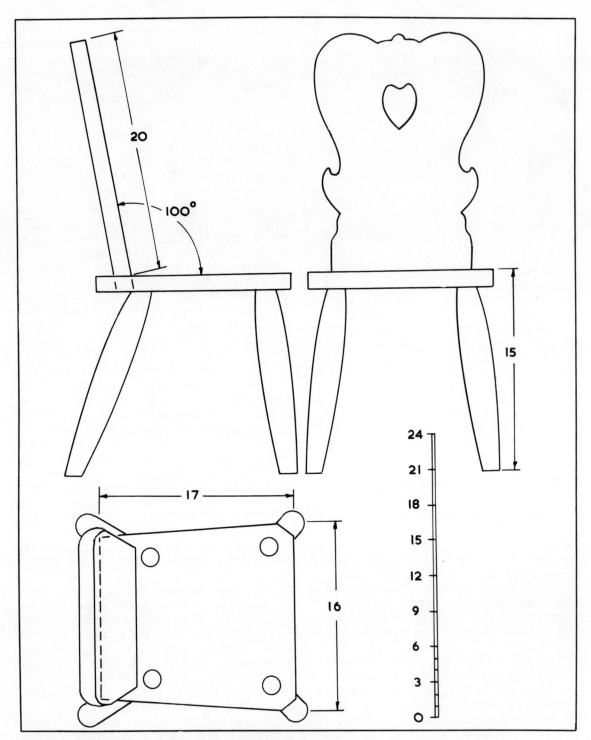

Fig. 5-9. The peasant chair has large sectioned wood and strong proportions.

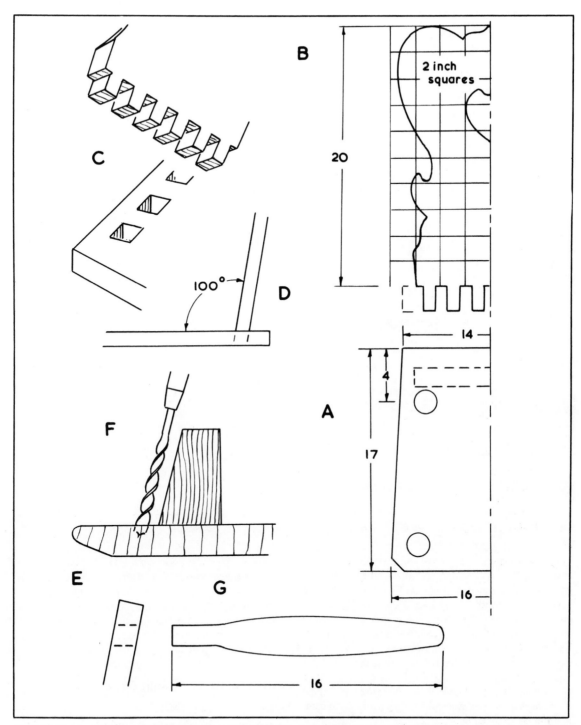

Fig. 5-10. The tapered seat (A) holds the shaped back (B) with multiple tenons (C and D). Holes are angles for the legs (E, F, and G).

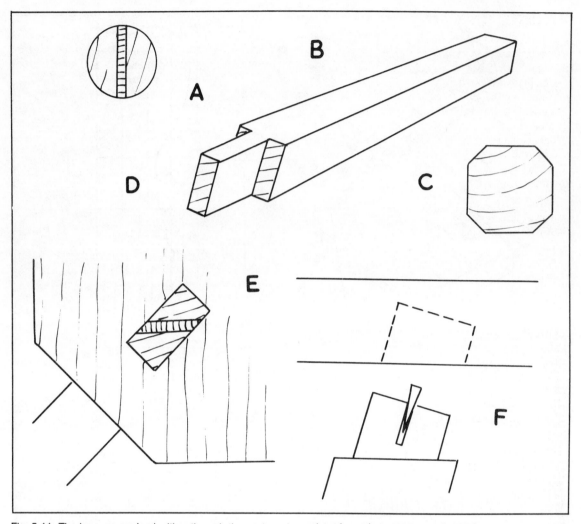

Fig. 5-11. The legs are wedged, either through the seat or stopped, and may be square or octagonal.

The curved shape may be sawed closely to the lines. The saw marks are removed by careful use of chisels and gouges. A Surform tool is useful. Tighter curves may have to be dealt with by coarse sanding. Thoroughly sand edges in any case. Edges can be rounded, but in the complex outlines that has to be done carefully and slowly if a reasonably even shape is to result.

To get the joint between the back and the seat tight, you will probably have to use a mallet or a hammer over scrap wood. It may be advisable to leave the top shaping of the back until after assembly, so any hammering damage can be trimmed off.

Trim off the extending tenon ends. Check the stand-

ing of the chair. If it rocks on a level surface, trim the bottom of a leg to correct this. The chair can be used as it is, but in the countries of its birth, it would usually have been provided with cushions. If you make cushions, provide the seat one with tapes at the rear corners to go around the back, and give the back cushion tapes to go around a hollow part of the outline.

Materials List for Peasant Chair

1 seat	16×17×1½
1 back	16×22×1½
4 legs	2¼×16×2¼

TALL CHECKER-TOPPED STOOL

If *seagrass* or other seat weaving material is worked in the traditional pattern, a comfortable seat is formed that goes down toward the center. If the material is woven in two separate directions, the result is flat. That may not conform quite so well to a sitter, but it allows many designs. It is also possible to use the flatter surface as a table, particularly at a bedside, where it can keep things within reach. It is possible to move the stool for use in front of a dresser when required.

Construction and Assembly

This stool (Fig. 5-12) is square and of a height that will suit as a bedside table and a dresser seat (Fig. 5-13A). It should be made of a hardwood to match existing furniture. Details of framework construction are very similar to those of the rush-topped stool. Refer to the drawings for the rush-topped stool.

The legs (Fig. 5-13B) are comparatively slender. Choose straight-grained wood that is unlikely to warp,

Fig. 5-12. A tall stool with double lower rails may have a checker pattern seagrass top.

and plane it straight. Mark the legs together. Mortises for the top rails are level, but the lower rail heights are staggered. Be careful to mark the legs in pairs to allow for this. Appearance can be improved by wagon beveling all round the upper part of each leg.

As the stool is square, all of the rails can be marked together. The top rails have central tenons, and their edges are rounded. The lower rails may be barefaced. The joints are arranged as for the rush-topped stool. Bevel the bottoms of the legs and treat the tops in a similar way to that suggested for the rush-topped stool after the mortises have been cut.

Assemble opposite sides of the stool first. Check squareness and freedom from twist, then add the other rails. Pay particular attention to squareness when viewed from above. See that the outline pattern made by the bottoms of the legs agrees with the top, as it is possible to get a twist during assembly. Stand back and view the framework from several directions. If the legs all appear parallel to each other when standing on a level surface, the framework is true.

Seating

Besides the shuttles and a pointed stick used in seating the rush-topped stool, you need a wooden needle (Fig. 5-14A). If possible, make it from ash or hickory, which will withstand the bending strains you will probably put on it. Exact size is not important, but ⅝ inch × ¼ inch is a suitable section. The needle should be longer than the distance across the stool. Give it a rounded point, and the two holes should be large enough to pass the seating material.

Besides seagrass and the alternatives suggested for the rush-topped stool, ordinary cord can be used. There are some attractive synthetic cords, either three-stranded or braided, that can be made into seats. Fine cords, whether seagrass or other material, make a pattern with more parts than if a coarse line is used. If you use very fine material, make sure it is strong enough. Synthetic cord of about ⅛-inch diameter will have ample strength, but in the natural materials it is better to have something slightly thicker.

Wind a few shuttles with seagrass or other material. Decide on the pattern to be worked. Lines across are divided by wraps around the rails. If you have many wraps, the pattern becomes more open and is easier and quicker to work. It is possible to have only one wrap between the lines across for a close top, but for a first attempt it is probably better to have two—four across and two wraps make a good pattern (Fig. 5-14B). Next, you

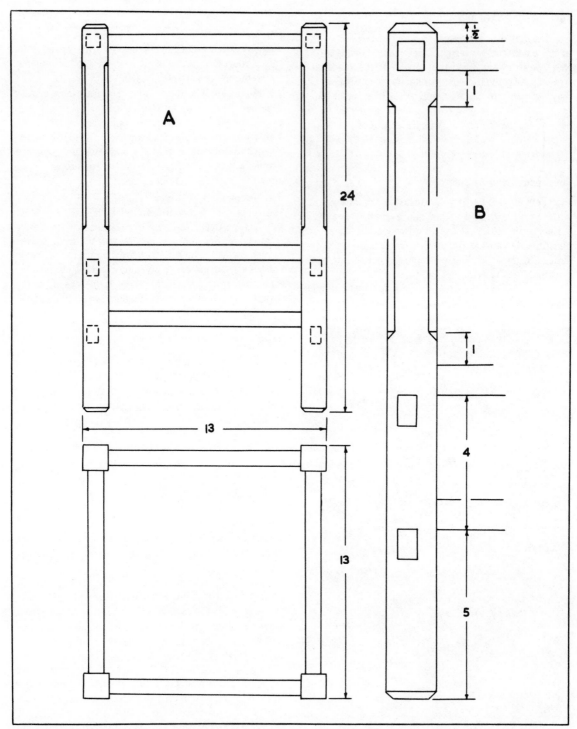

Fig. 5-13. The stool frame is tenoned, and the legs are decorated with wagon beveling.

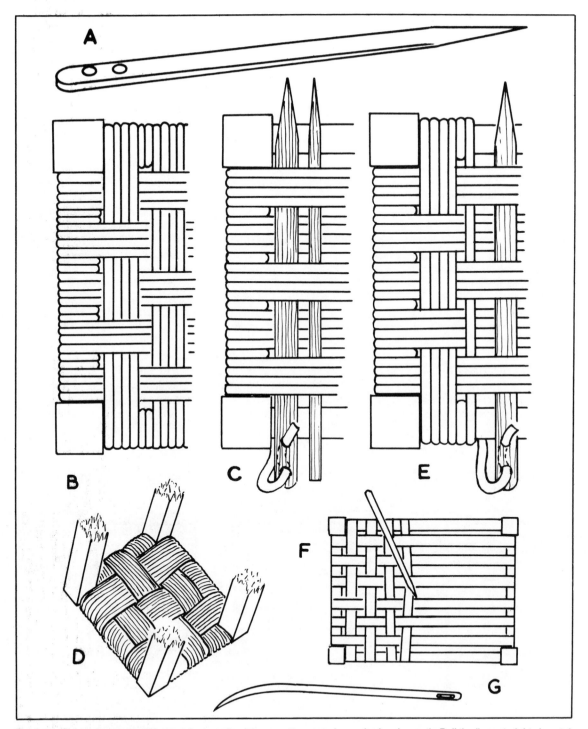

Fig. 5-14. The top is woven with a wooden needle. A large pattern may be worked underneath. Pull the lines straight. A metal needle will be needed for the last tucks.

have to decide on a color scheme. You can use natural or dyed material in both directions, and this may be a good choice to match other furnishings. You can use natural or one color in one direction and a different color the other way. That is the most popular arrangement (Fig. 5-15A). Another pattern has a color for the first and last bands each way, then the rest are natural (Fig. 5-15B). A neat arrangement has a band of natural followed by one or two bands of color framing the natural center (Fig. 5-15C).

Start with a knot in the end of the seagrass. Tack through near the knot into a leg close under a rail (Fig. 5-16A). Wind on four turns across the stool, then wrap twice (if that is the number chosen) at the far side (Fig. 5-16B). Return underneath and wrap twice on the near rail. You are ready to start across again with four turns (Fig. 5-16C). Getting the correct tension depends on experience. There must be some slackness, so the tucks can be made the other way. This has to be judged when putting on the first turns. With average materials, the first set of turns should be slack enough to be easily pushed down a couple of inches by hand.

You will have to make joints when you change color or run out of a spool of material. Knot underneath by using sheet bends. Do not cut off too closely at this stage. You can trim ends after completion of the top, but some longer ends are more easily hidden by tucking inside the pattern.

As you progress along the rails, push the turns tight with the edge of a piece of wood. No wood of the top rails should show between turns. If you are using a pattern that includes a border of a different color, you will have to judge how much of the remaining space to allow as you come near the ends of the rails. It is better to force the turns tight along a rail than to spread them when you finish. Finally, take the seagrass below a rail and tack it into a leg—in the same way as at the start.

You cannot use a shuttle in the other direction. Instead, there has to be a long length of seagrass fitted through the two holes in the needle. You will have to decide between having a long piece and pulling it all through, or having a shorter piece, with less to pull through, but more knots to tie. Start with a tacked knotted end under a rail.

Work the needle across, over, and under the groups of turns (Fig. 5-14C). If you push the pointed stick through first, that keeps the weave open. It is unnecessary to try to work the same pattern on the underside, but it strengthens the seat if you work a large pattern there. Dividing the area into three each way will do, so bring the needle back over and under groups of three underneath. When you have gone about one-third of the distance in the width underneath, change to weaving the other way. Eventually the underside will show a pattern of nine large squares (Fig. 5-14D).

Make four turns across, then wrap around the far rail before returning underneath to make the same number of wraps on the near rail. Weave the next group of four turns the alternate way (Fig. 5-14E) and so on across the seat. You will find that the lines you are making tend to curve.

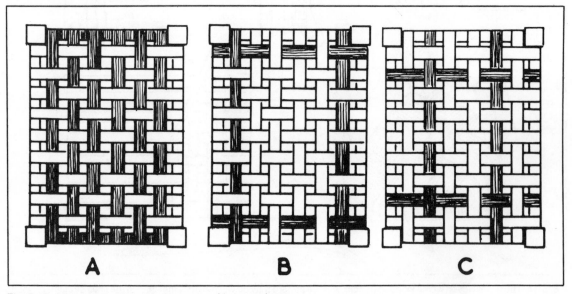

A   **B**   **C**

Fig. 5-15. A two-color pattern can be arranged in several ways.

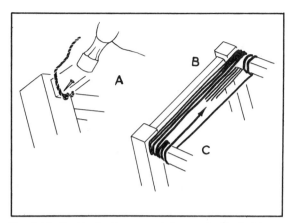

Fig. 5-16. Start by tacking an end, then make the first turns across.

After each set of four turns, use the pointed stick to pull the turns into line (Fig. 5-14F). With the early turns, you may even curve them slightly the other way to allow more room for the subsequent turns. Pull them straight later. As you progress, press the seagrass back toward the start along the rails, so the turns pack tightly. Lay a needle or a straight piece of wood across as a guide, so you can pull the turns into line.

If you put the right amount of tension into the first turns, you will find the pattern tightening as you progress. There will still be enough slackness for the needle to be pushed through, except that as you get to the last group of turns, there will not be enough give left, nor space allowed, for the wooden needle to go through. Pulling the worked turns back with the pointed stick helps, but having made all the spaces you can, you will still have to take the last turns through in a different manner. It is possible to work with just the end of the seagrass. Tuck it under a group at a time, but it helps to have a steel needle. This can be a *bagging needle*, which is intended for sewing string to close burlap bags. A needle about 6 inches long will have an eye large enough to take seagrass, and its curved point (Fig. 1-14G) makes tucking the last rows easier.

Pull the seagrass tight. Check the straightness of the rows in both directions. The gaps at the crossings should finish all about the same size. Tack the end to a leg below a rail.

Materials List for Tall Checker-topped Stool

4 legs	1½×25×1½
4 rails	⅞×13×⅞
8 rails	⅞×13×⅝

RUSH-TOPPED STOOL

A traditional method of seating that is still popular uses rushes, reeds, and grasses woven into ropes and worked into a pattern. Modern materials include prepared ropes of various natural and synthetic fibers that have been given a grasslike appearance. Some prepared natural materials can be bought dyed in a limited range of colors. One of these is described as seagrass and is imported from eastern countries. In the traditional method the reeds or rushes are twisted by hand into ropes as the work progresses, but this calls for more skill than when prepared ropes are used. Suitable rushes may not be easy to obtain, but gathering them from a riverside and drying them for use makes an interesting hobby. It is better to use prepared materials for most purposes. If it is a traditional piece of furniture that is being made, it is better to have the natural color—usually greenish brown—than to buy dyed material.

There are several interweaving patterns which produce a checkerboard effect, but the best one for chairs and stools is usually described as a rush pattern from its traditional form. In its finished appearance, the lines of rope are directed toward the center. The method of construction is not apparent. This makes a comfortable seat, due to the way it shapes downward to the center.

Seagrass may be in several thicknesses between about 3/16-inch and ⅛-inch diameter. The thicker seagrass is more durable for a much used seat and produces results more quickly. For an average chair or this stool, about 2 pounds should be sufficient. *Danish seat cord* is an alternative ropelike, brown fiber material and is about the same weight as seagrass. *Fiber rush* is based on paper and is lighter and not as strong as seagrass.

Construction and Assembly

The stool frame shown (Fig. 5-17) is of basic design and of a size that makes a seat for a child (Fig. 5-18). Many different proportions can be used without altering the method of construction. A low stool need only have single lower rails (Fig. 5-17A). If the legs are made longer to bring the stool to chair height or higher, it is better to have double lower rails (Fig. 5-17B). The stool can be square, but it is shown slightly longer one way. This improves appearance. It is possible to make a very long stool, providing the top rails are made stiff enough, but for a first stool a moderate size should be chosen.

As with any form of seating, the user may tend to rock the stool onto two legs. Joints should be strong enough to stand up to this rocking. It helps to stagger the heights of the lower rails. The tenons can then be taken

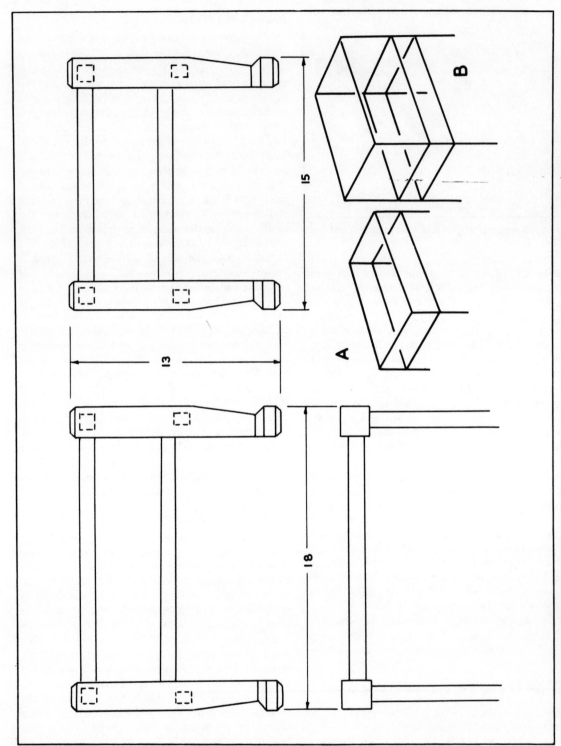

Fig. 5-17. Shaped legs are shown. Single lower rails can be used on a low stool (A), but double ones are needed to stiffen a higher one (B).

Fig. 5-18. A rush pattern makes a seat that goes down to the middle.

further into the legs instead of having to be mitered into each other. That has to be done at the top, but strong lower joints should keep the stool in shape.

The legs can be square for their whole length, but they are shown with a stylized form of the cabriole leg. In its full form this is a turned and carved claw and ball, but here it is made with a simplified square form that has only a trace of its origin. It makes a simple and interesting piece of cabinetwork.

Mark the lengths and joints of the legs together (Fig. 5-19A). Mark all the rails. Allow for the top rails being made with central tenons (Fig. 5-19B), with their ends mitered fairly close together. The lower rails are better with barefaced tenons (Fig. 5-19C). Mark and cut all the joints before shaping the legs. Round the edges of the top rails (Fig. 5-19D), but there is no need to sand them. They will not show in the finished stool, and a slight roughness helps to grip the seating material.

The inner corner of each leg remains straight, and that should be used for measuring from and putting the square against. Cut the bottoms of the legs to length. Do the shaping of all four legs in stages rather than completing one leg at a time, as that may lead to noticeable differences. Mark out one way (Fig. 5-20A) on opposite surfaces. Saw directly toward the deepest part (Fig. 5-20B). Carefully work down almost to the line on the top of the foot (Fig. 5-20C) with a chisel and mallet. Taper toward this in the same way (Fig. 5-20D). By doing the short slope first, there is less risk of the chisel going too far and marking the opposite slope. Finally, taper both slopes to the line. With most hardwoods, it should be

possible to pare finally with a broad chisel without using a mallet.

When the shape is satisfactory one way, mark the taper the other way on both surfaces (Fig. 5-20E). Cut that in the same manner. Mark around and bevel the underside of the foot (Fig. 5-20F). At the top bevel around (Fig. 5-20G) or taper to the center (Fig. 5-20H). The tops of the legs are very prominent in the finished stool, so be careful to get them symmetrical and sand them smooth. Do not trim the tops too low, or there is a risk of the short grain breaking out from the joints.

Assemble the stool in two stages. Make up opposite sides. Carefully square them and see that they are free from twist. When the glue has set, add the other rails to join these assemblies and complete the stool. Remove any glue that has squeezed out of the joints. Finish the woodwork almost completely before working the top. This can be stain followed by polish or varnish. There is no need to treat the top rails. The finish can be taken about ½ inch onto the ends of each rail, so there will be no plainness showing under the ends of the seat material. Leave a final coat of finish to apply after the seating has been done, in case there are any knocks or blemishes to touch up. If the entire finishing of the wood is left until after seating, there is a risk of marking the seat material.

Seating

Seagrass and other prepared materials may be supplied in *hanks*. Be careful of tangling when you extract pieces for use. Make a few spools or shuttles (Fig. 5-21A). They need not be very carefully shaped and finished. Keeping them narrow and long is better than making them wide. They will pass through the seat better after it has progressed to only having a small hole at the center. Scrap wood about 2 inches × 9 inches × ⅜ inch is suitable. You will also need a pointed piece of wood about ⅝ inch square and longer than the greater measurement of the stool (Fig. 5-21B).

Although the method of construction cannot be seen on a finished seat, the steps in working it are only the repetition of a simple action. Decide which way you want to go round the stool. A common beginner's mistake is to change direction. As described, the rope goes clockwise around the stool and counter clockwise around each leg. It can be done just as well the other way, providing you keep the same way all the time.

Have a shuttle full of seagrass ready. Tie a knot in its end. Use a thin nail or tack through the line near the knot into a rail (Fig. 5-21C). Go over the next rail at the corner, then up through the center of the stool, and back over the first rail (Fig. 5-21D). That is the complete action that has

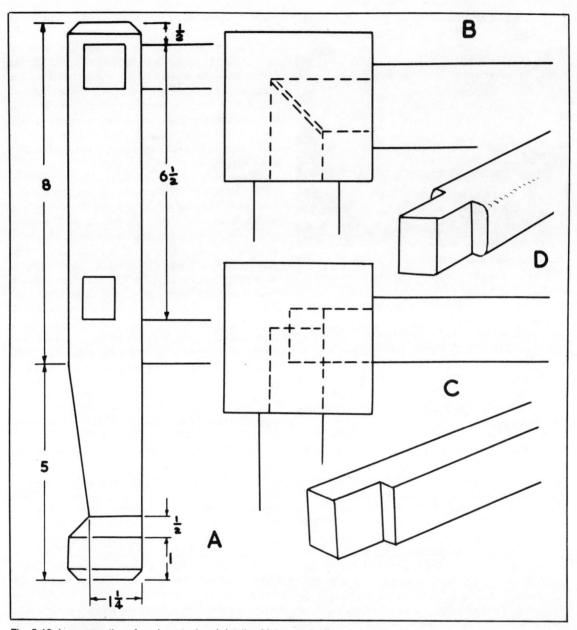

Fig. 5-19. Leg proportions for a low stool and details of joints and rails.

to be mastered. Subsequent work is a repeat of that procedure at each corner in turn, until the short sides of the stool are full.

Pull tight around that first leg. Bring the shuttle up through the center of the stool and do the same at the next corner (Fig. 5-21E). It helps to work with an assistant who can hold the tension on at a corner, while you go through the motions at the next corner and pull tight there before the previous corner is released.

Deal with all four corners, which brings the working end back to the corner on which you started. Repeat the action again inside the first round (Fig. 5-21F). Continue

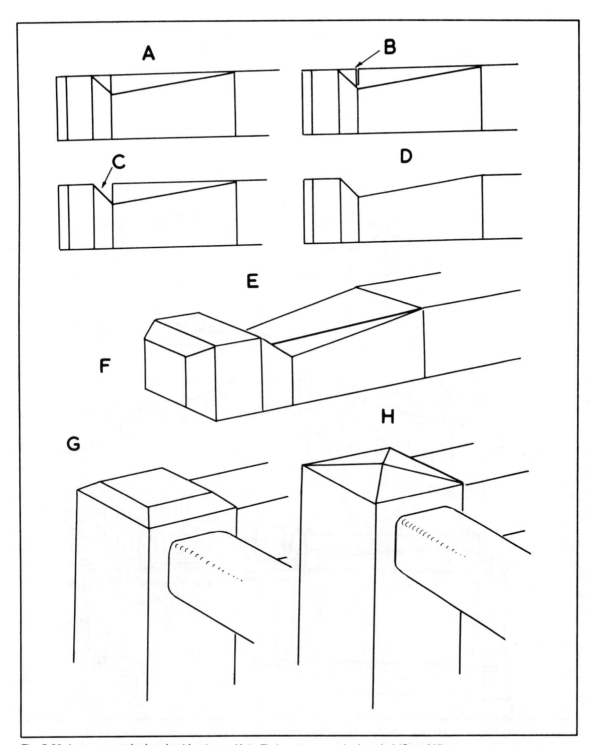

Fig. 5-20. Legs are marked and cut in stages (A to F). Leg tops may be beveled (G and H).

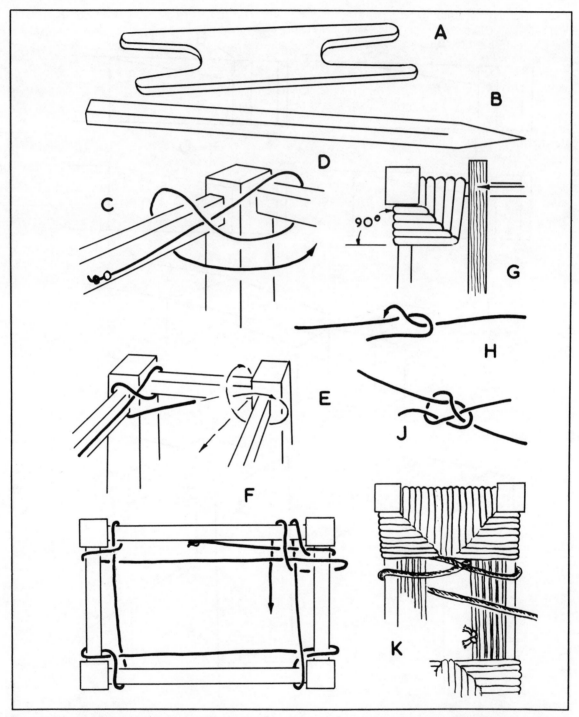

Fig. 5-21. A rush pattern is worked with a shuttle round each leg and round the stool (A to G). New lengths are knotted (H and J). The pattern changes for completion (K).

going round the stool inside the previous step each time. You will see that the pattern builds up the same on the top and bottom of the seat, with the parts between the corners hidden inside.

As you progress, get an even tension. See that the turns at the inner points of the pattern do not ride up over each other. After about every four times round, check that you are working squarely. Use the pointed stick or other piece of wood across the stool to push the turns tightly along the rails, so there are no gaps, and they are square (Fig. 5-21G).

Occasionally you will have to join in a new length of seagrass. Do that where the line is going from one corner to the next, then the knot will be hidden inside the seat. Some of this material is slippery, so make sure the knot is tight. If a knot comes adrift after a seat has been made, you cannot reknot unobtrusively. The best knot is the sheet bend. Bend back a loop in one part. Bring the other end toward it, up through it, and behind it (Fig. 5-21H). Go around the loop and across its front, so the end goes under its own part (Fig. 5-21J). Work it tight without altering its form. Do not cut off too closely.

Eventually you will have the short rails full. Make sure you cannot get any more turns in by pressing the strands toward the corners. At this point you cannot continue to use a shuttle. You will have to finish the seat with a loose end of seagrass. Try to allow enough to do all the finishing without knots, as any knot after this will have to be made underneath where it will show. Work in a figure eight fashion over the opposite rails (Fig. 5-21K). Pack tightly. The pointed piece of wood will be needed to open a central space for the final few tucks. When you have the rails full, fasten the last turn with a tack or small nail driven into the underside of a rail. Cut off a few inches from the tack and tuck the end into the underside of the seat.

Materials List for Rush-topped Stool

4 legs	1¾×14×1¾
2 rails	1×18×1
2 rails	1×15×1
2 rails	1×18×¾
2 rails	1×15×¾

RUSH-SEATED CHAIR

Traditionally, rush seating was used more for chairs than for stools. It used available natural materials to make a more attractive and more comfortable seat than a plain wooden one. It also avoided the need for the craftsman to prepare wide boards. This example is of simple form and typical of an early pioneer chair which still has uses in a modern home. It possesses a beauty different from that of a chair made in a more modern form and using modern materials.

The general shape is that of a stool with the rear legs extended upward to make the back. It is finished in the ladderback form with rails curved to match the sitter's back. Underneath there are deep side rails to provide stiffness and resist the loads applied by a sitter tilting the chair back. There are double rails across, set back so there is nothing to get in the way of the sitter's legs at the front. Use a close-grained hardwood. The legs are shown square and without decoration (Fig. 5-22). Appearance can be lightened by wagon beveling or carving the edges between joints. If a lathe is available, the parts between the seat and the lower rails can be turned.

Construction and Assembly

This chair, like most others, differs from most stools by being wider at the front. It suits the human body and makes for comfort. Differences in construction and in the method of working the seat are only slight. The angles of the sides are not far off 90°. A careful worker may choose to mark out joints to take account of the angles on the side rails, but the difference is so little that joints marked squarely will probably pull just as tight. In any case, the back and front of the chair are assembled squarely first. The side parts are then added.

Mark out the legs together (Fig. 5-23A). Notice that both sets have to be paired, with back rail positions and lower rail positions on adjoining faces. The seat rails are best with central tenons, but the back slats and the lower rails can have bareface tenons which will pull close better at the sloping sides. Draw a full-size plan view of the seat (Fig. 5-23B), with the sections of the legs square to back and front.

For seating with rushes that were twisted as the seat was made, it was common to make the rails slightly deeper at their centers. This is not essential when using seagrass or one of the other seating materials, but they are shown deepened to maintain a traditional appearance (Fig. 5-23C). Make these to the sizes obtained on the plan view. Also on the plan view, draw the side lower rails and the two that join them (Fig. 5-23D). Make the side rails and allow for mortises as deep as you can cut them without breaking through (Fig. 5-23E).

It is unwise to try to use dowels instead of mortise and tenon joints in rails of these sizes. It is possible to substitute round rods for the lower rails, so they go into drilled holes like dowels (Fig. 5-23F).

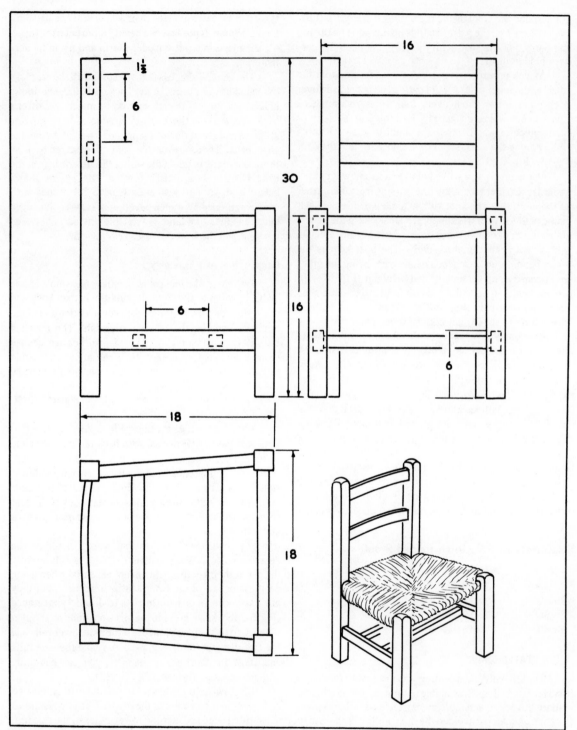

Fig. 5-22. A simple chair can have a rush pattern seat.

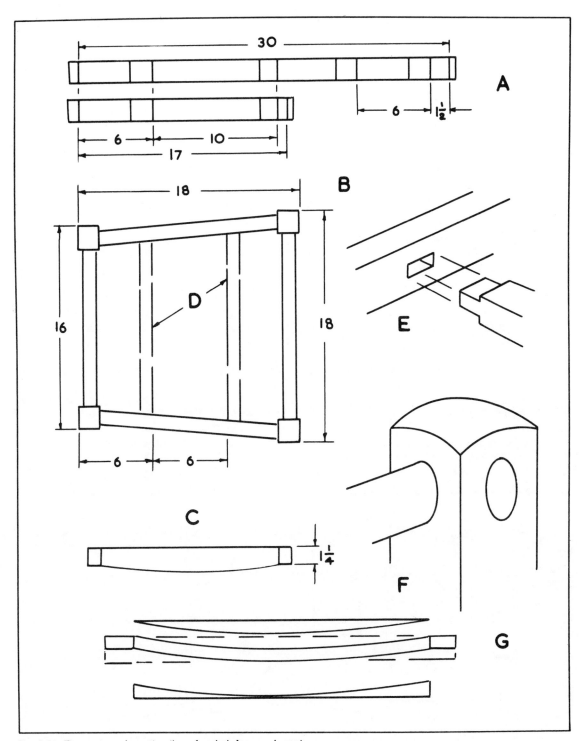

Fig. 5-23. The parts and construction of a chair for a rush seat.

The rails or *slats* at the back are cut from thicker wood and curved (Fig. 5-23G). A band saw is a useful tool, but otherwise the curves may be sawed by hand and smoothed with planes. Round the top and bottom edges. Notice that the tenons are cut squarely to the surface of the legs and not sloping to follow the curves.

Before assembly, remove the sharpness from all edges of legs and exposed rails. Although they may still look square, there should be no roughness when they are handled. The seat rails are better with rather more rounding on all four edges. In some types of chairs there can be angle brackets in the corners of the seat. They will interfere with rush seating, though, so you have to depend on tightly fitting joints.

If any joints are not as close fitting as you wish, it is possible to tighten them by fox wedging. This is a method of expanding the tenon within the mortise. Always do this in the direction of the grain of the mortised part and not the other way, which might split the wood. Make a saw cut across the end of the tenon (two if it is a wide one), then prepare a small wedge to fit into the cut (Fig. 5-24A). The wedge should extend so that when the joint is pulled tight, it presses against the bottom of the mortise and spreads the tenon (Fig. 5-24B). The size to make the wedge is a matter of judgment, depending on how much expansion is needed. If the joint is coated well with glue as it is clamped or hammered together, the whole thing should bond into a secure joint, unless it started exceptionally loose.

Put together the back and front assemblies separately. Check squareness and that the front matches the back when put over it in its correct relative position. Join the two lower cross rails into the side rails. If you think extra strengthening is needed, screws or nails driven from below will be inconspicuous (Fig. 5-24C). Assemble the lower and seat side rails to the two assemblies. Pull the joints close, but you cannot use a square to test the back to the front. Instead, see that the diagonals are the same (Fig. 5-24D), both at seat and lower rail levels. Check that the chair stands level and looks right when viewed from a distance. Finish the woodwork with stain and polish or varnish, except for the last coat, before working the top.

Seating

The basic method of making the seat is described for the rush pattern stool (Fig. 5-18). Those instructions should be used, except for the following variations. Use similar seagrass or other materials and have some shuttles loaded.

If the chair seat was worked in the same way as a square or rectangular stool, the back rail would be filled before the front one. There would be no easy way of filling the gap left there. Instead, there have to be extra turns worked around the front legs to make up the difference. If you decide to use the method on a tapered seat of a different size, make sure the side rails are not shorter than the front rail. Otherwise, there is a risk of filling them before you have done enough on the front rail. You are unlikely to do this, as a chair needs to be at least as deep back to front as it is wide for comfort.

Tack a knotted end to a side rail and work around all four corners as described for the stool (Fig. 5-25A). When you come to a front corner again, work around it in the

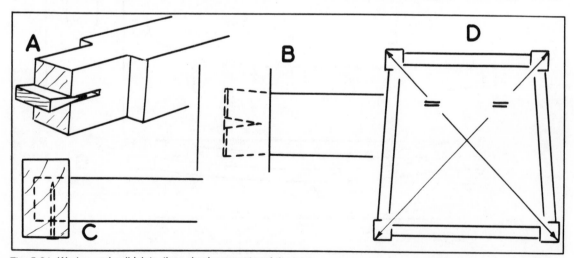

Fig. 5-24. Wedge and nail joints, then check symmetry of the seat.

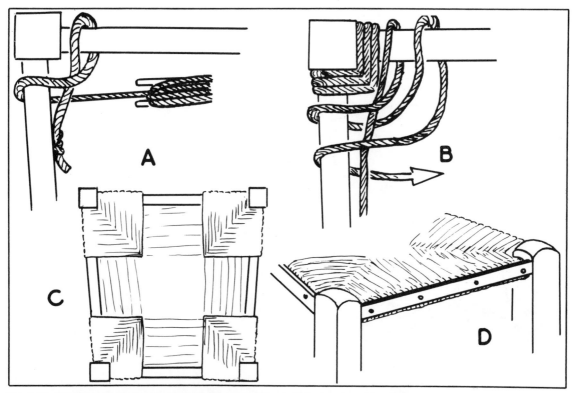

Fig. 5-25. Weaving the top has to allow for the taper. Wood strips can cover the edges.

usual way. Instead of going straight across to the other front corner, go around that leg again (Fig. 5-25B). Cross to the other front corner and go around that one twice. Never go around more than once at each rear corner.

You will have to make up by doubling around front corners more than once, but do not do this every time you come to them. After you have gone round the front legs twice, do perhaps another two circuits of the seat with only single turns at each corner. Follow this by going around the two front corners twice again. You should never go around just one front corner twice; always deal with both of them in the same way. Press the seagrass toward the corners so as to get the turns tight.

Continue in this way until the width of rail at the front is the same as that at the back (Fig. 5-25C). Then work around with single turns at each corner until the seat is filled. If more parts are needed, work in a figure eight manner as described for the stool.

That completes the chair, but if you want to follow tradition, there are two points you can consider. If an old rush-seated chair has worn out and the seat has begun to disintegrate, you will probably find more rush than you expected. This is because the seat was packed with odd pieces of rush. You find in working that as the top and bottom are formed, there is a space between. With tight seagrass, this does not matter. The seat should be satisfactory without padding. If you wish, you can push in oddments of seagrass when the seat is about three-fourths done. You can even use pieces of cloth. If you work the seat tightly and get in as many turns as you can along the rails, the padding should not show through.

With rushes, it helped to put strips along the edges to protect the material. It may not be so important with other seat materials, but there can be varnished strips of thin wood nailed through the edges of the seat into the rails and fitted tightly between the legs (Fig. 5-25D).

Materials List for Rush-seated Chair

2 legs	1¾×31×1¾
2 legs	1¾×18×1¾
5 rails	1¾×18×1
2 rails	1¾×16×1
2 rails	1×18×1
2 slats	1¾×16×1¼

Chapter 6

Simple Tables

Tables take many forms. Most tables have enough straight edges and square angles for setting out and assembly to be dealt with in the normal woodworking fashion, unlike some chairs, with their curves and compound angles. There are many ways of supporting tabletops—from the usual four legs to built-up structures that provide storage space and pedestals that give the main support centrally. There may be some shaping in the legs or supports, but the underlying forms are usually rectangular.

It is not always easy for a beginner to see from a design what sort of table is within his capabilities. Small tables are not necessarily simpler than large ones. The examples in this chapter all have straightforward construction. A capacity for taking care is more important than a high degree of skill. If there are four legs, they must match. If parts need to be straight and with square edges, take care to see that this is so.

You cannot get far with the making of tables and chairs without learning to make tight fitting mortise and tenon joints. It is possible to use dowels in many places where traditional construction called for mortises and tenons, but not everywhere. If you want to regard yourself as a craftsman, you should master the cutting of these joints. Some examples in this chapter provide practice without being too complicated. Other joints occur less often. You will have to cross rails with simple halving joints, and there are places where dovetails are the only joints acceptable to a craftsman. If you have little experience in joint making, select a few examples from this chapter to test your skill.

If you have a lathe, there will be plenty of opportunities for using it. Remember that for most tables you need to turn four legs that match. This is more difficult than making just one spindle.

BED OR TODDLER TABLE

This is a small table (Fig. 6-1A) that can be used by a child while sitting on the floor. It can be turned upside down and used as a doll's cot or an imaginary boat or car. Later, when the child no longer wants it, the table can be used on a bed where it, provides a support for food, books, or anything else needed there.

Construction is almost entirely of ½-inch plywood. The corners of the four sides are all cut the same way. They should match if the table is to look right, so it will

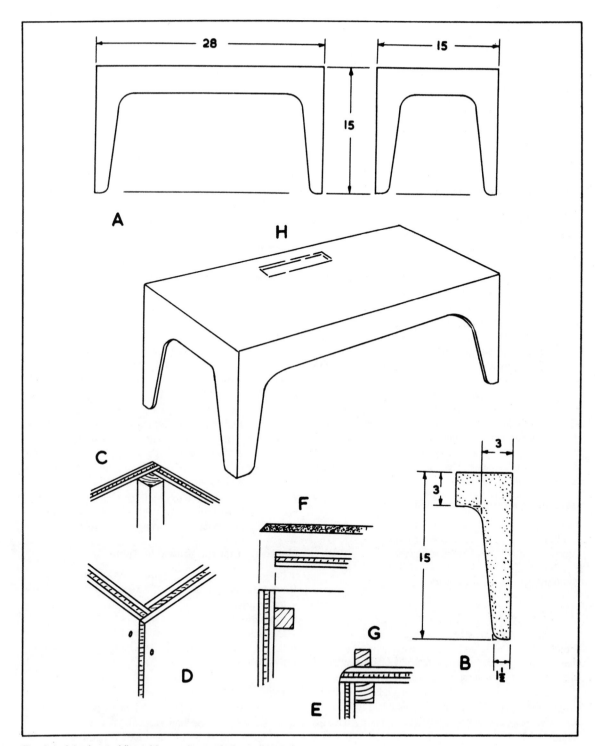

Fig. 6-1. A bed or toddler table can be made from plywood.

help to make a template of the legs (Fig. 6-1B). Make the four sides. Be careful of splintering edges as you cut them. Round the section of the inside shaping.

The simplest corner joint is made with a strip of solid wood inside (Fig. 6-1C). Glue and nail the strips to the edges of the short sides. Plane squarely after the glue has set, so you get close joints as you nail and glue on the long sides. Another way, if you have suitable tools to do it, is to cut a rabbet in one piece for the other part. Then the pieces can be brought together and glued with nails both ways (Fig. 6-1D) without the need of an inside strip.

For rigidity and a strong top, there should be more strips of solid wood around that joint. If the plywood will form the table surface, you can put strips around and fasten the plywood down (Fig. 6-1E). A top that is easy to clean is Formica or other laminated plastic. If you are to use laminated plastic, it is better to set the plywood top inside the legs and put the plastic over it (Fig. 6-1F).

If a child wants to turn the table over and drag it around, the top should be left smooth. Otherwise, it is better to have some edging to prevent things sliding off, particularly when used for drinks on a bed. The simplest way of providing edging is to attach strips to the top (Fig. 6-1G). They should not meet at the corners so crumbs and dust can be wiped off.

You can have a well to prevent a toddler's pencils from rolling off (Fig. 6-1H). Cut out a recess of suitable size in the top. Round its upper edges and fasten a piece of plywood underneath the opening to form its bottom. If that does not make a deep enough recess, you can cut a similar hole in another piece of plywood to fit under, and put the bottom below that.

Materials List for Bed or Toddler Table

2 sides	15×28×½ plywood
2 sides	15×15×½ plywood
1 top	15×28×½ plywood
6 stiffeners	⅝×15×⅝
2 stiffeners	⅝×28×⅝

STOWABLE TABLE

A table that takes up little space when it is not needed, yet can be brought out for parties or other occasions when there are crowds, has obvious advantages. The simplest type is a top with a pair of folding trestles. The idea dates back to the days of the feudal baron in his castle, where the tables in the great hall had to be taken down and stowed away when they were not being used for banquets. The top was not attached to its legs, but merely rested on supports made in the form of trestles that could be folded flat. The table described here follows the same design in a size more suitable for a modern home. There can be different top sizes. You can have two of these tables and an extra top to rest between them when you need that much space, possibly for entertainment outside or even a garage sale. The table itself is not intended to be decorative—the intention is pure utility—so it has to be covered with a cloth for more important occasions.

The top is drawn 78 inches long and 30 inches wide, which is the size of many doors. You may use a door panel (Fig. 6-2). The trestles give a working surface at normal height.

The simplest top is a single piece of thick plywood, but it is heavy and costly. It may be better to frame thin plywood with softwood strips (Fig. 6-3A). The plywood should not be thinner than ¼ inch. Plywood thinner than ¼ inch will require extra stiffening, which cancels any advantage of lightness in the top panel.

Put stiffening pieces across at each trestle's position, with two guide pieces to locate the trestle (Fig. 6-3B). Use halving or bridle joints in the framing (Fig. 6-3C).

The trestles can have parallel sides (Fig. 6-3D) or splayed legs (Fig. 6-3E). Both types are shown without diagonal bracing, so the strength to resist sideways collapse comes in the joints. Use dowels if you wish, although tenons should be stronger (Fig. 6-3F).

Make four identical frames and check them over each other during assembly. Hinge the tops. Do not bevel the top edges outward to match the underside of the top when in position. Bevel the other way, so the knuckles of the hinges come below the table line (Fig. 6-3G).

It may be possible to fit a folding strut between the bottom rails to hold each trestle open. The simplest control is a piece of rope through holes (Fig. 6-3H).

Materials List for Stowable Table

1 top	30×78×¼ plywood
2 top frames	2×79×1
2 top frames	2×31×1
2 top stiffeners	4×31×1
4 top guides	1×3×1
8 trestle legs	3×31×⅞
8 trestle rails	3×31×⅞

CHAIRSIDE TABLE

This is a small table or block of shelves intended to stand beside a lounge chair to take books, cups, and all the other oddments that you may need (Figs. 6-4 and 6-5). The table can be on glides to allow movement, but it will

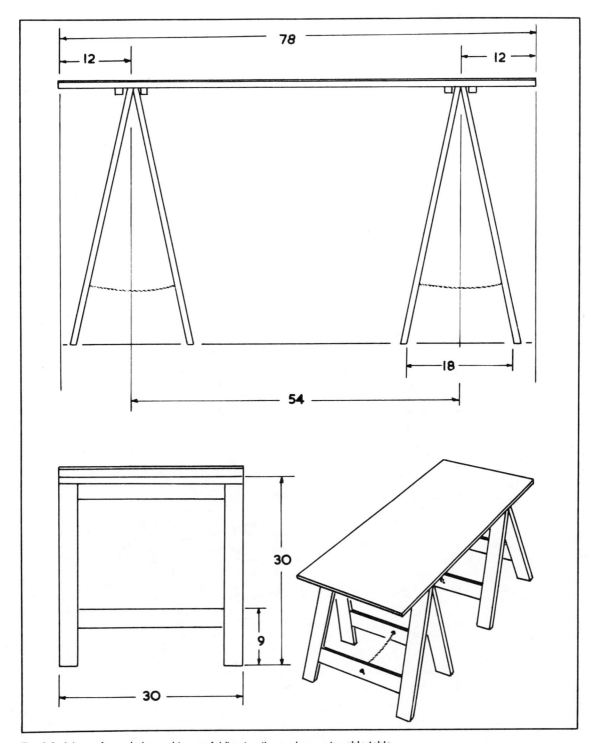

Fig. 6-2. A loose framed plywood top on folding trestles makes a stowable table.

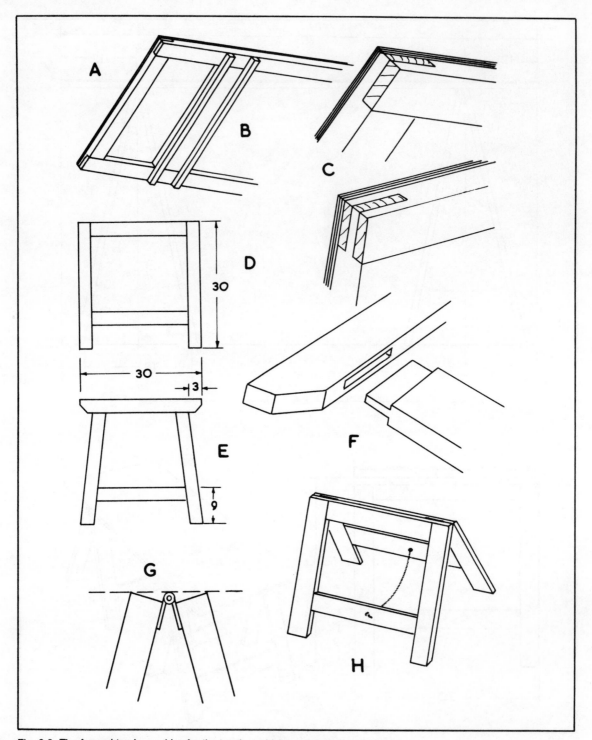

Fig. 6-3. The framed top has guides for the trestles, which are tenoned and hinged.

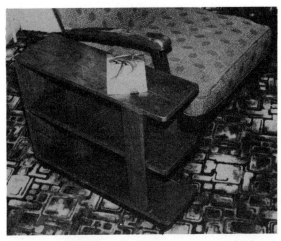

Fig. 6-4. A chairside table provides a place for many things within easy reach.

usually stand with its back level with the chair's back, so you can reach over the chair arm to it.

The top and bottom are the same, and the middle shelf differs in the joints. Curve all the front corners together, so they match. The best joint at the top and bottom of the back is a stopped dovetail (Fig. 6-6A). It will be exposed to the rear, but will not usually be on view. Even if the joint can be seen, it is evidence of your good craftsmanship. A simpler joint can be used if you do not trust your skill at dovetailing.

The middle shelf can fit into a dado joint. That can be carried right through, or you can stop both ends for a better appearance (Fig. 6-6B). That involves careful work with a chisel where the through dado is more easily cut with a saw or power *router*.

The two sides can be joined, so details of the joints do not show. Use short tenons into mortises at the top and bottom (Fig. 6-6C). At the middle shelf, cut dadoes in

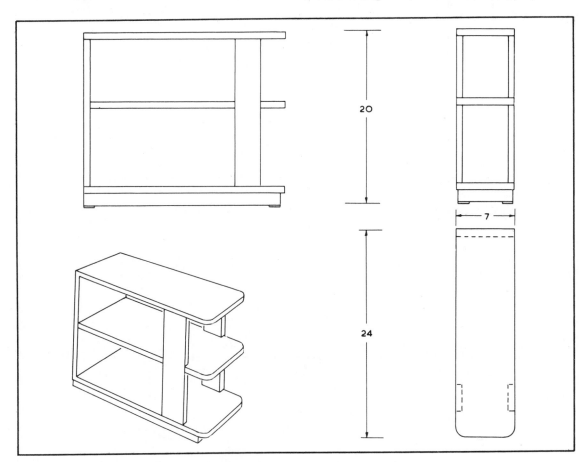

Fig. 6-5. A narrow chairside table takes up little space.

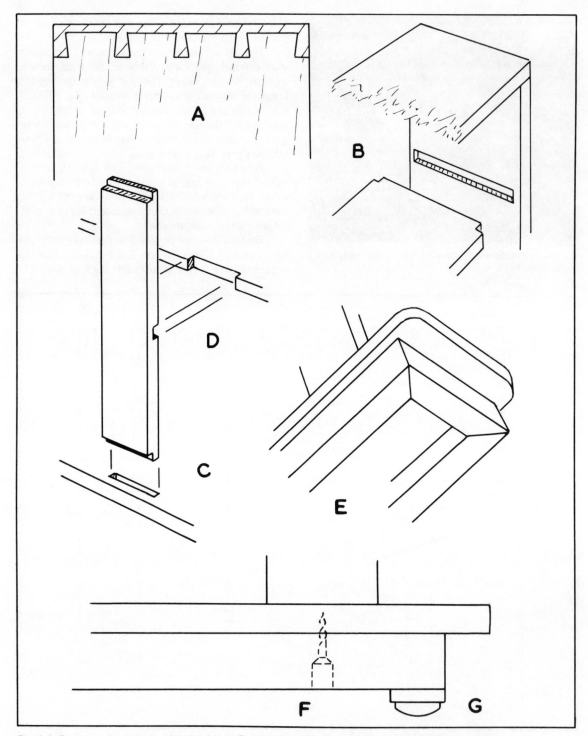

Fig. 6-6. Parts are dovetailed and dadoed (A to D), then the plinth is screwed underneath (E, F, and G).

the sides. Cut away enough shelf to bring it level (Fig. 6-6D). The sides should be flush with all outer edges.

If the table is to stand without glides, the *plinth* can be made of thinner strips on edge. To give width for glides, it is simplest to use square strips set back under the bottom. Miter the corners (Fig. 6-6E) and attach with screws upward into the bottom shelf (Fig. 6-6F). Small blocks may come under the corners to take the glides (Fig. 6-6G).

The table looks good if the main parts are finished in the natural color. The plinth is stained quite dark.

Materials List for Chairside Table

3 shelves	7×25×¾
1 back	7×20×¾
2 sides	3×20×¾
2 plinths	1½×24×1½
2 plinths	1½×7×1½

COLONIAL SIDE TABLE

Pioneer woodworkers were faced with the need to make furniture simply and quickly. Some of it was probably very crude, but other pieces had a certain basic beauty largely due to their proportions. Many things were made from wide boards with little decoration. This table is an example. It is not of a size for sitting at (Fig. 6-7), although it can be enlarged to make a dining table. It will then be necessary to keep the drawer shallow enough to

Fig. 6-7. This side table is on traditional Colonial lines.

allow spacer for a sitter's knees. It is a reproduction of a small table that would have been common in an early settler's home (Fig. 6-8). It still has uses today.

The wood is all in wide boards. It may be necessary to glue up pieces to make the width. With modern glues it should be satisfactory to rely only on glue between two true surfaces. If you want more strength, there can be dowels between the edges. Prepare any glued-up boards before starting on the general construction. To be authentic, the wood chosen should be a local hardwood.

Original tables may have been nailed together, or there could have been pegs driven into holes, like modern doweling, but taken right through. The original pegs would not have been perfectly circular. If you wish to use the method, drill as if for doweling. Take the holes through, then make pegs by whittling approximately round. Glue as you drive them in, then plane the ends flush. You probably will use dowels that do not show through, and that is the method illustrated. Similarly, the original drawer bottoms would be cut thin, with several pieces used to make up the width. A modern drawer would be more acceptable with a plywood bottom. That is shown, although such material would not have been available to the makers of the originals.

Prepare the boards that make up the main structure so they are flat and without twist. Carefully square ends to length. Errors in squaring are more obvious in a plain design than in one that has ornamentation to distract attention.

To provide feet so the table will stand evenly, although the floor may not be level, cut away the bottoms of the ends (Fig. 6-8A). Remove saw marks and slightly round the edges of the cut.

Make sure the parts that go between the ends are all exactly the same length (Fig. 6-9A), so the joints will all pull tight. All of the joints can be made with ⅜-inch dowels—taken as far into the thickness as you can drill without breaking through (Fig. 6-9B). Stand the assembly on a flat surface and check squareness before leaving the glued joints to set.

Put drawer guides between the rails on the ends (Fig. 6-9C). Make sure the surfaces that meet the front rails come level, so the drawer will run smoothly. Attach with screws and glue.

Prepare the tabletop, but do not fit it until the drawer has been made and found to slide and work properly. Make sure its overhang is the same all round. Take off sharpness, but otherwise leave the edges square. Drill for dowels to join the ends to the top (Fig. 6-9D). These will be the main attachments, but there should be two or three widely spaced dowels along the back rail. There can

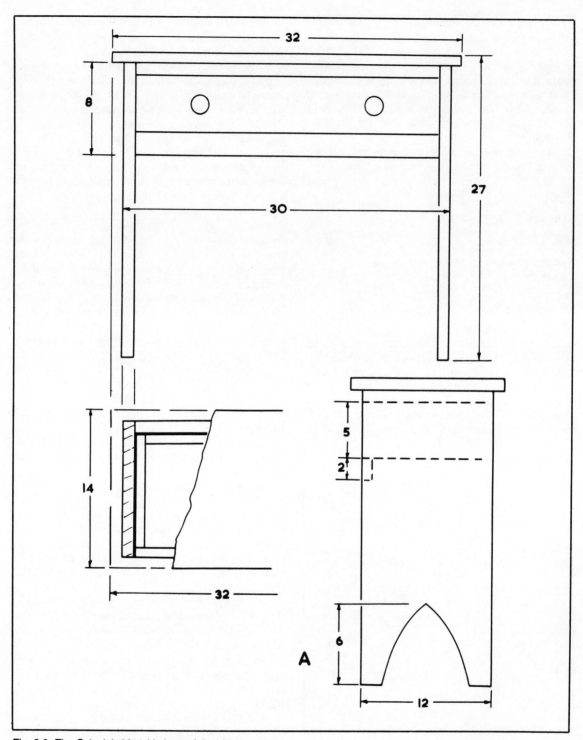

Fig. 6-8. The Colonial side table has a full-width drawer.

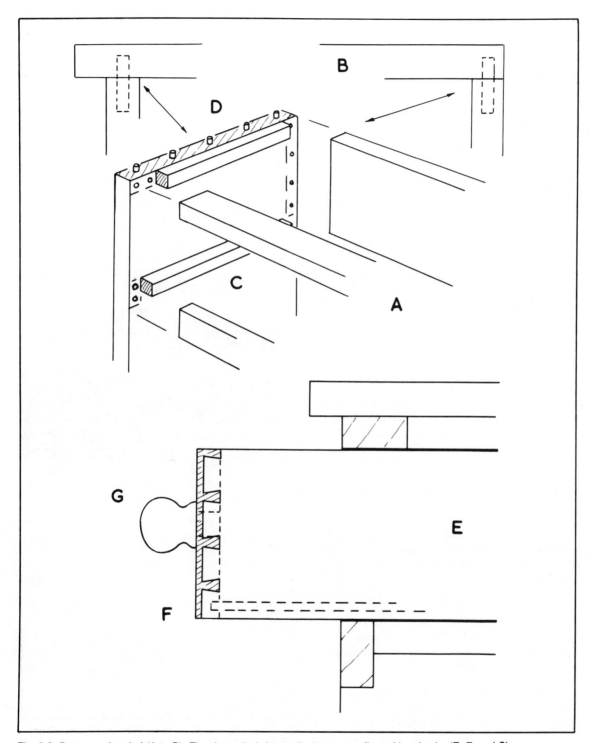

Fig. 6-9. Parts are doweled (A to D). The dovetailed drawer fits between rails and has knobs (E, F, and G).

be similarly spaced screws upward through the front rail. Do all the necessary drilling in the lower assembly and the top, so you are ready to put these parts together after working on the drawer.

Dowels in the main construction are hidden and do not detract from the authentic appearance of the table, but drawer details are visible. Most of the original makers of drawers used dovetails, unless they were so unskilled as to use nails. They would not have assembled a drawer with dowels or any of the special joints possible with modern power tools. For the best work the drawer corners should have hand-cut dovetail joints, and not the type which can be cut with a jig and show equal widths of tails and pins.

Cut the wood for the two drawer sides to be an easy sliding fit between the guides (Fig. 6-9E). Plow grooves for the plywood bottom. Prepare the drawer front to make an easy fit, but without any more clearance in the space than is necessary. Mark out and cut the front dovetail joints (Fig. 6-9F).

Allow for the drawer sides coming inside the back slightly when the drawer is pushed in, and the front comes level with its rails. Cut the dovetails for the back, which can come above the bottom, so the plywood may be slid in. After the drawer has been assembled, thin pieces of wood or even cardboard can be glued inside the rear rail to act as stops and bring the drawer front neatly level with its rails.

Drawer handles were nearly always turned. It is possible to make long handles hollowed to provide grip, but it is wrong to fit metal or plastic types to this traditional furniture. On a wide drawer there should be two handles, and the common shape is shown (Fig. 6-9G). Turn or buy the knobs with a dowel on the back to glue into holes in the drawer front.

Any polish on the first tables probably came from handling. Nothing particular was applied, unless wax or oil was available. It is unlikely that a table would have been stained. It is wrong to use varnish or similar finishing material on new work, if it is to retain a look comparable with an original. The grain can be filled and the surface sanded, then a rub with wax can be given at intervals of several weeks. Linseed oil can be used in the same way, but it takes longer to dry. The patina of old work can only come with age.

Materials List for Colonial Side Table

1 top	14×33×1
2 legs	12×27×1
1 back rail	8×30×1
2 front rails	2×30×1
4 drawer guides	1×12×1
1 drawer front	5×30×¾
1 drawer back	5×30×¾
2 drawer sides	5×12×¾
1 drawer bottom	12×30×¼ plywood

WINDOW TABLE

This is a straightforward small table of standard construction. In its original form it was intended to stand below a window, where it would accommodate pot plants and other items. It may be made with or without a shelf (Fig. 6-10) for magazines and other papers. The size given (Fig. 6-11) can be modified to make a table to suit its situation.

Fig. 6-10. This table is designed to go beneath a window.

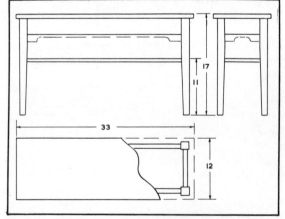

Fig. 6-11. The sizes of a window table can be adapted to its location.

The top can be made from solid wood, or it may be made of plywood with a solid wood border. A good alternative is veneered particle board, as there is then no risk of expansion and contraction due to varying moisture content. Adequately seasoned solid wood should not present any difficulties in this width. It is worthwhile keeping the wood for the top in the room that the table will be used in for a month, so it dries to a compatible degree before being made into the table.

The framework need not be the same wood as the top, but it should be hardwood and either naturally darker or stained darker than the top. If there is to be a shelf, the top rails need not be as deep as if the table is made without it. The shelf provides some stiffening. Joints between the rails and the legs may be mortise and tenon (Figs. 6-12A and 6-12B), or they can be doweled (Fig. 6-12C).

Make the legs parallel to below the rail positions, then taper the inner surfaces only to the bottom (Fig. 6-12D). Leave a little excess length at the top to trim off after assembly. Bevel the bottoms slightly (Fig. 6-12E).

Make the rails. Get lengths of opposite ones to match—between the shoulders if you are using tenons. Deep rails, for use without a shelf, look better if their lower edges are cut back (Fig. 6-12F). Leave enough full width at the ends to provide strength. Mark the joints in legs and rails together. Number matching parts.

If there is a shelf, it is notched into the legs. To get the sizes correct, draw a corner full-size (Fig. 6-13A). From this you can get the widths to mark from the outer square corners of the legs (Fig. 6-13B). The plywood shelf fits the notch, and its projecting corners are rounded (Fig. 6-13C). When the table is assembled, glue can be supplemented by a screw driven diagonally from below (Fig. 6-13D).

Assemble the framework in stages. Join the two long rails to their legs first. Take care to check squareness and that the two assemblies are the same. When the glue has set, join the sides with the short rails and take in the shelf, if there is one, at the same time. At this stage, check squareness as viewed from above. See that the legs stand evenly on a level surface. If necessary, put weights on boards over the rails to keep the table true while the glue sets.

The top is square-edged. It can be molded to match other furniture in the room. Make it to overlap the framework the same amount all round. There can be pocket screws to hold the framework to the top, but dowels are shown (Fig. 6-13E). Mark the dowel holes in the rails. A central one at each end, then others near the ends of the side rails, with more at about 9-inch intervals,

should be satisfactory. Invert the framework over the underside of the top and transfer the hole positions (Fig. 6-13F). Drill as deeply into the top as you can safely go without the point of the bit coming through. Glue the top on, using weights or clamps over wood strips to apply pressure.

Materials List for Window Table

1 top	12×33×¾
4 legs	1¼×20×1½
2 rails (with shelf)	3×33×¾
2 rails (with shelf)	3×12×¾
1 shelf	12×33×½ plywood
or without shelf:	
2 rails	4½×33×¾
2 rails	4½×12×¾

SEWING TABLE

A table with plenty of drawer storage capacity will keep tidy the many items needed for needlework. This table (Fig. 6-14) is of coffee table size, so it can be used for other things than needlework. The table is unusual in having a drawer that goes right through and can be opened from either end. This makes it possible to get at the contents either way, or the drawer can be used to store particular types of things at each end. An optional sliding tray will take care of small items.

An advantage of having one long drawer instead of two short ones is in the ease of running. A long narrow drawer will not seize as it slides through. Short drawers may twist and become temporarily jammed if not pulled straight. For anyone inexperienced at the making and fitting of drawers, this project is a simple practice piece that will show the principles involved.

The drawing (Fig. 6-15) shows a fairly deep drawer in relation to the other size. This does not leave much length of leg projecting. Legs can be left square, but a slight taper improves appearance (Fig. 6-15A). These short legs should be within the capacity of quite a small lathe, so the projecting parts can be turned (Fig. 6-15B). In any case, mark out the legs together (Fig. 6-16A). The rails at the long sides can be tenoned (Fig. 6-16B) or doweled (Fig. 6-16C).

In the other direction the rails above the drawer are best dovetailed into the tops of the legs (Fig. 6-16D). The lower drawer rails can be tenoned or doweled (Fig. 6-16E). Mark all rails in pairs to suit the chosen method of construction. The lower edges all round look best if cut back (Fig. 6-16F), but do not cut away very much. There must be enough depth for the drawer runners.

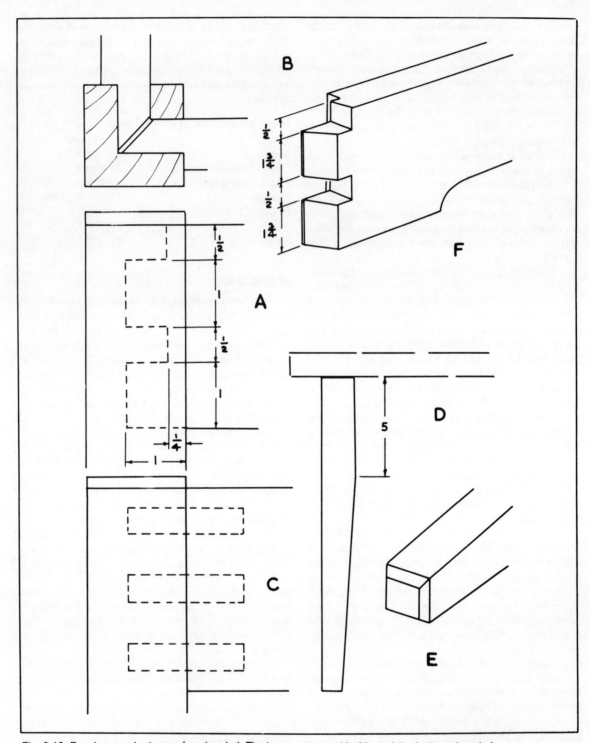

Fig. 6-12. Framing may be tenoned or doweled. The legs are tapered inside and the bottoms beveled.

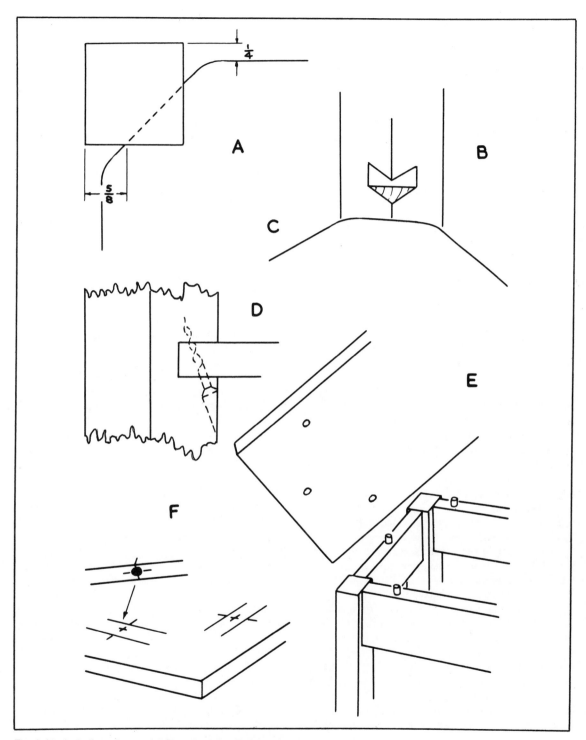

A

B

C

D

E

F

Fig. 6-13. A shelf can be notched into the legs. The top is doweled on.

Fig. 6-14. This sewing table has a drawer that can be opened from either end.

Make the two long side rails in the usual way. Cut the mortise and tenon joints (Fig. 6-17A). Along the top edges there has to be a kicker to come above the drawer sides, and this is made the length of its side between the tenon shoulders (Fig. 6-17B). Join it to the side with glue and a few screws.

Make the top short rails. Their lengths between the shoulders are the key measurements. Cut the dovetails on the rails and use them to mark the tops of the legs. Letter each pair of parts so there will be no confusion during assembly, as it is unlikely that you will make the joints interchangeable.

The lower short rails should have their bottom edges level with the bottoms of the side rails. The joints to the legs can be dowels, but they are better tenoned (Fig. 6-17C). Use barefaced tenons and make sure the outer surfaces finish level.

The drawer runners are strips similar to the kickers, but they have to be cut around the legs to finish level with the lower drawer rails (Fig. 6-17D). Leave fitting them until after the legs and rails have been joined.

Assemble the legs to the side rails first. Add the short rails. Be careful to check squareness in all directions. Fit the drawer runners with glue and screws to the side rails, but watch the close fitting of the ends around the legs and level with the lower drawer rails. It will help to drill them for screws into the legs inside (Fig. 6-17E). Fill above the runners with guides brought out to the inner surfaces of the legs (Fig. 6-17F). The guides, runners, and kickers will provide a smooth enclosure for the drawer.

The top may be a piece of veneered particle board (Fig. 6-18A), a piece of plywood with a solid wood edging (Fig. 6-18B), or solid wood with its edges left square or molded (Fig. 6-18C). Prepare the top and make a trial assembly if you wish, but it is easier to fit the drawer without the top in position. The top is easily fitted with screws upward through the short top rails and the kickers (Fig. 6-18D).

Drawer

When making this or any drawer, it is usually advisable to start with one side. Fit it to slide easily between runner and kicker, and cut approximately to length. It then serves as a pattern for the other side and other parts. The drawer described here is made by the traditional dovetailed method. Alternatively, one of the methods described elsewhere for drawers can be used.

Make the two ends. Carefully fit them to their openings, with enough clearance for them to pass easily. Plow grooves for the plywood or hardboard bottom in the sides and ends (Fig. 6-19A). This small table can have ⅛-inch hardboard for the drawer bottom.

The sides of the drawers should stop ⅛ inch in from the outsides of the ends (Fig. 6-19B). Mark the amount of overlap of each joint on the sides. Mark the dovetails, arranging the bottom ones to contain the groove (Fig. 6-19C). It should be possible to cut the sides of all dovetails through two thicknesses with the wood held in a vise (Fig. 6-19D), then chop out the waste.

Mark around the dovetails on the ends and square down to a line marking the thickness of the side (Fig. 6-19E). Letter each joint, so you assemble correctly. Saw down the sides of the sockets, with the saw on the waste side of each line. Chop out the waste while the wood is supported on a firm flat surface to prevent breaking out.

An experienced woodworker does not test joints before assembling them. A trail assembly tends to wear the joint loose, but if you want to try yours, only enter the dovetails a short distance into their sockets. Make sure there are no fibers or other obstructions that may prevent a joint from pulling tight.

Cut the drawer bottom. Get its size by measurement, but it need not press tightly into the bottom of the groove. Otherwise, it may prevent the other joints from coming tight.

When you are satisfied that all of the joints are cleanly cut, glue the parts together. You can put one long side on the ends, then slide in the bottom before adding the other side. Only a few spots of glue in the grooves are needed to secure the bottom. Check squareness. Sight along the sides and see that they are not bowed, as that

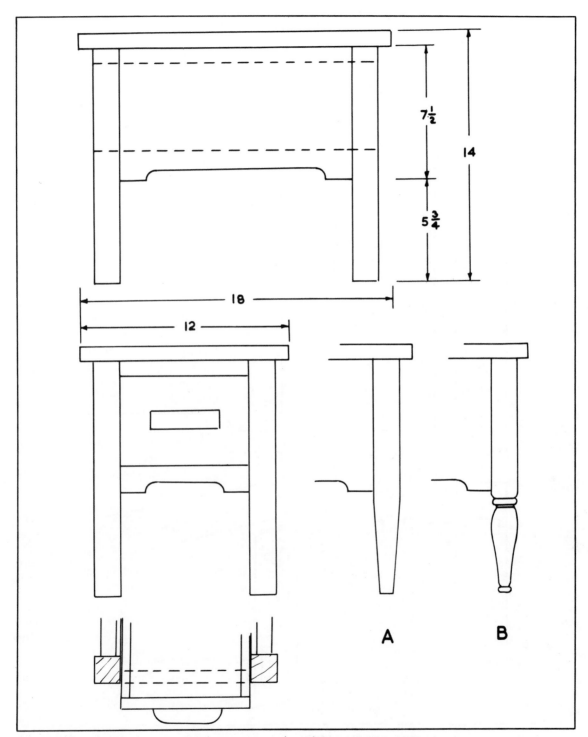

Fig. 6-15. The solid sides provide stiffness. The legs can be square, tapered, or turned.

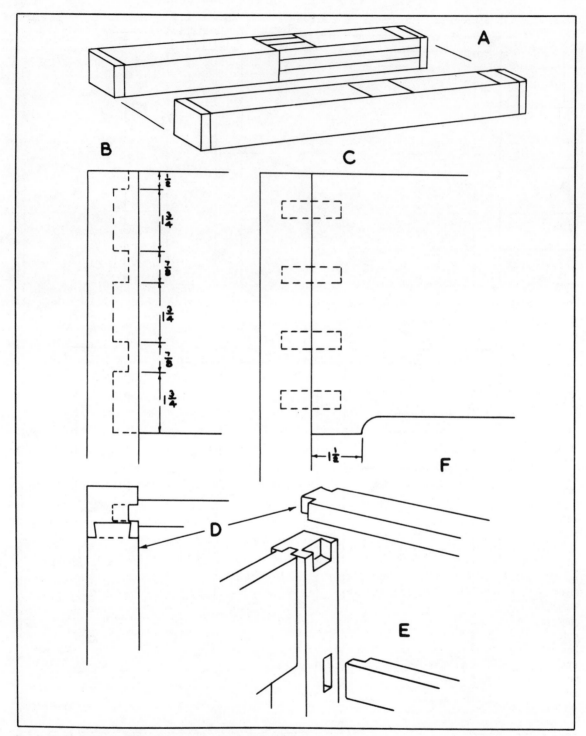

Fig. 6-16. Mark legs together and tenon or dowel the framing.

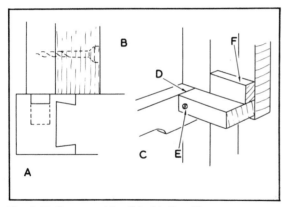

Fig. 6-17. Drawer guides fit inside the sides.

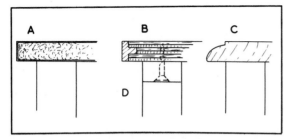

Fig. 6-18. The top may be veneered chipboard, lipped plywood, or solid and screwed from below.

will interfere with sliding through the table. You cannot put the drawer through the table at this stage. If you stand it on top, though, you will see that it is not out of shape.

When the glue has set, remove any surplus at the joints. Try the drawer in position. You will probably have to use a sharp, finely set smoothing plane to get the drawer running smoothly. Rub some candle fat on the bearing surfaces for a smooth action.

There will have to be a handle at each end. It can be a bought plastic or metal one, but wooden drawer pulls seem particularly appropriate. A simple shape allows fingers to be put underneath (Fig. 6-20A). The best way of making them is on the edge of a wider board, rather longer than will be needed for two handles (Fig. 6-20B). A router will make the hollow, or it can be plowed out and shaped with planes (Fig. 6-20C). The outside shaping is simple planing and sanding (Fig. 6-20D). Cut the strip off the wider board, separate the handles, and round their ends. Glue them in place, but use two screws to resist the pull (Fig. 6-20E).

The drawer can be left as it is, but there is nothing to keep it in the closed position. A simple way of holding it closed is to put a small spring ball catch under one end.

Use the type that goes into a hole. Let its striker plate into the rail below the drawer.

When you have the drawer fitted to your satisfaction, remove it and screw on the tabletop. Make sure all holes are countersunk enough for the screwheads not to interfere with the action of the drawer.

Sliding Tray

A sliding tray can be fitted to the drawer. Its size will depend on the small items you want to store in it. Obviously, its depth will affect what can be put below it, so it should not be deeper than necessary. The tray can be made to suit reels or other things of standard depth. Use wood about ¼ inch thick, with ⅛-inch hardboard for the bottom. Put strips inside the drawer as runners for the full length (Fig. 6-21A). Corners may be glued and nailed, or the tray will look good with small dovetails. A comb joint (Fig. 6-21B) is easier to make. If you want to add divisions, V-shaped notches (Fig. 6-21C) will make joints without weakening the thin tray sides. Felt or other stout cloth can be glued to the bottom of the tray, either fitted into the compartments, or put all over the bottom before the divisions are glued in.

Materials List for Sewing Table

4 legs	1½×14×½
2 rails	7½×16×¾
2 top end rails	1½×10×¾
2 bottom end rails	1½×10×¾
2 drawer runners	1⅛×16×¾
2 drawer kickers	1⅛×16×¾
2 drawer guides	¾×16×½
1 top	12×18×¾
2 drawer sides	5¼×16×½
2 drawer ends	5¼×10×⅝
1 drawer bottom	9×18×⅛ hardboard
4 tray sides	1½×8×¼
1 tray bottom	8×8×⅛ hardboard
2 tray divisions	1½×8×3/16

PEDESTAL TABLE

This is a full-size *octagonal* table with a central support (Fig. 6-22). It can be used as a dining table for four in the sizes given (Fig. 6-23). A smaller version will make a coffee table. The parts are of fairly thick wood, and this is essential to provide weight and rigidity. The top and part of the *pedestal* will almost certainly have to be made up by gluing boards together. With modern guides a simple butt joint between accurately planed edges will usually be strong enough, but suggestions for stronger joints are given in the next paragraph.

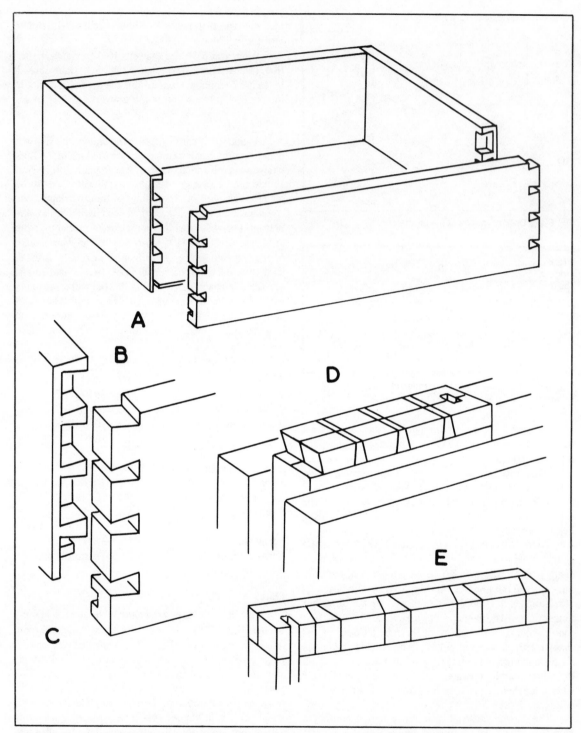

Fig. 6-19. The double-ended drawer has similar dovetails which can be marked and cut together.

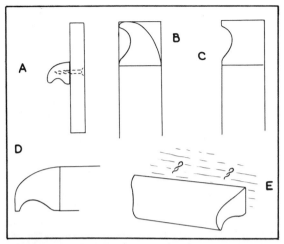

Fig. 6-20. A wood handle or drawer pull may be worked on the edge of a wide board and cut off. Attach it with screws from inside the drawer.

Boards can be joined with dowels—½-inch diameter going into each piece about 1 inch will do. Space them at about 6-inch intervals (Fig. 6-24A). Mark across the boards together and gauge the centers from the face sides (Fig. 6-24B). Another method is *secret slot screwing*. This method uses ordinary wood screws instead of dowels and draws the boards together without the use of clamps while the glue sets. Use fairly thick screws; 14 gauge and 1½ inches long will do for this table. Mark across the boards together in the same way as for the centers of dowel holes, but on one edge measure ½ inch further at each position (Fig. 6-24C).

Drive a screw into the edge with single markings at each position and to a depth that leaves about ¼ inch of the head projecting (Fig. 6-24D). Drill slightly deeper than this in the other board with a diameter that will admit the screwhead at the second marks. At the other positions, drill to a diameter that will clear the neck of the screw (Fig. 6-24E). Join this to the large hole with a slot

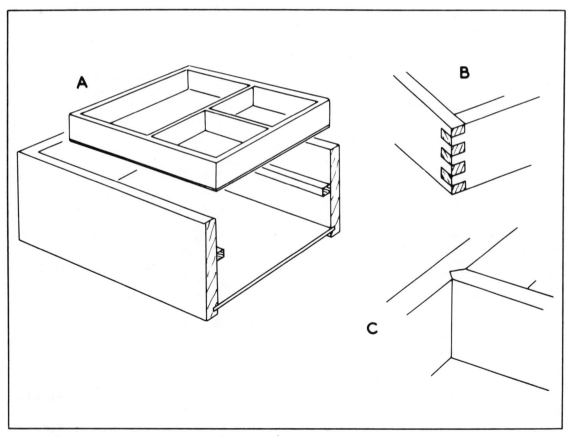

Fig. 6-21. A tray can slide in the drawer and may have divisions.

Fig. 6-22. A pedestal table has crossed supports and feet.

the pedestal edges provide places for the clamps to press over scrap wood.

Clean the edges of saw marks and leave them square across, except for slight rounding to remove sharpness (Fig. 6-25C). This looks better than larger edge curves. If you want to round the edges, a full curve is best. This looks better as part of an ellipse (Fig. 6-25D) than a semicircle (Fig. 6-25E). It is difficult to shape this accurately by hand. A square edge is better, unless you have a spindle molder with a suitable cutter.

It is possible to join the pedestal parts with dowels right through, but it is easier to fit the joints accurately if the dowels are separate and slightly staggered (Fig. 6-25F). Before assembly, mark and drill the doweled holes at top and bottom. Normal clamps can be used to pull the joints together at the ends of the parts, but not within the length of them. It helps in getting tight joints if the edges of the narrow parts are planed very slightly convex, so when the ends are pulled in there is more pressure due to the curve near the center. Do not overdo it. If you try a straightedge on the planed wood, the curve in the length need not be more than 1/16 inch.

Top and Bottom Frameworks and Ends

The top and bottom frameworks are made in a similar way. Mark each pair of parts out together (Fig. 6-26A) and gauge both parts of the halving joints from the face sides, so the depths of the parts to be cut out match (Fig. 6-26B). Cut the slots with the saw on the waste sides of the lines to get a tight fit. Make the bottoms of the slots flat or very slightly hollow, so surfaces come level when joined.

Prepare the ends. Put feet under the bottom assembly (Fig. 6-26C). If the pedestal edges are square, the ends may be straight tapers. If you have rounded them, it will look better if the ends are shaped (Fig. 6-26D). They can be made like this, in any case, if you wish. A fine band saw blade will do the shaping, but be careful to remove all saw marks afterward.

To get the positions of dowel holes in the frameworks, mark on the pedestal projections a short distance up the surfaces at each hole position. Put the pedestal on a framework. Check by measuring that you have it symmetrically placed. Pencil around the wood and mark at each dowel position. Put identifying marks at two adjoining positions, so you will put the parts together the same way again. Remove the pedestal and locate the hole centers (Fig. 6-26E). Drill the holes and make the joints with glue and dowels. You will probably find it easier to deal with one end at a time.

of the same width (Fig. 6-24F). This is most easily done by drilling more holes and cutting away the waste with a chisel.

Bring the edges together and enter the screwheads in the large holes. Drive one board along the other, so the screwhead cuts along behind the slot (Fig. 6-24G). If this proves the joint is satisfactory, knock the boards back the other way and take them apart. Give each screw one quarter turn, apply glue, and drive the joint together again. Be careful not to position the screws anywhere that will be cut. It helps to have some screws near what will be the ends of finished parts. If there are several boards making up the top, and it is possible to arrange things so the curves of grain at the ends are opposite ways in alternate boards, that will reduce any risk of overall warping.

Pedestal

The pedestal is made with one piece full width and two others doweled to it. More dowels are used at top and bottom (Fig. 6-25A). It is important that all external edges match, if the table is to look right. Either make one of the narrow parts completely first and use that as a template for the others, or cut a scrap piece of plywood to shape and mark each edge from that. Get the shape by enlarging squares (Fig. 6-25B). Besides their function in the appearance of the table, the flats at top and bottom of

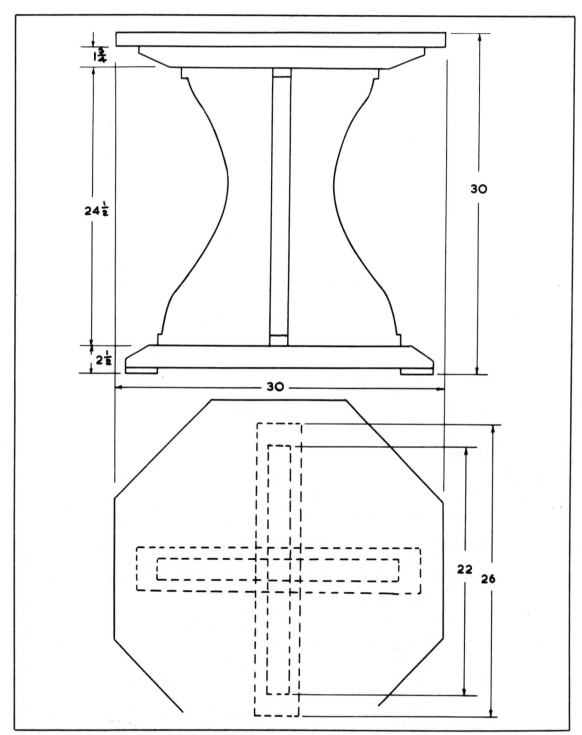

Fig. 6-23. The octagonal top has supports with a broad base.

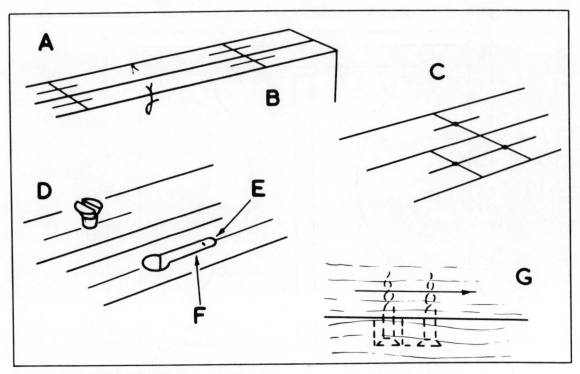

Fig. 6-24. Secret slot screwing pulls glued edges together.

Top

The top is the prominent part, and it needs a good surface. When leveling by hand, it helps to plane across the grain first, then diagonally, and finally along the grain. In that way you can lower high spots in all directions. Check that the bottom surface is also level, although you do not need such a high quality finish. Watch in leveling the top that you do not plane off excessively at one edge, and have to remove a lot over the rest of the surface to keep the thickness even.

One way of drawing a regular octagon is to first mark out the top as a square. Measure a diagonal and halve it. Use this measurement along each edge of the square from each corner, then join the marks (Fig. 6-26F). Check that you have done this accurately by measuring all eight sides. It may help to give an even appearance to the thickness of the edges to bevel slightly below (Fig. 6-26G). Deal with the top edges in the same way as the edges of the pedestal—leaving them square or fully rounding them. Join the pedestal to the top with counterbored screws driven upward (Fig. 6-26H).

Materials List for Pedestal Table

1 top	30×30×1¼
2 top frames	4×27×1¾
4 bottom frames	4×29×1¾
4 feet	3×4×¾
1 pedestal	22×25×2
2 pedestals	10×25×2

CABINET TABLE

This is a table of moderate size that has some enclosed storage space accessible by dropping flaps at the ends and another shelf lower down. It can be used to keep sewing or knitting things out of sight or to store hobby equipment. It can be placed beside a bed, particularly for an ill person who needs easy access to many things. Access to the storage compartment is from either end, and it is open right through. This will suit most purposes, but there can be a central division so different things may be kept at opposite ends.

The main large parts are shown as plywood, but they can be veneered particle board. Legs and other solid wood parts should be of hardwood to match the plywood. It may be possible to buy legs with ends already turned or otherwise shaped, but those shown are given a simple taper (Fig. 6-27).

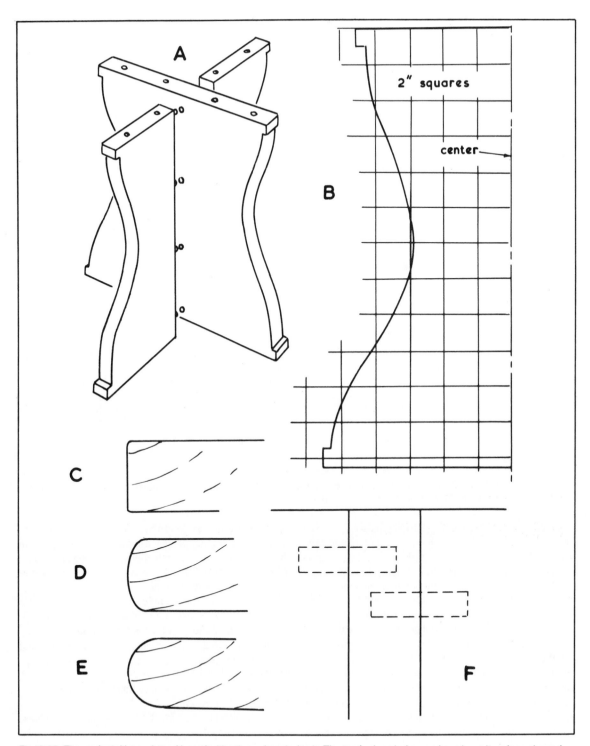

A

B

2" squares

center

C

D

E

F

Fig. 6-25. The pedestal has a broad board with others doweled to it. The top is doweled on and can have its edges shaped.

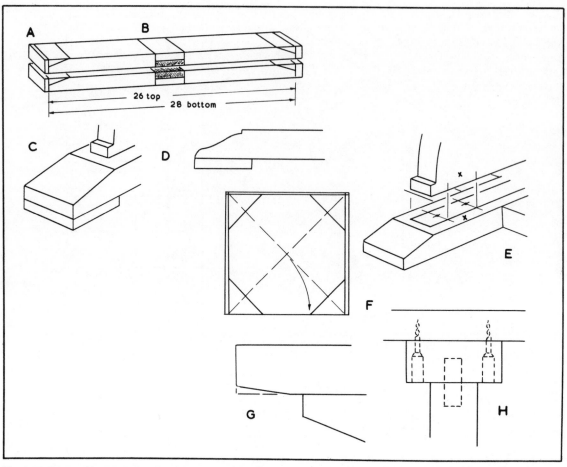

Fig. 6-26. The matched feet have shaped ends (A to E). The top is a regular octagon (F) and can be thinned round the edges (G). It is held to the pedestal with screws from below (H).

Start by making the legs. Either make a full-size drawing (Fig. 6-28A), or do this marking on one leg and transfer the spacings to the other three legs. Leave some excess wood at the top until after the joints have been cut, but the bottoms can be tapered, either on the inner faces, or all round. If there are to be glides on the bottoms of the legs, adjust the amount of taper to their size.

The side rails need plowed grooves for the plywood panels (Fig. 6-28B) and rabbets below in the lower ones for the bottom of the cabinet. This is necessary, so the bottom can be added after the top has been fitted. If the bottom was in grooves or otherwise joined in a way that had to be dealt with during first assembly, it is difficult or impossible to attach the top from inside. Make matching grooves in the tops of the legs where the side panels will come.

Prepare mortise and tenon joints for the rails into the legs (Fig. 6-28C). Because of the groove and rabbet in the lower rails, the size of the tenon cannot be very great. When the panel and rails are glued together, the assembly will be of ample strength.

Drill and countersink holes at about 6-inch intervals in the top rails for use later in attaching the top (Fig. 6-29A). Prepare the legs for taking the bottom shelf by notching (Fig. 6-28D). You can now cut the panels and assemble the opposite sides. Cut the plywood so it does not quite touch the bottoms of the grooves, then glue it and the rail to leg joints. Check squareness and that the two assemblies match.

If plywood is used for the top and the two shelves, the exposed edges should be lipped to obscure the plies. There can be strips tongued and grooved in, as described for some other projects, but it is satisfactory to glue and pin on narrow strips (Fig. 6-28E). Go all round the top with mitered corners. For the bottom of the cabinet, only the two ends needed be lipped. The lower shelf will have its corners cut off, so there is no need to take the lips right to them, providing there is enough left to trim with the plywood. It helps to have the lip strips slightly too wide. They can then be leveled with the plywood surfaces after gluing.

Make the bottom of the cabinet to fit in the rabbets, then notch around the legs with space left for the ends (Fig. 6-29B). Cut the lower shelf to match the cuts in the legs. Make the two ends that function as doors which flap downward. They are plywood and look best if their sides

and top edges are lipped. Because they do not show in the closed position, lipping is not quite so important.

The hinges are short lengths of iron or brass rod— about ⅛-inch diameter. They can be cut from nails. Drive them into the ends and have the holes ready in the legs (Fig. 6-29C). The hole location must allow the bottom edge of the end to swing under the bottom of the cabinet (Fig. 6-28F).

Mark the location of the legs on the underside of the top. Invert one side assembly over its marks. Glue and screw it to the top. You now have to bring in the two end flaps by putting their pivot rods into the leg holes. Add the lower shelf when you put the other side assembly into place on the top. Besides glue, there can be a screw

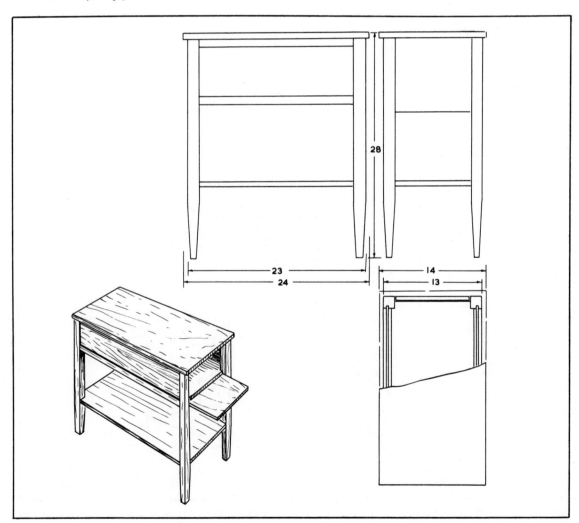

Fig. 6-27. A cabinet table has a storage compartment and a lower shelf.

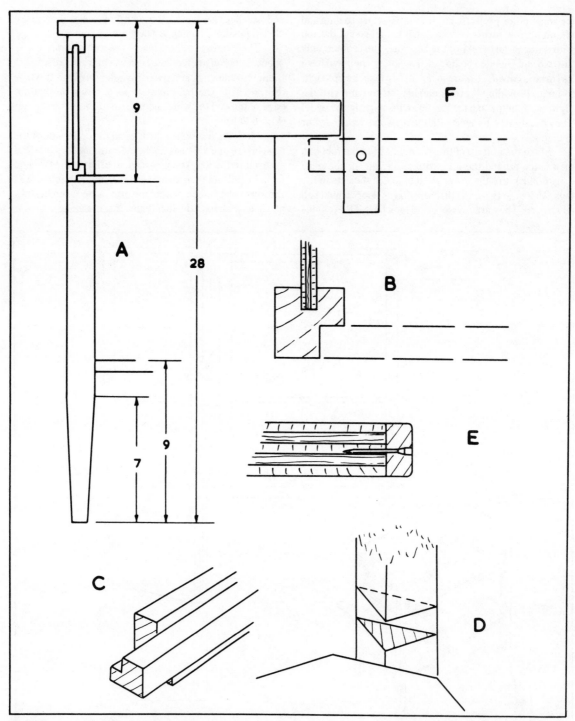

Fig. 6-28. An end detail shows sizes (A). Rails and panels are let in (B and C). The shelf goes in a notch (D) and can have its edge lipped (E). End flaps swing under (F).

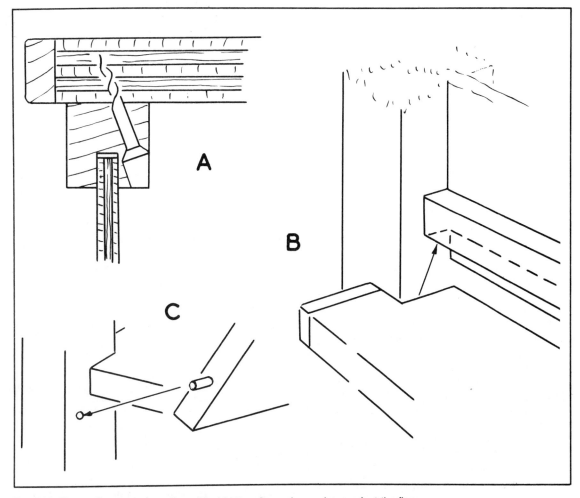

Fig. 6-29. The top is screwed on, the cabinet bottom fits under, and pegs pivot the flaps.

driven diagonally upward through each corner of the lower shelf when you put the other side assembly into place on the top. You can add the bottom of the cabinet after all screws have been driven into the tabletop, with screws and glue into the rail rabbets. There may be a certain amount of wobble in the assemble up to this point, so be careful that the ends are squared before glue sets by measuring diagonals and seeing that the end flaps work correctly.

For light use the end flaps can be merely supported by their slight projection under the cabinet bottom, but if much pressure is put on the end of a flap, it can break at the pivot rods. There can be folding struts to take this weight. One at each end should be enough. Use the type that fits against the leg and has an angled end to screw to

the flap. As the flap is raised, the strut folds at its center into the cabinet.

It should be possible to open a flap by pushing its bottom. There can be a small knob or handle added near its top for pulling open.

Materials List for Cabinet Table

4 legs	1½×28×1½
4 rails	1×22×1
1 top	14×24×¾ plywood
2 top lips	¾×25×⅜
2 top lips	¾×15×⅜
2 shelves	14×24×½ plywood
2 ends	9×11×½ plywood
2 panels	7×22×¼ plywood

95

STORAGE TABLE

A table of a size that can be stood beside a chair and opened to expose sewing and knitting things may also serve as a coffee table. If space is limited, it is low enough to slide under another table. With a height slightly more than the seat of a dining chair, it can also be cushioned and used for a child's seat at the table.

This table (Fig. 6-30) is of framed construction with plywood panels. If possible, get plywood already veneered to match the solid wood. Otherwise you will have to match the parts by staining.

The legs are shaped so that the reduced lower parts are clear of the grooves for the plywood. It is possible to plow the grooves right through and cut them away, making this part of the work easier than if the grooves had to be stopped. The plywood panels come central in the rails, which are flush with the outsides of the legs. Set your plow plane, wobble saw, or router so you can cut the grooves along all the rails. Keep it at the same setting to make the grooves in the legs (Fig. 6-31A). A depth of ¼ inch will be enough.

Mark the positions of the rails on all the legs together (Fig. 6-31B) and gauge for the mortises on the legs and the rails. These will be wider than the plywood grooves. At the bottom rails, cut back to the bottom of the grooves (Fig. 6-31C). Otherwise, the tenons are the full depth. As the tops of the legs will show when the lid is lifted, it will be better to cut down the tenons so they will not show (Fig. 6-31D).

Below the bottom rail line, cut back the inner surfaces of the legs (Fig. 6-31E) as far as the bottoms of the grooves. In that way the grooves will flow out just under the rails, where they will not show. The legs will be given a more graceful appearance. Round or bevel the bottoms of the legs to reduce marking of carpets. Otherwise, leave the bottoms square and fit glides when the table has been finished.

Prepare the plywood panels, slightly undersize, so they do not bottom on the grooves and prevent the mortise and tenon joints from being pulled tight. Assemble two opposite sides in the usual way and then make up in the other direction.

For the bottom of the box, put strips around inside the bottom rails and cut plywood to fit closely over them (Fig. 6-31F). Assemble with glue and pins.

Check flatness of the top surfaces by putting a straightedge across in several directions and by sighting across to see that an opposite surface is parallel with a near one. Getting the top true is important if the lid is to rest level.

The simplest lid is solid wood or a piece of plywood or particle board, preferably edged with a flat lip or a molding (Fig. 6-32A). Another lid can have thinner plywood on a frame, then a lip outside (Fig. 6-32B). This allows you to put fabric or elastic strips across the recess underneath to hold small items, or you can arrange holes for knitting pins or other long thin items (Fig. 6-32C). An attractive top can be made with a plywood panel in a rabbeted frame (Fig. 6-32D). The panel may be one with a rare wood veneer, or it can display some of your own marquetry. The wider frame with mitered corners shows off the panel better than putting plywood all over with just a narrow lip around.

Use plain hinges; 3-inch brass ones are suitable. It is simplest to let the whole thickness of the hinge into the back rail, so the upper part goes flat on the surface of the lid (Fig. 6-32E). Allow just a little clearance, so the lid falls flat and does not bind at hinges which are too deep.

For sewing or knitting things, the inside of the box can have the panels lined with cloth. For the sides and ends, glue the cloth to the plywood before it goes into the grooves, which may have to be a little wider to allow for this. Similarly, wrap the cloth over the edges of the bottom before it is put in place. The top of the box may have felt or other cloth glued on the rails and leg tops to provide a bed for the lid to close on. Allow for this when settling on the depth to let in the hinges.

Without anything to restrain it, the lid can be forced back and strain the hinges. To limit movement you can fit a folding strut, but that will take up space inside. Instead, there can be two screw eyes with a cord between. This will adapt to the contents as the lid is closed.

Materials List for Storage Table

4 legs	1½×20×1½
4 rails	1¼×21×1
4 rails	1¼×9×1
2 panels	9×23×¼ plywood
2 panels	9×9×¼ plywood
1 bottom	9×22×¼ plywood
2 bottom strips	½×22×½
2 bottom strips	½×9×½
1 lid	12×25×½

LIBRARY TABLE

A *library table* can have at least two uses. In a large library it serves as a place for sorting books before putting them on shelves. In a home with fewer books it can be the only storage place for books and magazines. A

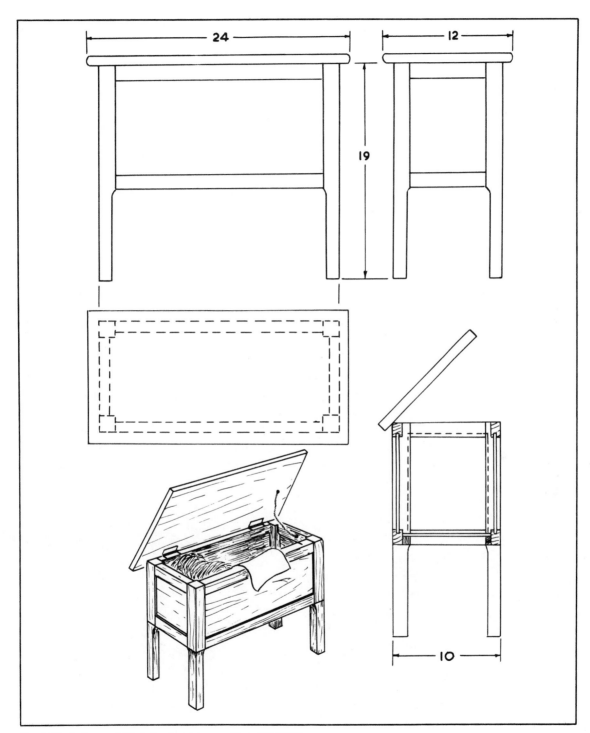

Fig. 6-30. A storage table has a large box under a hinged lid.

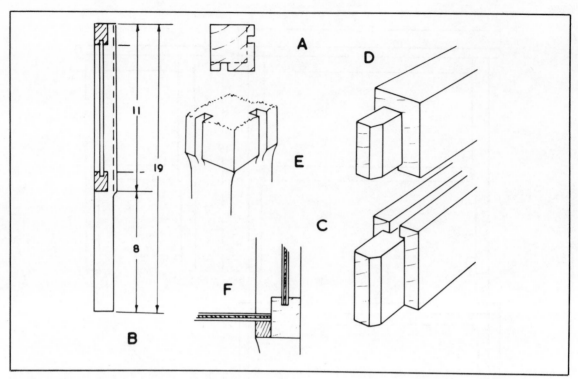

Fig. 6-31. Reducing the leg section allows for grooving for plywood. Rails have the tenons cut back to allow for grooving.

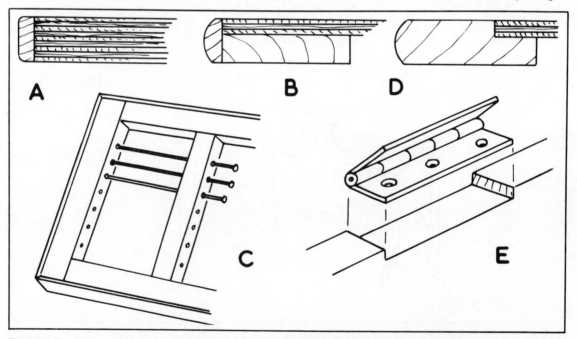

Fig. 6-32. The top can be made in several ways and may be arranged to provide storage. Hinges are let into the side only.

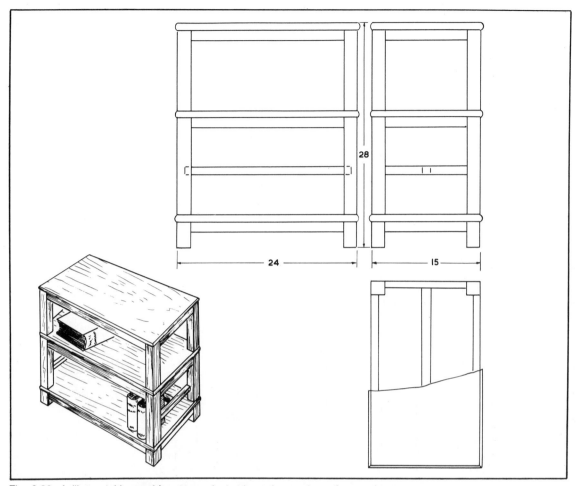

Fig. 6-33. A library table provides storage for books and magazines of many sizes.

full load of books can be quite heavy, so it needs to be substantial. In a large library it may be mounted on wheels or casters, so it can be taken where needed.

The table shown (Fig. 6-33) has a flush top for spreading or reading books or magazines. It can be used for writing. The middle shelf is without obstructions and can be used for magazines or large books laid flat. It will also take phonograph records. The bottom compartment has a central rail that will divide books stood on edge, with their backs to either side.

Construction is straightforward, with nearly all joints the same. The framework has plywood shelves resting on the rails and not in rabbets, then the plywood edges are covered with molding. If made in a good hardwood, this is an attractive piece of useful furniture. A similar construction in softwood may make a good hobby

bench or be used in the laundry room or an outside shed or shop.

Start with a drawing of one leg full-size (Fig. 6-34A) to get the spacing of rails and other parts. Mark out all the legs together and square around the lines for the mortises on both inner faces. The rails are half the thickness of the legs and finish with their outer surfaces level (Fig. 6-34B). They are most conveniently fitted with barefaced tenons (Fig. 6-34D). Later there will be plywood over the joints and molding at the edges (Fig. 6-34C). The top joints may be open, will full-width tenons, as they will be hidden.

Mark and cut all the rails each way together, so their lengths match. Cut all the mortises for these rails.

The divider in the lower compartment has the two short rails flush with the inner surfaces of the legs to

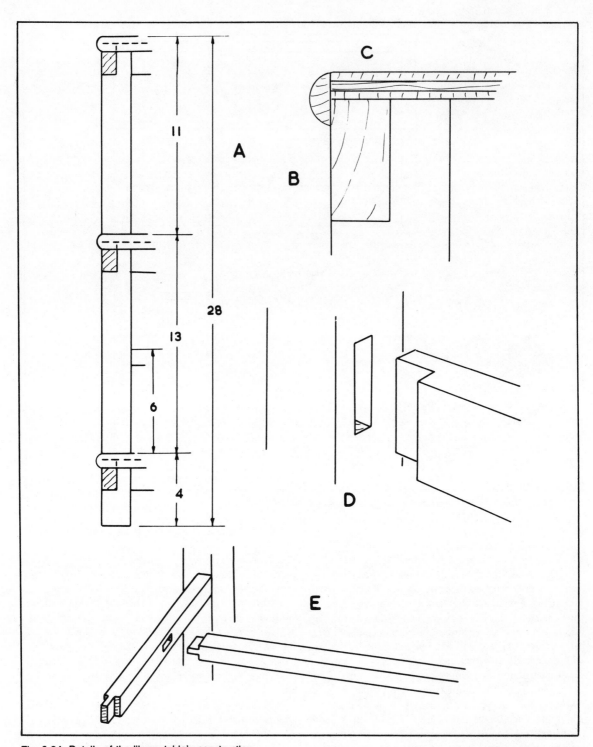

Fig. 6-34. Details of the library table's construction.

provide a level rest for a book. The lengthwise rail is tenoned centrally (Fig. 6-34E).

Assemble the two end frames, then add the lengthwise rails including the divider in the lower compartment. You should then have a substantial framework that is square in all directions.

Start fitting the plywood shelves from the bottom upward, so you do not restrict access to each shelf with the one above as you work on it. The edges can be slightly full for planing level after fitting. Attach each shelf with glue and pins around the edges, punched below the surface and covered with stopping. The molding at the top will obviously have to be taken all round and mitered. At the other shelves it can be stopped at the inner edges of the legs, but it may look better if taken to the outer edges of the legs and mitered there like the top. Half-round ¼-inch molding is suggested, but it can have another section. Keep the top edges level with the plywood as you glue and pin it on.

There are some possible modifications that may be worthwhile depending on the use of the table. There can be flaps hanging between the legs at one or both ends that can be raised to give additional working surfaces. A flap is a piece of plywood fitting loosely between the legs and hanging far enough down to almost reach the middle shelf. It is held by hinges to the underside of the top and rail (Fig. 6-35A). There are triangular pieces of plywood hinged to the legs to hold it up (Fig. 6-35B). The pieces are hidden by the flap when it is down, but they swing out at the correct level to hold it up.

Another possible addition is a flap that slides out to one side for extra space, particularly for writing on (Fig. 6-35C). There can be two of these—on opposite sides and ends or both on the same side. The flap is a piece of plywood that goes the full width under the top, through a slot cut in the top rail during construction, and located to come just below the edge.

Make guides to go inside. They can be built up from odd pieces of plywood (Fig. 6-35D) and should allow the flap to slide easily. Fit them from rail to rail under the plywood top. Try the flap movement as you secure them.

Put a piece of half-round molding across the front of the flap to provide a grip for pulling out. To prevent the flap falling out and to leave enough inside to hold it level, screw a short strip of wood under it to act as a stop against the top rail.

Materials List for Library Table

4 legs	1¾×29×1¾
6 rails	1¾×23×⅞
6 rails	1¾×14×⅞
1 rail	⅞×23×⅞
2 rails	⅞×14×⅞
3 shelves	15×24×⅜ plywood
6 moldings	¾×26×half-round
6 moldings	¾×17×half-round

PEDESTAL SIDE TABLE

Much of the beauty of many furniture pieces comes from the inclusion of curves, but there is one form of modern design that relies on straight lines. This table has no curves, the quality of appearance comes from its proportions and the use of bevels. One advantage of this is in simplicity of construction, as all cuts are straight and can be made by the simplest hand or power equipment.

The legs and rails can be decorated by wagon beveling or left square. The legs can be chamfered for their full lengths—an easier task than the stopped chamfers of wagon beveling.

The sizes are for a side table (Fig. 6-36), but the same design can be enlarged to make a dining table or reduced for a coffee table. Start by making a full-size drawing of one end; half the width will do (Fig. 6-37A). Mark all similar parts together. Get all legs identical and the spacings of their joints on other pieces the same distance apart.

Dowels can be used, but the leg ends can be given tenons to go right through (Fig. 6-37B), as their ends will not show in the finished table. If wedges are driven into saw cuts across the ends of the tenons, exceptionally strong joints should result (Fig. 6-37C). Cut the joints before beveling the ends. Do all wagon beveling (Fig. 6-37D), if it is to be included, before fitting any parts together. The feet are attached with glue and screws from below. They extend outside the line of the top for stability.

The top and bottom rails may be tenoned into the ends, but dowels are simpler and satisfactory (Fig. 6-37E). The bottom rail can be beveled to match the ends. In any case, take off the sharpness along the exposed edges of all rails.

The top can be a piece of veneered particle board. Its edges should be square and veneered. If solid wood is used, a bevel can be taken around the top edge (Fig. 6-37F), or both edges, to continue the style used on the supports. Attachment of the top may be with pocket screws driven upward. One screw near the end of each pedestal top and two or three from the insides of the top rails should be sufficient. If you wish, the insides of the top rails can be plowed to take buttons, but it will still be necessary to use pocket screws at the ends.

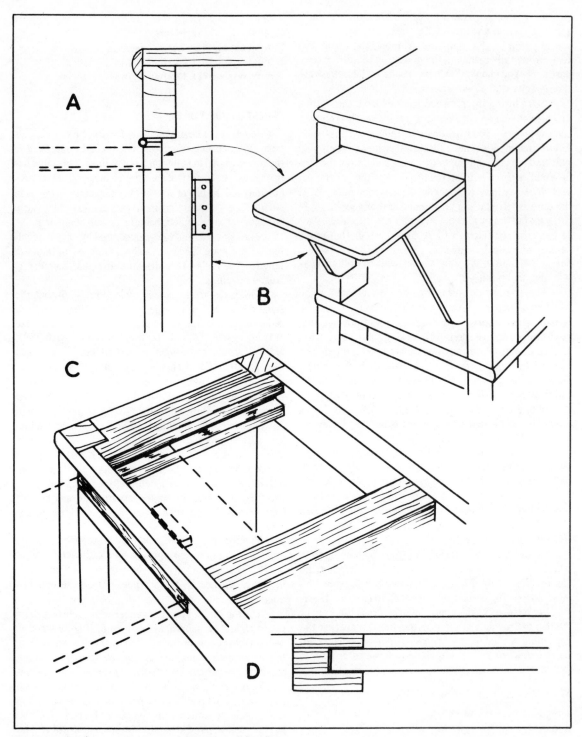

Fig. 6-35. The library table can have hinged or sliding flaps.

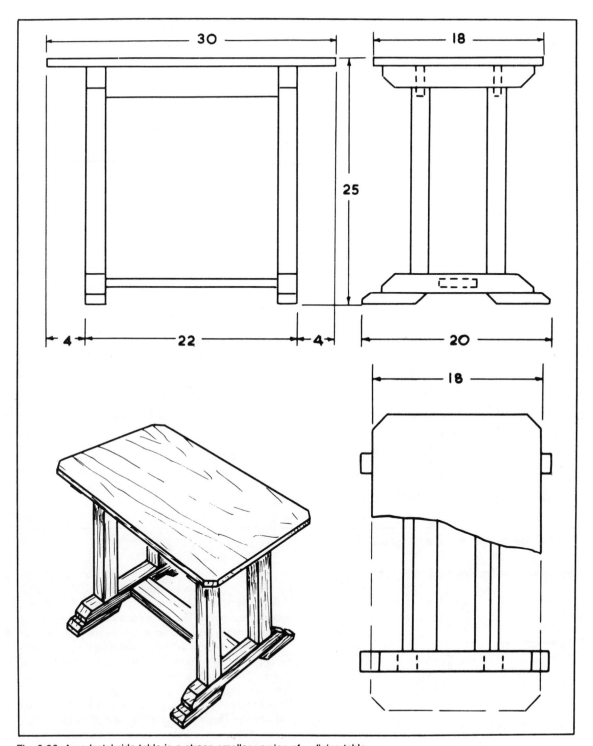

Fig. 6-36. A pedestal side table is a strong smaller version of a dining table.

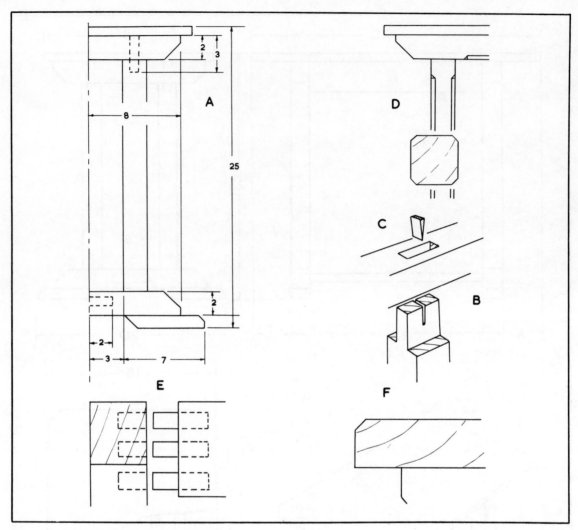

Fig. 6-37. Details of the pedestal's construction.

Materials List for Pedestal Side Table

4 legs	2×26×2
4 feet	2×9×1
2 bases	2×17×2
2 pedestal tops	2×17×2
2 top rails	3×22×¾
1 bottom rail	4×22×¾
1 top	18×31×¾

HEXAGONAL CANDLE TABLE

You may not have a use for a table on which to set a candle—at least not in the way our ancestors would have located a candle alongside them for reading. Such a table makes a suitable way of displaying one of the modern decorative candles. The more common use today is as a side table near a lounge chair or as a stand for a pot plant.

Many of these tables have most of their parts turned. Such a table is described elsewhere, but this table is designed to be made without the use of a lathe (Fig. 6-38). It has a hexagonal post with three legs. The advantage of three legs is in their ability to stand without wobbling on any surface. That would have been important in the days of candlelit homes, where floors were more uneven than today. A modern table can be made with an octagonal post

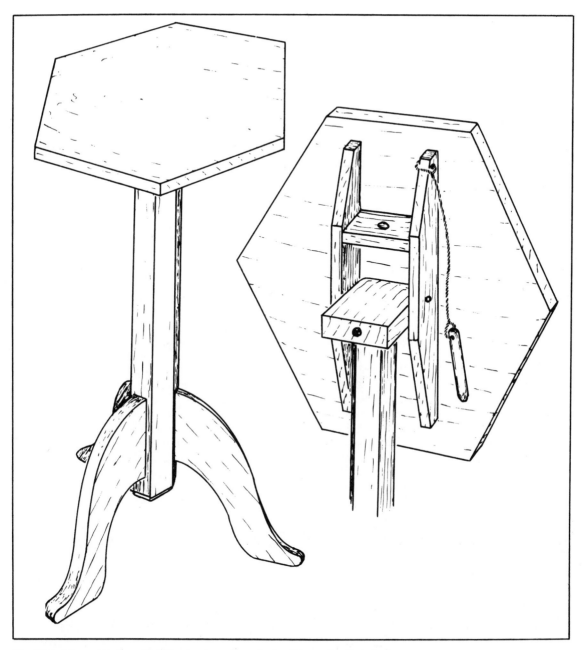

Fig. 6-38. A hexagonal candle table stands on three feet and has a top that pivots.

and four legs, but most people consider three legs more attractive. This arrangement is easier to make and avoids congestion in the joints between legs and post. The top can be round, but it is shown hexagonal to match the lower parts.

It was common to make a top that would tilt. The reason is not very apparent, but the top would be swung upright when the table was out of use. That construction is described, but if you prefer a fixed top, the braces can be screwed to the support and the peg arrangement

105

omitted. The sizes given (Fig. 6-39) bring the top to the same level as other tables, and this should suit use beside a chair. The top is of sufficient area for that purpose and big enough to take the base of a fairly elaborate ornamental candle. If sizes are altered, keep the spread of the feet at least the same size of the top for stability.

Start with the post, which has to be made into a regular octagonal section. Draw an end view of the wood, with a centerline the long way (Fig. 6-40A). Draw a circle on its center to touch the sides. If you step off the radius from each end of the line onto the circumference (Fig. 6-40B), that should come close to the other edges. You can join them to make the hexagon (Fig. 6-40C). Plane the wood to this section and check that all faces finish to the same width.

At the top the support is a plain rectangular piece, with a mortise and tenon joint to the post. The tenon need not go right through (Fig. 6-40D). The top will pivot on two screws driven into the support, and the edge has to be rounded to provide clearance (Fig. 6-40E). Take off too much rather than too little. At the other side there will be a hole for a peg, but delay drilling this until you can drill through both parts during assembly. It is important that the support is square in all directions with the post, so cut the joint carefully and check when you assemble.

The bottom of the post extends below the leg joints. Cut it square and bevel the edges (Fig. 6-40F). The legs are mortised into the post, but mark the mortises at the same time as the tenons on the legs.

Draw the shape of a leg on a pattern of 2-inch squares (Fig. 6-39A). Allow for tenons going about ¾ inch into the post (Fig. 6-39B). One problem with this type of leg is clamping the joint tightly. It helps to leave on the projection shown (Fig. 6-39C), so a clamp can be put across it and a scrap wood pad placed on the other side of the post. Draw the shape of the leg across this, then it is a fairly simple job to cut off the projection and finish the outline after the glued joint has set. When you assemble, deal with one leg at a time. Do not glue and clamp the next joint until the previous one has set.

Cut the legs to their outlines. One leg may be finished first and used as a pattern for the others. You can also make a template of the shape, particularly if you expect to be making more of these legs. Clean up the edges. Check that the section is square across, then take off sharpness of the angles. When all legs have been assembled to the post, glue the support to the top of the post.

Get the shape of the top by drawing a circle of the size across the points. Step off the radius around it (Fig. 6-39D). Cut it to shape and deal with the edges as you wish. They can be molded, although it will be more like the traditional form if they are left square or moderately rounded. It is possible to decorate the top in many ways. It may be veneered in a geometric or other pattern. There can be some surface carving. A piece of leather or leather cloth may be glued on or let in. One simple decoration that is in keeping with the general design is an incised border of parallel lines (Fig. 6-41A).

Mark the pattern with pencil, then use a sharp knife against a steel straightedge. A single cut along each line will do. You can get a more prominent result if you make two passes on each line with the knife blade tilted opposite ways (Fig. 6-41B), so you actually remove a tiny sliver of wood. When you finish the wood, the lines will show darker, whether you stain or finish with polish in the natural color.

The braces beneath the top (Fig. 6-41C) come on each side of the support, and there is a piece tenoned across opposite where the pivot will be (Fig. 6-41D). The assembly swings up on two roundhead screws (Fig. 6-41E). If you do not want the top to pivot, the crosspiece between the braces can be omitted. The braces can be screwed into the support. Glue and screw the braces to the top (Fig. 6-41F). Arrange them pointing toward the sides, not points, and preferably across the grain of the top, so they resist any tendency of the wood to warp.

The peg is a piece of ⅝-inch dowel rod. Drill for it through the cross brace into the support. Also, drill through it for a cord, which can also go through a hole at the end of a brace or to a screw eye driven into it (Fig. 6-41G). For easy fitting, taper and round the end of the peg. Obviously, it is important that the peg goes in far enough and is tight enough not to come out unintentionally, but you should be able to remove it without tools. Rubbing it with candle grease or wax will make it work smoothly.

Materials List for Hexagonal Candle Table

1 post	2½×30×1⅛
3 legs	8×18×1
1 top	20×20×1
1 support	4×5×1½
2 braces	1½×15×¾
1 brace	1½×5×¾
1 peg	⅝×4×round rod

SOFTWOOD DINING TABLE

Furniture is sometimes made of softwoods and may be described as "knotty pine" or something similar, al-

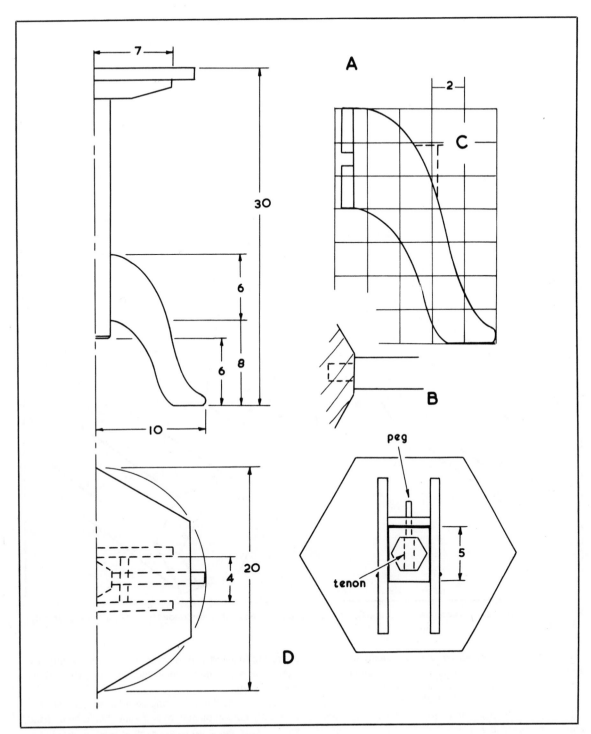

Fig. 6-39. Sizes of the hexagonal candle table parts.

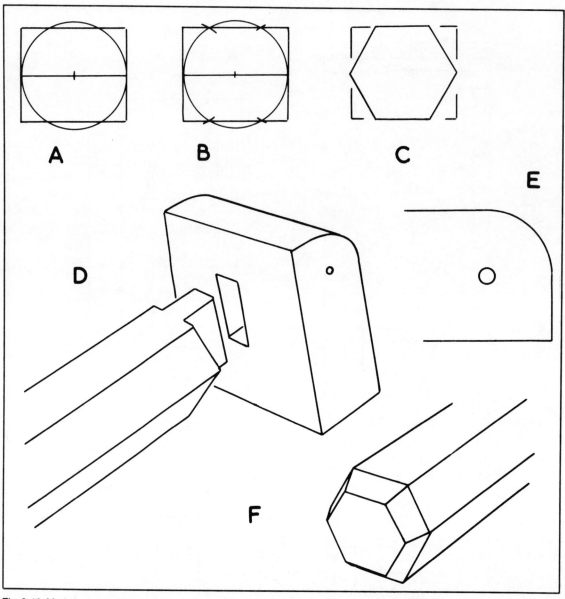

Fig. 6-40. Mark the hexagon accurately (A, B, and C). The post tenons to the top which is rounded (D and E), and its other end is beveled (F).

though the wood may not be pine. The many knots are regarded as a design feature, and the wood is given a clear finish so all of the grain details are exposed. It is important that the wood is sound. Much softwood that is suitable for constructional and house use has flaws besides knots, and open *shakes* or other defects will spoil its appearance in furniture. If there are many knots, it is

important to avoid stressing the wood in the vicinity of a knot. The wood there does not have the strength of normal grain.

Another problem is bringing a knotty surface to a good finish. Final planing over a knot should be by hand with a finely set sharp plane, used in several directions, to reduce the tendency of the knot grain tearing up.

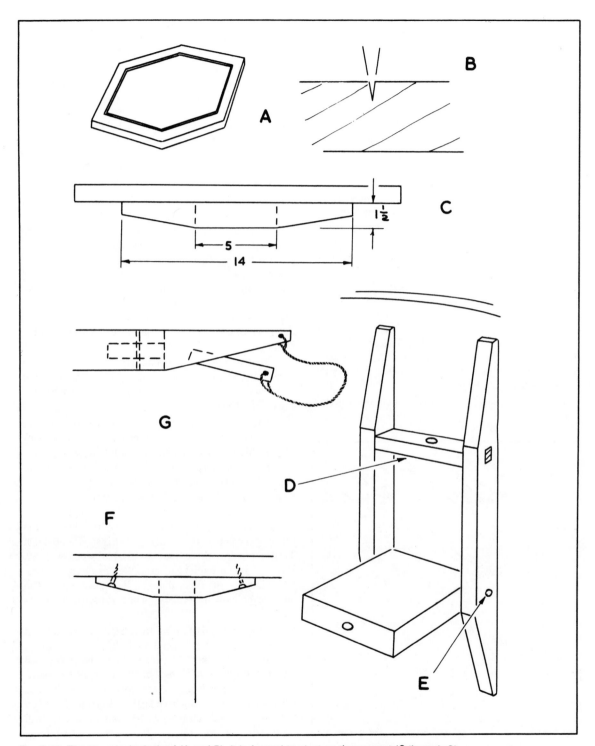

Fig. 6-41. The top may be incised (A and B). It is framed to pivot on the support (C through G).

Although the surrounding wood may have its grain parallel with the surface, the knot is the remains of a branch leading off the trunk and is end grain. There is also the problem of finish to be applied. Many knots in softwood will exude resin for some time after the work has been finished. To prevent this coming through the applied finish, the usual treatment is to give the knot one or two coats of shellac dissolved in alcohol. Some synthetic finishes are not compatible with shellac, but they may resist resin from the knot themselves. Check with the finish instructions.

So far as possible in a softwood table, use knotty boards in the top. Avoid large knots in the legs and underframing. Apart from any weakness, they may cause warping. There can be small knots anywhere without causing trouble, but in structural parts be suspicious of any knot that is more than about one-fifth of a surface's width.

Softwood is not as strong as most hardwoods, so it is common to make sections a little bigger. Softwoods do not look as good in slender sections. As softwoods are lighter, the larger sections do not make the table heavier.

This table is of dining size (Fig. 6-42), but the same method of construction can be used for other sizes. Softwood legs are best braced with lower rails, so this table has end rails and a central stretcher. Construction is generally similar to standard tables of other designs (Fig. 6-43).

Fig. 6-42. A dining table may have turned legs.

Start with the legs. They can be square, but without other treatment that tends to look clumsy. Corners may be beveled full length, either just the outsides or all round. There can be wagon beveling between the rail positions. Carving or fine decoration is inappropriate for softwoods. The best treatment is turning. Softwood turns easily. It is not so forgiving as hardwood to slight errors, though as the grain will tear out. Keep your turning tools sharp and have the lathe rotating at its highest speed for most work. Do not attempt very fine detail. The softer grain may break out, either during turning or when knocked later.

Turn the legs with squares left where the joints come (Fig. 6-44A). Cut in with the skew chisel having its long point downward to sever the grain where you change from square to round, so slivers do not break off the square corners. Turn one leg and use it as a pattern for the others, with the aid of a rod marked with key parts of the turning, so you can pencil their positions on the revolving wood. Have the bottoms of the legs toward the tailstock and turn the ends slightly hollow there. The other end can be left overlong until after you have cut the joints.

Mark all the joint positions across all four legs at the same time. Square around for the top joints, but the lower rail joints are on meeting faces only. Be careful to pair the legs (Fig. 6-44B).

The top rails are made in the usual way and are grooved for buttons. If you cut tenons, have them as thick as possible to get maximum strength (Fig. 6-44D).

The lower rails at the ends are also tenoned into the legs (Fig. 6-44E). The stretcher between them needs to be joined as strongly as possible. The wood can be horizontal and the tenon taken through. Arrange for two wedges and bevel the mortise slightly to allow for the tenon spreading as the wedges are driven (Fig. 6-44F). This is a place where you can use hardwood wedges. Have the tenon too long at first, then use long wedges. Glue them as you drive them in, then plane level. The different color of the wedges can be regarded as a decorative feature.

Another way is to have the stretcher vertical, but give it a tusk tenon through the rail (Fig. 6-45A). Do not cut the wood too short. Driving in the wedge puts a load on the end grain, which may break out if cut too short. During the first assembly the wedge may be used dry, and you may find that it will drive further after a while. When the table has been in use for some time, the wood will have stabilized. You can glue the wedge in place if you wish.

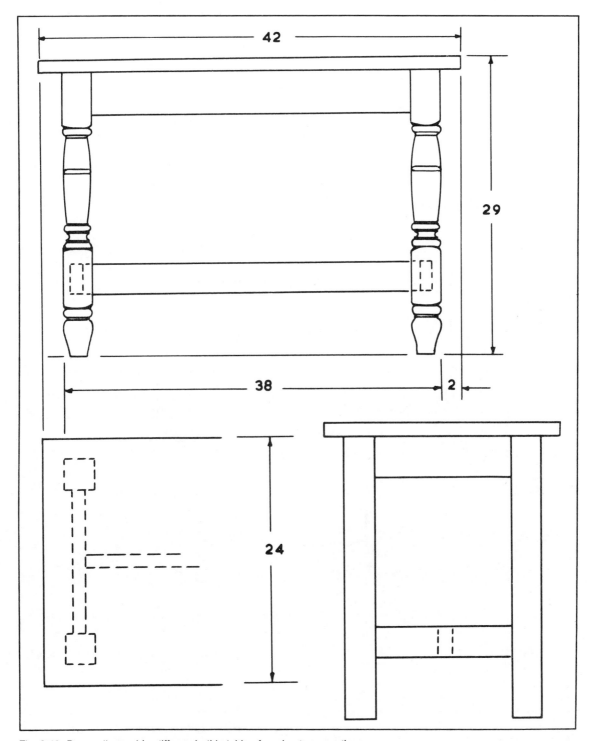

Fig. 6-43. Deep rails provide stiffness in this table of moderate proportions.

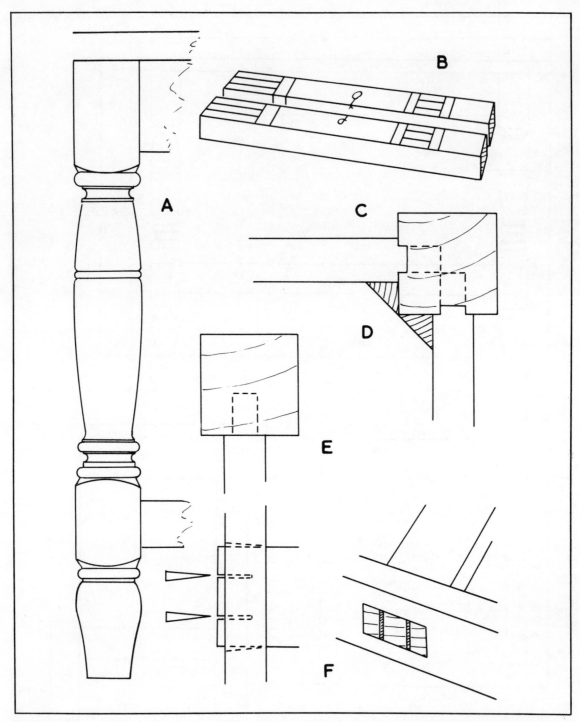

Fig. 6-44. A turned pattern is suggested. Mark legs together and tenon the rails, with fillets inside the joints. The center rail can be tenoned and wedged.

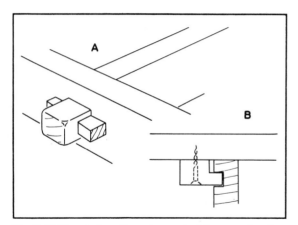

Fig. 6-45. The center rail may have a tusk tenon and wedge. The top is held to the top rails with buttons.

The top has to be made of several boards glued together. Make sure meeting edges are planed straight. Modern glue should hold without other treatment, but you can put dowels between the parts if you wish. The outer edge can be molded or left square, with slight softening of the corners. Join the top to the frame with buttons into the grooves (Fig. 6-45B). Use plenty of them, so there is no fear of the top moving or coming away. Buttons about 9 inches apart should be adequate.

Materials List for Softwood Dining Table

1 top	24×43×1¼
4 legs	3×30×3
2 rails	4×38×1¼
2 rails	4×21×1¼
2 rails	3×21×1¼
1 stretcher	3×38×1¼

Chapter 7

Advanced Seating

The most comfortable chairs are the ones that come closest to conforming to the human form. If a person sat without moving, the chair could be made to fit his figure. As we have to allow for movement, there has to be tolerance all round. Varying positions are allowed for in upholstered chairs, as described in Chapter 10. Other chairs have their seats, backs, and arms arranged to allow for the sitter's posture. There may be loose cushions to provide padding.

Many of the more advanced chairs have turned parts, and one example is given here with full use of the lathe. Anyone relaxing welcomes the chance to rock a chair. Many chairs can be adapted by adding rockers, but it is better to start with the intention of rocking, as in the example given.

Many folding chairs today are made of metal and designed so they fold ingeniously and compactly. There is still a place for chairs with wooden frames, where slung canvas makes comfortable seats and backs.

There have been many examples of combination seats, where they can be converted to something else, so they often do neither job very successfully. The monk's bench is a historic example of a seat that can be made into a table while providing storage space underneath. It is an interesting reminder of the days when storage chests had to double as seats.

The selection of designs in this chapter should be considered alongside the upholstered ones and the Windsor chairs described later. Chairmaking in an even more advanced form calls for increasing skill that only comes by practice. It would have been possible to show examples of chairs by Chippendale and the other great cabinetmakers, but few readers would be able to make similar ones successfully. If you gain the skills that come from making the chairs described in this book, you may then obtain a copy of the pattern books of those golden days and adapt your technical skill and manual ability to producing reproductions.

HARDTOP CHAIR

One or more general-purpose chairs are useful around the home. They can be used as dining chairs if you have to accommodate guests, but their main purpose is for occasions when you do not want to risk soiling your best chairs. This chair has a flat wood seat, but it can be softened with a cushion. The seat can be removed or turned back when you want to stand on the chair to reach a high shelf. Such a chair also has uses in a shop where you

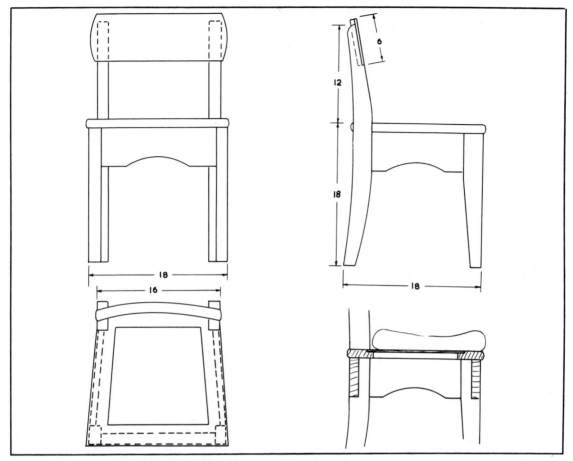

Fig. 7-1. A simple chair has a hard top which can be cushioned.

sit to carry out your hobby. If it has to double as a sawing stool or is used to support the object on which you are working, there is not the same worry about looking after it as there would be if you had borrowed one of the family's better chairs.

There is no reason why this design should not be used to make a set of dining chairs, using attractive wood and a good finish, if the straightforward design suits your decor. The sizes shown (Fig. 7-1) are for sitting at a normal table, but you may want to shorten the legs if your hobby work is low—as when using a spinning wheel—or lengthen them if that allows better handling of tools over a bench.

Rear Legs

The rear leg shape is the key one, so mark out a leg (Fig. 7-2A) and use this as a guide for marking the front legs (Fig. 7-2B). The rear leg outline must be straight and parallel where the seat and rails come. The part of the upper slope that will take the back must also be straight, but you can get smooth curves elsewhere by springing a lath through the points and drawing around that. Although you draw the shapes, do not cut them until after you have cut the joints. Similarly, mark the taper of the front legs, but delay cutting in until the joints have been cut.

The rail joints can be mortise and tenons (Fig. 7-2C), or there is enough depth for three or four dowels (Fig. 7-2D). The rails can have straight lower edges, but they are shown with curves which lighten appearances (Fig. 7-2E). Do not reduce the width of the wood too close to the ends. As you will probably often lift the chair by putting your hands under the rails, round the hollowed parts in cross section.

115

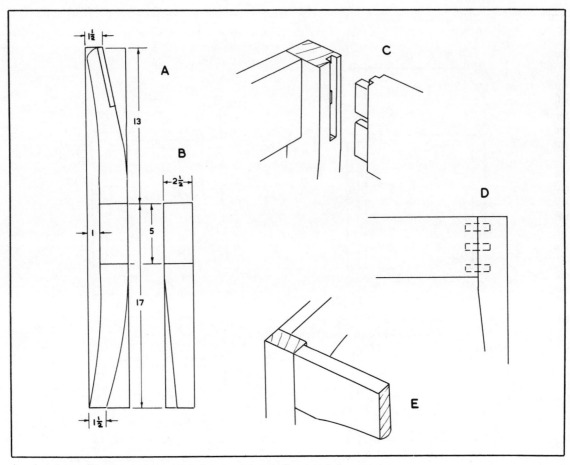

Fig. 7-2. The rear leg is shaped, and the joints are tenoned or doweled.

The tops of the rear legs have to be shaped to take the hollow back. The final fitting is best done after the chair has been assembled. The recesses have to match the curve of the back, which may not be exactly the same on all chairs. After you have shaped the rear legs, the recesses can be cut square across. The top of the leg can be rounded. Without cutting into the outer line, you can make a start at beveling. Leave some wood for final trimming (Fig. 7-3A).

Assembly

Assemble the chair, first by making up the rear and front assemblies so they are square and match. Add the side rails. The amount of slope is very slight, but you may have to trim the ends a little for a close fit against the legs on the outside. Check diagonals across the seat, so you get it symmetrical. Stand back and see that the chair

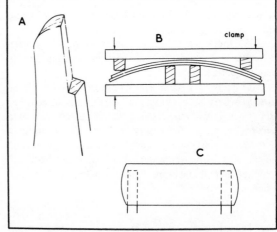

Fig. 7-3. The curved back is laminated and sprung to a curve.

116

stands upright on a level surface and looks correct from all angles.

Back

The back is made of two pieces of thin plywood, cut with the grain of the outer veneers the short way, so they will bend easier. By gluing two pieces together while forced to a curved shape, they will hold their shape when the glue has set. Choose a strong glue. A fully waterproof one intended for boatbuilding is best.

The two pieces of plywood can be cut to width, but leave some extra on the length. There is to be about 1 inch of curve across the chair back. You will have to bend a little more than that to allow for springing back. Have two stout strips of scrap wood bigger than the plywood. With it go four pieces about 1½ inches square. Round their corners so they will not mark the plywood.

Have all these parts ready and four C-clamps large enough to go over everything. Put glue on the meeting surfaces, then squeeze the curve (Fig. 7-3B). Pieces of cardboard between the wood and plywood will reduce the risk of marking. Squeeze deliberately to the curve you want, then leave the assembly for a couple of days. Do not be tempted to try tightening later. That would make the meeting surfaces slide and weaken the glue line after setting had started.

Cut the back to shape (Fig. 7-3C) and round the edges. Trim the leg recesses to make a close fit, then fit the back with glue and a few screws. As the screwheads will show, brass will look better than steel. Chromium plating will look even better. Try to countersink exactly level. Screws pulled in too far look ugly. In typical plywood, a screw will pull in to make its own countersink without using a bit first.

Seat

The seat is independent of the chair frame, but screwed to it. Prepare the strips with rabbets for the plywood (Fig. 7-4A). Round the outer edges or allow enough there for rounding after assembly. At the corners

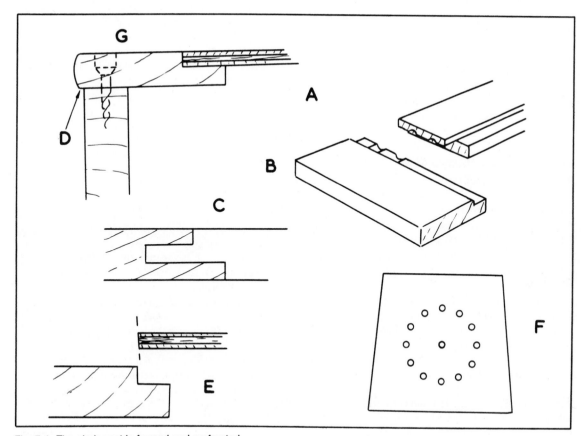

Fig. 7-4. The chair seat is framed and perforated.

117

the crosswise members can either be doweled into the side pieces, or there can be tenons. If you choose dowels, it is easier to drill for them before cutting the rabbets. The holes overlap the two different depths (Fig. 7-4B). Tenons can be cut to come below the rabbet (Fig. 7-4C).

Use the actual chair as a guide to the sizes of the seat frame, which should overlap about ¼ inch (Fig. 7-4D). Cut around the rear legs. Make up the seat frame, then cut the plywood panel to fit in. To get a close fit, bevel the edges very slightly (Fig. 7-4E), so the joint tightens as it is pulled together. There can be a pattern of small holes in the plywood (Fig. 7-4F), either arranged geometrically or as a badge or initials. Glue the plywood in and clamp it. That should be sufficient, but you can use fine nails, too.

Check the seat in position. Examine it from below. The overlap should be the same all round. You may have to do some planing of edges to get them parallel with the parts below. There need not be many screws holding the seat down. One screw a short distance along each rail from each corner will do. If you plan to remove the seat later, let the screws be on the surface and do not glue down. Otherwise, the screws may be counterbored and plugged (Fig. 7-4G).

If a cushion is made to fit, there is no need for it to be cut around the rear legs. A sitter's body does not go that far back, but the rear corners of the cushion may have tapes to tie around the legs. A cushion made the same below and on top can be turned over occasionally to equalize wear and any tendency of the filling to settle one way.

Materials List for Hardtop Chair

2 legs	2½×18×1½
2 legs	3½×31×1½
4 rails	5×18×1
4 seats	3½×19×¾
1 seat	14×13×¼ plywood
2 backs	6×19×¼

FOLDING CHAIR

A folding chair has the advantage of being available as an extra piece of furniture, yet it takes up little room when stored. This folding armchair (Fig. 7-5) follows a well-tried design and has a canvas seat and back. It has ample size for comfort when opened, but packs to only a few inches thick, although its side view is the same size whether opened or closed.

It is possible to complete the chair with a cabinet-making finish and suitable seat and back material for use indoors, when it should not look out of place with other

Fig. 7-5. This chair folds flat and opens to make a comfortable armchair.

room furniture. Alternatively, it can be made for use outdoors. The finish will be plainer, and the canvas is chosen more for its durability if left out in wet weather than for its appearance. There are some attractive waterproof canvas available. Construction should be with one of the straighter-grained hardwoods. The finish may be with a waterproof boat varnish over stain.

Nearly all of the construction is wood. There are some metal links and spacers to make, but they involve simple sawing, filing, and drilling.

The design (Fig. 7-6) consists of two main assemblies: a folding stool with a canvas top, and a pair of sides joined to the stool and their backs linked with the canvas rear part. You can make the stool first and fit the sides to it. It is probably easier to get a good fit if you start with the pair of sides, then adjust the spacing of the stool sides or legs to suit.

Sides

Set out a chair side full-size (Fig. 7-6A). Its parts are made with square edges, but before assembly round all exposed edges to an arc section (Fig. 7-7A) for comfort when handling. Most joints can be dowels, although tenons may be used.

Mark out the legs together (Fig. 7-7B). The stool will pivot on ¼-inch bolts 1 inch up from the bottom. The side rails have dowels into the legs, and there are dowels upward into the arms (Fig. 7-7C).

Round the forward ends of the arms and taper at the back. The side slats are too thin for dowels, and it is better to slot them into the arm and the rail (Fig. 7-7D). The joint between the end of the arm and the back has to resist the thrust of a person leaning back. If too much is cut from the back in the joint, that may be the weak point

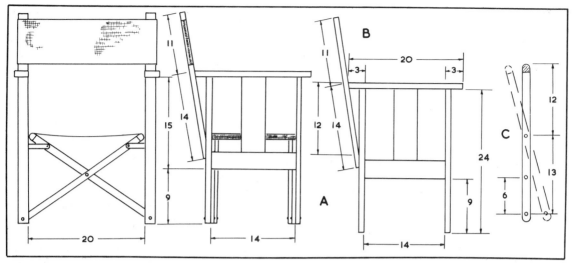

Fig. 7-6. Sizes of the folding chair.

that will give way. To insure that there is plenty of wood left in the back, join with a single ⅝-inch dowel and put a wedge in a slot behind (Fig. 7-7E).

The back (Fig. 7-6B) has to be cut to fit against the rear leg, but it need not go down to a featheredge. Round the top. The load on the chair normally pushes the lower joint together as the canvas is pushed back, so there is not much load at the bottom of the back. Glue it and drive a screw through it into the leg.

See that the two sides assemble to make a matching pair. Remove any blobs of glue and thoroughly sand all parts.

Stool

The stool consists of two crossbars that take the canvas, with four crossed sides held below the pivot with pieces of dowel rod (Fig. 7-8A). The sizes shown (Fig. 7-6C) will give a convenient spread when opened. When laying out the stool, it is the spacing of the side joints to the crossbars that is important. One pair of outside stool sides or legs should fit between the rigid side legs, with just enough clearance for thin washers. The inside legs must fit between them with similar clearance. The sides may be joined to the crossbars with a pair of small dowels, but it is better to use stub tenons (Fig. 7-8B). Round the top edges of the crossbars (Fig. 7-8C). Drill for ¼-inch bolts 1 inch from the bottoms of the sides and again at the pivot points. Drill to suit the dowel rods.

The central pivot of the stool is a ¼-inch bolt or rivet taken through washers. The pivot of the outside stool legs to the rigid legs is the same (Fig. 7-8D). When you

finally assemble, have the manufactured head of the rivet or bolt on the outside. Hammer the rivet end over the washer at the other side. If a bolt is used, hammer over the end of the screw part to prevent the nut working loose, or use a friction locknut.

There is a gap to be filled at the bottom of the other leg. Use short pieces of tube on the rivet, making the length enough to take up the thickness of the outer stool leg (Fig. 7-8E). You can make a trial assembly with the rivets loose, but do not fit them permanently until you have the canvas on and the other metal parts ready.

Links

The links that join the stool to the sides and permit folding are pieces of strip iron about ⅝ inch wide and under ⅛ inch thick; 3/32 inch would be ideal, but any strip of about this section can be used. There are two straight links which join the outside stool legs to the rigid legs (Fig. 7-8F). Mark the centers of the holes and draw curves for the ends before drilling. At the other side of the chair, the links have the same distance between the holes when finished. They have to be cranked to allow for the legs being in a different plane (Fig. 7-8G). Bending can be done by hammering each bend while the strip is projecting above the vise jaws. Drill holes to suit the screws used. There should not be much strain on the links, but allow for using 10-gauge screws. Countersink the holes, so the heads will not interfere with folding.

The best positions for the links are found by a trial assembly. Have the rivets put in loosely and open the chair to the sitting position. Attach the links temporarily

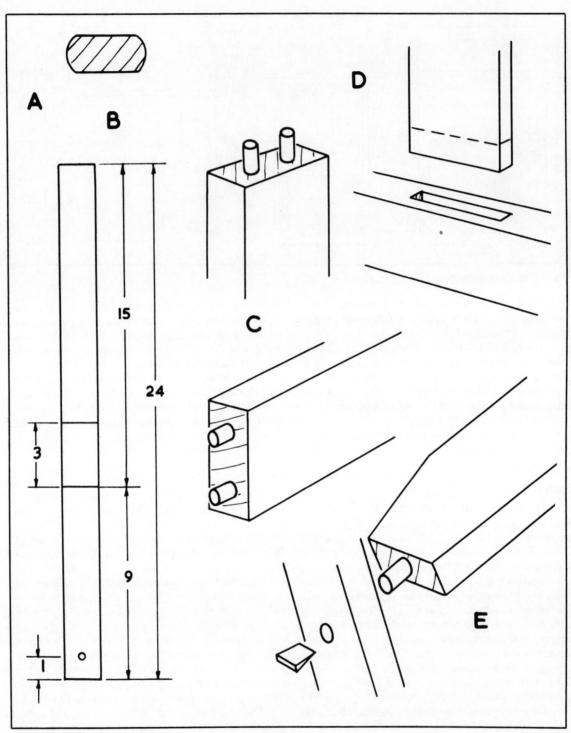

Fig. 7-7. Chair parts are doweled.

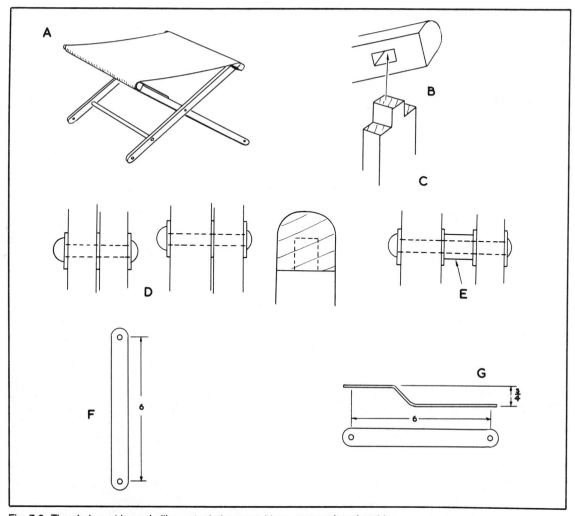

Fig. 7-8. The chair seat is made like a stool, then metal bars connect it to the sides.

to the rear stool legs only, about 3 inches down from the crossbar. Put screws into the side legs when the links are about horizontal. Try the folding action, then alter screw positions until the action is correct. Mark similar positions for screws at the front. Measure across the top of the stool in the open position as a guide to the length of canvas to fit.

Seat Canvas

The seat canvas may be 15 or 16 inches wide. If this standard width cannot be obtained, wider canvas has to be cut and turned under the edges. If the cut is made with pinking shears, simple stitching can be used (Fig. 7-9A). For an ordinary cut, it is better to turn in the edge to

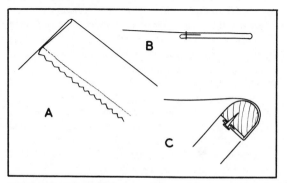

Fig. 7-9. Canvas edges are turned in, and the tacks come underneath rails.

prevent fraying (Fig. 7-9B). At the ends, take the canvas to the underside of each crossbar. Turn it under and tack through (Fig. 7-9C). The roll over the wood will take some of the strain off the tacks, but they should be fairly close for trouble-free use—a spacing of 1 inch or less.

Do any finishing to the woodwork before attaching the canvas. For outdoor furniture, the parts that will be under the canvas should be treated as well as the exposed parts, for the sake of protection and the prevention of water soakage. When you have added the seat canvas, you can assemble with rivets and screws. When you are satisfied with the appearance of the chair, add the back canvas. When the seat canvas is first fitted, it should be taut in the open position. It will soon stretch and sag to a comfortable curve in use. The back strip need not be stretched as much. It should start with some slight slackness. The width is between 7 and 8 inches. If you have to cut and sew, treat the edges in the same way as described for the seat. Wrap the ends so you tack closely on the inner edges.

Materials List for Folding Chair

4 stool sides	1¼×26×⅝
2 stool crossbars	1¼×18×1¼
2 stool rods	⅝×18×round rods
4 side legs	1¾×26×⅞
2 side rails	3×18×⅞
2 side slats	4×15×½
2 arms	3×22×⅞
2 backs	1¾×26×⅞

ROCKING CHAIR

Many chairs can be converted to rocking chairs during construction by tenoning the feet into the rocking bases. It is necessary for the back legs to be about the same distance apart as the front legs, although being slightly narrower does not matter. The rockers can come closer together at the rear without affecting the stability of the chair, providing the taper is not much. If the chair legs slope outward much, it is difficult to make satisfactory joints to the rockers, which would have to be either upright in section or tilted and the bottoms beveled.

It is better to start with a design that is intended to be a rocking chair. One constructional advantage is that you do not have to bother about arranging legs that would stand upright without the rockers. The rear legs can continue down the line of the back in a way that would not be stable in a chair standing only on its legs.

This chair (Fig. 7-10) can be made to match other room furniture, or it may be considered as a semioutdoor

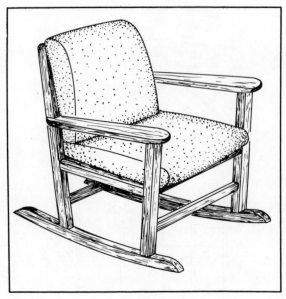

Fig. 7-10. This rocker is fitted with loose cushions.

chair for use on the porch. The seat and the back can be upholstered in the way described in Chapter 10. These parts can be given springs or rubber webbing strips across to support cushions. There can be plywood for the seat and back. With modern thick foam padding, cushions over plywood can be soft enough. For a porch chair with loose cushions to take indoors, plywood may still serve as an occasional seat without padding.

The sizes shown (Fig. 7-11) make a roomy chair with parallel sides and a modern effect due to the straightness of parts and the proportions. Allowance has been made for cushions about 4 inches thick. If the chair is intended to be used without cushions, the seat may be reduced, back to front, by a few inches, bringing the front legs and the fronts of the rockers back by the same amount.

Making the Seat Frame

Start by making the seat frame. Other sizes have to be related to it. Corners can be dovetailed (Fig. 7-12A), or there can be comb or finger joints (Fig. 7-12B). Decide on the method of seating before making up the frame. You may groove the sides for springs (Fig. 7-12C) or rabbet them to take a metal strip (Fig. 7-12D). The spring ends can be hooked around screws. Rubber webbing may be tacked to the top surfaces, but it is better to use the metal pieces intended to go into an angled groove (Fig. 7-12E). An interesting treatment is the use of broad strips of leather interwoven and wrapped around to tack inside

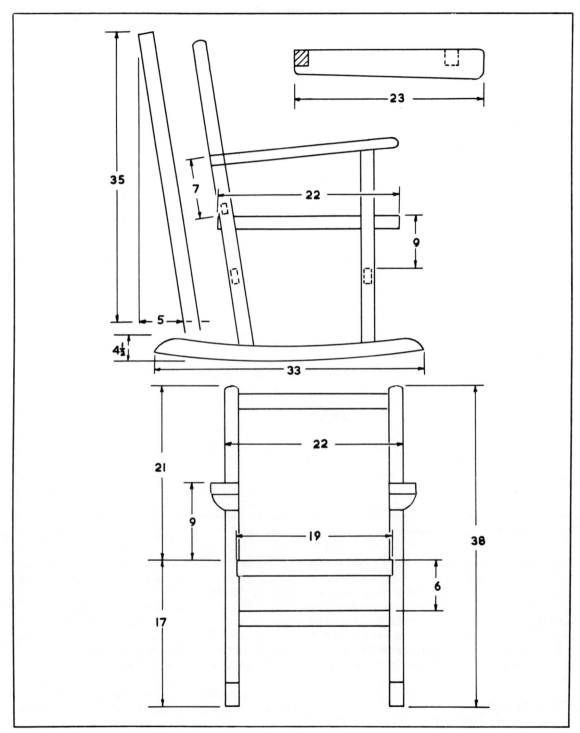

Fig. 7-11. Sizes of the rocker.

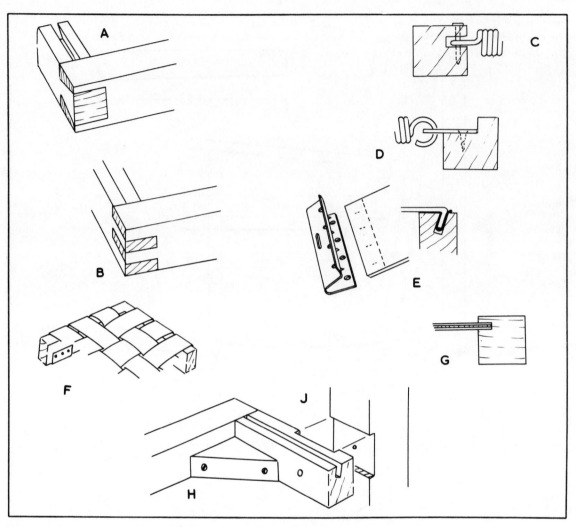

Fig. 7-12. The rocker seat is framed and may have springs or webbing.

(Fig. 7-12F). Wrapping under relieves the tacks of some strain, so do not stop at the under surface. Instead of leather you can use plastic-coated fabric, possibly with different colors each way. If the seat is to be plywood, that may be nailed on top, but it is better let into a groove (Fig. 7-12G). Plywood will stiffen the frame, but for the other treatments you may put triangular blocks in each corner, kept low enough to be clear of the seating supports (Fig. 7-12H).

Legs, Arms, and Rails

Draw a side view of the main lines full-size. That will give you the slope and size of the back and arms. The legs

are notched into the sides of the seat, with the front legs crossing squarely and the back ones at the angle obtained from the full-size drawing. The notching is very shallow (Fig. 7-12J), only going ⅛ inch into each part. The front legs are held by glue and one large screw from inside at each position. The rear legs are better screwed from outside, with the heads sunk and plugged over.

Prepare the wood for the arms (Fig. 7-13A). The best joint into the back is a combination of a tenon and notch (Fig. 7-13B). For the front leg into the arm, you can use a rather similar joint right through (Fig. 7-13C). If you want to keep the top surface clear, it is better to use one or two stub tenons with fox wedging as well, if that seems

124

necessary (Fig. 7-13D). Away from the joints, round the edges of the arms, particularly around their fronts.

Make the top rail to a length that will keep the sides parallel when attached to the seat. Make the other rail above the seat to match it. Prepare these in the same way as the side seat rails. Springs or rubber webbing will be arranged vertically between these rails. If the back is to be plywood, groove these rails and the sides. For woven leather there is no special treatment, but keep the lower rail far enough above the seat to allow you to get the strips through easily.

The lower rails are the same length as the upper ones. Mark them together, so lengths between shoulders are the same. Simple mortise and tenon joints take them into the legs. Round the tops of the back legs. Take the

sharpness off all exposed edges. If you are springing the seat and back, round inner edges so no hard angle can be met when supports are fully compressed.

Rockers

At this stage, there should be some excess length left at the bottoms of the legs for joints into the rockers. The rockers are cut from solid wood, or they can be laminated. Exact geometric accuracy of the curve may not be important, providing the two pieces match. The radius of a suitable curve is about 84 inches. You can draw it with a compass made from a strip of wood. Put an awl through for a center. Allow for a pencil at the end and in a notch 2 inches back for the thickness (Fig. 7-14A). Mark the thickness at the end and center of the wood. Manipu-

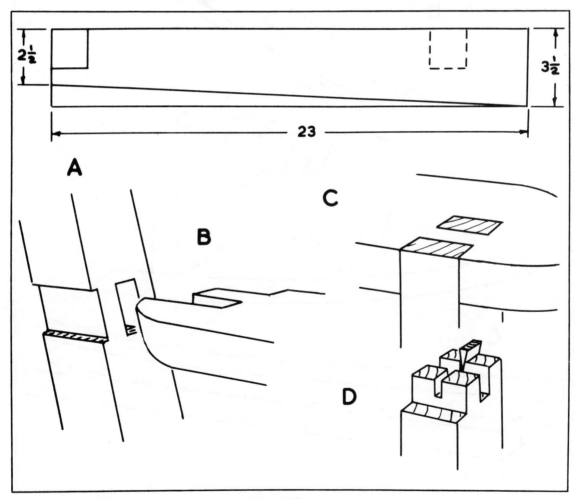

Fig. 7-13. Arms are securely attached to the back and front legs.

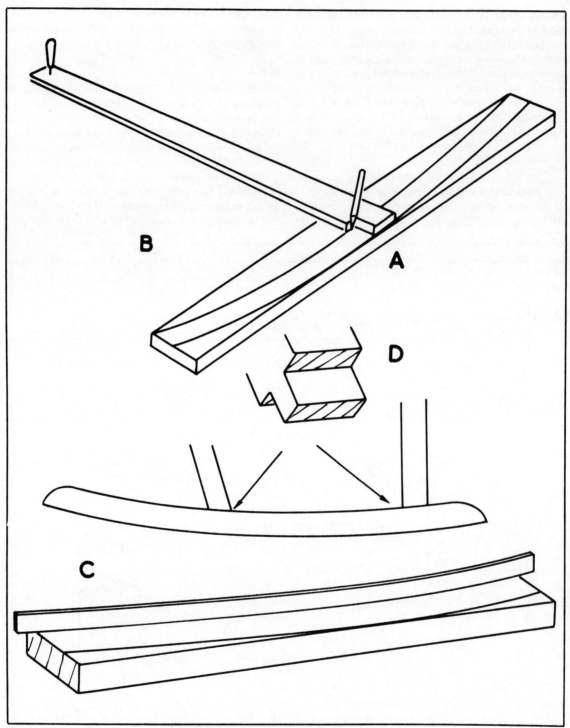

Fig. 7-14. The rocker curve can be drawn with an improvised compass or a sprung lath.

late the wood so the compass will go through the points before drawing the curve on one piece (Fig. 7-14B). Cut that piece and use it to mark its partner.

Another way of marking the curve is with a sprung lath (Fig. 7-14C). Have the lath longer than the wood. Otherwise, there is a risk of getting too much curve at the center and almost straight slopes toward the ends. Get an assistant to help hold the lath to shape, so it goes through the marks indicating width at the center and ends.

Arrange the chair to come with the front legs about 6 inches back from the ends of the rockers and the other legs. The balance of the rocker length extends to the rear. Round the tops of the rockers down to the ends.

Check the height of the seat before cutting the joints for the legs into the rockers. Allow for the thickness of the cushion. The height shown is probably the maximum anyone will want, and it may be reduced. Use stub tenons into the rockers (Fig. 7-14D). Round the tops of the rockers away from the joints and take the sharpness off the lower edges. Small pads of leather about 1 inch across and ¼ inch thick can be glued and tacked under the ends of the rockers to act as stops.

Assembly

Assemble the seat frame first and check diagonals. If there is a plywood panel, use exterior or marine grade for porch or patio use. You can drill a pattern of holes in the plywood. They will drain rain away and will help in allowing air through as the cushion contracts and expands in use.

Put the rails between the back legs and assemble them to the seat frame. Check squareness and that the back is without twist. If there is to be a plywood back, it should be included at this stage, with a pattern of holes to match those in the seat. Join the arms to the back legs, then the front legs to them and to the seat. Finally, add the rockers.

Cushions

If cushions are to be fitted, make them as described in Chapter 10. Let the seat cushion go to the back and overlap an inch or so at the front. Make the cushion fairly tight between the front legs to prevent it from slipping. There can be tapes at the rear corners for tying around the back legs. The back cushions rest on the seat cushion and may go above the top rail, where tapes at the corners keep it in place. Alternatively, a strip sewed across its back and brought down about 6 inches can act as a pocket to go over the top of the back framework.

Materials List for Rocking Chair

2 front legs	1¾×27×1¾
2 back legs	1¾×39×1¾
2 seat frames	1¾×23×1¼
2 seat frames	1¾×20×1¼
2 arms	3½×24×1¼
2 top rails	1¾×22×1¾
2 lower rails	1¾×22×1
2 rockers	5×34×1¾

TURNED CHAIR

There are parts of many chairs that can be turned, but this design is intended for the wood turning enthusiast. All parts except the back can be made on a lathe. The limiting size is the seat. The lathe has to be able to swing 16 inches in diameter, so it will probably have to be a lathe that can take a faceplate at the outboard end of the headstock. If a turned seat is beyond the capacity of the available lathe, the chair can be made with the tapered seat similar to those described for Windsor chairs, either left flat or with a scooped top.

The chair (Fig. 7-15) follows a traditional design, but you can use your own ideas for the turned parts. The general drawing (Fig. 7-16) gives the centerlines of the turned parts only. Set out a similar drawing of the front and side views full-size on a piece of plywood or hardboard to serve as a guide to actual sizes and the angles they come in with relation to others, particularly when you drill holes.

Seat

The seat (Fig. 7-17A) is flat underneath, so it can be screwed to a faceplate. The width will probably have to be made up from several pieces. Using four or more pieces glued together helps to reduce the risk of subsequent warping, particularly if you can arrange them with the curves of end grains in opposite directions in alternate pieces. Do not use very narrow pieces at the outsides, where there may be a risk of tearing out during turning.

Plane the underside of the seat flat. Unevenness of the other side will be taken care of when you turn it. Mark the center on the underside and draw circles to match the faceplate and the outer circumference. Saw fairly closely to the outside. An irregular outline at this diameter will set up vibrations in the lathe, and wood may break out when you use the tools on it. Screw through the faceplate securely into the seat. The load on the screws is consid-

Fig. 7-15. A chair can be made almost completely on a lathe. Only the back of this chair is not turned.

erable, and any movement there after partial turning may spoil the work.

Turn to the beaded outline and hollow the top surface slightly (Fig. 7-17B). Put a straightedge across the work and check that the hollow goes down evenly. It is easy to find that the section rises toward the middle. It should be like a regular shallow bowl. When the seat has been turned and you have finished sanding in the lathe, hold a pencil against the rotating wood and lightly draw the circle on which the holes for the back uprights come.

Unscrew the faceplate. Although the underside of the chair will not often be seen, it will look better if you glue plugs into the screw holes. If you plane them and the bottom level, be careful not to remove the mark showing the center.

The seat has to be marked out on the underside for the leg holes. Although the holes for the back can be marked and drilled on the underside, there is a risk of breaking out as the drill goes through and spoiling the look of the top. Mark the back holes on the top. You have to get the leg and back holes correctly related.

Have the seat grain running back to front. On the underside, draw a line through the center mark—back to front. Draw another square to it. From these lines, measure the positions of the leg holes (Fig. 7-17C). To get the top marking symmetrical, square over the back to front line onto the top surface and lightly draw it across. This mark and the curve on which the holes come will have to be cleaned off, so do not pencil any harder than necessary. The center hole for the back comes where this line crosses the curve (Fig. 7-17D). Mark the positions of the outer holes on the curve (Fig. 7-17E) and space the other holes evenly between them. Locate the centers of all holes on both sides of the seat by pushing in an awl, but do not drill any holes yet.

Spindles and Rails

The various spindles that have to be turned (Fig. 7-18) are located on the general drawing by circled letters. The legs splay outward under the seat, but those at the back have a greater slope. This affects their lengths, but all the legs are shown the same length (Fig. 7-18A) as they will be trimmed after assembly.

Make a hole with the drill you will use for the seat in a piece of scrap wood to test the leg tops. Turn the legs with their tops toward the tailstock for ease in testing, as the diameter of the foot end is not as critical. Keep the top end parallel for a short distance, so it will still fit if you do any trimming of length there.

The three rails (Fig. 7-18B) are shown all the same, but there will have to be some trimming of lengths during assembly. The center parts are parallel, and the ends are turned parallel for a short distance to allow for retaining diameters after trimming. Drill the two side rails to take the ends of the center rail.

The two outer back spindles are the main supports (Fig. 7-18C). The upper end is a smaller diameter than the bottom. The greatest diameter is about one-third up. Be careful that the long sweeps are smooth curves without straight parts.

The other spindles (Fig. 7-18D) are also thinner at the top than at the bottom. Their greatest diameters should come opposite the greatest diameters of the outer spindles. Be careful to get smooth flowing curves, without straight sections, and have them all matching. As they assemble close together, variations may be noticeable.

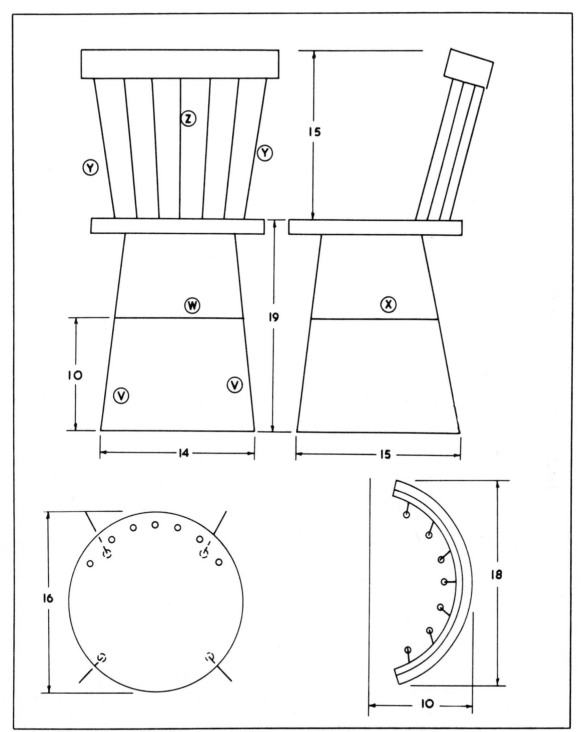

Fig. 7-16. The main sizes of the turned chair, with only the centerlines of turned parts shown.

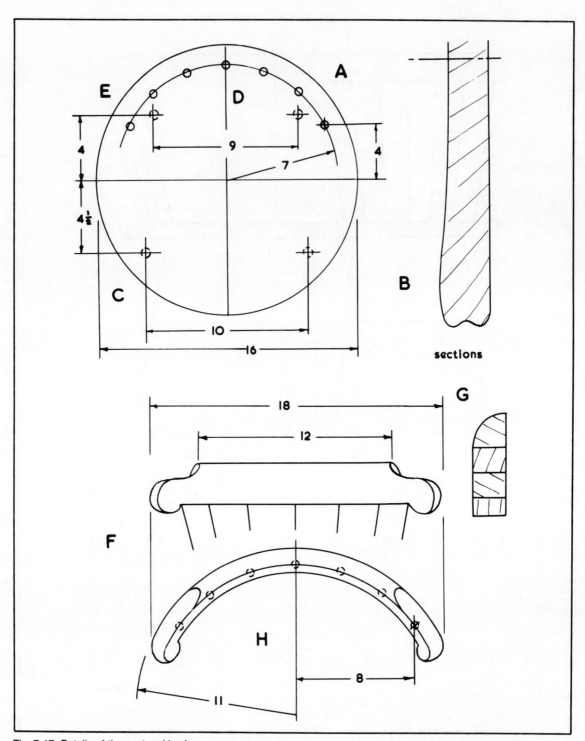

Fig. 7-17. Details of the seat and back.

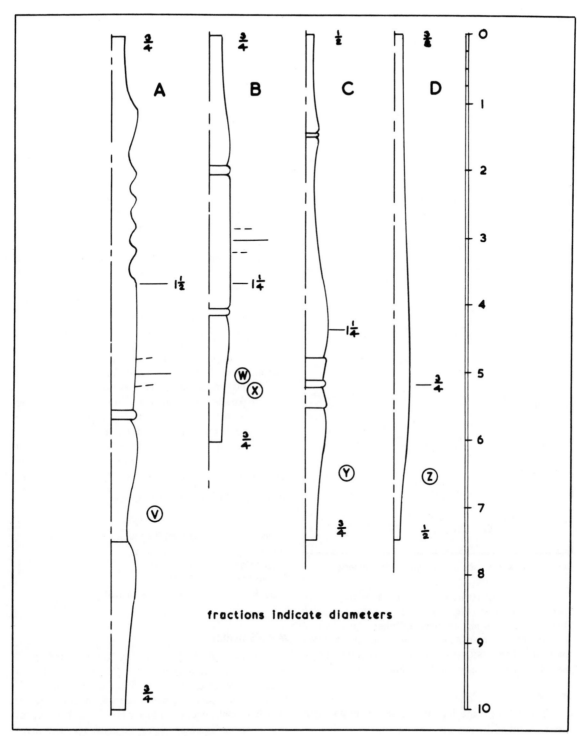

Fig. 7-18. Suggested designs for the turned parts.

Back and Central Part

The top part of the back is tilted, so its actual curve is greater than when viewed directly from above. Set it out full-size (Fig. 7-17F). There is a central part 1½ inches deep that goes all round. A piece above it forms the shaped top, and there are small pieces at the ends to form the lower curves. You can laminate the curve and cut the outline from it, but that involves fairly wide strips for pulling around a simple former. Most craftsmen find it simpler and just as satisfactory to make the back by layering.

The full-length central part can be made by three or more pieces in each layer (Fig. 7-19A), with joints in the top part coming under the shaped top piece, which is best if in one piece (Fig. 7-19B). The curves at the ends are small solid pieces (Fig. 7-19C).

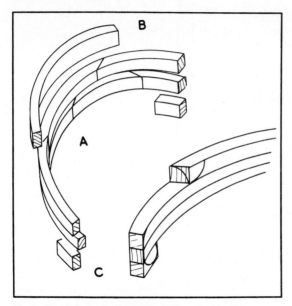

Fig. 7-19. How the back can be built up by layering.

Get the section to a uniform thickness all round, then round the top part (Fig. 7-17G). Except for removing sharpness, there is no need to round other edges. Draw a line around the center of the thickness underneath. Mark the central hole position and the outer ones, then space the others evenly between them (Fig. 7-17H).

Drilling

The holes for the legs in the seat may go about three-fourths of the way through, but the back holes can go through. Use your full-size outline drawing as a guide

to the angles to drill for the legs. When viewed from the front, the legs slope outward the same amount, but when viewed from the side the rear legs have more slope than the front ones. A trial assembly will show if the angles are correct and allow you to first cut the side rails to size, then cut and fit the one between them.

When drilling the seat for the back spindles, allow for them all being at the same angle as viewed from the side. The central one is upright when viewed from the front, so its hole can be drilled first. Use an adjustable bevel as a guide to the drill angle. If you put the spindle in its hole while drilling for the other spindles, it serves as a guide to the angle in side view. The other spindles have to flare out progressively. Holding the curved back above the central spindle will help you estimate drill angles. Drill the back to match.

If any of the drilled holes finish rather loose due to corrections, the legs can have fox wedges. The back spindles can be wedged from under the seat. Assemble the legs and their rails to the seat first and let the glue set. Invert the assembly on a flat surface and measure vertically to the ends of the legs to mark them all at the same level. This will result in diagonal cuts across the ends. When the chair will stand without rocking, take the sharpness off all round the leg ends.

As the back spindles go through the seat, it is possible to make some adjustment at that level. Assemble the spindles into the back and into the seat. Let some go through further until you have the shaped back with both ends at the same height above the seat, and the assembly looking correct when viewed from the side. Wait until the glue has set before leveling any projecting ends below.

Materials List for Turned Chair

1 seat	17×17×1½
4 legs	1¾×20×1¾
3 rails	1½×12×1½
2 spindles	1½×15×1½
5 spindles	1×15×1
1 back	layered as drawing

MONK'S BENCH

This is a piece of combination furniture. It forms a seat with arms when the top is tilted back. Underneath is a roomy storage chest with a lifting lid. The top can be brought back level to make the bench into a table. Whether monks ever used such a bench is debatable, but it is an attractive name. Some old monk's benches have turned and carved parts. This one is shown with some

Fig. 7-20. A monk's bench is a combination of the seat, table, and chest.

turned parts, but the turning can be omitted and the wood left square. There is no carving, but some edge shaping is included, although that can be simplified if you wish. Many old benches were made completely of oak, with the number of panels and their sizes arranged to suit the available widths of wood. In this example all panels are plywood, preferably bought already veneered to match the solid wood parts.

The design (Fig. 7-20) is arranged so the best effect is when the top becomes a seat back, and the sizes (Fig. 7-21) make a double seat suitable for use in most homes. Early monk's benches were often much larger. Draw the main sizes of an end view (Fig. 7-22A) full-size as a guide to the dimensions of parts, particularly the legs (Fig. 7-22B) and arms (Fig. 7-22C). If a lathe with sufficient capacity is unavailable, the spindle parts can be turned separately, with dowel ends to fit into holes in the chest parts of the legs (Fig. 7-22D).

Mark the legs together. Allow for the usual mortise and tenon joints for rails and for tenons into the arms (Fig. 7-23A). Groove all rails to take the plywood panels, with the central dividing pieces tenoned (Fig. 7-23B). The outside surfaces of the rails should finish flush with the legs (Fig. 7-23C). The legs can be grooved, but that means stopping at the mortises. It is difficult to cut by the

usual plowing methods, unless you have a suitable router. The alternative is to make up with strips on the legs (Fig. 7-23D) shown square, but they can be molded.

To support the plywood bottom, put strips around inside the rails and cut a piece of plywood to fit on them and around the legs (Fig. 7-23E). All of the parts described up to this stage can be assembled. Put together the back and front first, checking their squareness and that they match, and then add the end parts. Cut the panels very slightly undersize, so they do not bear on the bottoms of the grooves and prevent joints from pulling tight. This also allows a little tolerance for squaring after checking diagonals.

The seat lid comes between two pieces cut around the legs and attached to the rails (Fig. 7-24A). A simple way of making the lid is to use plywood over a frame (Fig. 7-24B), with the ply edges in rabbets (Fig. 7-24C) or hidden by quarter-round moldings (Fig. 7-24D). Allow for a strip along the back of the chest for hinges (Fig. 7-24E). Without this, the cross bearers under the tabletop would prevent the chest lid from opening properly.

The tabletop has to be linked to the arms with dowels. In the tilted position the top has to swing on the dowels (Fig. 7-25A). For the table position, each dowel slides in a groove to the center of its arm (Fig. 7-25B). The rear end of each arm has to be rounded enough to clear the tabletop (Fig. 7-25C). The other end can match. The tops of the arms are cut down for comfort and to leave the ends as supports. There are mortises for legs, and the dowel grooves must not be so deep as to cut into them (Fig. 7-25D). Make the arms and round the prominent parts of their sections.

The tabletop can be made in a similar way to the seat lid (Fig. 7-26A). Make up a framework with mortise and tenon joints. Put a plywood top over this, either in rabbets or with molding around (Fig. 7-26B). The spacing of the bearers must suit the width between the arms. Either cut the bearers to fit into the framework or use filler pieces. Shaped edges are shown on the bearers (Fig. 7-26C), but you can use plainer curves. The dowels come central in the length and at a height that lets the tabletop rest on the arms. Note where the bearing surfaces are and put fillers in the top to take the pressure on the arms (Fig. 7-26D).

Check the bearer spacing and the action of the tabletop by a trial assembly without glue. When you are satisfied that you have it right, attach the bearers to the tabletop. Link the dowels into the slots as you put the arms on the leg tenons. You cannot add the top after the arms are attached to the legs because of the projecting dowels.

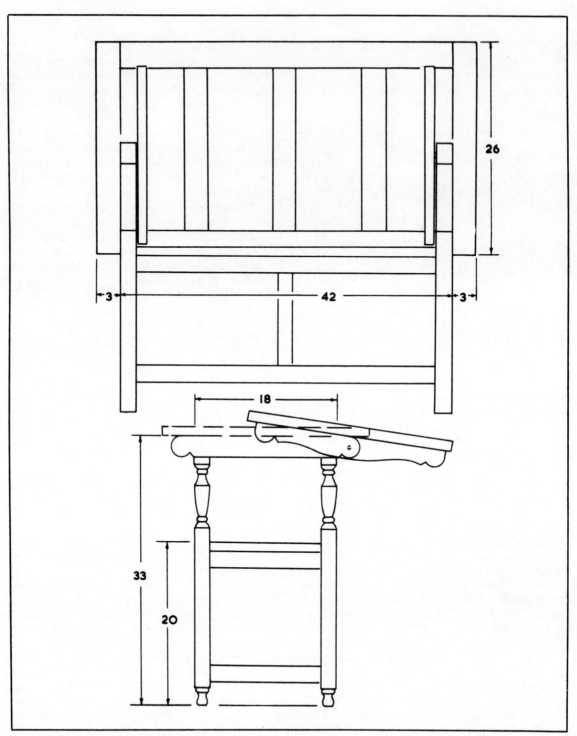

Fig. 7-21. The main sizes of a monk's bench.

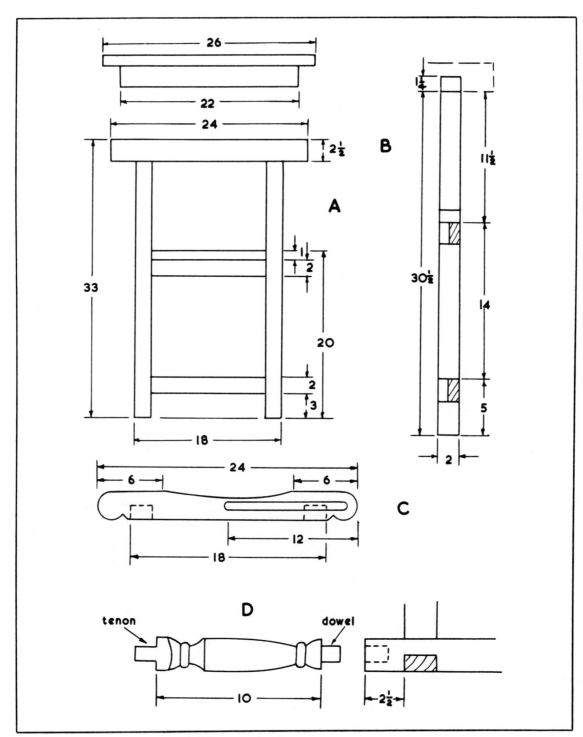

Fig. 7-22. Ends, arms, and spindles for the monk's bench.

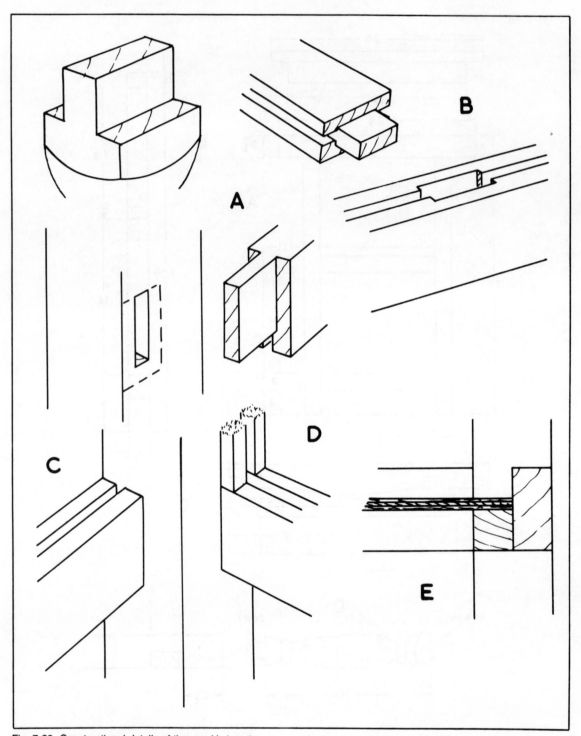

Fig. 7-23. Constructional details of the monk's bench.

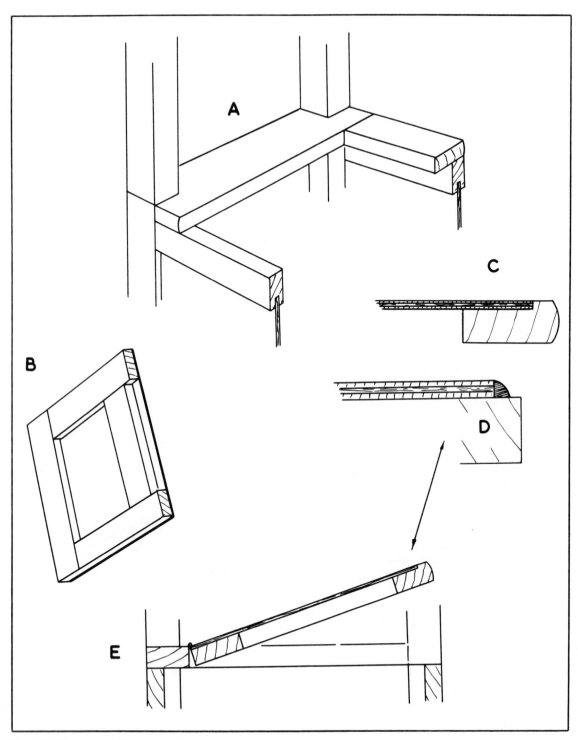

Fig. 7-24. The seat and its surroundings.

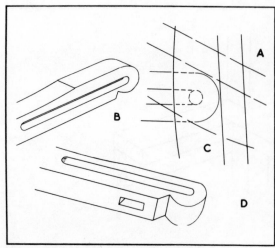

Fig. 7-25. The grooved arms allow the tabletop to swing down as a seat back or to slide central as a table.

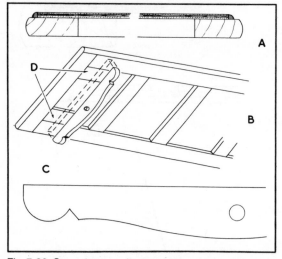

Fig. 7-26. Crosspieces under the tabletop pivot on the arms.

Materials List for Monk's Bench

4 legs	2	×31×2
4 chest rails	2	×42×1
4 chest rails	2	×18×1
2 chest dividers	2	×18×1
2 chest bottom supports	1	×42×1
2 chest bottom supports	1	×18×1
1 chest bottom	18	×42×¼ plywood
2 chest panels	16	×18×¼ plywood
2 chest panels	16	×20×¼ plywood
2 seat ends	3	×18×1¼
2 seat sides	3	×38×1
2 seat ends	3	×18×1
2 seat dividers	3	×18×1
1 seat back	2	×40×1¼
1 seat top	18	×40×¼ plywood
2 arms	2½×25×2	
2 table rails	3	×42×1
5 table rails	3	×27×1
1 tabletop	26	×42×¼ plywood
2 table bearers	2½×23×1	

Chapter 8

Advanced Tables

Table design has probably provided more opportunities for ingenious inventors than anything else in furniture making. The variety of table patterns is endless. Some typical examples are given in this chapter.

Supports may consist of corner legs, but many tables either have a central pedestal or pedestals at each end. A cross between the two is a *sawbuck table*. Some very large tables have six or more legs or three pedestals, but these arrangements are best avoided as they depend on a floor being absolutely level. In many tables the end pedestals become the ends of storage spaces, or the whole table may be in the form of a box. Tables with drawers are obviously useful.

If you examine old tables, or illustrations of them, some of the legs are elaborately shaped and often carved, usually with feet in the form of claw and ball. There was a period when cabinetmakers almost wanted to carve every piece of wood within sight. Those designs are too ornate for modern usage. The basic leg shape in more streamlined form, known as a *cabriole leg*, has survived. You should learn how to make these legs, as they can only be copied in a stylized and less attractive form by machine. The ones you make will add the distinction of hand craftsmanship to your work.

There are many uses for small tables, often called coffee tables, although that name does not describe all of their uses. There are side tables and others that find a place beside lounge chairs. These tables are often made like miniatures of full-size tables, and they are usually quite attractive. Many designs can be reduced.

BOOK TABLE

This is a table which is almost a cube. It can house books of normal proportions in four sections. There is an upper compartment to take the oversize so-called "coffee table books" (Fig. 8-1). The table can be stationary in a position where there is access all round, but for most positions it is better on four casters, so it can be turned round or moved about. It then becomes a sort of mobile compact library, which can be used beside a chair and turned round to allow any compartment to be reached without leaving the chair. The top is also at a suitable height for holding coffee or other drinks, or it may take magazines or newspapers.

Construction should be with flat panels, either thick plywood or veneered particle board, which can have self-adhesive veneer strips fitted to cut edges. All of the joints are doweled, and it is helpful to have a doweling jig

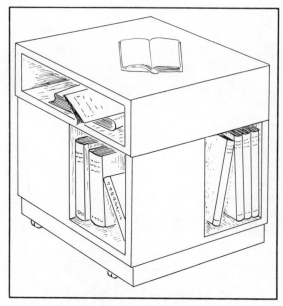

Fig. 8-1. This book table holds books on all four sides as well as in the top.

or template that allows pairs of holes to be drilled to match. The holes can be positioned by careful marking out without a doweling jig or template. Holes for dowels must be drilled squarely to surfaces and to controlled depths. A drill press is advisable if the doweling jig does not control the direction of the drill, and there should be a depth stop on the drill or the press. All of the dowels may be ¼-inch diameter. Prepared dowels should be 1 inch or slightly longer, but they can be cut from longer dowel rods as you need them.

The proportions given (Fig. 8-2) are intended to suit plywood ¾ inch thick or slightly thinner veneered particle board. Solid wood of about the same thickness can be used and joined in the same way.

Use the crossed book compartments as the guide sizes to which other parts have to be matched. Make the baseboard 18 inches square. Either draw on this or on a scrap piece of plywood the layout shown in Section x-x (Fig. 8-2). Make the central piece (Fig. 8-3A). Cut the pieces that make this into a cross (Fig. 8-3B), then those that go round the outside (Fig. 8-3C). When brought together after veneering exposed edges, these parts should fit on to the base without overlapping its edges.

At the center it is unwise to try to fit dowels right through and into both crosspieces. It is easier to get the parts located correctly if you drill from both sides, so the dowels are staggered (Fig. 8-3D). At the corners, drill as

far as possible without the drill breaking through (Fig. 8-3E). Mark adjoining parts as you drill them, so you assemble them correctly later.

Drill for more dowels downward into the base. As the underside will not show, the dowels may go right through (Fig. 8-3F). Support with flat wood close to the surface to prevent the material from breaking out when the drill goes through.

Put this assembly together with glue and dowels. Get the crossed parts tight, then the outside pieces, and finally join on the base.

The *plinth* that goes underneath is set in about ¼ inch all round. The corners overlap and are doweled, but inside there should be wood strips screwed in so the plinth can be screwed upward into the base (Fig. 8-4A). The wood strips need not be full length inside, but they should go most of the distance along each part, so there is a good spread of screws.

The top compartment is open-ended, so large books or magazines can be reached from both ends (Fig. 8-4B). Make the top and bottom identical and veneer the cut edges. Make the two sides and drill for dowels. Also, drill and dowel into the edges that come below. Take care to get the assembly symmetrical.

If casters are used, they should be fairly widely spaced. If they are a large rubber-tired type, set them inside the plinth slightly so they do not lift the table too far. For small casters, there may be strips across for screwing on about 3 inches from each corner. Put packings inside the plinth and screw the strips to them (Fig. 8-4C). If you are using deep casters that should be set into the plinth, you can attach the strips to the pieces being used for attaching the plinth to the base. Strips across will take casters with flat bases intended to be screwed on. If you have the type intended to go into a hole in a chair or table leg, there can be pieces screwed inside the plinth, drilled with suitable holes (Fig. 8-4D).

The finish you apply will have to suit the material used and the surroundings. You can give a distinctive appearance by staining the plinth block black or a dark brown before applying polish or varnish.

Materials List for Book Table

All plywood or particle board ⅝ or ¾ inch thick

1 base	18 × 18
1 divider	12 × 18
2 dividers	9 × 12
4 sides	9 × 12
4 plinths	2 × 18
2 top parts	20 × 20

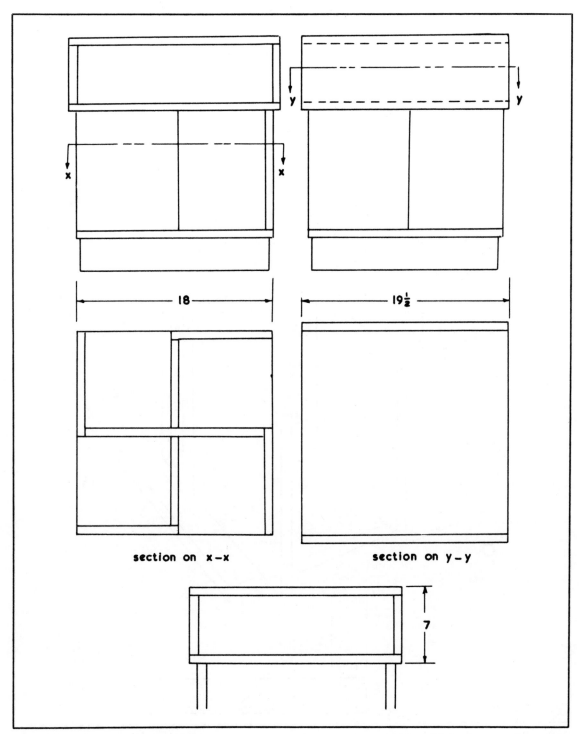

Fig. 8-2. Suggested sizes for a book table.

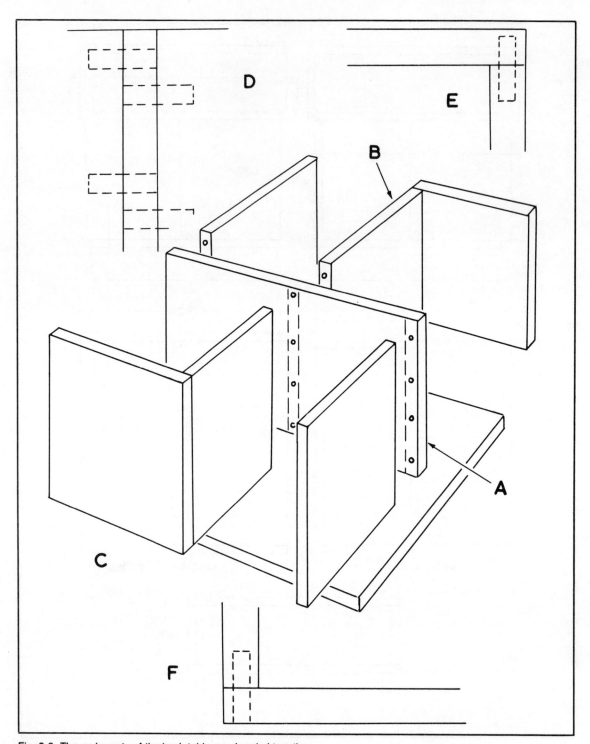

Fig. 8-3. The main parts of the book table are doweled together.

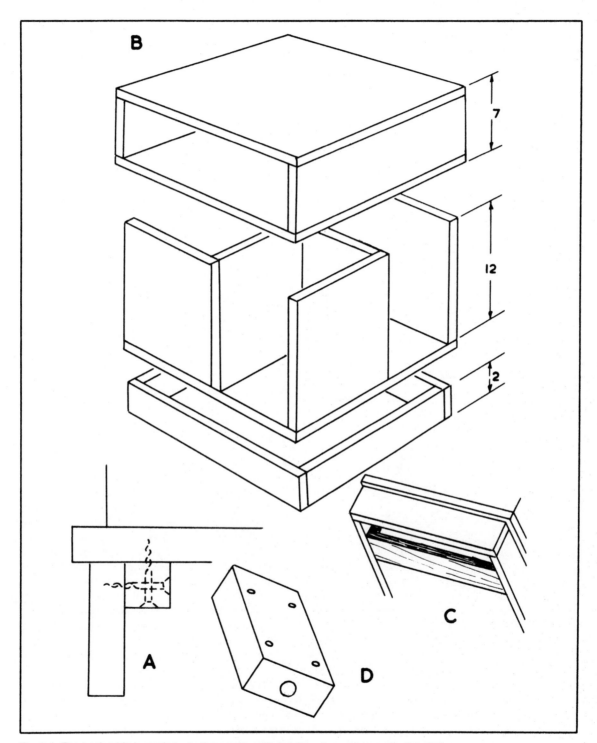

Fig. 8-4. The book table is made up in three units, with locations for casters under the plinth.

2 top parts	¾ × 18 × ¾ wood
4 plinth pieces	3 × 18 × ¾ wood
2 caster supports	

GLASS-TOPPED TABLE

The use of transparent glass in tables is a modern idea. Some earlier tables had obscured glass, but good quality strong glass is a fairly recent product. There are tables with thick glass that has free edges for much of its perimeter, but that involves rounding and polishing edges. This makes the tabletop fairly expensive, both because of the work involved and the need to use a thickness that will resist breaking. If the glass is framed all round, the need for shaped and polished edges is avoided. With all edges supported, ¼-inch plate glass should be strong enough for the tops of small tables.

This example (Fig. 8-5) is of coffee table size with the glass in a frame, although it can be lifted out for cleaning, and crossed rails below (Fig. 8-6). As the top can be seen through, the crossed rails look more interesting than other rail arrangements.

Fig. 8-5. This table has a wood frame and a glass top.

You should get the glass top before starting on the woodwork. If the supplier makes two sides marginally out of square, you can allow for that in the woodwork without it being noticeable in the finished table. If you complete the woodwork before ordering the glass, you may find the glass not quite parallel with the wood or slightly inexact in some other way.

Prepare the rails by cutting rabbets for the glass (Fig. 8-7A). You can let the glass rest directly on the wood or allow for a strip of sponge plastic in the recess (Fig. 8-7B). The type sold for sealing drafts round windows and doors is suitable. Get a good surface inside the rabbets by sanding after cutting with a fillister or other means.

The legs are plain rectangle sections. Make sure the faces are truly square to each other, as the whole of each leg's top will be visible. Corner joints can be doweled, but they are better made with tenons (Fig. 8-7C). Cut the joints while there is some excess length at the top of each leg. Letter inside each joint, so the same parts will be brought together again during assembly. Cut the tops of the legs just a bit too long at this stage (1/16 inch is more than enough), so you can level the legs to the rails after assembly. Mark and cut the recesses in the tops of the legs to match the rabbets in the rails (Fig. 8-7D). Pare carefully with a sharp chisel to get the final surfaces smooth.

The diagonal rails have to mate with the legs, so the legs are not pulled out of square with the top, even if you have made the top rails marginally different lengths to allow for the shape of the glass. To allow for adjustment, the rails go into the legs in their full section instead of being cut down to tenons. When assembling, you can pull a rail in or out a little to bring the leg upright. From the top rail lengths and the sizes of the leg section, set out the leg locations. Draw diagonals. These are the centers of the rails, and you can draw in the thicknesses of the rails (Fig. 8-8A) and get their lengths. Allow for entering the rails about ⅞ inch, but the mortises will be slightly deeper to allow for adjustment (Fig. 8-8B).

Mark the heights of the rails on the legs together, then square round enough to mark the widths of the rails across the corners (Fig. 8-8C). Cut to this depth (Fig. 8-8D). Check this against the end of the rail. Drill and chisel each mortise. An adjustable bevel, set to the angle that a rail will come, provides a guide to the drilling and cutting angle. If you drill on a drill press, a tilting table or packings will keep the wood at the correct angle.

Cut a halving joint where the rails cross (Fig. 8-8E). Use your drawn layout as a guide to angles. Trim the rails to length. Allow for each end going to a particular corner if there are slight variations.

The whole table can be left with square edges and corners, but appearance can be improved with wagon beveling. Put a stopped bevel on the outer corner only of each leg (Fig. 8-9A). Bevel the lower outer edge of each top rail, stopped a short distance from each leg (Fig.

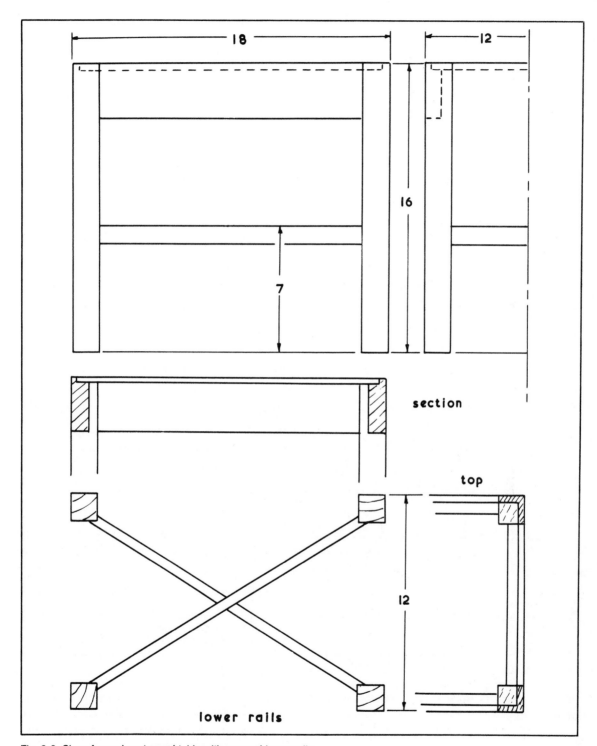

Fig. 8-6. Sizes for a glass-topped table with crossed lower rails.

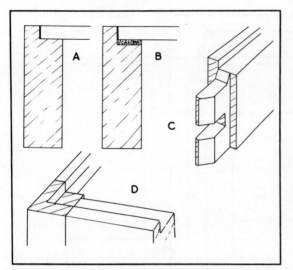

Fig. 8-7. The glass top fits into recesses in the rails and legs.

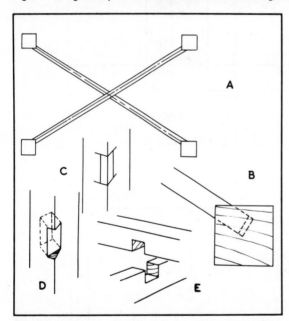

Fig. 8-8. The crossed lower rails are notched into each other and into the legs.

8-9B). These bevels can be about ¼ inch wide. If you continue the treatment on the lower rails, the bevels there should be only about ⅛ inch, stopping each side of the crossing and only working on the top surfaces (Fig. 8-9C).

Assemble the opposite long sides with the top rail between its legs, squaring and matching the pair. Glue

the crossing of the lower rails. Assemble the shorter top rails and enter the diagonal lower rails in their mortises at the same time. Check the squareness of the top as viewed from the sides, but use the glass to settle the shape when viewed from above. Let the diagonal rails adjust to allow the legs to be upright in relation to the top. Make sure there is enough of each end in its mortise, standing on a level surface, and then allow the glue to set.

Clean out any surplus glue from the recesses in the tops of the legs. Level the legs with the adjoining rails. Plane the outsides of the rails and legs level, if there is any unevenness. Lightly round the top edges of the rails and legs, but be careful to not go below the level of the glass.

If the rabbets are not to be lined with plastic foam, the assembly looks good if the rabbets are stained or painted black or dark brown, even if the rest of the wood is left its natural color or only stained lightly before polishing or varnishing.

Materials List for Glass-Topped Table

4 legs	1½ × 17 × 1½
2 rails	3 × 18 × 1
2 rails	3 × 12 × 1
2 lower rails	1 × 21 × ½

TRESTLE DINING TABLE

Tables of this general design have been used in all sizes from small side tables to long tables suitable for a

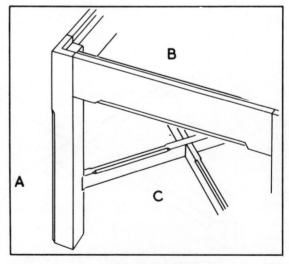

Fig. 8-9. Legs and rails can be decorated with wagon beveling.

baronial hall. The method of construction lends itself to the making of strong tables of any size. The example (Fig. 8-10) is of a size that makes it suitable for the dining room (Fig. 8-11), but it can be scaled up or down, while keeping the height if it is intended for use with a normal chair.

Fig. 8-10. A trestle dining table has its end supports braced with rails.

There is a deep central rail under the top (Fig. 8-11A), and this provides lengthwise stiffness in conjunction with the wedged stretcher lower down (Fig. 8-11B). The fairly heavy sections make a strong, steady table.

The trestle ends are built up. The central upright part looks best with a shaped outline (Fig. 8-11C), although it can be made parallel or tapered with straight sides. Whatever shape is chosen, do not reduce the widths at the ends of the wood where maximum sizes are needed for strength in the joints. The stretcher is shown straight, but it can be given some edge shaping to match the trestles, providing it is not made too thin at any point.

Make a full-size drawing of a trestle (Fig. 8-11D). Mark and cut the joints before doing any shaping of edges. Allow for tenons going well into the other parts. When you assemble, there can be dowels driven through the tenons.

The stretcher goes into each trestle with a form of mortise and tenon joint. Locate this just above center height for the best effect. The joint is a wedged tusk tenon (Fig. 8-12A). Besides the tenon, which goes right through, there is a step cut in the shoulder below the tenon and a wedge from the shoulder line above the tenon. Allow for a sufficient length of tenon for cutting the wedge slot. Let the inner edge of the slot come slightly within the mortise, so driving the wedge pulls the stretcher tight.

The joints at top and bottom are multiple mortise and tenons (Fig. 8-12B), although you can use dowels. Mark out opposite ends togehter. Arrange the joints so the inner surfaces come level, for convenience in fitting the central top rail. You can do the shaping with the joints cut. To ensure symmetry, it helps to make card or plywood templates (Fig. 8-12C). The bottoms are cut back to form feet.

The way that you attach the lengthwise rail to the trestles depends on your skill and personal preference. Whatever method is used, the joint will not be apparent in the finished table. The simplest method is to cut the ends of the rail squarely and use dowels (Fig. 8-13A). Another way is to have short tenons (Fig. 8-13B). They cannot be very long, unless they are allowed to go right through. A simple groove for the rail (Fig. 8-13C) will not be very strong, but one of the strongest joints will make it a dovetail section (Fig. 8-13D). The end of the rail can slide in from the top.

The top can be thick plywood or particle board framed around. It can consist of several pieces of wide thick boards with battens across underneath. The top shown follows traditional methods. It is a broad piece of wood or several pieces glued to make up the width. The top is shown with cleated ends. Well-seasoned hardwood should not expand and contract much. If softwood is used, leave the ends free as the wood can vary in width.

The cleat is shown grooved and with tenons (Fig. 8-14A). Make the cleat slightly too long and too thick, so it can be planed to size after fitting. Round the outer corners and take sharpness off the edges, but for this type of table it is improper to round or mold the wood in section. If you want to make the thick top look thinner, it can be beveled on the underside (Fig. 8-14B).

The tabletop should be held down firmly along the central rail. That can be done with screws driven from above in counterbored holes, which are plugged, but to avoid marking the top surface it is better to drive screws through pockets from alternate sides (Fig. 8-14C).

With the top held along its center, there must also be attachments near the extremities of the trestles to prevent warping. To allow for slight movement in the width of the top, the screws at these points should be in slots in the direction of the top's width. You can make slot holes through the wood and let the screwheads in below (Fig. 8-14D).

A neat way of arranging these screws is to make or buy metal plates with slot holes at one or both sides. Notch the wood to take the plates, which are screwed down before you add the top, and screw upward with round head screws (Fig. 8-14E).

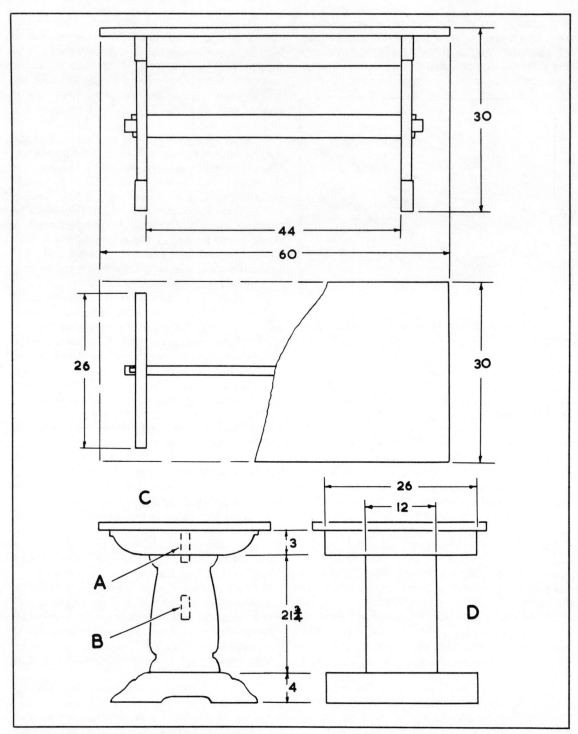

Fig. 8-11. Suggested sizes for a trestle dining table.

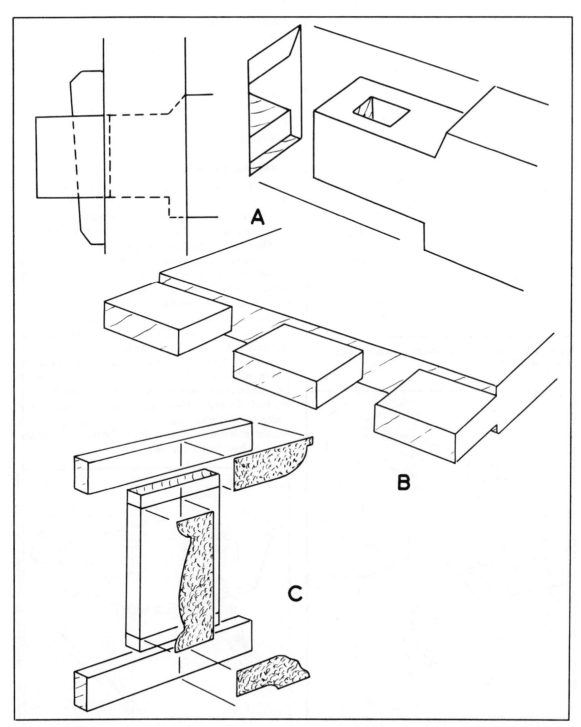

Fig. 8-12. The lower rail has a tusk tenon (A). The ends are joined with multiple tenons (B), and shapes are marked from templates (C).

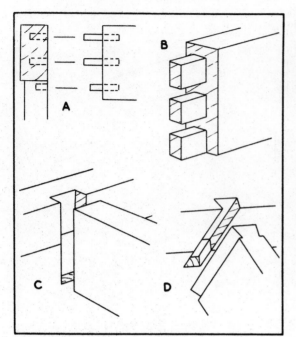

Fig. 8-13. Rail joints can be doweled (A), tenoned (B), housed (C), or dovetailed (D).

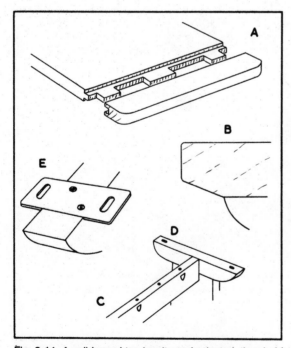

Fig. 8-14. A solid wood top has its ends cleated, then held down with pocket screws and screws through slots.

Materials List for Trestle Dining Table

1 top	30 × 60 × 1¼
2 top cleats	3 × 30 × 1¼
2 top rails	4 × 24 × 1¾
2 bottom rails	5 × 24 × 2
2 posts	12 × 27 × 1½
1 long rail	5 × 48 × 1½
1 stretcher	4 × 56 × 1½

OCTAGONAL BOX TABLE

There is a central area under any table which does not get in the way of a sitter's knees and serves no function except to support the top. If there are drawers under the tabletop, they may extend through this area. Another way of using the space is to build in a box. It can have a useful storage capacity. If the top serves as a lid, as it usualy has to, access to the box is blocked when the top is being used as a table. Many tables are made with boxes that are accessible when the top is tilted, so many things can be put in them.

This table (Fig. 8-15) has an octagonal top at a height that makes it suitable for dining or other use with chairs of normal height. The box is about 8 inches deep, 16 inches wide, and 18 inches long (Fig. 8-16). The lid hinges to one side, so it is vertical when the box has to be reached. To match the angular top, decoration of the lower parts is also angular and with straight lines. A similar table can be made with a round top, then decoration will look better curved.

Fig. 8-15. This octagonal box table has angular decorations.

150

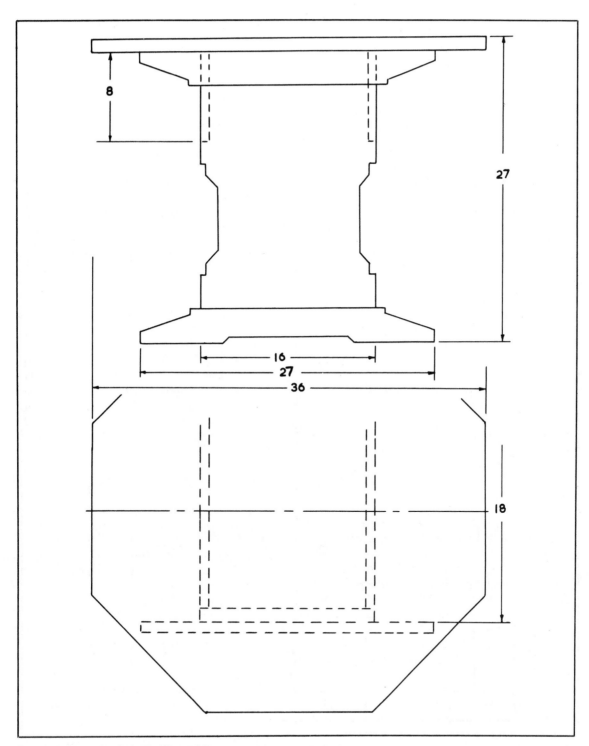

Fig. 8-16. Sizes of an octagonal box table.

Start by making the ends (Fig. 8-17A). At the bottom there can be a series of tenons into the feet (Fig. 8-17B), or the end can be cut level and dowels used (Fig. 8-17C). In both cases, penetration of the feet about 1 inch should be sufficient. Mark where the box sides will come and cut the decorative edges.

Prepare the feet (Fig. 8-17D). Cut the mortises or drill for dowels. Trim the ends and cut out the bottom edge. Be careful that cuts are square across and that both feet match, as they are prominent in the finished table. Any discrepancy will be obvious.

Make the box sides. The lengthwise grain of the sides has to meet the sideways grain of the ends. Although a dovetail joint may seem right, this is not appropriate as the pins are cross-grained and not very strong. It is better to groove the ends and make tongues on the sides (Fig. 8-17E). An alternative is to cut rabbets in the sides, so they overlap the ends. You can glue and drive pins both ways (Fig. 8-17F).

The plywood box bottom can be fitted in grooves (Fig. 8-17G) all round. It may be grooved into the sides and supported by strips across the ends (Fig. 8-17H), or strips can be used under it all round.

Make up the parts so far, with the box built into the ends. Check that the assembly stands level. Sight across the top both ways to see that there is no twist on the top edges, and the lid will close level.

The supporting braces under the top have the same outlines as the feet, except for the cutout (Fig. 8-18A). Make both of them. The pivots for the top are dowels or

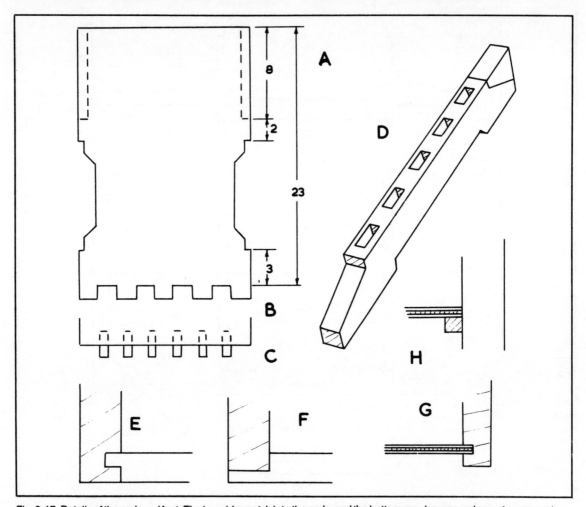

Fig. 8-17. Details of the ends and feet. The box sides notch into the ends, and the bottom may be grooved or rest on supports.

152

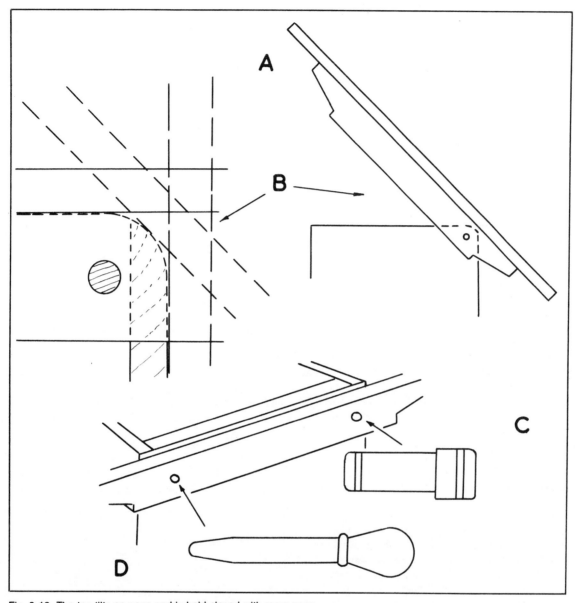

Fig. 8-18. The top tilts on pegs and is held closed with more pegs.

pegs through the braces into the ends. The top will be quite heavy, and the pegs should be ¾-inch hardwood or thicker.

The back of the box at the pivot has to be rounded, so the top will clear it when it swings on its pivots (Fig. 8-18B). You can mark the amount of curving by temporarily mounting a brace on its peg and swinging it from horizontal to vertical, with a pencil against its edge.

Round the edge slightly below this line to provide clearance. To prevent the tabletop tilting unintentionally, there should be more pegs near the other side of each end. If a lathe is available, you can make pivot pegs with heads (Fig. 8-18C). The other pegs can have knobs for easy withdrawal (Fig. 8-18D). You can drill through these pegs in the lathe for cords to retain them to screw eyes when loose.

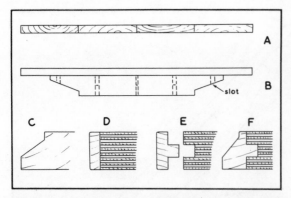

Fig. 8-19. A solid top may be made with boards having the grain alternate ways (A), then the support is screwed on (B). The edge can be shaped whether solid wood or plywood is used.

There are several ways of making the top. It can be solid wood, with several boards glued together to make up the width. End grain alternate ways (Fig. 8-19A) will minimize any overall tendency to warp. In this width you must expect some expansion and contraction, so the braces should be screwed and not glued. The central screws may be in round holes, but others should be through slots to permit slight sideways movement (Fig. 8-19B). Sink the screwheads and plug over them.

The table edges may be left square or rounded, but you can continue the theme of the lower decoration with an angular molding (Fig. 8-19C). This can be made by cutting a rabbet, then tilting the plane.

The top can be veneered particle board, with veneered edges. That top is very heavy, and a better top can be made from plywood or blockboard that is veneered to match the wood chosen for the underparts. Because of the partial end grain, veneer will not glue satisfactorily around the edges. The simplest treatment is to use thin strips of wood (Fig. 8-19D) glued and held with pins punched below the surface and covered with stopping. Cut the strips slightly wide, so they can be trimmed to the top thickness and rounded.

A better cover has a plowed groove around the edge. The added strip is given a tongue to fit in (Fig. 8-19E). The strip should also be slightly wide, so it can be trimmed to the thickness. If a molded edge is intended, this tongue and groove joint is the best choice. The outer edge can be molded without fear of breaking the joint (Fig. 8-19F).

None of the manufactured boards will be troubled by expansion and contraction, so the braces can be attached rigidly by gluing. The pivot pegs can be put in dry, so they

can be removed if you ever want to dismantle the table, possibly for transport. They can also be glued in the braces and allowed to turn in the holes in the box ends.

Materials List for Octagonal Box Table

2 legs	16 × 25 × 1¼
2 feet	3 × 28 × 1¼
2 braces	3 × 28 × 1
2 sides	8 × 19 × ⅞
1 bottom	16 × 18 × ¼ plywood
1 top	36 × 36 × 1

SAWBUCK TABLE

Crossed legs give a table a distinctive appearance and are quite satisfactory functionally, if they are properly made. This construction is called sawbuck from the similarity of appearance to the method of supporting a log for hand sawing. The table (Fig. 8-20) is drawn as a dining table (Fig. 8-21), but it can be made smaller as a side or coffee table. A small sawbuck table has a neat and unusual appearance among other furniture.

The important parts are the two end trestles, and they should be set out and made first. Draw an end view (Fig. 8-22A) full-size on a piece of plywood or hardboard, and use that to get sizes and as a base for assembly. Note that the bottom parts extend to the width of the tabletop, but the top pieces set in. All of the parts are 2 inch by 3 inch section on edge, except the tops have the 3-inch way against the tabletop.

Cut the sloping pieces too long at first, then mark and cut the halving joints (Fig. 8-22B). Assemble them temporarily dry and put a pair over the full-size drawing to pick up the marks for the top and bottom joints (Fig.

Fig. 8-20. A sawbuck table with a solid wood top.

154

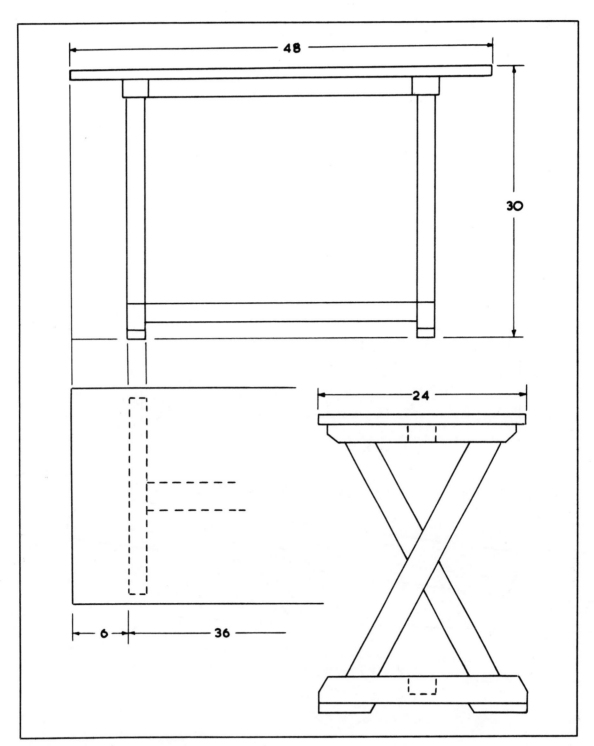

Fig. 8-21. Sizes of the sawbuck table.

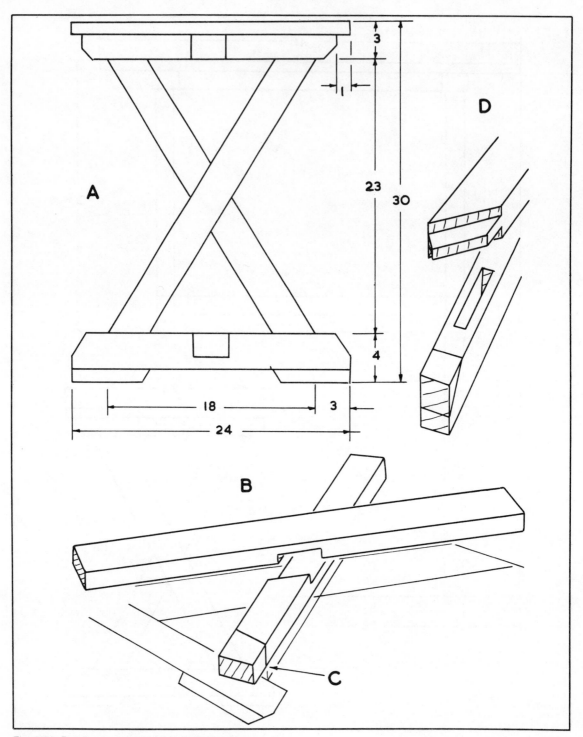

Fig. 8-22. Details of one end of the sawbuck table.

8-22C). From these points, mark out and cut the joints (Fig. 8-22D). One end of the mortise and tenon joint is cut square, but the other end follows the slope. Mortise and tenon joints are preferable to doweling, as the slope of a leg limits the area available for positioning dowels across its end.

After making the joints in the bottoms, cut the ends to length. Bevel them at the same angle as the legs. The tops will not normally show, and they can be cut at 45°. Make the feet to go under the bottoms. They are cut square at their outer ends and at the same angle as the inner ends (Fig. 8-23A).

The bottom rail is the main support to resist lengthwise loads on the table, and it should be tenoned into the end (Fig. 8-23B). The top rail can also be tenoned, although it is easier to notch and screw it (Fig. 8-23C). The joint will be covered by the top.

All of the parts can be left with square edges, but this is a design that can be improved by wagon beveling between joints and with bevels at the ends. Adopt a standard width of bevel throughout—¼ inch should be enough. Arrange the stopped bevels on the end assemblies (Fig. 8-23D), then bevel down to the feet outside (Fig. 8-23E). The wagon beveling can be done on both sides or kept to the outer faces only.

The top is a plain rectangle of glued-up boards. Alternate the directions of end grain, if possible, to minimize any tendency to warp. If the leg assemblies are left square-sectioned, the top should also be square-edged. Otherwise, similar beveling should be used around the top (Fig. 8-23F) on the top surface only, or underneath as well. Outer corners may be cut off (Fig. 8-23G). If sections are left square, take off sharpness of edges and corners before assembly.

There can be a line of screws up through the central rail into the top (Fig. 8-23H), but further out you have to allow for possible expansion and contraction of the top. One way is to use slotted metal plates (Fig. 8-23J) for screws. You can groove the top pieces either right across during making, or a short distance, to take buttons (Fig. 8-23K). With the central screws holding down the top, you should only need other fastenings near the extremities of the supports.

Materials List for Sawbuck Table

1 top	24 × 49 × 1
4 legs	3 × 36 × 2
2 tops	3 × 24 × 2
2 bottoms	3 × 25 ×2
4 feet	2 × 8 × 1
2 rails	3 × 36 × 2

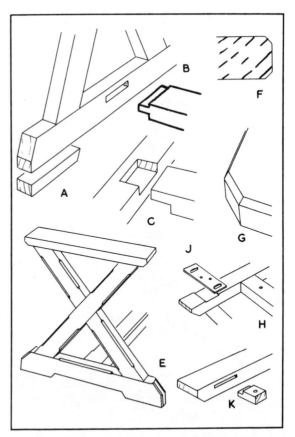

Fig. 8-23. Attachment of rails and top to the sawbuck ends.

TURNED CANDLE TABLE

The post and top of a candle table make interesting lathe projects (Fig. 8-24). The size that is possible depends on the capacity of the lathe. The controlling limit is usually the largest diameter that can be swung. This table has a 12-inch diameter top, which should be within the capacity of most lathes. To give a proportion that looks right, the height is limited to about 20 inches. If the table is to be used for a pot plant, the spindle can be lengthed. The standard table has possibilities as a coffee table or for use beside a lounge chair. The design is shown with a tilt top, so the top can be swung vertical when out of use as a table. That action is optional. If tilting is not wanted, the braces may be screwed to the support.

The general drawing (Fig. 8-25) shows a suggested design for the spindle or post. Note that where the legs are attached the wood is reduced slightly to a parallel cylinder (Fig. 8-25A). At the top turn a dowel to fit into the support (Fig. 8-25B). When turning the spindle, get

Fig. 8-24. A mahogany candle table.

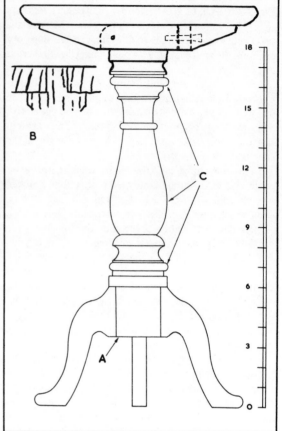

Fig. 8-25. Sizes of a candle table with a tilt top.

the right proportions by keeping the wood at its maximum diameter at the two main beads and the largest part of the bulbous center (Fig. 8-25C). The sweep of the curve from the bulbous part is shown broken by a single bead. Be careful that the wood on each side of the bead continues the same flowing curve.

Saw the wood for the top to a circle slightly oversize and mount it by screwing through a circle of plywood on the faceplate (Fig. 8-26A). Make sure the underside of the top is planed flat. There should be no need for any later work on that surface. It will probably be possible to locate the screws from the faceplate where they will be hidden by the braces. If not, their holes can be filled with glued plugs later. Turn the rim circular, then work it to a tapered rounded section (Fig. 8-26B). Move the tool rest across the surface and turn the top. It can be flat across, but it looks better and will hold things placed on it if you

turn it to a shallow hollow (Fig. 8-26C). Except for the curve up to the rim, the surface should finish flat. It is easy to find that you are making it deeper toward the middle. That is better than having the center higher, but check it frequently to get it flat.

Some of these tables have a leather disc let into the top. Turn the inside so there is a step down inside the rim (Fig. 8-26D). When you fit the leather or leathercloth, choose a suitable glue. Some wood glues do not have a very good grip on leather. Read the maker's recommendations. Watch for trapped air. Rub down from the center outward.

Another thing you can make while at the lathe is the peg that holds the tilt top. It can be a piece of dowel rod, but with a lathe available you can give it a knob for easy withdrawal (Fig. 8-26E). You may also be able to drill through it in the lathe to take the securing cord.

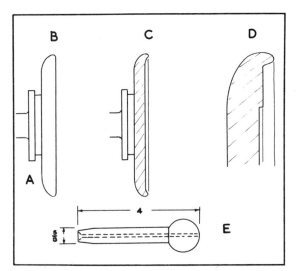

Fig. 8-26. Turning the top of a candle table, and the peg for the tilt top.

Draw a leg shape on a pattern of squares (Fig. 8-27A). The legs can be tenoned into the post in a similar way to that described for the hexagonal candle table. In that case, leave on a projection for clamping (Fig. 8-27B). Follow the instructions for fitting the legs to the hexagonal table. Instead, a type of dovetailed dado is described here. As can be seen, this provides a lock in addition to that provided by the glue, but you may want to allow for clamping.

Make a template of a leg, or complete one leg and use it as a pattern for the other two. As the main parts of the table are turned, the legs should not be left with square edges. They will match the other parts if they are rounded, either to a completely semicircular section or to a lesser curve. This can be done with a suitable spindle molder, but tool marks should be removed by sanding. Otherwise, shaping can be done by hand. When the edge has been trued square across, do the rounding in steps to keep a uniform shape. Draw guidelines with the aid of a notched piece of wood (Fig. 8-27C), then plane and chisel to these lines (Fig. 8-27D). Remove the angles and sand across with a strip of abrasive paper (Fig. 8-27E), until you have removed tool marks and have a regular curve (Fig. 8-27F).

The leg positions have to be marked at equal spacings around the bottom of the post. If there is a dividing head on the lathe, you may be able to mark 120° divisions with it. There is a simple way with a strip of paper. Wrap the paper round and prick through the overlap with any sharp point (Fig. 8-27G). Open the paper and divide the

distance between the holes into three (Fig. 8-27H). Put the paper back round the wood and mark the three divisions.

A further marking problem is drawing lines along the cylinder through these points and for other details of the joints. Join two pieces of parallel wood and use that (Fig. 8-27J). If the wood can be mounted in the lathe again, it is possible to bring the tool rest close to the wood and draw along its edges in the marked positions.

At each leg position, flatten the wood to about the thickness of a leg (Fig. 8-28A). Use guidelines drawn along the strips. The legs have to be cut with shoulders that will bear against these flats and with dovetail-section pieces to go into grooves (Fig. 8-28B). Cut the legs before cutting the post, in case you have to do any adapting to suit individual leg joints that are not the same as their neighbors.

Mark the shapes of the dovetails on the end of the post. Use these as guides when sawing the sides of the dadoes (Fig. 8-28C). It will be easier to cut the far ends of the dadoes by careful chisel work, if the legs and grooves are cut back there (Fig. 8-28D). The legs should slide in from below and hold by their own shape. If you do not get a perfect fit, it will help to clamp, as if for tenons.

The support at the top is a square piece with a hole for the dowel on the post. One side is rounded to give clearance when the top is tilted (Fig. 8-29A). Make the braces to go on each side of the support. Round their outer ends to make them inconspicuous (Fig. 8-29B). Arrange a piece between them to take the peg (Fig. 8-29C). Join these parts with mortise and tenon joints. Glue and screw the braces to the top. Drive the pivot screws and check the action of tilting, then drill through the two thicknesses for the peg. Secure the peg with a cord, either to a hole at the end of a brace or to a screw eye in a brace or the crosspiece.

Materials List for Turned Candle Table

1 post	3 × 16 × 3
3 legs	4 × 10 × 1
1 top	12 × 12 × 1
1 support	4 × 4 × 1½
2 braces	1½ × 10 × ¾
1 brace	1½ × 6 × ¾
1 peg	⅝ × 4 × round rod

SMALL CABRIOLE TABLE

The *cabriole* leg shape can be made quite slender to produce a graceful small table. The fairly small sections of wood needed make it possible to fashion the legs with

159

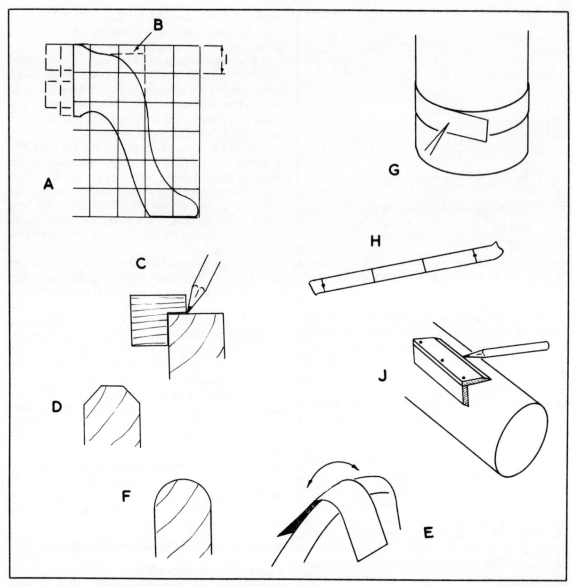

Fig. 8-27. The legs and a method of marking the spindle.

simple equipment on a small bench. This type of leg on a chair may require heavier work, but a light, small table lets you test your skill on these legs, possibly as a preliminary to tackling larger versions.

The table shown is intended to have a ceramic tile as a centerpiece (Fig. 8-30). Overall sizes depend on the chosen tile, but those shown are intended for a tile 6 inches square (Fig. 8-31A). It is common when making a table to build the framing first and match top sizes to it,

but here it is better to draw the layout of the top, even if you do not make it first, to get the other sizes.

The top is based on a piece of ½-inch plywood, 11 inches square (Fig. 8-32A). Solid wood strips go over this as a frame. Their thickness depends on the thickness of the tile (Fig. 8-32B). Miter their corners and glue them to the plywood. Check that the tile fits, but do not glue that in until the table has been finished, stained, and polished. Trim the outer edges square, if necessary. Frame the top

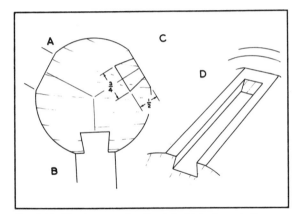

Fig. 8-28. The legs can be dovetailed into the spindle.

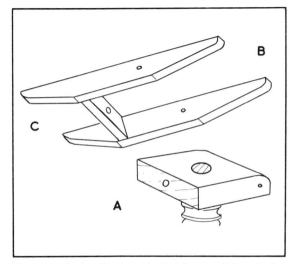

Fig. 8-29. The top tilts on a block at the top of the spindle.

Fig. 8-30. A small cabriole table with a tile center.

with strips of wood ¼ inch thick, also mitered at the corners (Fig. 8-31B). They can be level with the surfaces, but giving them a rounded raised edge looks good and prevents items from sliding off (Fig. 8-32C).

Mark the layout of the framing on the top's underside. The square tops of the legs come in 1 inch, but that brings the curve of a leg and its foot about level with the top's outside edges.

Choose straight-grained wood that has no flaws for the legs. The slender legs have no bracing within their lengths to prevent movement, and warping of imperfect wood after completion cannot be corrected. Make all four legs together, doing the same work on each, rather than carrying through the work on one before starting on the next. This is the best way to insure uniformity. First,

mark the lengths together and square around. Cut the bottom end to length. There can be a little extra left above the top line.

Make a full-size drawing of a leg side view based on a pattern of squares (Fig. 8-31C). From this drawing make a template from thin plywood or hardwood. Be careful that the curves flow smoothly without obvious kinks. You will be reproducing the outline at least eight times, and probably 16, so inaccuracies will be repeated that number of times.

Shaping

Use the template to mark the top and bottom of each leg surface (Fig. 8-32D). With a band saw you can cut closely to the lines and retain the offcuts, so you can mark on the other surfaces at the same time (Fig. 8-32E). If you have to remove the waste by hand sawing and work with a chisel and other tools, the waste will not be sufficiently intact for use when cutting the other way. If you have band sawed one way, put the offcuts back in place, with a few fine nails in the waste parts to retain them. Bandsaw the other way. Otherwise, use the template to mark the

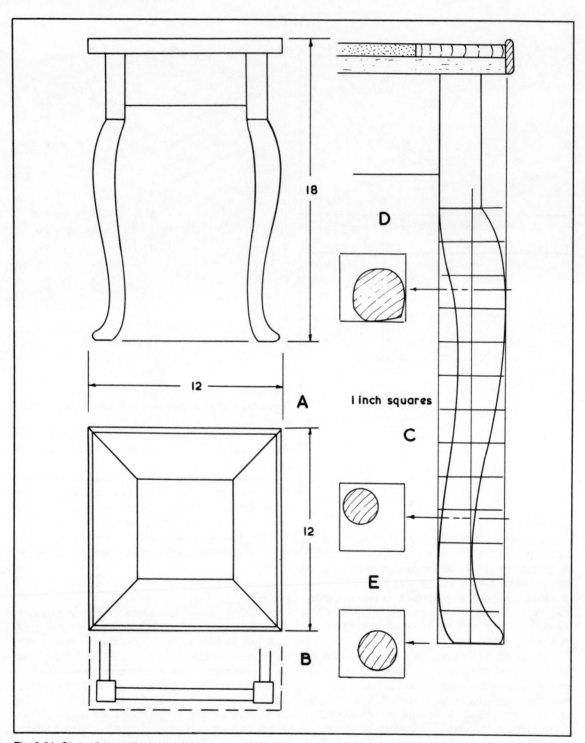

A

B

D

1 inch squares

C

E

18

12

12

Fig. 8-31. Sizes of a small cabriole table.

162

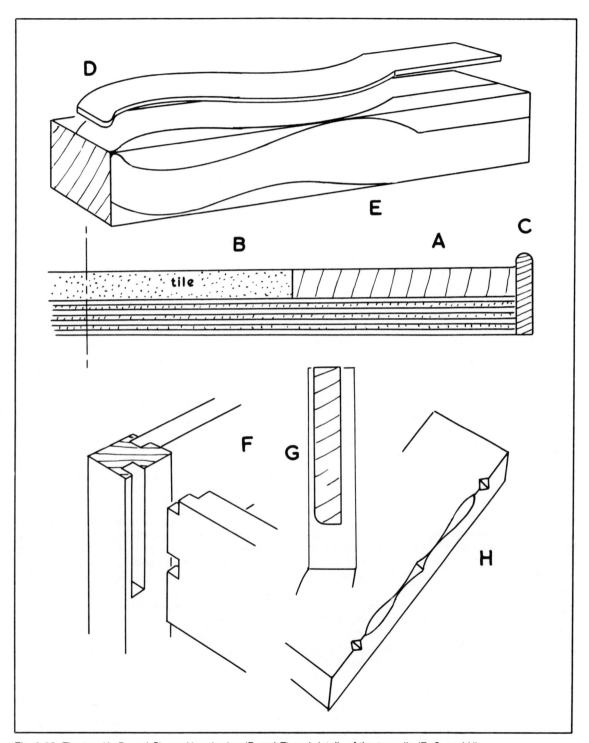

Fig. 8-32. The top (A, B, and C), marking the leg (D and E) and details of the top rails (F, G, and H).

shape on the cut surfaces. A flexible template helps in getting the shape right.

Finish the curves before smoothing the square top surfaces. You can hold the square ends in a vise while working on the curves. If a chisel slips into the square part while shaping a curve, it may not matter if that surface has yet to be level.

True the surfaces where necessary, while the wood is still a square section. It is difficult to get the shape right when curved, if the square sectioned wood is inaccurate. You may pare with a wide chisel. A spokeshave is useful, but for this part of the shaping flat and curved Surform tools allow you to follow the curves and correct the outline without fear of splitting or taking off too much.

In the finished leg the outer corner is angular from the square top over the curved knee, until it blends into a curve about 5 inches down. Its sharpness will be removed in final sanding, but until then keep it as cut. All other angles have to be taken off. Surform tools may be used, but final shaping is best done with a spokeshave.

The higher parts of the leg can be regarded as a square with the corners rounded, except for the outer corner (Fig. 8-31D). As the shaping gets lower, the section has to be nearer round until at the thinnest point, and from there to the foot you should aim at a round section (Fig. 8-31E).

Start by shaping to octagonal sections. Where the final section will be round, aim at regular octagons. Leave spaces between the cuts the same width as the cuts. Do not take off so much in the higher parts. Look at the leg from all directions. See that what you have taken off leaves cuts that show flowing curves. Correct any unevenness. Next, take off the angles of the octagons, so you produce 16 faces. By then you will be working by eye rather than geometrically.

Use strips of abrasive paper across the grain. With the square end in the vise and the leg standing up, use the paper around all parts, except the upper sharp corner, until you have removed all tool marks. Use a fairly coarse abrasive at first, but no rougher than you find necessary to complete the shaping. The marks from it will have to be removed by further sanding—at first with a finer grade pulled around the leg, then with fine sanding along the grain until you are certain there are no cross-grain scratches left. Cross-grain scratches that may not be apparent until you apply a finish may become darker with stain and show as lines under polish or varnish.

Level the surfaces of the square tops. Make the rails with barefaced tenons into the legs (Fig. 8-32F). Round the outer lower edge for its full length (Fig. 8-32G), or it can be decorated by bevel cuts (Fig. 8-32H). Assemble the framing in the usual way. Attach the top with pocket screws driven from inside the rails.

There is an opportunity to use a lathe for making the foot of each leg, but it cannot be used far above it if you are to get the authentic shape. With a leg marked out, locate the center of the foot and make a center punch mark there for the tailstock center. The other end of the wood can be driven by the usual headstock fork center. In this way you can ensure getting the foot truly circular (Fig. 8-33A), but you have to blend the turned work into the further shaping.

Club-footed Leg

An alternative to a full cabriole or *Queen Anne* leg is a tapered leg with a club foot. The leg may not be as attractive (Fig. 8-33B), but it can be made almost completely on a lathe. The leg tapers toward the inner part of the leg. The club foot is concentric with the square top, although it appears to project cornerwise in the finished table.

To make a club-footed leg, have the wood carefully squared. Allow about ¼ inch of waste wood below the foot. Draw a diagonal on this and mark the center of the end with a center punch mark. That will be the tailstock center position for turning the foot. Make another dot a short distance along the diagonal toward what will be the inner corner of the leg (Fig. 8-33C). The distance to go depends on the amount of taper and intended appearance of the leg, but on 1½ inches square, ¼ inch from the other mark may be about right. To get an appearance you like, roughly turn a leg from scrap wood to see the effect. If the leg is not slender enough above the foot, locate the center a little further from the first.

To turn the club foot, first mount with the tailstock center on the middle dot. Turn the foot without going very far over the curve toward the main part (Fig. 8-33D). Change to the offset center and turn the taper, going only far enough into the inner surfaces near the foot to remove the flats. The two sets of turned curves have to be blended into each other. You may have to go back to the other center and turn a little further from the foot. You cannot get a perfect blending, but you can get to the stage where not much work with a chisel and sandpaper has to be done to get a good shape (Fig. 8-33E).

Materials List for Small Cabriole Table.

2 legs	2 × 18 × 2
4 rails	3 × 11 × ¾
1 top	12 × 12 × ½ plywood
4 top frames	3 × 12 × ⅜
4 borders	1⅛ × 13 × ¼

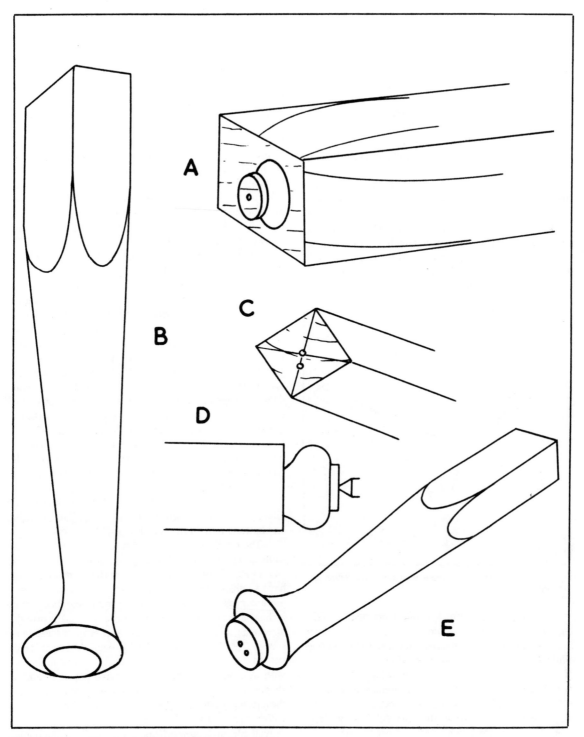

Fig. 8-33. A leg with a club foot that can be turned on a lathe.

QUEEN ANNE TABLE

In the eighteenth century a fashion developed for furniture that was mostly curved. Queen Anne was on the English throne, and this type of furniture carries her name. The style usually includes cabriole legs, which are something like the leg of an animal with a pronounced knee and foot. The graceful S-shaped outline can have many variations, and there are elaborately carved examples. The claw and ball foot, with talons gripping a ball, was one type. Much furniture was and still is made with the legs given smooth sweeps.

The table described here (Fig. 8-34) follows the Queen Anne form, with cabriole legs made in the traditional way. The overall sizes suggested (Fig. 8-35) make it suitable as a side table, but tables can be made larger or smaller using similar construction methods. Besides the legs, the edges of the top and the rails are also shaped. Straightening the edges of the top is simpler, but it is a departure from the traditional treatment.

Fig. 8-34. A Queen Anne table with pie crust edge and cabriole legs.

The original cabinetmakers did all the shaping of the legs by hand. That can be done again, but a band saw lessens the labor and insures cuts that follow curves while being square to the surface. After sawing, the rest of the shaping will have to be done by hand. Shaping is described in stages, and dealing systematically in this way is not as difficult as may be expected.

The best legs are made from solid wood (Fig. 8-36A). You can start with a square piece the size of the top and glue on other pieces to make up the widths of the curves. It is difficult to match grain. A visible glue line and different grain can spoil the finished appearance. It is important that all legs match. Thus, the outline, which has to be marked eight times, should be drawn around a hardboard or stout card template. Use this to mark the shape both ways on each leg (Fig. 8-36B).

Saw the outline in one direction (Fig. 8-36C). Careful cutting close to the line will reduce the amount of further work. This will remove some of the marking out of the shape in the other direction. You can use the template to mark the lines again on the shaped part, but it is better for band sawing to have flat surfaces. The waste pieces can be lightly nailed back into place, with the nails into what will be cut off. The cuts are then made in the second direction (Fig. 8-36D).

Get the top part of the leg truly square and straight. It should be overlong at this stage. Use a spokeshave or Surform tool on the other parts. The foot is made circular at the bottom. The narrow part above it is also circular in section. As you shape further up the leg, the outer corner is allowed to remain progressively more angular (with just a slight rounding), so it meets the square top sharply. Leave final shaping of the top few inches until after the ears have been glued on (Fig. 8-36E). Get the ears approximately to shape and join them to the legs with dowels. Shape the surfaces of the ears with the top of the leg to matching curves, but make sure their top surfaces are square to match the lines of the rails (Fig. 8-37A).

There is a temptation to want to go ahead and complete one leg. To insure uniformity, do similar work to all four legs at the same time. Compare the legs as you progress toward completion.

Assembly of the table framework is the same as for tables of simpler construction. Tenons go into the legs and buttons to hold the top (Fig. 8-37B).

The top is made from solid wood using strips glued to make up the width. The edge is scalloped or given a "pie crust." Start with the wood carefully squared. You have to design the edge, so the scalloping makes complete curves with outward curves at the corners. Four inches between the crests of the curves go equally in both directions. Make a template that will span at least two curves (Fig. 8-37C), so you get a regular pattern. Band saw to the shape as evenly as possible. You can follow with a drum sander or loose abrasive paper around a shaped block of wood. Making a suitable molding around the shaping is difficult by hand, but it can be accomplished with patience. If a spindle with a suitable molding cutter is available, an accurate shape is easy to work. A simple

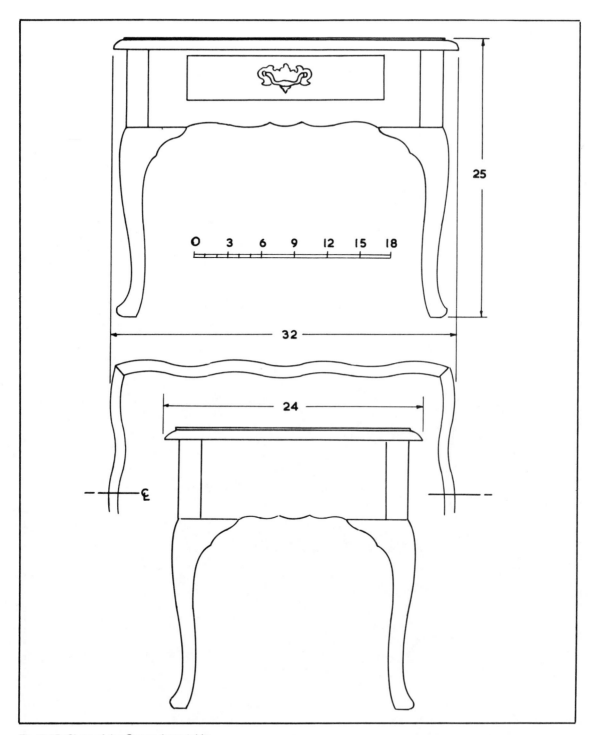

25

O 3 6 9 12 15 18

32

24

3

Fig. 8-35. Sizes of the Queen Anne table.

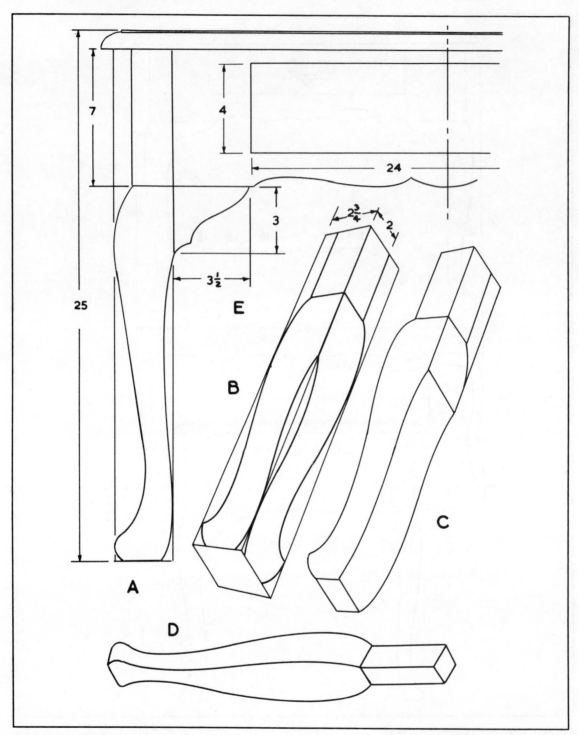

Fig. 8-36. Leg details of the Queen Anne table.

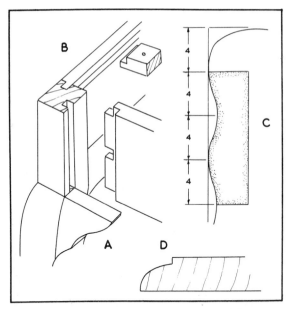

Fig. 8-37. Corner details and the edge shape of the top.

section (Fig. 8-37D) is suitable whether the edge is scalloped or straight.

The table can be completed without a drawer, but traditional Queen Anne tables had a drawer in the long side. Cut the hole for the drawer in one long rail before assembly. Be careful to get all edges straight and square. Further work is done after the table has been assembled. Make two guides long enough to fit between the two rails and deep enough to take the drawer runners (Fig. 8-38A). Space the runners parallel and to match the depth of the

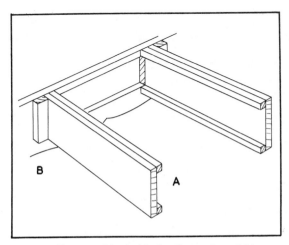

Fig. 8-38. Drawer guides inside the Queen Anne table.

opening. Attach the guides with blocks of wood screwed inside the rails (Fig. 8-38B).

Construction of the drawer is by the usual method, with the sides dovetailed to the front and a plywood bottom in grooves. This method of construction is described in several other projects. Use Fig. 8-39 as a guide.

Traditionally the drawers in Queen Anne furniture were given decorative brass pulls. You should not make a wood handle.

Materials List for Queen Anne Table

4 legs	2¾ × 26 × 2¾
8 ears	3 × 4 × 1½
2 rails	7 × 27 × ¾
2 rails	7 × 20 ×¾
1 top	24 × 33 ×⅞
8 buttons	1½ × 3 × ¾
1 drawer front	4 × 25 × ¾
2 drawer sides	4 × 20 × ⅝
1 drawer back	3½ × 25 × ⅝
1 drawer bottom	20 × 25 × ¼ plywood

WORKTABLE

In most homes there is a need for a strong utility table. The table may serve as a desk for a child to do schoolwork, or it may be needed for hobby material. It need not be strong enough to stand up to the planing and hammering of heavy woodworking. If the table is of normal height, it may be pressed into use as a dining table with a cloth over it.

This table is shown at a normal height (Fig. 8-40). If it is intended only for children's use, the legs can be shortened. It is kept narrow enough to be carried through doorways and is shown with two drawers, which are not so deep as to interfere with the knees of anyone sitting on a chair. The sections of wood shown suit hardwood, but softwood can be used if most of the sizes are increased by about ¼ inch. Several methods of making the top are given. If tools are to be used on the table, it should be solid, but otherwise framed plywood is lighter.

Sizes are not critical (Fig. 8-39), and the table can be made to fit a vacant space or a recess. Prepare the wood for framing. Construction is shown with mortise and tenon joints, but dowels can be used in many places. Start with the legs (Fig. 8-41A). Mark them out together. The rails on three sides come to the same depth as the front drawer rails and are joined with haunched mortise and tenon joints (Fig. 8-41B). At the front the rails above and below the drawers go round the legs to butt against the

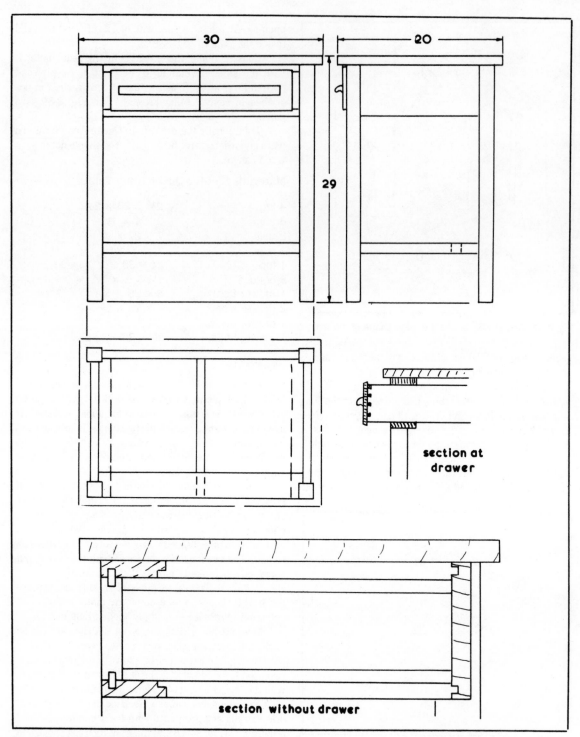

Fig. 8-39. Sizes of the worktable.

section at drawer

section without drawer

170

Fig. 8-40. A worktable with two drawers.

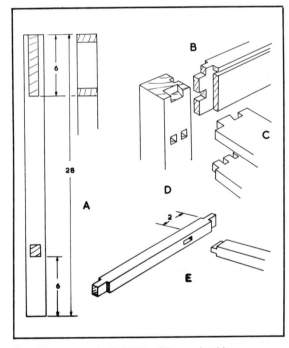

Fig. 8-41. Leg and rail details of the work table.

side rails. The top one has a dovetail into the top of the leg (Fig. 8-41C), but the lower one is tenoned (Fig. 8-41D). This arrangement gives rigidity across the front, where the stiffness of a solid rail is lacking. If the top is to be secured with buttons, plow grooves near the top edges of the side rails before assembly.

There are lower rails between the front and rear legs with plain tenon joints. A single rail or stretcher goes

between them toward the back (Fig. 8-41E), where it is out of the way of anyone sitting. It is in a suitable position to act as a footrest.

Mark the drawer spacing along the pair of front rails. Three pieces with their grain upright go between these parts and separate the drawers. They can be cut to length and joined with glue and screws, but you can use tenons (Fig. 8-42A) or dowels (Fig. 8-42B) for more strength.

The drawers travel on *runners* at the bottom and are prevented from tilting by *kickers* at the top. In this case they are made in the same way. Strips are lapped into the front rails and tenoned or doweled into the back rails (Fig. 8-42C). Strips go on them to prevent the drawers from moving sideways. The central pieces extend each way to support both drawers (Fig. 8-42D). For the smooth running of the drawers, get the meeting surfaces level at the front. Make sure the runners and kickers are fitted parallel and square across the table. Even if there are slight errors elsewhere, it is important that the drawers run squarely to the front rails.

You can assemble the framework at this stage. First, put together the back and front and compare them with each other. Add the end rails and the drawer guides. You can leave cutting the guides to length until this stage, as you enter rear joints to allow marking at the front before finally dropping the guides into the halved notches.

The drawers are best made and fitted before you add the top to the table. Thus, you can see how they work and deal with any corrections. There are overlapping fronts to the drawers, which cover the gaps around the edges. This allows you to make the drawers in several ways, as the design of each is a box with the front added. In the simplest form the boxes can be nailed together, or you can use comb or other joints. It is best if the bottom is grooved into the sides, and the back comes above it (Fig. 8-42E). The back can then be notched into the sides and screwed or nailed through, as well as glued (Fig. 8-42F).

At the front the best traditional joints are dovetails (Fig. 8-42G). When you pull a drawer out and see dovetails, it is always a matter of pride to the maker. Notch the plywood bottom into the front and make the lowest dovetail to enclose it.

Use the positions of runners and kickers as guides to the drawer sizes. Allow only slight clearances in the height and width of each drawer, then they will run smoothly. From back to front, the drawer length should not quite reach the back rail when the front is level. The added false front will also act as a stop when it comes tight against the front rails.

The false drawer fronts (Fig. 8-42H) meet at the center, but they overlap elsewhere by about ¼ inch. Any

171

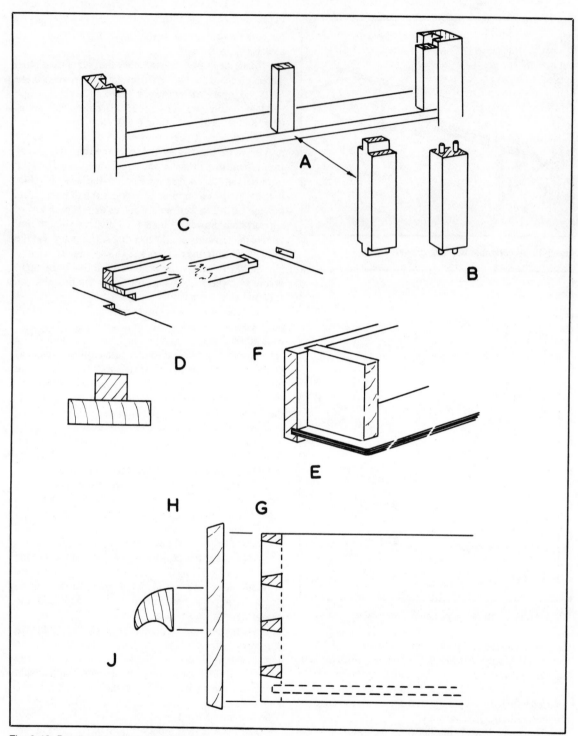

Fig. 8-42. Details of front rails and drawers.

work on their edges should match what you do to the edges of the tabletop, with similar molding or rounding.

Drawer handles can be bought metal or plastic ones, but a wood bar type (Fig. 8-42J) can go most of the way across the drawers, so it can be reached and pulled at almost any position. Attach this type of handle to the false drawer front before that, in turn, is screwed from inside the drawer.

If the tabletop is to be solid wood, glue boards to make up the width. For hobby use it is best to leave the edges square, so you can hold work down with clamps or use other screw or clip-on devices. Otherwise, there can be a simple beading or molding.

If you do not need a light bench top, it is probably better to make a top of framed plywood. Thick plywood can be fitted into a grooved frame (Fig. 8-43A). Thinner plywood may go into rabbets (Fig. 8-43B), where it is held by glue. You can drive pins and punch them below the surface. They are covered by stopping. If the top is thin plywood, it may need intermediate stiffening. You can put a piece across above the central drawer kicker to give that support as well as the top.

A solid wood top should be held down by buttons into grooves in the back and side rails, but it can be held at the front by screws up through the top drawer rail. The buttons then allow for expansion and contraction of the solid wood. You can use buttons for a framed plywood top (Fig. 8-43C), with packings under the plywood, or there can be pocket screws (Fig. 8-43D). If you make the frame so its inner edges come level with the side and back rails, small pieces of plywood will act as cleats to hold it (Fig. 8-43E).

Materials List for Worktable

1 top	20×30×1
	solid wood or plywood
4 legs	2×30×2
1 back top rail	6×27×1
2 side top rails	6×18×1
2 front rails	3×27×¾
3 drawer spacers	1×6×¾
2 drawer guides	1½×18×¾
1 drawer guide	2×18×¾
2 drawer guides	¾×18×¾
1 drawer guide	1×18×¾
2 bottom rails	1¼×18×1¼
1 bottom rail	1¼×28×1¼
4 drawer sides	4½×19×⅝
2 drawer fronts	4½×14×⅝
2 drawer backs	4×14×⅝
2 false fronts	5×14×½
2 handles	1¼×14×1¼
2 drawer bottoms	14×19×¼
	plywood

STUDENT'S TABLE

This is a small table or desk of sufficient size for a student to spread books and papers (Fig. 8-44). There are two fairly deep drawers for storage, but they can be extended to the floor. These are shown on the right (Fig. 8-45), but the table can be made the opposite way for a left-handed person.

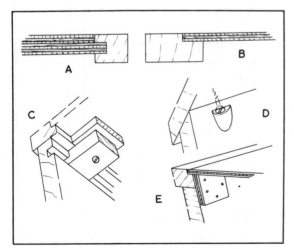

Fig. 8-43. Construction and attachment of the tabletop.

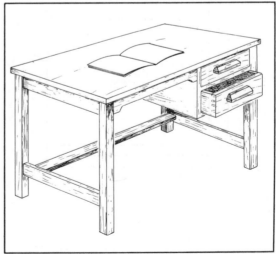

Fig. 8-44. A student's table provides a good work surface and drawers for storage.

173

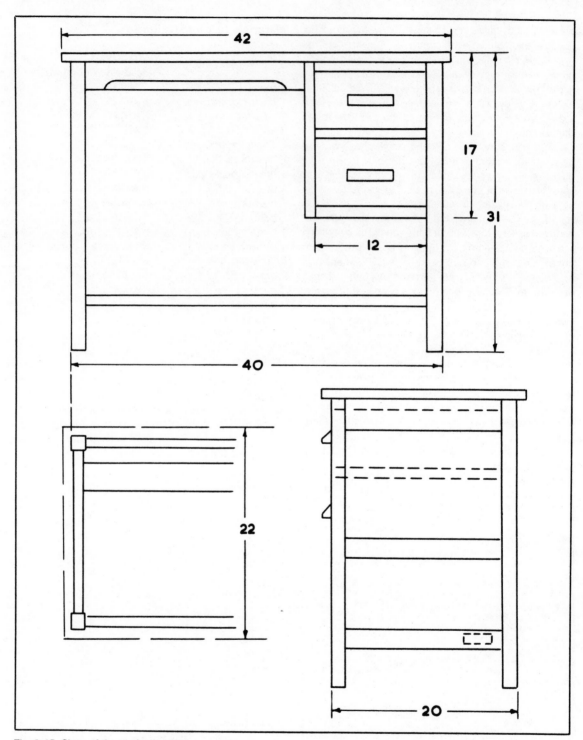

Fig. 8-45. Sizes of the student's table.

The desk will also be suitable for typing. In that case it may be made slightly lower, unless a tall chair is to be used. Construction is simplified with plywood panels that do not need grooves. Mortise and tenon joints make a better table than doweled joints.

Start with the legs. Those at the open end take upper and lower rails (Fig. 8-46A), but at the other end you have to allow for the drawer dividers and the extra rail outside (Fig. 8-46B). There will be ¼-inch plywood inside the back and the end of the table that has to come flush with the legs, so arrange the positions of the mortises for the tenons to suit the actual plywood (Fig. 8-46C). There are top rails in three of the legs both ways, but the one at the right front has the drawer dividers (Fig. 8-46D).

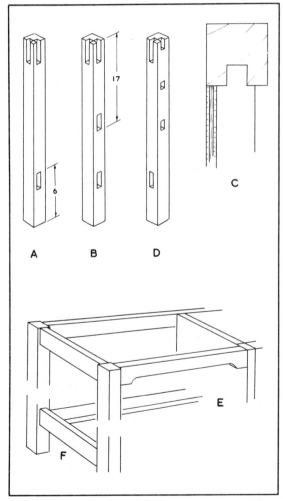

Fig. 8-46. Legs and constructional details of the student's table.

The back top rail and the two short end top rails are straight. The front top rail stops at the block of drawers where it is tenoned, and its lower edge may be cut away to provide knee space (Fig. 8-46E). At the lower level two edgewise end rails go between the legs. There is a flat rail between them, positioned towards the back (Fig. 8-46F), where it can act as a footrest.

A rail crosses between the legs at the bottom of the drawer block, and piywood fits between the legs and against this and the top rail (Fig. 8-47A). Use glue and pins from inside to fit the plywood. If the plywood is made a close fit between the legs, there is no need for any support on the legs between the rails. You can put small quarter-round molding there.

The drawer spacers (Fig. 8-47B) are all the same, with tenons at both ends. The inner side of the drawer block is made of uprights 1 inch thick and horizontal pieces ¾ inch thick, so ¼-inch plywood can be fitted level inside (Fig. 8-47C), like the other side of the drawers. Having the plywood level at both sides avoids the need to fit drawer guides. There are tenons three ways at the top and bottom front corners, but there is just enough space for them (Fig. 8-47D). There will be another piece of plywood at the back of the drawer compartment. It is fitted to the top rail, with a stiffening piece put across its bottom edge.

Make the drawer runners the same thickness as the front dividers. Fit them so the drawers will slide smoothly over the joints between them (Fig. 8-47E). It will probably be best to adopt the following assembly sequence. Put together the two ends and check that they match. Put together the inner side of the drawer block. When the glue on these parts has set, fit the drawer guides. Use the mortises as indications of levels. Make sure they are parallel and square with the front. Otherwise, the drawers will not run smoothly. Now add the parts that go across the table, starting with the back and bottom rails. With the framework standing squarely, add the parts of the drawer block. Screw through the top rail into the back of the block's inner part. Use clamps where necessary. In some parts you can drive a nail or screw through a joint where it will not show in order to hold the joint while the glue sets. Check squareness, particularly at the parts where the drawers will fit.

The top can be made at this stage, but its final fitting may be left until after you have made the drawers. You can see how they fit and check what adjustments, if necessary, have to be made by viewing from above.

The suggested top is a piece of plywood, ⅜ inch thick, over a solid wood frame and edged around (Fig. 8-48A). The framework will not show in the finished

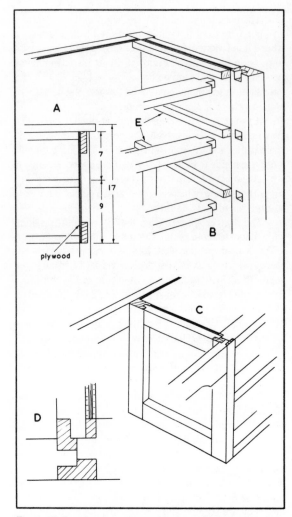

Fig. 8-47. Details of the drawer block of the student's table.

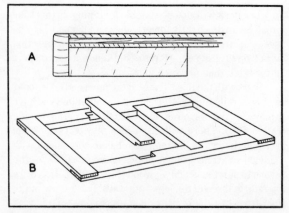

Fig. 8-48. Construction of the framed top of the student's table.

that they will slide properly. Cut the wood for the fronts, so they fit easily into the spaces. Groove all of these pieces for the bottom and make the joints between them. The drawer backs can fit into dado grooves above the plywood bottom. This gives you a projection at the back that can be planed off to get the drawer the right length to stop with its front level, as the drawer hits the back plywood (Fig. 8-49B).

The drawer handles may be metal or plastic, but wooden ones are attractive. Those shown (Fig. 8-49C) are angular. Have a piece of wood long enough for both

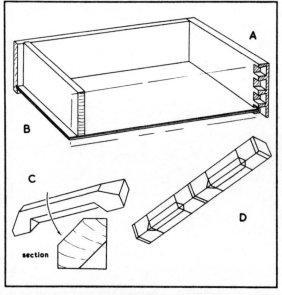

Fig. 8-49. Suggested drawer construction and how to make wooden handles or drawer pulls.

table, so corner joints can be halved for simplicity. To stiffen the top, allow for an intermediate crossbar over the edge of the drawer compartment and another between that and the end (Fig. 8-48B). Put the framework together, then attach it to the plywood. Plane the edges true and add a flat or half-round lip.

When the top is fitted, you may be able to drive screws up through the top drawer guides. Use pocket screws elsewhere that are driven from inside the top rails.

The drawers can be made by any of the usual methods, but the best construction has dovetails at the front. The plywood bottom is then slid into grooves (Fig. 8-49A). Cut the wood for the drawer sides first and check handles and cut the finger recesses first, while the wood is square and can be gripped in a vise (Fig. 8-49D). You can plane the bevel and separate the pieces to cut the ends. Attach the handles with glue and screws from inside the drawers.

Materials List for Student's Table

4 legs	1½×31×1½
1 back rail	3 ×40×1
2 end rails	3 ×20×1
1 front rail	3 ×26×1
2 lower rails	2 ×20×1
1 lower rail	3 ×40×1
2 drawer block strips	1½×18×1
2 drawer block strips	1½×20×¾
2 drawer block panels	17 ×20×¼ plywood
3 drawer dividers	1½×14×1
6 drawer runners	1 ×20×1
1 top panel	20 ×42×⅜ plywood
2 top frames	3 ×42×¾
4 top frames	3 ×23×¾
2 top lips	1⅛×43×⅜
2 top lips	1⅛×23×⅜
1 drawer front	6 ×13×¾
1 drawer front	7 ×13×¾
2 drawer sides	6 ×20×⅝
2 drawer sides	7 ×20×⅝
1 drawer back	5½×13×⅝
1 drawer back	6½×13×⅝
2 drawer bottoms	12 ×20×¼ plywood

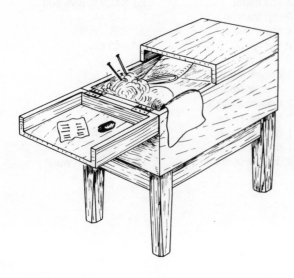

Chapter 9

Extension Tables

When a table is not being used, it is sensible to reduce its size for storage if possible. Ways to do this have exercised the ingenuity of man over many centuries. The earliest tables were just boards on trestles, so the method of stowage was obvious. Later tables mostly had their tops in several parts, so flaps or leaves could swing down when not required. It is in the method of supporting the flaps that designs vary tremendously.

Flaps can be supported with hinged brackets, so the framed legs on which the table stands do not vary in size. There are limitations in this arrangement, as flaps that are too large for the narrow base can make the table top-heavy. The method of providing support for large flaps is the use of gatelegs, where an additional leg swings out under each flap. It is then possible to have the main framework and its top quite narrow, so the flaps provide the major top area.

Another way of providing support is to revolve the hinged and sectioned top over a long framed leg part, so its ends hold up the flaps.

There are several ways of making table legs to fold into the top, but many of these methods require special metal fittings. Two examples that do not require anything that you cannot make are described here. Nesting tables

take care of extended needs in having two extra tables hung under the main one. Compared with many other ways of enlarging and reducing table sizes, they are modern ideas, but in our compact homes they can play a valuable part. The method of nesting described can be adapted to other designs.

BOX TABLE

This table is intended to hold sewing things, but it can have other uses (Fig. 9-1). The container is a box with a lid in two parts that swing to the sides and can be used as trays when open. The box stands on a table framework where it has locating pieces, but it can be lifted off and moved elsewhere if required (Fig. 9-2).

To get the lid to match the box, the two are made together. Making a separate lid to fit a box exactly is a difficult job. By making the box and lid as a unit, then separating them, the two parts are made to match with minimum trouble.

There is a choice of methods for making a box. Nailing together may be considered too crude, although it can be done if you want to reproduce Colonial style. Screwing is more acceptable than you may think. Polished hardwood can have exposed brass screwheads

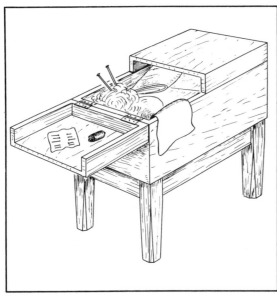

Fig. 9-1. The box part of this table will lift off, and the lid opens to provide working surfaces.

for a traditional nautical appearance. Many things used at sea were made of polished mahogany with brass fastenings. If you do not want to have screwheads visible, they can be sunk and covered with stopping to match the wood.

There are several ways of fitting box corners together that can be done by machine. One machine method is a *comb joint* (Fig. 9-3A). The truly craftsmanlike joint is a dovetail (Fig. 9-3B). Even when the corners are joined in this way, the top and bottom will be glued and nailed or screwed on. The bottom can be plywood with its edges hidden in a rabbet (Fig. 9-3C), but the top parts are better made of solid wood to match the sides (Fig. 9-3D). Solid wood is the obvious choice for the box. It is possible to use veneered particle board, but then the joints are better made with dowels spaced fairly closely (Fig. 9-3E).

Make the box sides and ends by the chosen method. Mark where the cut between the lid and box will come, with lines spaced wide enough to allow for sawing and cleaning off (Fig. 9-3F). With some methods of jointing, you can let this come as it will. For dovetails, arrange them so the cut does not break across one (Fig. 9-3G). The corners will look best if you space the tails to suit the box and lid widths separately, rather than if you merely divide the full width evenly.

Prepare the parts and join the corners. Fit the plywood bottom in tightly to keep the assembly truly square. Add the top. It can be slightly oversize and then planed level. Mark the division across the lid. Plane and sand all parts completely and round all edges and corners, so the box is comfortable to handle.

Carefully saw the lid from the box, keeping the cut between the lines. This can be done with a table saw, holding the box against the fence, but a fine handsaw can be used as you turn the box to bring the part being cut upward as you progress. Mark the matching sides as you separate them. It is unlikely that the lid will still fit exactly if turned around. Plane the meeting surface to the marked lines and check that the lid rests level on the box.

Saw the lid into two and plane those edges. Try the parts together. Use two hinges at each end. Let them into both lid and box edges. Assemble with the lid held closely to the box and the knuckle of the hinge over the meeting edges (Fig. 9-3H). This ensures that each half of the lid hangs horizontal when it is open. If there is a gap, it will sag. Try an assembly with only one screw in each flap of the hinges. See that the lid parts close properly. If they do not, you can try a slight movement at a hinge by putting a screw in a different hole, until the action is correct and all screws may be driven.

The supporting part is made like many other tables, with rails doweled or tenoned into the legs (Fig. 9-4A). The lower parts of the legs can be turned, if you have a lathe, or they can be shaped in one of the ways described for other tables. The shaping shown (Fig. 9-4B) goes from square to octagonal by tapering to the bottom. Be careful to keep the starts of the tapers level. Use pencil marks around below the rails as guides.

Use the box as a guide to the size of the lower part. It should overhang the same amount all round—½ inch is suggested. No matter how carefully you have worked, it is unlikely that both the box and support will be perfectly symmetrical and match each other both ways. Make the support to fit one way on the box. Put permanent marks under the box and inside a rail to show the right way to assemble.

When the supporting assembly has been made, invert it on the bottom of the box. Use it as a guide to fitting locating strips under the box (Fig. 9-4C). They come inside the rails and reach almost to the legs at the corners. If the outer surfaces are given a slight taper. You can make the assembly a push fit, so the box cannot be inadvertently lifted off its supports.

All of the parts can be finished the same color. The table looks good with the box a lighter color than its supports, even if they are the same wood.

The box part can be lifted off as it is. There can be brass handles on the ends, located low enough not to

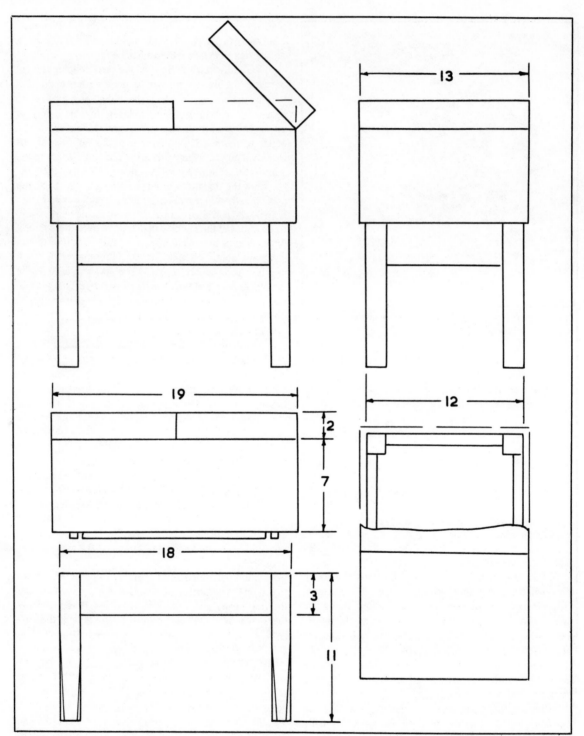

Fig. 9-2. Sizes of the box table.

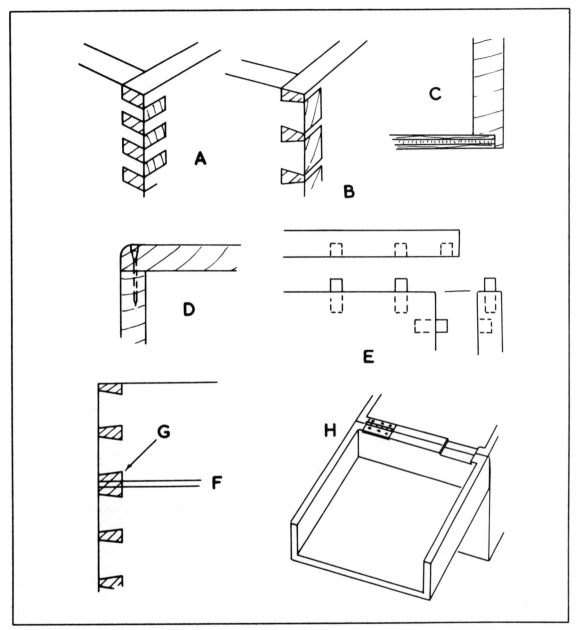

Fig. 9-3. Joints for the box part of the table.

interfere with the opened lids. Wooden handles may be made, and little more than straight pieces are needed for a finger grip at each end.

If this is to be a sewing box, the owner may wish to line it. That can be done with each part fitted separately to get a neater finish than would be obtained by trying to fit cloth continuously all round. Cut stiff card to the size of a panel. Cover it with the lining cloth. A particularly luxurious effect can be obtained by putting the cloth over foam plastic about ⅛ inch thick. Wrap the cloth over the card and glue it to the back (Fig. 9-4D), then glue the card to the wood. Put the bottom in before the sides.

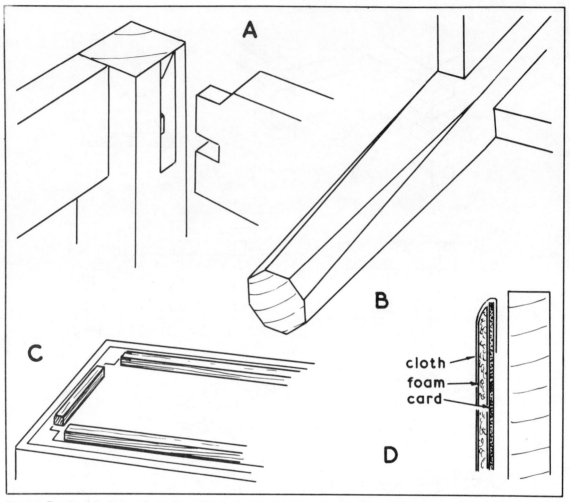

Fig. 9-4. Details of the legs and rails (A and B), the locating blocks on the box (C), and the possible lining for the box (D).

Materials List for Box Table

2 sides	9×19×9/16
2 ends	9×14×9/16
1 top	13×20×9/16
1 bottom	13×20×¼ plywood
4 legs	1½×12×1½
2 rails	3×17×¾
2 rails	3×11×¾
2 strips	½×15×½
2 strips	½×9×½

FLAT SIDE TABLE

This is a table intended to stand where there is little spare space, and it need only be about 13 inches from the wall. If more top area is needed, a flap on one side lifts to make the top 20 inches wide. It also incorporates a simple method of holding up the flap, which was popular in some light antique furniture. The table is not suitable for a large and heavy table leaf, but it holds a small one neatly.

The table can be made with all square legs and rails, but they may be turned to give a lighter and more individual appearance. Sizes can be adapted to suit situations. The table is particularly suitable for a recess or a vacant space between other furniture. If it is to be kept against a wall, there can be a rim along the back. If it is ever to be brought into the room for use all round, the top should be left level. The sizes shown (Fig. 9-5) make an attractive table. The design is not intended to be enlarged to make a dining table.

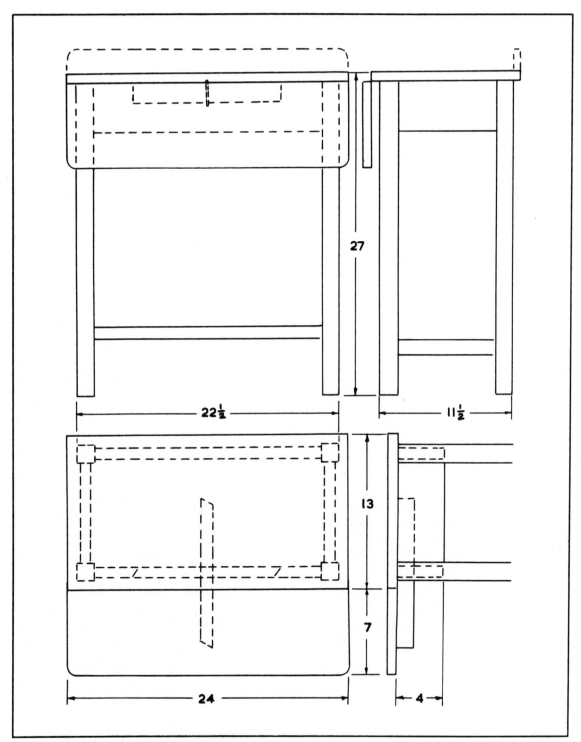

Fig. 9-5. A flap side table has one hinged flap and a pivoted support.

Start with the legs. Mark them out together. If they are to be turned, allow for them remaining square to below the level of the flap when it is down (Fig. 9-6A). Leave sufficient squareness in the area of the bottom rails for them to come in at different levels.

The top rails tenon into the legs in the usual way (Fig. 9-6B). Prepare them and use them as guides for the lengths of the bottom turned rails. The turned patterns shown (Figs. 9-6C and 9-6D) are complementary to those of the legs. If you adopt another turned design for the legs, try to make the rails with rather similar patterns. The holes into the legs can be ¾-inch diameter. Drill a hole with the bit you will use in scrap wood and use that to test the rail ends as you turn them.

The flap support is actually part of the front top rail, but you may prefer to cut it from a separate piece. It is difficult to get it from the rail without removing too much width when sawing. Mark the shape on the rail (Fig. 9-7A). The ends cut across at an angle, which is not critical, but 60° is about right (Fig. 9-7B).

Cut out the shape (Fig. 9-7C), being careful to get the bottom level and parallel with the top. Make a piece of the same thickness as the rail to fit in, so its top edge comes level with or very slightly below the top edge of the rail (Fig. 9-7D). Drill centrally through the piece to take a pivot rod. This should be about 3/16 inch thick and can be cut from a suitable large nail. Mark out on both edges and drill from both sides to get the hole exactly central. Put the piece in the recess and drill downward through it about ½ inch into the rail. Make the pivot long enough to go into that hole and upward about ¼ inch into the tabletop.

The top is best made with square edges or moderate rounding. The edge must be straight at the flap. Check this and the meeting edge of the flap with a straightedge and by sighting along. Fit hinges to the underside just outside the limits of the support. They can be ordinary hinges with their knuckles downward or backflap hinges with the knuckles sunk in the wood (Figs. 9-6E and 9-6F).

If there is to be a rear rail, attach it before putting top on the framework. It can be screwed upward (Fig. 9-7E) or doweled. If you want to make it removable so the top can be without obstruction when needed, you can glue dowels in the rail. Let them be a push fit into the tabletop (Fig. 9-7F). Taper and round the ends of the dowels for easy fitting.

The tabletop can be fitted with buttons engaging with grooves in the rails, but this small width may be fitted with pocket screws upward from the inner edges of the top rails. Drill a hole for the pivot rod (Fig. 9-7G) and enter this as the top is assembled to the framework. It

may be advisable to make a trial assembly to check action before screwing down all round. Watch squareness. See that the top goes on parallel; otherwise, lack of truth may be apparent in the hanging flap.

Materials List for Flap Side Table

4 legs	1½×27×1½
2 rails	1½×22×1½
2 rails	1½×11×1½
2 rails	4×22×1
2 rails	4×11×1
1 top	13×25×¾
1 flap	7×25×¾
1 support	1½×13×1
1 rear rail	2×25×¾

FOLDING CARD TABLE

This is a light table, easily carried and stored flat, that will suit most card games for four players. If veneered plywood is used for the top, a natural finish may be preferred. Otherwise, thick felt, baize, or other cloth makes a better playing surface. If the table will also have to serve other uses, it may be better to have a plain wood top and use a loose cloth over it.

The top is framed plywood, and the crossed legs fold against it (Fig. 9-8). The sizes and sections of wood (Fig. 9-9) should ensure enough rigidity without too much weight. It is possible to use softwood and finish it by painting, but hardwood looks better and is less liable to wear in the moving joints after long use.

Start with the square top (Fig. 9-10A). There can be comb joints (Fig. 9-10B) cut with a suitable attachment, or open bridle joints (Fig. 9-10C) cut by hand sawing. Have the plywood slightly oversize and attach it to the framework with glue and pins, punched and covered with stopping (Fig. 9-10D). Plane the plywood level with the framing, but do not round its edges.

The legs are all 32 inches long, with their ends rounded (Fig. 9-11A). Mark them together. Drill at the centers for pivot bolts. These are best countersunk outside, but the shallow heads of coach bolts will do. In any case, assembly is with washers (Fig. 9-11B). At the tops of the outer legs the pivots are stout wood screws into the top (Fig. 9-11C), but the inner legs are joined with a round rail. A ¾-inch rod can be turned down at the ends, or ½-inch dowels can be fitted into its ends (Fig. 9-11D). The rod length should give the inner legs an easy clearance inside the outer legs, when these are fitted to the top.

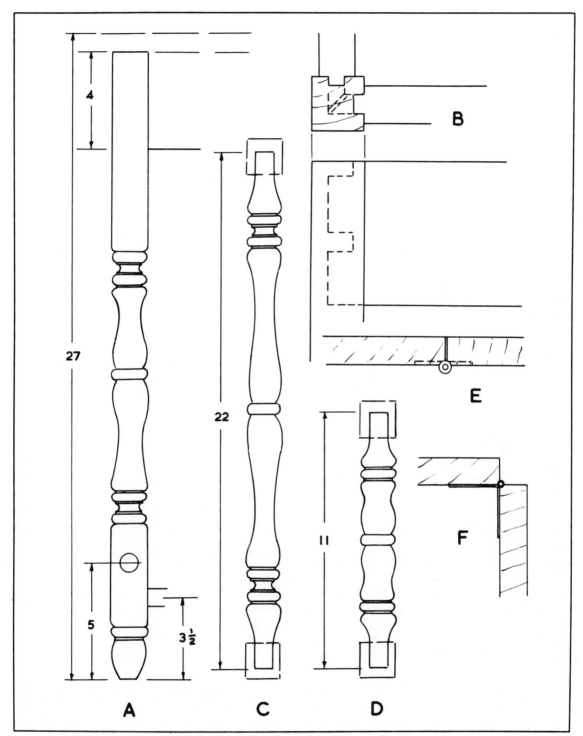

Fig. 9-6. Legs and rails may be turned. The flap is hinged, and the top rail is tenoned.

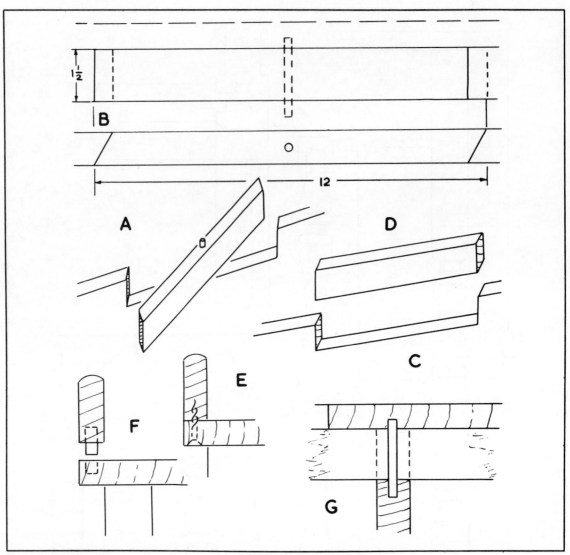

Fig. 9-7. Details of the pivoted flap support and optional back rail.

On the lower parts of both pairs of legs, there are stays and braces to maintain the leg widths and prevent wobble of the fairly light structure (Fig. 9-12A). For the best construction these parts should be halved together (Fig. 9-12B), possibly with screws as well as glue. For simplicity, particularly if a large number of these tables are being produced, the ends can be rounded and screwed (Fig. 9-12C). The ends of the braces will not then come in the same plane.

When the table is opened, the rod across the tops of the inner legs has to be gripped by a spring (Fig. 9-13). A suitable one may be bought, or it can be made from a strip of springy brass or steel. Curl back the end so the rod will enter as the table is pulled open. Make a trial assembly with the bolts loose in their holes to see that the table folds and opens correctly, then take it apart for finishing the woodwork.

If the top is to finish showing the wood surface, cover the plywood edge with a half-round molding (Fig. 9-14A) or a flat strip with a rounded edge. Miter the corners and attach with glue and pins. If there is to be a cloth covering, it has to be stretched evenly. Use ⅜-inch

Fig. 9-8. A light folding card table.

tacks. Put the cloth over the plywood and tack about ½ inch down at the center of one side, then stretch across and do the same at the other side. Repeat the action the other way (Fig. 9-14B). Tack again each side of these first tacks and work outward toward the corners. The distance apart you need to space the tacks depends on the cloth, but 2 inches should be about right. The amount of stretch to apply depends on the cloth, but aim to get it flat without puckers, yet without the weave being distorted. Cover the edges with strips (Fig. 9-14C).

In the final assembly, put locknuts on the bolts. You can also lightly rivet over the ends of the bolts to prevent plain nuts from coming off.

Materials List for Folding Card Table

4 legs	1¼×33×¾
4 top frames	1¼×22×¾
4 top edges	¾×23×¼
1 top panel	22×22×¼ plywood
2 stays	¾×22×¼
4 braces	¾×10×¼
1 inner top rail	¾×22 round rod

FOLDING TABLE

This is a small table that folds flat for storage. If made in an attractive hardwood and given a good finish, it will serve as a coffee table indoors. Without the special finish, it is useful outdoors or when camping. The top is like an inverted box, and the end pairs of legs will fold into it (Fig. 9-15). They are kept in the open or closed positions by a spring action, and there are no parts to adjust or screws to turn.

The sizes shown (Fig. 9-16A) will make a coffee table. If any other size is made, you have to arrange the length and height so the legs will fold without the leg ends overlapping. Using parts with the sections given, the table has to be at least 7 inches longer that it is high.

The legs are arranged to stand sloping outward at 5° from vertical. They are hinged to crosspieces under the top. The rail between the tops of the legs is notched at its center, so a springy piece of wood, held to a block at the center of the table, can press into it and hold the legs in position. If the legs are moved inward, they fold into the box. The springy strip presses against the side of the rails (Fig. 9-16B). General construction may be of almost any wood, but the spring should be made of ash or hickory, if possible, to get suitable springiness without risk of the wood breaking.

The top is a piece of ½-inch plywood, with its upper surface veneered for a good quality finish, or Formica laminated plastic can be used for other purposes. Put the strips across under the ends (Fig. 9-17A) and frame around with strips (Fig. 9-17B), glued and held with thin nails, punched below the surface and stopped. Miter the corners.

The leg assemblies are made in the same way, but the parts at one end should be narrow enough to go inside the other (Fig. 9-17C). Both should be the same height. Bevel the tops and bottoms to 5° (Fig. 9-17D). Join the leg with dowels or tenons and keep the inner surfaces flush (Fig. 9-17E).

Be careful about checking squareness, as any inaccuracy will affect the fit when folding. Hinge the end assemblies near the outside edges with 3-inch hinges. Check the folding action. The narrow assembly goes inside the other, and both sides should close to touch the top.

For the spring, put a block under the center of the top. The thickness that the spring is made depends on the wood chosen. Start with about 5/16 inch, but if that proves too stiff, plane it thinner. Make the spring just long enough to come inside the top framing when folded. To avoid weakening the spring with large holes, secure the spring to the block with 4-gauge screws through a cover piece (Fig. 9-16C). Two screws may be enough. Mark where the spring comes on the edges of the leg rails and cut away to allow it to bed down level (Fig. 9-17F). Allow a little clearance in the width.

When you are satisfied with the table, disassemble it to clean up. Sand the wood prior to finishing.

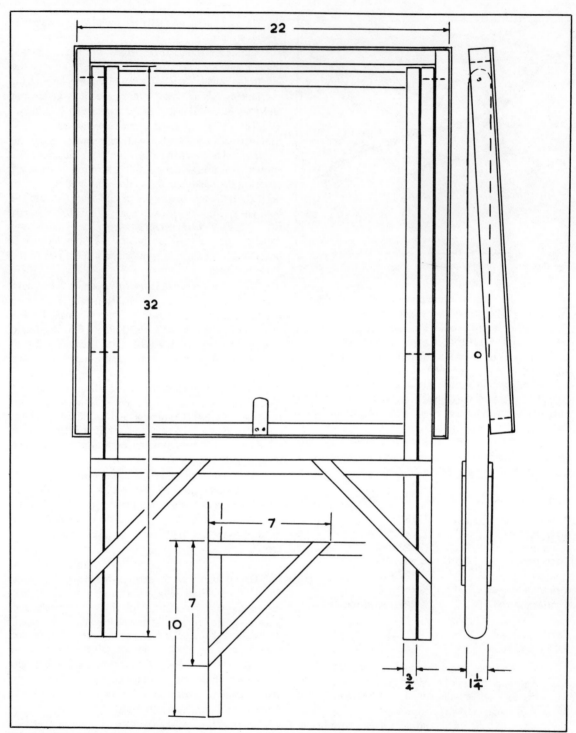

Fig. 9-9. Sizes of the folding card table.

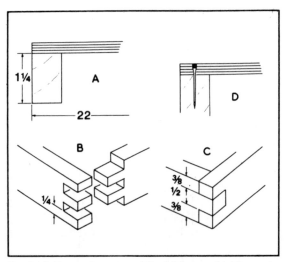

Fig. 9-10. Top and corners of the folding card table.

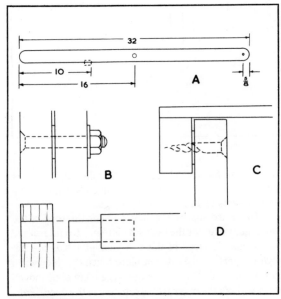

Fig. 9-11. Leg size and pivoting details.

Materials List for Folding Table

1 top	5×23×½
2 frames	3×23×½
2 frames	3×15×½
2 end strips	2×15×¾
4 legs	1½×15×1⅛
2 leg rails	2½×14×¾
1 spring	2½×23×5/16

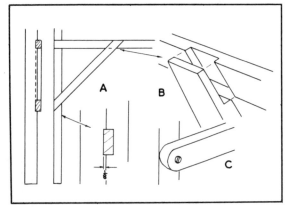

Fig. 9-12. Leg bracing of the folding card table.

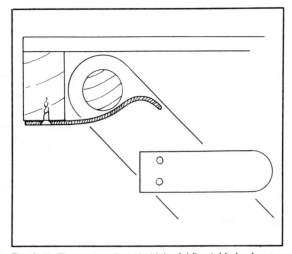

Fig. 9-13. The spring clip to hold the folding table in shape.

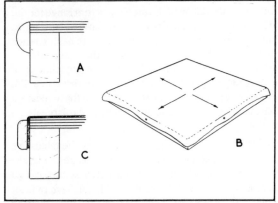

Fig. 9-14. The card table with an uncovered top (A) or with cloth stretched over (B and C).

189

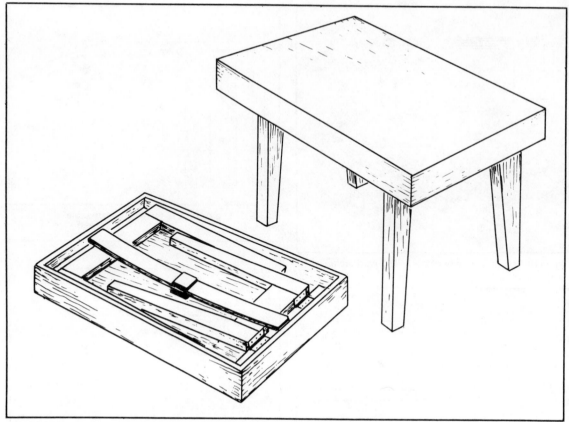

Fig. 9-15. The legs of this small folding table fit inside the top.

NESTING COFFEE TABLES

It is useful to have several coffee tables available when many people have uses for them, but it is not always convenient to have them around when they are out of use. One way of dealing with the problem is to arrange for the tables to be of different sizes, so they can stand in a stack. A further step is to arrange for the tables to nest, so each hangs inside the next one larger. If the outer table is lifted, the others go with it. There can be any number of nesting tables, but it is common to have three in a set. There can be only two, but any more than three means a considerable difference in size between the largest and smallest.

There are some variations in the way the tables are arranged to nest, but it is necessary to make the larger tables without front rails at top and bottom so they can go together compactly. The smallest table can have rails all round in the usual way. The rails that have to be omitted would have added some strength, but there will be ample

strength left for normal use providing the other work is done properly. Obviously, these tables should not be used as seats and rocked on two legs.

There are supporting pieces under the tops of the two larger tables for the next smaller ones to slide on and hang from. The legs of the two smaller tables are cut slightly short, so they do not quite touch the floor when they are nested. This allows the large table to be moved about without the other tables catching in the floor covering and pulling out.

The original nest of tables was made with turned legs (Fig. 9-18). As can be seen, the range of sizes shows quite a difference (Fig. 9-19). The smallest is big enough for normal coffee table use, while the large table has plenty of room for other purposes as well. If other sizes are chosen, it is the clearance needed for one tabletop to fit between the legs of another that determines the limitations. There will be about 9 inches difference in length and 4 inches in width between the largest and the smallest tabletops.

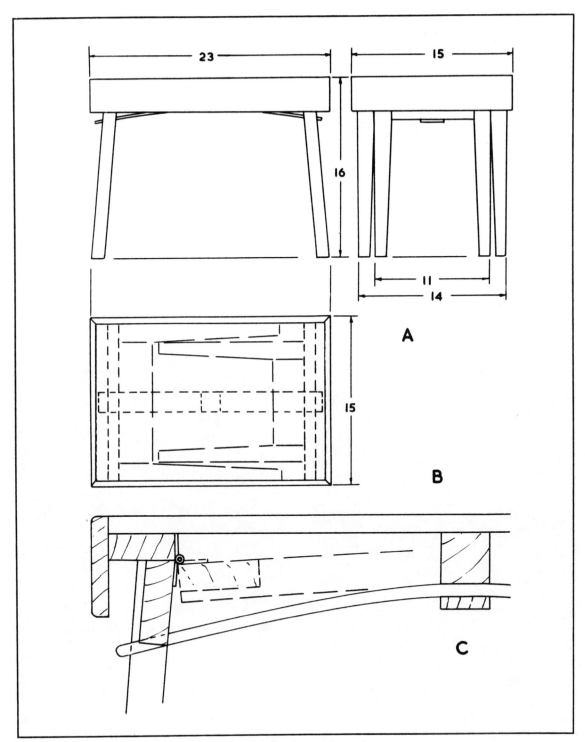

Fig. 9-16. Sizes of the folding table and a section showing the wooden spring.

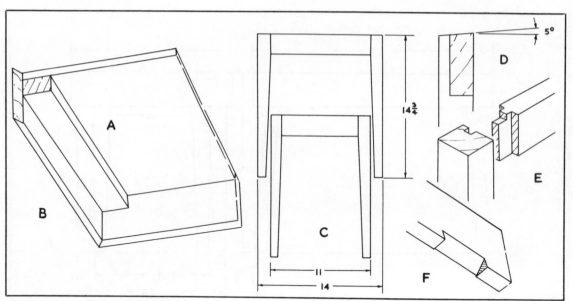

Fig. 9-17. Top and leg construction.

Fig. 9-18. These three tables nest so the inner ones hang inside the large one.

Fig. 9-19. The nest separates into three useful tables.

Viewed from the front, the tables are symmetrical (Fig. 9-20A). When viewed from the side, the rear legs have to come in steps like the front view, but at the front the legs are all level (Fig. 9-20B). The relative positions at the back can be seen in the view from above (Fig. 9-20C). The table widths are arranged so the edges of the tops are level at the front, with their legs in the same plane.

The key drawing, which governs the proportions of your tables, is a section showing how the tables fit into each other (Fig. 9-21). Reproduce this full-size on a piece of plywood or hardboard, then use it for reference as the table parts are made. Draw it with the actual sizes of wood that you have. It may not matter in the final set of tables if your wood at some place is slightly thicker or thinner than specified. It does matter if it comes in the nesting part of the assembly, so make the drawing accordingly.

The section only applies at the sides. There is no need for supports at the back, where the tabletops inside

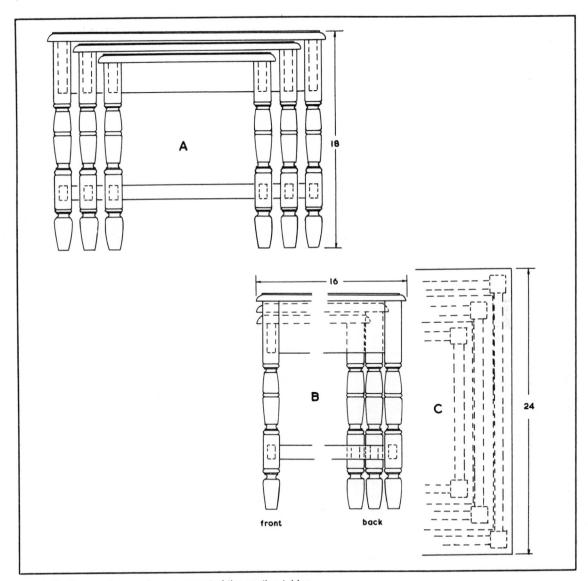

Fig. 9-20. Sizes and general arrangement of the nesting tables.

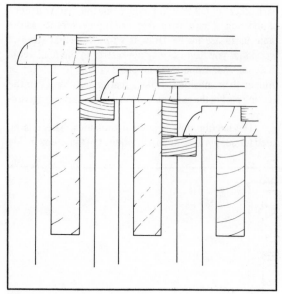

Fig. 9-21. Section at a top corner showing how the tables nest.

go against the rear rails. Notice that the edges of the tabletops have a slight clearance between the legs. Supports hold and guide them as they slide in.

Figures 9-18 and 9-19 show the tables with turned legs, but it is possible to use plain square legs or to decorate them with beveling or carving. Whatever decoration is used, you should match it on all tables. When the tables are nested, the decorated parts should be at the same level on all three tables. The top rails are of different depths, so their lower edges come level. The lower rails are all at the same level, so decoration should come at the same heights between the rail edges on all legs. Extra length for the outer tables has to be allowed at the top.

A simple treatment for square legs is to chamfer the outer corners only (Fig. 9-22A), either for the full length, or stopped below the top rail (Fig. 9-22B). A development of this is wagon beveling, stopped at both ends within the limits of the rails (Fig. 9-22C), and either on the outer corners only or all round each leg. A simple way of getting a comparable appearance is to scoop hollows (Fig. 9-22D), which can be done with a chisel held bevel downward and used toward the center of each hollow.

Legs can be left square and tapered to their feet (Fig. 9-22E). Tapering at corners only is quite effective and simple (Fig. 9-22F). If equipment is available, outer surfaces can be beaded or reeded (Fig. 9-22G), or corners can be molded (Fig. 9-22H).

Turning the Legs

Turning the legs is probably the most attractive treatment. Much depends on your ability and patience. You have to make 12 legs—all with patterns that match. Slight variations in detail may not matter. Turning a full set of legs is an interesting project and well worth the effort.

There are many possible turning designs, and you can use your own ideas for individual designs. Some are shown (Fig. 9-23A). A leg can be square to the floor, or there may be turned feet. The leg should remain square at the top to below the rail level, then be square again where the bottom rails come. Be careful when turning not to damage the squareness by chipping off corners. Although all the patterns must be the same and at the same distance from the bottom, remember to allow enough squareness at the tops for the different heights of tables.

The best plan is to turn one leg completely. With experience, you can probably make the design by eye. Otherwise, sketch what you have in mind. Be prepared to make variations from it, as you find the wood looks better with slightly different spacings or curves. Do not weaken the leg by making any part too thin. When you are satisfied that your first leg is how you want it, make a rod with key measurements marked on it (Fig. 9-23B). Use this as you turn the other legs. Rest it on the tool rest and mark the revolving wood with a pencil (Fig. 9-23C). If you mark and cut beads correctly located, other more sweeping curves are easier to make between them (Fig. 9-23D). Use *calipers* to compare diameters. If you arrange for the larger parts to be as big as the wood will allow, other sizes can be related to them by eye to get matching turnings. Be careful that each leg is truly square before you mount it in the lathe. Make sure you get the lathe centers into dots exactly central in the ends. Lack of squareness or inaccurate centering will cause a reduction of diameter to turn off the flats and an uneven blending of the curves into the square parts. Lack of squareness will also lead to difficulties in assembly.

Preparing the Rails

Make all the legs in whatever style you choose before making other parts. It helps to prepare a rod showing the location of the lower rails, the lower edges of the top rails, and the overall lengths of the legs in each table. Legs can then be marked in groups of four from the rod, so they match each other (Fig. 9-23E) and will be the same as the other sets at key points.

Prepare the wood for rails and other parts of the framing. With all of the wood ready, it is best to then

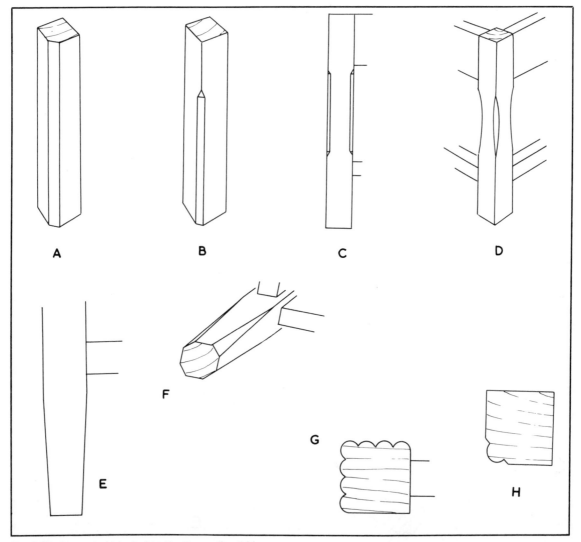

Fig. 9-22. Suggested leg designs for the nesting tables.

make one table at a time to get a smooth fitting. If you make the largest table first, you can assemble it without its top. Check on the fit of the top of the next table inside it.

Mark out the set of legs for the large table (Fig. 9-24A). Remember there are no rails across the front. Corner joints at the top may be mortise and tenon, with the smaller rails dealt with in a similar but reduced manner (Fig. 9-24B). They can be doweled (Fig. 9-24C). The bottom rails are better tenoned (Fig. 9-24D).

Prepare the rails for the large table. Check that distances between shoulders are all exactly the same

where they have to match. Truth of assembly is very important in a nest, where inaccuracy of one table can affect nesting or, at the least, be rather obvious. Assemble the two ends as a pair (Fig. 9-24E). Check with a square, measure diagonals, and see that there is no twist.

Fit the supports for the next one inside the top rails. One strip acts as a width guide and should be level with the insides of the leg surfaces. The other projects as a slide for the next tabletop (Fig. 9-24F). There is no need to extend the slide over the legs. Take off sharpness and round the front corners where the next table has to be hooked on (Fig. 9-24G).

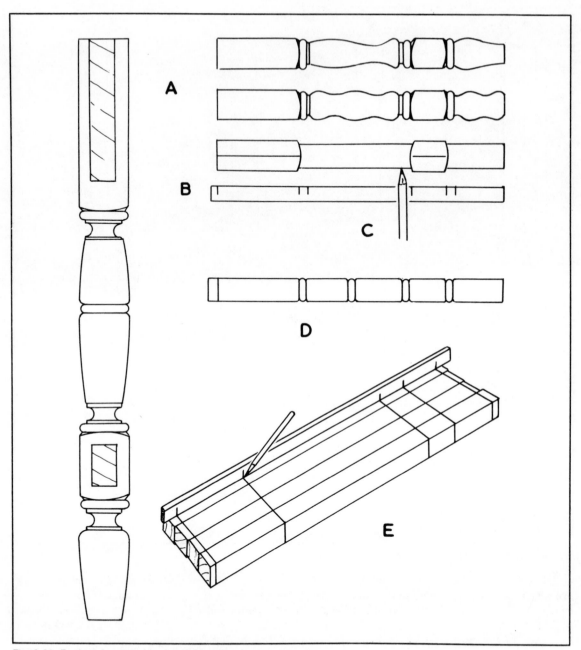

Fig. 9-23. Designs for turned legs and the methods of marking out.

Join the end frames with the upper and lower back rails. As with the end frames, check squareness carefully. Lightly nail a temporary strut across the tops of the front legs to keep them at the right distance. See that this assembly stands squarely and level.

Making the Tops

The tops may be solid wood. The tops can be plywood with edge strips or molding to cover the plies, or they can be blockboard dealt with in a similar way. Top surfaces can be veneered. The tops shown consist of

196

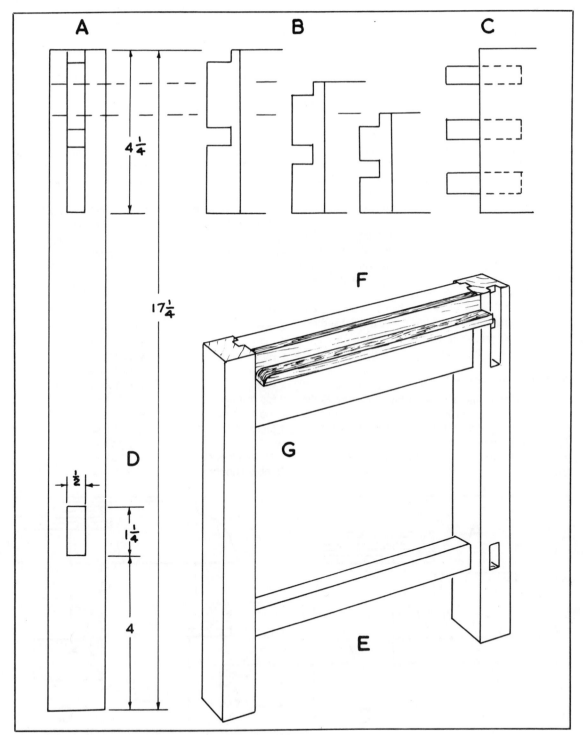

Fig. 9-24. Constructional details of the legs at different heights.

197

framed plywood panels, which can be of the type supplied with veneered surfaces. The frame has a rabbet into which the plywood fits (Fig. 9-25A). The plywood can be glued and clamped into the rabbets, but if it is thick enough to take them, screws can be driven upward as well. The corners of the frames are miters. The plywood in rabbets will strengthen the corners, and they will be further strengthened when they are attached to their frames. If there is any doubt about the strength of simple miters, their lower parts can also be lapped.

The edge is shown with a simple molding. Other moldings can be used, but there should be a flat surface underneath to slide on the guides. Although that does not apply to the large table, its molding ought to look the same as the others.

Make the tops for the large and second tables. Use the framework you have made as a guide to the size of the second top, while giving the large tabletop an even overhand on its frame. The tops can be attached with pocket screws driven through the rails along the back from inside (Fig. 9-25B), or screws can be taken through the guide rails at the sides (Fig. 9-25C). Be careful that there is nothing left projecting that may interfere with the smooth sliding of the tabletops.

Constructing the Smaller Tables

The second table is made in the same way as the outer table. Set the framing in by the same amount from the top edges. This table should finish with its front edge level with the front edge of the outer table and its legs level with the outer ones, when the top is against the back rail.

Mark out the legs for the second table with the lower rail joints level with those of the outer table and the patterns level. The top is adjusted to suit the different height and the width of rails. At this stage it is simplest to have the bottoms of the legs level with the others. You can take off a little for floor clearance later, when you have tried the nesting action.

Making the smallest table is almost a repeat of the second one, except that this one does not have to take another one inside it. There will be a full set of rails all round. Mark out the legs. Check that the bottom rails will be level with the others, and that the lower edges of the top rails also match those outside them.

With the tables nested, check that the large table stands level. Trim the legs of the other tables, so they hang with about ⅛-inch clearance at the floor. Make sure there are no rough edges left at the bottoms.

Materials List for Nesting Coffee Tables

Outer Table

4 legs	1½×18×1½
1 rail	4¼×23×¾
2 rails	4¼×15×¾
1 rail	1¼×23×¾
2 rails	1¼×15×¾
2 top frames	2×25×¾
2 top frames	2×17×¾
1 top panel	14×22×⅜ plywood
2 table supports	⅞×15×½
2 table supports	⅞×15×⅜

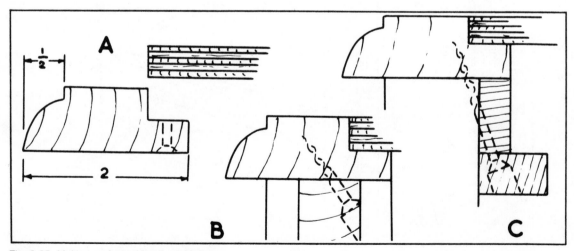

Fig. 9-25. Making and attaching the tabletops.

Second Table

4 legs	1½×17×1½
1 rail	3⅜×21×¾
2 rails	3⅜×14×¾
1 rail	1¼×21×¾
2 rails	1¼×13×¾
2 top frames	2×21×¾
2 top frames	2×15×¾
1 top panel	11×18×⅜
	plywood
2 table supports	⅞×15×½
2 table supports	⅞×15×⅜

Inner Table

4 legs	1½×16×1½
2 rails	2½×19×¾
2 rails	2½×13×¾
2 rails	1¼×19×¾
2 rails	1¼×13×¾
2 top frames	2×14×¾
2 top frames	2×14×¾
1 top panel	7×15×⅜
	plywood

REVOLVING DROP FLAP TABLE

There are many ways that a tabletop may be made, so its size can be altered. Most of them involve the use of struts or other supports, such as the gates of a gateleg table. If the top can be made to revolve, it is possible to obtain support without extra parts to adjust as the extended flaps rest on the main structure. Although it is possible to make the top square or other shape, it is more common for this type of table to be given a round top. The proportions of the top must be such as to not make too great an overhang when extended, or there need to be very long feet to provide stability. A round top is most suitable for getting satisfactory proportions. The flaps hang at the sides. They can then be lifted level, and the whole top is rotated 90° to make the framework support the flaps.

This table (Fig. 9-26) is of dining table size when extended, but the reduced top comes down to one-third of the full width. Measurements can be altered to make a side or even a coffee table.

As drawn (Fig. 9-27), the top makes a circle of 48 inches in diameter and is formed from three pieces 16 inches wide. The supporting framework is very similar to that for a gateleg table, with end pedestals on broad feet. Two top rails go between the end parts and support a board that provides the pivot (Fig. 9-28A). There is a

Fig. 9-26. A revolving top table with the flaps raised.

central lower rail, and feet project each side (Fig. 9-28B).

Doweled construction is suggested. If you want to build the table by more traditional methods, you may prefer to use mortise and tenon joints. Use ½-inch dowels spaced fairly closely in the rails (Fig. 9-28C) and into the feet (Fig. 9-28D).

The ends can be left with straight sides, but some shaping is suggested (Fig. 9-28E). Work about a centerline and either cut one edge to mark the others or make a template, so the patterns match. Be careful that the cuts are square across and finished, so no saw marks are visible.

Deal with the feet in a similar way (Fig. 9-28F). Mark the curves from a template of half a foot. Be careful to get meeting surfaces flat and the dowel holes marked truly, then drill them square to the surfaces. Clamp tightly, so no gaps show in the finished joints.

The central board that makes the pivot can be doweled or tenoned into the side rails. Because the board will not show, it is simpler to notch it into the rails and screw down through (Fig. 9-28G). Prepare the board, but do not screw it down until the pivot parts are completed.

As the top has to rotate over the central framework, there must be no projections that will catch on the other parts. The hinges should be backflaps let in with their knuckles upward (Fig. 9-29A) and preferably slightly

199

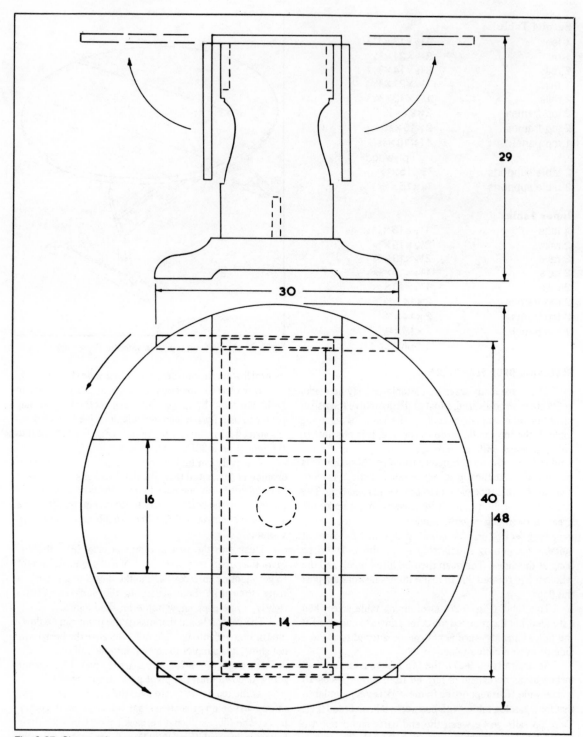

Fig. 9-27. Sizes and arrangements of the revolving table.

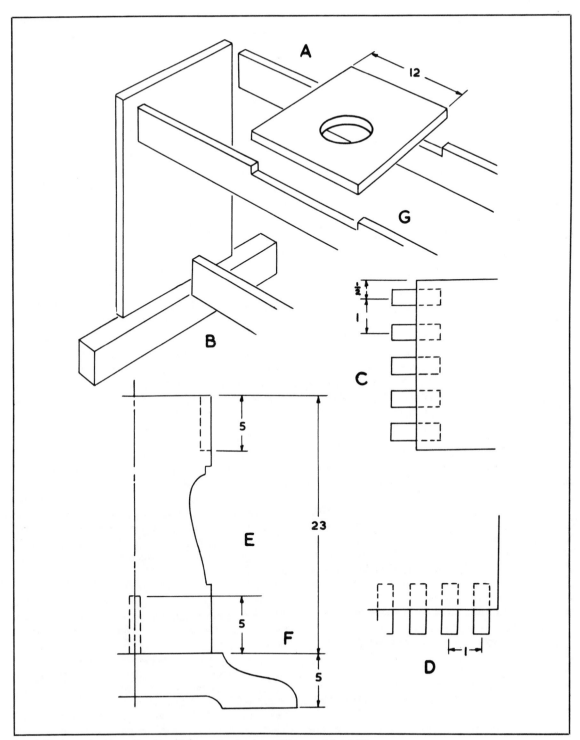

Fig. 9-28. Layout and construction of the main structure of the revolving table.

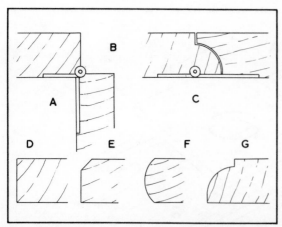

Fig. 9-29. The flap joints and suggested tabletop edge details.

below the surface. The meeting edges of the top can be cut square (Fig. 9-29B) or prepared as knuckle joints (Fig. 9-29C). Obviously, the meeting edges must be straight and a good fit. To prevent movement, two hinges should be fairly close to their ends, with either one or two intermediately.

Prepare the meeting edges before marking out the shape of the top's three parts. A piece of wood with an awl through it, and a pencil against its end, will serve as a compass. The curved edge can be left square in section (Fig. 9-29D) or given a beveled top (Fig. 9-29E), a curve (Fig. 9-29F), or a molding worked to match that of the knuckle joint (Fig. 9-29G). Getting that molding exact by handwork is difficult and should only be attempted on this curve if you have a suitable spindle molder or router cutter.

The pivot consists of a disc through a hole, with a larger disc to retain it (Fig. 9-30A). The exact size is not important, but it is shown as 4 inches (Fig. 9-30B). If you have an expansive bit that will drill near that size, the hole can be made with it. If not, you can cut the hole with a jigsaw or similar tool after drilling many ½-inch holes just inside the circle indicating the finished diameter. Fortunately, the pivot will work when the hole is not a perfect circle, but get it as accurate as you can.

The pivot disc should be thicker than the board with the hole to provide clearance as the top is turned, but this need only be slight. Make sure the disc turns easily in the hole without catching at any point. It does not have to be a precision fit, but try not to let it have much sideways movement.

Glue and screw the pivot disc to the middle of the top's center part. Try the action. The retaining disc may

be plywood, but it would last longer if it was a close-grained hardwood attached to the pivot disc with its grain crossing. Screw the discs together (Fig. 9-30C). Do not use glue, as you may need to remove the disc after long use for maintenance.

The top will soon rotate smoothly, but it will help in the initial stages to use wax polish on the parts that will rub before assembling them. In particular, put beeswax fairly liberally around the pivot before screwing on the retaining disc.

Materials List for Revolving Drop Flap Table

3 tops	16×48×1
2 ends	14×24×1
2 feet	5×31×1½
3 rails	5×40×1
1 pad	12×15×1
1 pivot	5×5×1
1 pivot	7×7×½

SIMPLE GATELEG TABLE

There are many methods of making adjustable tables, but one simple and satisfactory way is to provide leaves or flaps that fold down. Smaller flaps can be supported by brackets. If there is much area to the extension when it is up, it is better to support it from the floor, making the whole table much steadier. A gateleg table gets its name from the fact that the supporting legs swing in and out like a gate. It is possible to arrange for a flat table on one side only, but it is more common to have a flap on each side of a central top.

This table has a central part which is 18 inches wide and 42 inches long. That is the fixed size and is the floor area that the table occupies when standing with its flaps hanging down. The two flaps are the same size as the central part, so with one flap up the total top area becomes 36 inches by 42 inches. With both flaps up, it is 54 inches by 42 inches. As drawn, the top is 30 inches from the floor.

Construction is simple, with all parts of fairly light section (Fig. 9-31). The general drawing (Fig. 9-32) should be read in conjunction with the other drawings, so the method of construction is understood before starting work.

The table frame is made around two identical assemblies (Fig. 9-33A). Any of the usual corner joints can be used between the parts, but dovetails (Fig. 9-33B) are best. The top frame only can have a central crossbar to aid in securing the top and keep that frame in shape under load (Fig. 9-33C). Check the two assemblies against each other as you make them.

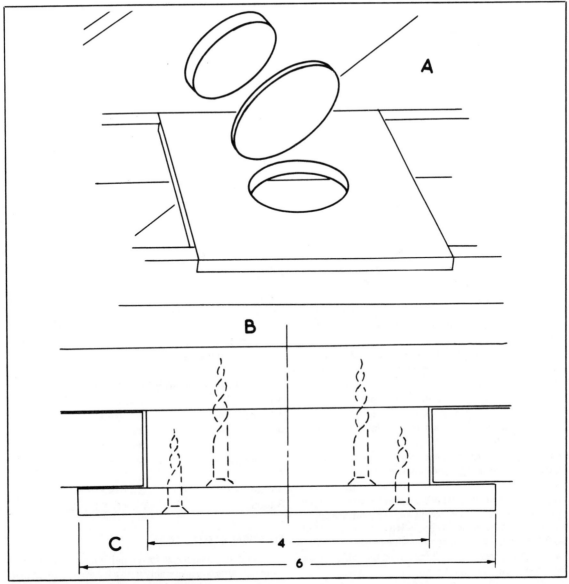

Fig. 9-30. The pivot of the revolving tabletop.

The legs are straight pieces (Fig. 9-33D) that overlap the frames, so they stand out 1 inch each side. Mark the joint positions on all the legs together, and join them to the upper and lower assemblies with glue and screws driven from inside. The tabletop will be attached with pocket screws (Fig. 9-34A). You may cut these recesses and drill the holes before assembly if you wish.

The two gates are the same (Fig. 9-33E) and made of narrower parts than the main assembly. Check that the legs are the same length as those of the central assembly, so the top will be supported level. It is possible to dowel the gate parts, but mortise and tenon joints are better (Fig. 9-34B). Attach the gates to the central part with butt hinges, so they swing with ample clearance inside the main legs (Fig. 9-33F). Make a trial assembly, then disassemble to sand and finish the wood.

The three parts of the top can be made from solid wood. You must be certain that the top was thoroughly

Fig. 9-31. A simple gateleg table with one flap raised.

seasoned and preferably kept in the atmosphere in which it will be used for several months before using it for the table. This will insure that it settles into a stable condition, and the risk of warping is minimized.

The central part will be held flat by the screws to the framework. There can be strips across the undersides of the flaps to prevent them from warping, but attach them with screws only. Do not glue, as that may cause cracking if the wood expanded or contracted. The central screws can be in round holes, but those at the extremes are better in slots (Fig. 9-34C).

Alternative tops can be made from plywood ¾ inch or more thick. If this is obtained already veneered to match the solid wood, it will make a tabletop that should remain flat and look good, except for the edges. The best treatment there is to provide a lip of solid wood, preferably with a tongue and groove joint (Fig. 9-34D). If the lip is made slightly too thick at first, it can be planed level after fitting. The edge, whether lipped plywood or solid wood, may be left square, except for taking off sharpness. It may also be rounded (Fig. 9-34E) or molded (Fig. 9-34F). Do not make molding too wide or elaborate, or it may affect the safety of anything put on the table. Round the outer corners of the flaps.

There are ways of molding the meeting surfaces between the tabletop parts. The usual way is described in more advanced tables, but here the meeting edges are best left square.

Ordinary butt hinges can be used under the joint (Fig. 9-34G), with the flaps let in for neatness. Four 4-inch butt hinges will do. Be careful to locate them where the one near where the gate closes does not get in its way.

Better hinges are backflaps. They swing back more than *butt hinges,* so they can be mounted with the knuckle

upward, leaving the lower surface level (Fig. 9-34H). With wider flaps, the screw holes are staggered and make a stronger attachment where they enter different lines of grain.

Invert the table over the center section of the top and screw it on. See that the edges are parallel and there is clearance at each side for the gates to fold clear of the flaps. Attach the hinges while an assistant keeps the inverted parts pressed close together. When the table is fully opened, there should be no gaps along the hinge lines.

The legs will probably open and stay square to the center part without any restriction. If you wish, there can be small blocks screwed under the flaps to act as stops at the fully extended positions. Round the tops of the gatelegs, so there is no roughness or sharp edges to scratch the flaps.

The table as shown is plain. If good wood that is attractively finished is used, the simple lines will accentuate the quality of the wood. You can provide some shaping of the legs' edges and of the underside of the two first assemblies, but they do not show much, except at the ends. It is possible to put a shelf on the lower assembly if you want some storage space, but it is only accessible easily from the ends when the table is closed.

Materials List for Simple Gateleg Table

4 legs	4×30×1
4 frame sides	4×36×1
4 frame sides	4×16×1
1 top bar	4×16×1
2 gate legs	3×30×1
2 gate uprights	3×25×1
4 gate rails	3×16×1
3 tops	18×43×1

ELLIPTICAL GATELEG TABLE

A table of useful size for a family meal needs to be of sufficient area and preferably with a leg arrangement that does not interfere with the way that sitters arrange their chairs. The gateleg arrangement of a folding table keeps the legs out of the way. It has the advantage of allowing the table to be reduced in size when not needed to its full area. This example (Fig. 9-35) has an elliptical top, which gives an attractive appearance and is suitable for comfortably seating several people. Keeping to a rectangular outline may give a larger top area if that is essential, but the method of construction is basically the same.

There is a central fixed top of about 36 inches long and 16 inches wide on legs that support 29 inches from

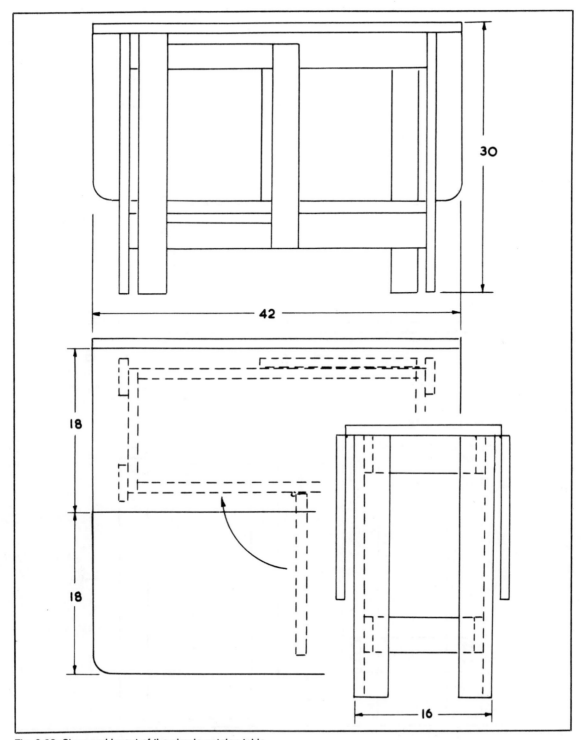

Fig. 9-32. Sizes and layout of the simple gateleg table.

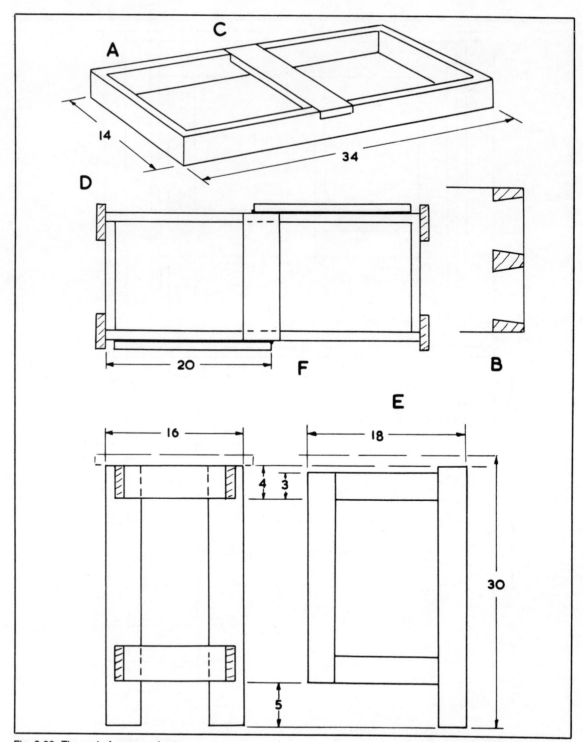

Fig. 9-33. The main frames and gates.

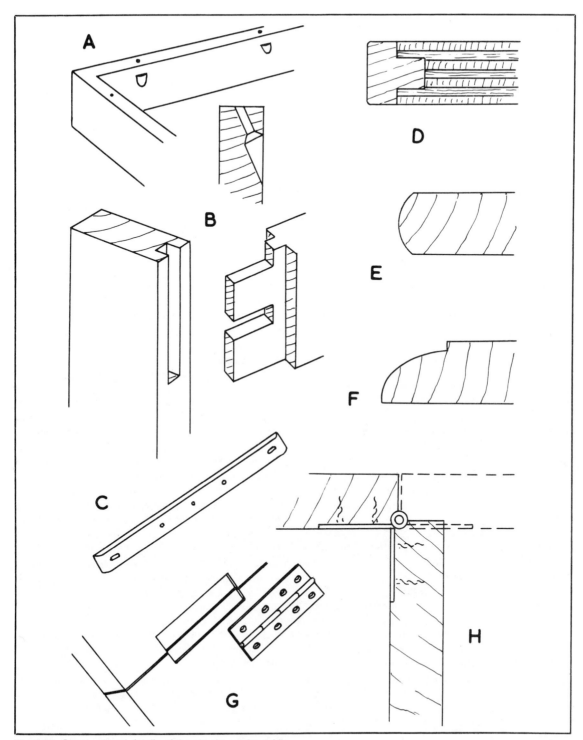

Fig. 9-34. Constructional details of the simple gateleg table.

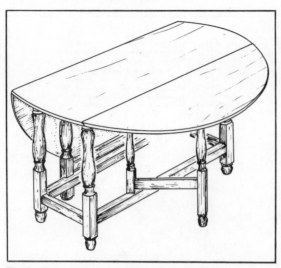

Fig. 9-35. An elliptical gateleg table with turned legs and one flap raised.

the floor. With both flaps up, the top measures 36 inches by 48 inches (Fig. 9-36). With only one flap raised, the top is 36 inches by 32 inches. The arrangement of supports has four legs as main supports, then the gates swing out two other legs.

The legs can be left square in the simplest form. Some decoration may be applied as wagon beveling on exposed edges. The best appearance is with turned legs if a lathe is available. There are six legs and four pilasters at the inner ends of the gates. All are to be turned with matching and identical patterns. If you do not feel able to produce eight pieces of turning that are sufficiently alike, it may be better to settle for square legs. The capacity of the lathe has to be considered. Most lathes will take the suggested leg length.

Start by marking out a leg (Fig. 9-37A). The rails in the narrow direction are deeper to provide stiffness. The other way the rails are as wide as the legs, for convenience in arranging the swinging gates.

Mark all of the legs from the first by squaring across. The legs at the extremities of the gates are the same length as the others, but the arrangement of joint positions is different (Fig. 9-37B). The top has to be notched into the top rail (Fig. 9-37C). The pilaster fits between top and bottom rails, then has the same joint arrangement as the outer legs (Fig. 9-37D). If the legs are to be turned, it is the part within the length of the pilaster that sets the length of the turned part (Fig. 9-37E). This should be matched on the legs. If you decide to decorate with wagon beveling, this is also the distance to deal with (Fig.

9-37F) on the pilaster and in the same relative positions on the legs. There will be turned feet on the turned legs that relate to each other, although not to the pilaster which does not go as low.

Turn one leg, using the drawing as a guide. If you find you get a more pleasing shape on the actual wood by varying from the drawing, that does not matter. You have to treat the other legs the same way. It helps to make a rod from the first leg, with lengths marked on its edge (Fig. 9-37G). This can be held against the wood that has been turned cylindrical in the appropriate part. Lines are penciled on the revolving wood to give you the positions of the cut. Keep the first leg nearby and refer to it for diameters and the sweeps of curves, as you do further turning to make up the set of legs.

Parts of the Central Table

Make the parts of the central table before making the gates. There are deeper rails in the short direction to provide stiffness. They can be tenoned or doweled into the legs (Fig. 9-38A). The lower rails are arranged similarly (Fig. 9-38B). The top long rails are the full width of the legs (Fig. 9-38C). Make the joints to the legs—either tenons or dowels.

Draw a plan view of one side, with the gate position and the overhang of the top shown. The pilasters come within the width of the rails, but the outer legs need only swing back far enough to clear the hanging flaps (Fig. 9-38D). Notice that the gate comes toward one end, so the swinging leg swings approximately central under the flap when opened. This means that the two gates are not opposite each other when closed.

From this drawing, note how much to cut out of the legs and the rails for the gate to close enough to clear the lowered flap (Fig. 9-38E). This means cutting something like a sloping halving joint in each position (Fig. 9-38F). The joints do not have to be a tight fit, as they would be in making a glued joint, but the gates should swing comfortably into slightly oversize cuts (Fig. 9-38G).

Make up the central table in the usual way. Glue up two opposite frames. Join them with the rails in the other direction, so the assembly is square and stands firmly.

From this assembly, get the lengths of the pilasters to fit between the rails. Make up the gates (Fig. 9-39A). Note that the top rail is kept down from the top of the pilaster to give clearance under the top table rail (Fig. 9-39B). The gates have to be arranged to pivot on pieces of dowel rod. Drill the rails and the ends of the pilasters carefully. Allow for the dowel rods to go into the pilasters sufficiently. They will be glued in later, but obviously

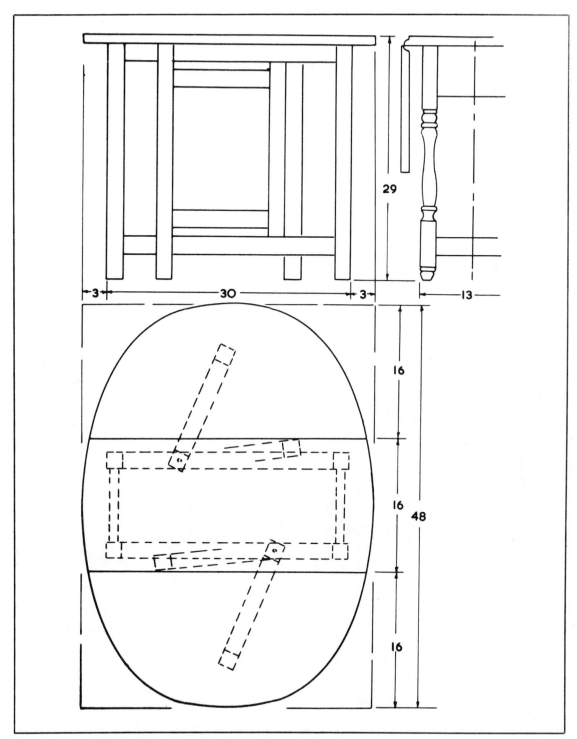

Fig. 9-36. Sizes of the elliptical gateleg table with both flaps raised.

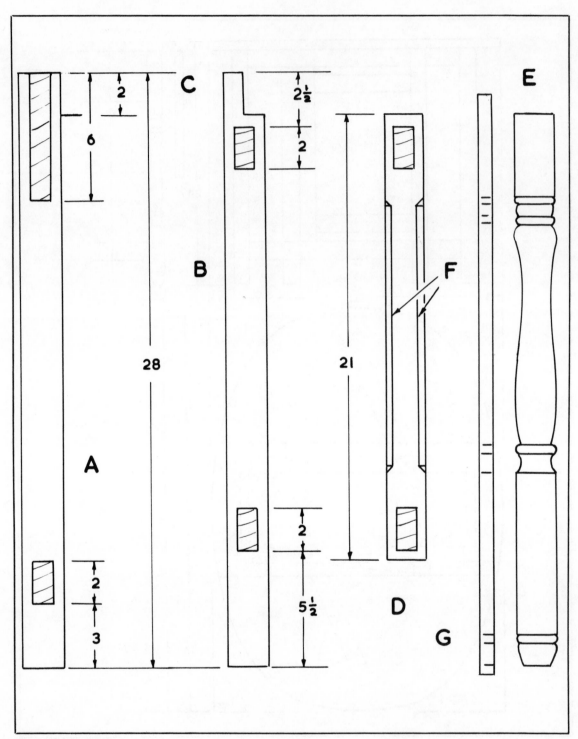

Fig. 9-37. Leg details.

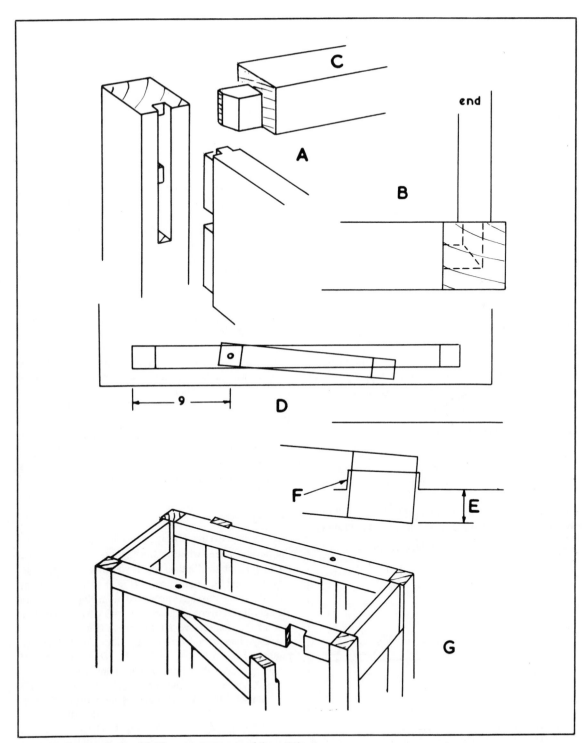

Fig. 9-38. Construction and folding arrangements of the gatelegs.

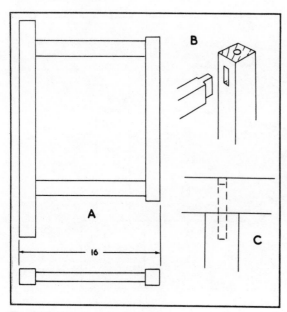

Fig. 9-39. How to make the gates.

must be free to rotate in the rail holes. The top dowel rods must finish below the top surface of the table rail (Fig. 9-39C). Make a temporary assembly, if you wish, and check the action of the gates. Keep the dowel rods overlong so you can pull them out again.

Rule Joints and Backflap Hinges

The three parts of the top are solid wood with the grain running in the 36-inch direction. The joint between them can be cut square and ordinary hinges used underneath, but that leaves square edges exposed. You may find that acceptable, but for the best looking result there is a *rule joint* (Fig. 9-40A). This leaves a molded appear-

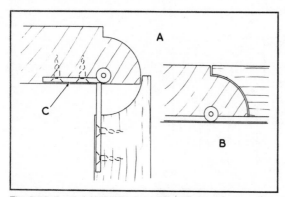

Fig. 9-40. A rule joint for the top of the elliptical gateleg table.

ance along the joint when a flap is lowered, and the parts fit when it is raised (Fig. 9-40B). The name comes from the similarity of a section to the joint used in some types of folding rules.

A problem in this type of joint is the choice of hinge. If an ordinary hinge is used with its knuckle downward, the flap drops with a gap between it and the top. The point on which the joint swings is the center of the hinge knuckle, and that is below the underside of the top. If an ordinary hinge is put the other way up, so its knuckle is buried and the pivot point comes higher, it will not swing back far enough. *Backflap hinges* are made for this purpose and will swing back. They also have one flap extended, so the screw holes are far enough from the knuckle to allow for the hollowing on the edge.

To make a rule joint, first draw a full-size section. Use the size of the wood and the actual hinge as a pattern. Allow for the hinge being let in level or slightly below the under surface (Fig. 9-40C). The curves of the two parts have to be drawn with compasses about the center of the hinge knuckle. Allow for some clearance between the two curves, but that can be slight if you work carefully.

Traditionally, the curves are cut with hollow and round planes. A modern method uses a spindle molder or a router with suitable cutters. Some of the waste can be removed with a rabbet or fillister plane. The convex curve may be cut almost entirely with a rabbet plane followed by sanding.

It will be advisable to use four backflap hinges along each joint, with the outer ones not very far in from the ends and the others evenly spaced. As they come entirely within the wood, they will not interfere with the action of the gatelegs.

The Top

It is best to cut and fit the rule joints before trimming the parts to size, whether the table is to finish with a rectangular or an elliptical top. If you choose a rectangular top, round the outer corners (Fig. 9-41A). If you want something like the shape produced by an ellipse, but with straight lines, there is an octagon with corners trimmed toward the greater overall dimension (Fig. 9-41B).

If you want to make the top elliptical, it has to be regular shape if it is to look right. There are several geometric methods of finding many points on the circumference, which can then be joined up. Whatever method is used, it is best to make a template of one-fourth of the top. Use that to mark the shape and get it uniform.

A practical method of drawing the shape uses string and two nails. Draw a centerline, which will be the major

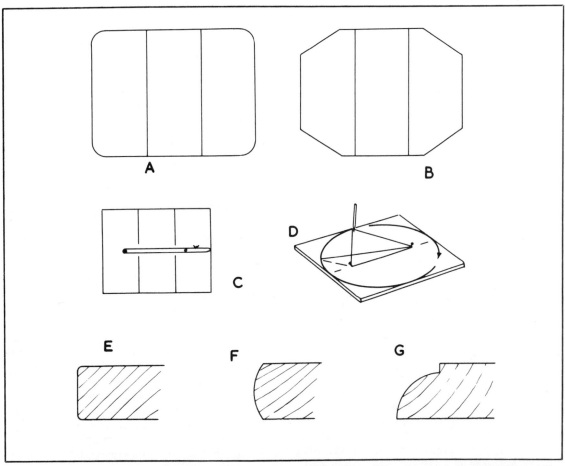

Fig. 9-41. Alternative shapes for the top (A and B), how to draw an ellipse (C and D), and suggested edges (E, F, and G).

axis of the ellipse. A centerline the other way will be the minor axis, and these two mark the limits of your one-fourth template. On the major axis, drive in two nails the same distance from each end. This distance will have to be found by experimenting but start with 12 inches. Make a loop of string around the nails to reach to one end (Fig. 9-41C). Put a pencil in the end of the loop and move it around, keeping a tension between it and the nails (Fig. 9-41D). Move the nails closer together if your ellipse does not go wide enough. Adjust the loop size to the end again, or move the nails further out to get it narrower.

What you do to the edge depends on your skill and available equipment. Molding a curved edge by hand is not easy. It may be better to leave the edge square or rounded (Figs. 9-41E and 9-41F).

If you have a suitable cutter for a spindle molder or a router, the edge will look good if given a section similar to the rule joint (Fig. 9-41G). Be careful at the joints that the section follows through, so you do not break out the grain.

The top can be attached with pocket screws (Fig. 9-42A), but in this width, with a risk of expansion and contraction, it may be better to use buttons in slotted top rails (Fig. 9-42B). Before fitting the top, put the dowels into the top rails and pilasters.

The position each gateleg swings to is not critical. You may find that you pull it out to the right position without difficulty, but there can be a block of wood screwed under each flap to act as a stop for the gate. When the table is standing on a level floor, the flaps should come level with the center top. Try a straightedge across the top. If the flaps do not lift high enough, you can put a piece of veneer or card next to the stop block as packing.

213

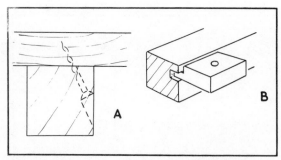

Fig. 9-42. The top of the central part of the table is screwed and buttoned.

Materials List for Elliptical Gateleg Table

6 legs	2×29×2
4 pilasters	2×22×2
4 rails	2×30×2
2 rails	2×13×1
2 rails	6×13×1
4 gate rails	2×16×1
3 tops	16×37×1

STUDY CORNER TABLE

Anyone studying or looking after household accounts needs a place to work where papers can be kept together with pens and other equipment, perhaps including a typewriter. One problem is often lack of space. This table is intended to fit in a corner. It can be extended to an L-shape when maximum space is needed. The extension is particularly useful for a typewriter, as it allows you to turn to use it without disturbing the papers on the main top. The extension is shown on the right (Fig. 9-43), but it will work just as well on the other side. It does not matter if you are right or left-handed.

There is a basic table that has a drawer and an extending part which slides in a similar way to a drawer, while on top there may be a rack for papers and books (Fig. 9-44). The rack is a separate construction that can be made and fitted later or removed when not required.

Construction of the table frame follows normal methods, except for the need to allow for the sliding part. Make the four legs, which are shown square (Fig. 9-45A), but they can be turned between the rails. Their appearance will also be improved by wagon beveling or tapering below the bottom rails. The back and side top rails are joined to the legs with haunched tenons (Fig. 9-45B). At the front the rail is narrower to allow for the horizontal piece below. That forms a bearer for the drawer and is

tenoned into the legs (Fig. 9-45C). The rail is cut out for the drawer and the sliding top (Fig. 9-45D).

The lower side rails are tenoned into the legs. The single stretcher near the back serves as a footrest (Fig. 9-45E).

The main tabletop can be solid wood or framed plywood. It is then held to the framing with buttons or pocket screws as described for the worktable.

The making of the drawer and its guides can be similar to those in the worktable. Tenon the guides into the back rail and lap into the horizontal rail at the front. At the top you can tenon into the front or arrange another lap there. Make the drawer with a false front. It is set further under the tabletop because of the need for clearance for the sliding part. Provide it with a handle that can be felt and gripped when you may not be able to see it from above. A wood bar handle is shown, but a metal type with a swinging ball may be preferred.

The sliding extension top has to be self-supporting. It is best made of thick plywood or chipboard, which will not twist or warp like solid wood. Cut this to width, although it can be left too long at this stage. Guides for it need to be stronger than those for the drawer. Pack out from the side rail to the thickness of the front leg and continue with a support for the slide (Fig. 9-46A). This can be made from two pieces, or a single piece may be rabbeted. Make a similar support for the other side (Fig. 9-46B). The ends can be tenoned or lapped into front and back rails. If the tabletop is solid, that will act as a kicker for the slide. If the top is framed plywood, pack it to thickness above the inner slide position and above the other side if the frame is narrow to prevent the slide from tilting as it is pulled out.

As the extension slides, its weight should be taken by the two guides and not by the cutout in the front rail. Trim the cutout to give a slight clearance, but not so much as to look ugly.

Cut the extension top so when it is fully in, its front edge comes under the front edge of the main tabletop. The legs are similar to the main legs, except for being slightly shorter. Make the top rails with reduced width, so its lower edge will come level with the main rails. Position the bottom rail at the same level as the main lower rails (Fig. 9-46C).

Assemble the framework of the main table in the usual way, but do not add the top yet. Fit the drawer and its guides, so you can check its action while able to view from the top. Fit the slide guides and check the action to the extension.

As there can be no framing to stiffen the extension legs in the direction that they pull out, the top joint needs

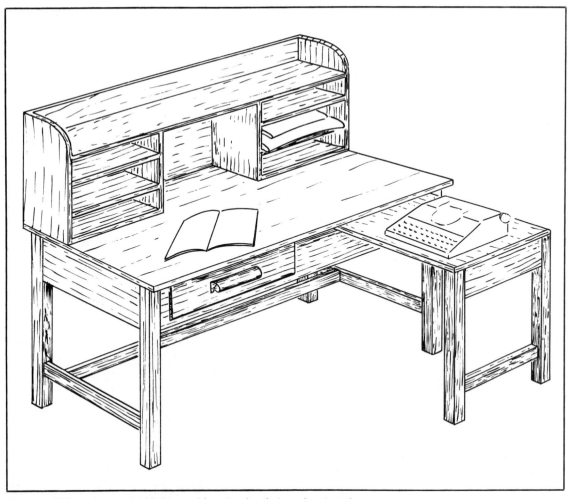

Fig. 9-43. This study corner table has a side extension that can be stowed.

to be as strong as possible. You can screw down through the extension top into the rail, counterboring the holes and plugging them, or you can use pocket screws driven upward from inside. Nearly 2 inches of space are left when the extension is stowed, and that can be made up with a block of wood in the angle (Fig. 9-46D).

Try the action of the extension. When you are satisfied that you have it right, put a stop block under the inner end to prevent the extension being pulled right out (Fig. 9-46E). Screw it without glue, so it can be removed without damage if you ever need to disassemble the table.

You can use your own ideas for the top rack, but the one shown has space on top for books and other things and racks on each side for papers, magazines, and files. The central space will take larger books, or it can just be a place to push things that accumulate on a desk.

Suitable sizes are suggested (Fig. 9-47A). The main part of the back is plywood, but the piece above the top shelf will look better if it is solid wood. This means that the ends should be rabbeted to take the plywood, then deeper for the top (Fig. 9-47B). The shelves all fit into stopped dadoes (Fig. 9-47C), with the bottom ones into rabbets with screws upward (Fig. 9-47D). The inner upright parts go into dadoes in the long shelf (Fig. 9-47E).

The back will provide rigidity and hold the joints together, but at the front it is advisable to use thin screws diagonally upward (Fig. 9-47F). To do this, have the holes already drilled in the shelves and assemble with the rack upside down, sliding the shelves in turn after the next

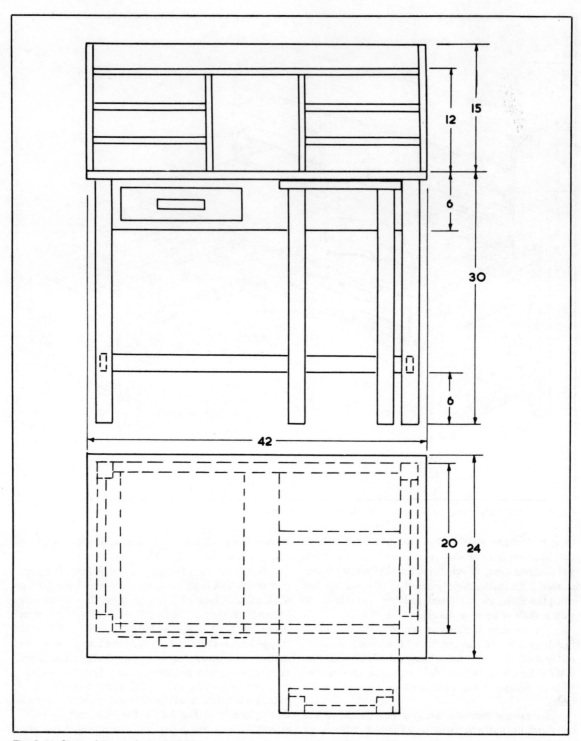

Fig. 9-44. Sizes of the study corner table.

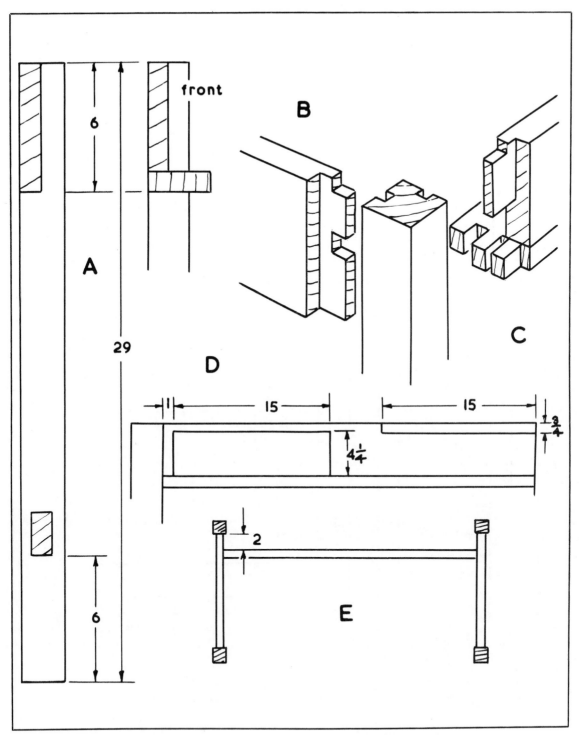

Fig. 9-45. Construction at the corners (A, B and C), the front (D), and lower rail (E) layouts.

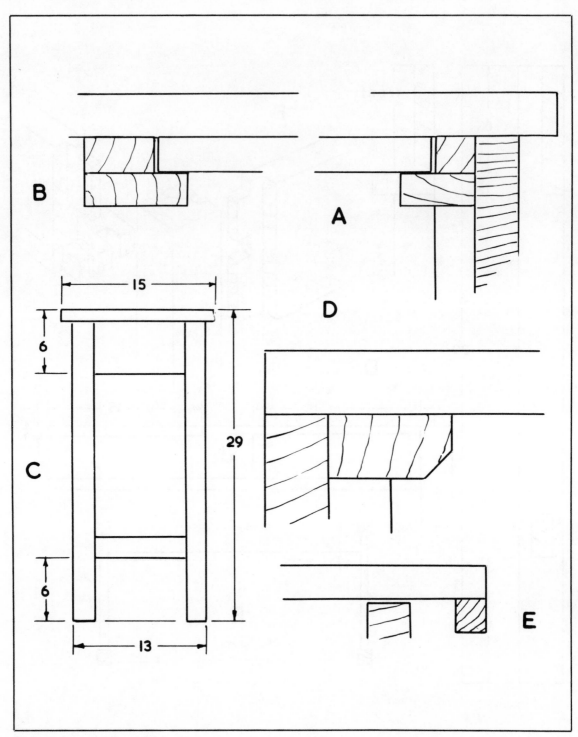

Fig. 9-46. Side extension details.

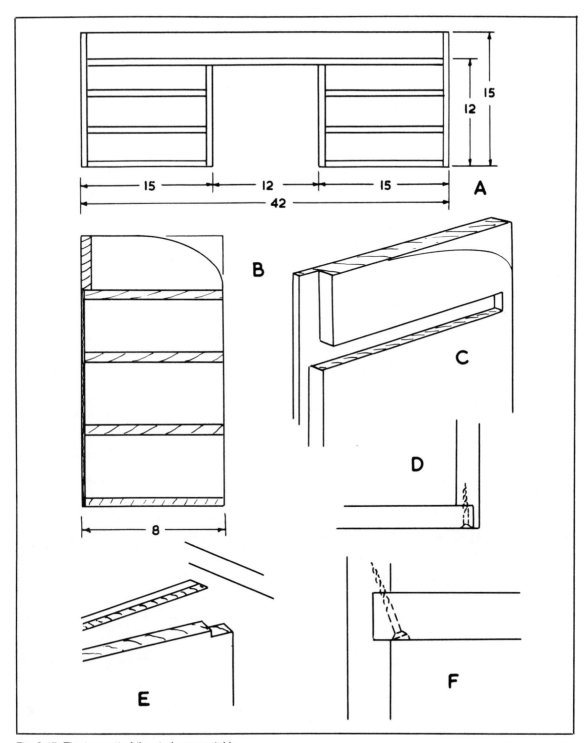

Fig. 9-47. The top part of the study corner table.

shelf has been screwed. If you do not do this at every level, drive screws into the top shelf. With the screws in the bottom rabbets, the other shelves will be held as well.

Screw the solid top piece of the back upward through the top shelf. Nail and screw the plywood into the rabbets and to the shelves. One screw downward at each end will locate the rack on the table and allow easy removal.

Materials List for Study Corner Table

1 top	20×42×1
6 legs	2×30×2
1 rail	6×439×1
2 rails	6×17×1
1 rail	5×39×1
1 rail	3×39×1
2 lower rails	2×17×1
1 stretcher	2×40×1
2 drawer sides	4¼×20×⅝
2 drawer ends	4¼×16×⅝
1 drawer bottom	16×20×¼ plywood
1 false front	5×16×½
1 extension top	15×24×¾ plywood
1 extension rail	5×12×1
1 extension rail	2×12×1
2 extension guides	2×20×1
1 extension guide	1×20×1
1 extension guide	3×20×1
1 extension stop	1×15×1
2 rack ends	8×15×⅝
1 rack top	8×42×⅝
1 rack top	3×42×⅝
2 rack uprights	8×12×⅝
6 rack shelves	8×15×⅝
1 rack back	12×42×¼ plywood

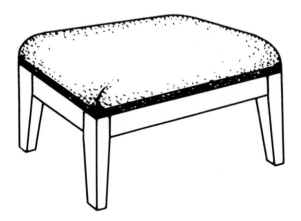

Chapter 10

Upholstered Seats

Traditional upholstery required considerable skill and knowledge of materials and their behavior. In recent years the place of many of the traditional materials has been taken by rubber and plastic foam of a spongelike texture that is available in many sizes and thicknesses. These materials can be cut with a knife and are easily shaped. There is still a place for traditional methods, and anyone interested in going further into upholstery of all kinds will find it a fascinating activity. Complete instructions are outside the scope of this book, but anyone wanting to know more about all kinds of upholstery will find information in my book *The Upholsterer's Bible* (Tab Book No. 1004). In this chapter there are examples of the application of plastic and rubber foam material used on stools, chairs, and other seats. Instructions on different aspects of upholstery are given. If you want to make some other example of upholstered furniture, read through the upholstery instructions of the many projects to see which technique is applicable.

TOOLS

If you already possess the tools needed to make wooden furniture, you will have suitable tools for upholstery as well. Thick foam can be cut with a knife having

a long thin blade, such as a carving knife. Moistening it will help on rubber. Many cuts in cloth can be made with a knife of the type used for marking out wood, but there will also be a use for scissors. Ideally they will be quite large, such as the ones that are used for tailoring or cutting wallpaper. Smaller ones are suitable for occasional use.

Any small hammer will do for driving tacks, but an *upholsterer's hammer* has a longer head (Fig. 10-1A) for getting into confined spaces. It is usually strengthened with cheeks on each side of the handle, and the other end may be forked to lift tacks. An upholsterer's ripping chisel is not a cutting tool, but it has a forked or wide end for levering out tacks (Fig. 10-1B). You can do that with a screwdriver pushed under the tack head and twisted sideways. There are special *pincers* with wide jaws for pulling webbing and cloth (Fig. 10-1C), but you can use pliers for a small amount of work.

Be prepared to sew some upholstery material. Much of it can be sewed with a domestic sewing machine, preferably with a foot that allows the stitches to come quite close to an angle in the cloth. You must do hand sewing for some work. *Curved needles* are made that way, so you can enter them and pull them out from the same side (Fig. 10-1D). They may have points at one or both

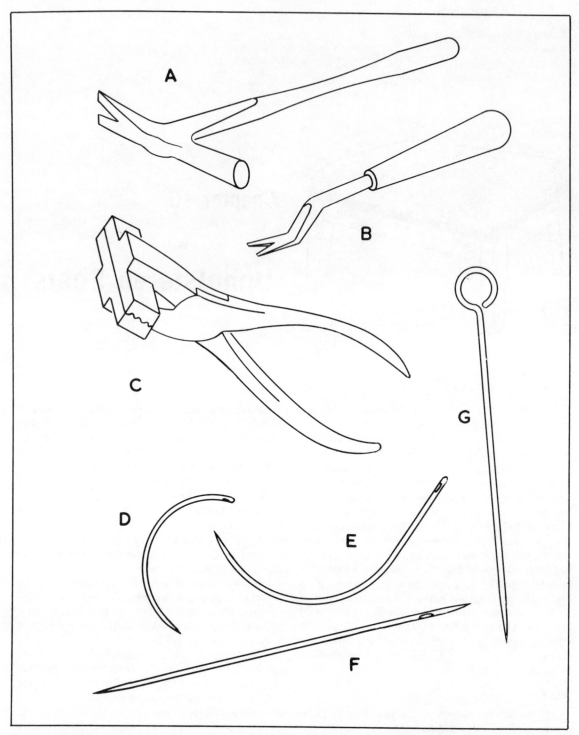

Fig. 10-1. Upholstery tools include a hammer (A), tack lifter (B), pincers (C), needles (D, E, and F), and a skewer (G).

ends. Sizes are by length around the curve and by a gauge thickness. For average work, a needle 3 inches long and 16 gauge may be the first choice. *Spring needles* are similar, but the eye end is straight for a short distance (Fig. 10-1E). They are intended for sewing springs to webbing, but you can use them elsewhere.

For buttoning, you need a straight needle longer than the thickness you have to penetrate. That is a *mattress needle* (Fig. 10-1F) made in lengths from 4 to 16 inches. For general work, 6 or 8 inches in length and 14 gauge will be suitable. An upholsterer's *skewer* (Fig. 10-1G) is like a large straight needle with a loop at one end. It is used in the way a dressmaker uses pins—to keep cloth temporarily in place.

COVERING

Modern upholstery does not have as many stages in it as the traditional form. The foam is not liable to move or settle, nor does it disintegrate and try to come out through the covering. It is helpful to understand the form of older upholstery. The simpler modern work can then be understood.

In section (Fig. 10-2) the base is interlaced strips of webbing attached all round to a wooden frame. The webbing is drawn tight, but there is some residual elasticity. Coil springs are sewed to the webbing, possibly at each crossing or spaced to suit what goes above. There may be smaller springs at the edge, and the tops of the springs are kept in place by an often quite complicated pattern of

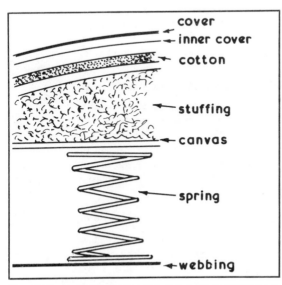

Fig. 10-2. Section showing the layers in traditional upholstery.

knotted twine. The object is to keep the springs from tilting, as the user moves on the seat.

Canvas, which is sometimes as coarse as burlap is stretched over the springs. That forms the base for the stuffing, which is the primary source of softening for the user. Many things have been used for stuffing, but the most popular has been hair followed by fiber, wool, kapok, and feathers. Its softening comes from being curled, so there are many air pockets. Hair may be horsehair, but it is more likely a mixture of hairs from cattle. Many of the older stuffing materials lost their capacity to return to full-size after being compressed, so seats went out of shape and became uncomfortable. Rubber and plastic foam do not have this disadvantage.

Traditional stuffing needed a piece of cotton cloth over it to keep it in shape and minimize the risk of any of it working through. A layer of cotton batting went over it. Besides providing a little more padding, this helped to even the appearance by disguising any small bumps and hollows in the stuffing.

Some covering materials, such as leather or plastic imitation leather, can go directly over the batting. For woven cloth, there is an inner cover of plain cloth. Over this goes the cover, making the visible part of the upholstery. Around its edges, if they go directly on to wood, there is a strip of *gimp*, which is a tapelike material obtainable in many colors and with a patterned surface. This is attached with *gimp pins*, which are small black nails that are inconspicuous after they have been driven.

In modern upholstery some of the stages described can be omitted, as the foam filling takes the place of the stuffing which had to be built up and held in place and in shape. For the best work, cloth and springs have their uses. Webbing still makes a good base, and it is common to finish edges with gimp. There are some special springs to stretch across frames, something like webbing that provides springing without using coils. Rubber webbing has also taken the place of some earlier springing.

There is an almost unlimited range of outer materials. For ease in covering, some stretch in both directions is desirable. Leather is rarely used, but there are simulated leathers consisting of plastic on a fabric backing. Most of these are usually much more flexible if fitted when warm. Woven cloths usually have enough stretch for easy fitting. Usually the weave is parallel to the frame sides, but if there is a taper it will be square to the centerline. If you choose a fabric with a prominent pattern, you must allow for cutting some waste. You will have to center a pattern on the seat or back.

Zip fasteners are much used today. They allow a filling to be removed, so the cover can be laundered. In some cases they merely take the place of a line of sewing that would otherwise have to be done by hand after assembly.

UPHOLSTERED STOOL

A stool at a height rather less than that of a normal chair is useful for a child or for an adult needing to sit low. It can also become a footstool for use with a chair. An upholstered top adds to comfort, but it should not be used if the stool is intended to be stood on. There are many possible ways of making stools, but this one gets its stiffness from deep top rails, so there is no need for lower rails. The upholstered top is given an appearance of sumptuousness by taking the covering cloth deeper than the padding it encloses (Fig. 10-3).

The legs taper below the rails on the inner surfaces only (Fig. 10-4A). Mark the four legs together to get matching lengths and joint details. For the best construction use mortise and tenon joints, but the rails can be doweled to the legs. The joints are shown with wide barefaced tenons (Fig. 10-4B). Alternatively use four ⅜-inch dowels in each joint (Fig. 10-4C). Mark all cut edges with a knife and see that opposite rails are marked together, so their lengths are the same.

As there are no lower rails to hold the parts squarely, be careful that legs and rails are assembled square with each other and remain so while the glue is setting. If clamps are unavailable, hammer joints together with scrap wood to avoid hammer marks. Drive thin nails into the tenons from inside the legs to hold them while the glue sets.

The outsides of the rails should finish level with the outsides of the legs. Make a plywood top and drill a few holes in it to allow air through as the filling expands and contracts in use. Glue and screw or nail the top on (Fig. 10-4D), then plane the plywood level with the frame. Remove its sharp edges, but do not round it excessively.

Use a piece of plastic foam or sponge rubber about 2 inches thick for the filling, and trim this to about ½-inch overlap all round. Use a sharp knife to bevel the underside all round (Fig. 10-5A). If the covering is to be plastic-coated fabric or simulated leather, that can be put on direct. If a cloth is chosen for the covering, it is advisable to use a piece of *calico* or other plain flexible cloth first. Tack its center to one rail and stretch over the foam to tack at the other side. Do the same centrally the other way. From these central tacks, work outward toward the corners. Pull each place against an opposing tack at the other side and try to get the foam drawn down evenly. Tacks will probably have to be 1½ inches or a little less apart. Work a short distance down from the top plywood and keep the tacks in line (Fig. 10-5B).

Pull down diagonally at the corners to get a neat shape. Fold as necessary to allow tacks to hold the shape. Use a knife to cut the surplus cloth below the tacks. Use the same method with the outer material, but let the lines of tacks come just below the first ones (Fig. 10-5C). As far as possible, arrange the tacks to come between as well as below the first ones, so they tend to level out any unevenness still apparent in the padding after the first layer of cloth. If the outer cloth has a bold pattern, you may have to arrange the cloth so the pattern is central or symmetrical.

Be careful to get all the tacks in straight lines and at the same level all round. When you are satisfied with the tacking, trim the cloth below the line of tacks. Cover this with a strip of *gimp*, which is a tapelike material available in many patterns to match the covering cloth. Fasten the gimp with small nails, preferably the type colored black and sold as gimp pins (Fig. 10-5D). If you have covered with plastic-coated fabric, a strip of that can be used instead of gimp. It may be held with nails having decorative heads.

Any staining, varnishing, or polishing is best done before the upholstery. Because handling may affect the finish on the wood, it is advisable to leave the last coat or a final rub with polish until the covering has been completed.

Materials List for the Upholstered Stool

4 legs	1½ × 13 × 1½
2 rails	4 × 18 × ¾
2 rails	4 × 11 × ¾
1 top	11 × 18 × ½ plywood

UPHOLSTERED STOOL WITH A LOOSE SEAT

One of the commonest chair forms has a seat that lifts out. A stool with a similar upholstered lift-out seat is an interesting and useful project to tackle before making a chair, with its more complicated construction. If the stool is at chair height, it can be used as an extra seat at the table, a piano stool, a seat before a dresser, or as a spare seat for adult use.

Legs and Rails

The example is shown with turned legs (Figs. 10-6 and 10-7). The lower rails are also turned, and the general effect with the patterned upholstered top is of richness and quality. A similar stool can be made with square legs and rails, but a craftsman with a small lathe will find this a

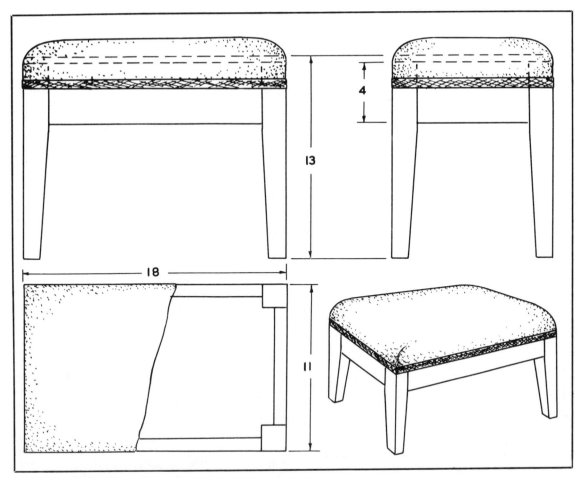

Fig. 10-3. A stool with an upholstered top.

worthwhile piece of furniture on which to exercise his skill at wood turning.

The turned legs are left square where the joints come (Fig. 10-8A). Carefully center the wood in the lathe. Otherwise, the square parts will not be concentric with the round parts, and the curves where they meet will be uneven. Turn the legs with their tops toward the lathe headstock. Leave an inch or so of extra length there to be trimmed off later. Turn one leg without too much regard to the measurements of details. Use this as a pattern while making the other three legs to match. It helps to mark a rod to use as a gauge when turning the other legs (Fig. 10-8B).

The lower rails have to be matched in pairs, but the longer ones are the same as the shorter ones, with extra length at the ends (Fig. 10-8C). Be careful to get the beads central. Lengths need not be cut in the lathe, as a

little excess can be sawed off later. It is important that the diameters at the ends fit the holes that will be drilled in the legs. Use the same bit in a piece of scrap wood to make a template for trying on the rail ends.

The top rails are the same thickness as the tops of the legs, but a rabbet is cut to take the lift-out seat (Fig. 10-9A). Tenons at the corners have one face level with the rim and are haunched (Fig. 10-9B).

Mark out all four legs together. Get their bottoms level and use a square to mark the tops, including the sizes of the mortises and the positions of the holes for the lower rails. These holes are staggered just enough for the rail ends to overlap (Fig. 10-9C). When you cut the mortises, also cut down the inner corners of the legs to the level of the rabbets to take the top (Fig. 10-9D).

Assemble the pair of opposite long sides first. As there is no definite stop when the lower rails go into their

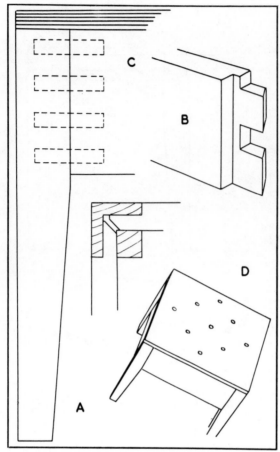

Fig. 10-4. Constructional details of a stool with an upholstered top.

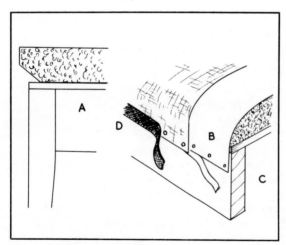

Fig. 10-5. Steps in upholstering the stool.

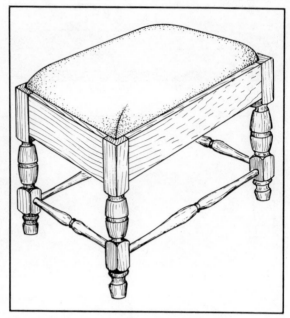

Fig. 10-6. A stool with a lift-out upholstered top.

holes, check with a square at the top and measure between the squares at the lower positions. It will help to compare diagonals. Besides clamping the top joints, drive thin nails or pins into the insides of the legs through the ends of the lower rails.

Assemble the rails the other way. Because the stool will be without a permanent top to keep it in shape, there should be some stiffening gussets put in the corners (Fig. 10-9E). Cut then with the grain diagonally across the angle. Make sure the faces that go across the corners are truly square. It helps in getting a close fit to cut off a small amount in the corner. Attach these gussets with glue and screws, but keep them below the level of the rabbets.

Seat

It is possible to make the seat of a piece of plywood and upholster over it, but a more comfortable seat can be made with webbing over a frame. This is commonly used on chairs, and the stool makes a good practice piece for anyone hoping to go on to more advanced upholstery.

The frame has to fit in the recess, so it is reasonably tight after the upholstery has been done. Both pieces of covering material should be obtained before making the frame to allow for the total thickness. It will be possible to plane something off the frame after it is assembled, but it is better not to have to remove much. You cannot adjust the size of the frame after covering has been done, except

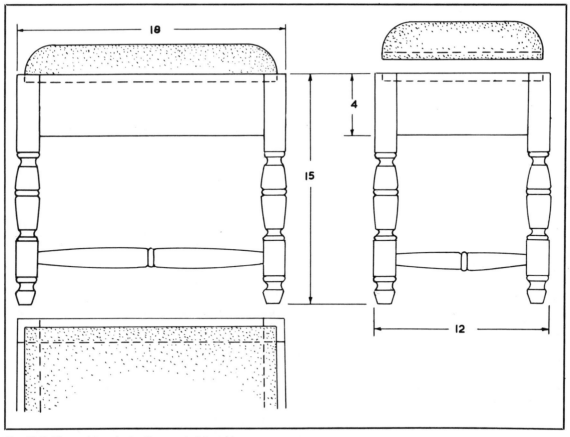

Fig. 10-7. Sizes of the stool with an upholstered top.

for packing with cardboard or cloth if the seat will otherwise finish too loose.

Frame corners can be doweled (Fig. 10-10A). Haunched mortise and tenon joints can be used, but there is little strain and the joints will not show. Open mortise and tenon, or bridle, joints can be cut (Fig. 10-10B). Besides glue, a screw can be put through each corner. Trim the frame to fit the stool recess. If your workmanship has not been perfect, you may have to settle for the top going in one way only. That does not matter, but reference marks underneath will show which way to put the top in. The frame is thicker than the lip of the stool top. Taper around the top for a neat finish (Fig. 10-10C). Take sharpness off the wood at the edges and corners, but do not round it.

Most upholstery webbing is about 2 inches wide. Space the webbing so the gaps between pieces are not much more than the width of the webbing. Use tacks ⅜ inch or ½ inch long for attaching the webbing. Small

large-headed nails can be used. It is possible to strain the webbing with a short length of wood. If you are unlikely to be doing more upholstery, that is a satisfactory method. If you expect to do more upholstery, it is worthwhile making or buying a proper webbing strainer.

There are several types of strainer, but a simple one is a slotted piece of wood used with a dowel rod (Fig. 10-11A). Sizes are suggested, but the important consideration is the slot rather wider than the webbing and with space to easily pass a loop (Fig. 10-11B). Secure the rod with a piece of cord so it does not get lost.

Tack near the end of a piece of webbing with two or three tacks (Fig. 10-12A). Fold over the end and tack through that (Fig. 10-12B). You have to stretch each piece of webbing across the frame with as much tension as can reasonably be applied. If a piece of scrap wood is used, fold the webbing over it and lever downward (Fig. 10-12C). Otherwise, use the strainer you have made for the same purpose. With the first piece of webbing, put a

227

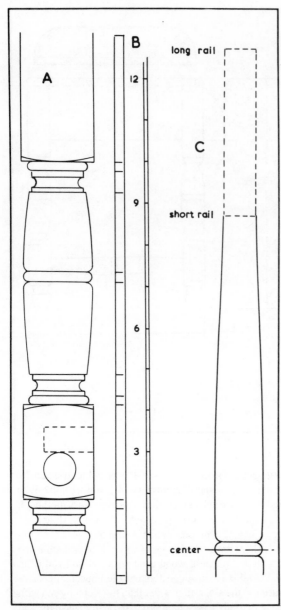

Fig. 10-8. The turned stool leg and rail shapes.

You can tack a piece of plain cloth directly over the webbing, but it should be satisfactory to put most types of plastic or rubber foam directly on the webbing. Foam 2 inches thick should be satisfactory. Have it slightly oversize and bevel all round its lower edges. Cover it first with a piece of plain cloth, stretching first near the centers of opposite sides to pull the foam to shape (Fig. 10-12G). Tack underneath far enough in for the lines of tacks to come inside the lines of the stool rails (Fig. 10-12). When putting on the outside covering material, get sufficient tension. The inner cloth should be pulling the foam to shape. Take this cloth further in underneath the frame and turn in its edge for tacking (Fig. 10-12J).

At each corner pull diagonally over the point to get the visible part free from creases, or as free as the particular material will allow. Cut into the cloth on the underside to avoid the buildup of thicknesses that will occur with folds there (Fig. 10-12K).

The top should fit in the stool tight enough to stay in place in normal use, but a push from below should release it. If the finished top is found to be too loose, release the cloth from one side and put a strip of cardboard or cloth underneath to increase the size.

Materials List for the
Upholstered Stool with a Loose Seat

4 legs	1¾×16×1¾
2 top rails	4×18×¾
2 top rails	4×12×¾
2 bottom rails	1½×18×1½
2 bottom rails	1½×12×1½
2 seat frames	1¾×18×¾
2 seat frames	1¾×12×¾

DRESSER STOOL

This seat is intended for use in the bedroom, particularly for sitting in front of a dresser. The stool is light and has hand grips at the ends, so it can be easily carried for use elsewhere. It can be used for general seating at a table or will serve as a piano stool. Construction is entirely with dowels. All of the wood is ⅞ inch thick, and ½-inch dowels are suitable.

The woodwork should match other furniture (Fig. 10-13), and the covering of the seat should not conflict with other cloth used for bed covering or drapes. The sizes given (Fig. 10-14) should suit most situations, but they can be adapted. If the stool is made much bigger, the sections of wood have to be increased.

There are two similar end frames which should be made first—joined by lengthwise rails and with the upholstered seat screwed on. The seat is not intended to be

pencil mark on its edge level with the edge of the frame before stretching, then another pencil mark after stretching. Use this as a guide to the amount of stretch to put in the other pieces. Tack the stretched webbing (Fig. 10-12D), then cut it off with enough to fold back and tack again (Fig. 10-12E). Interweave the strips of webbing (Fig. 10-12F).

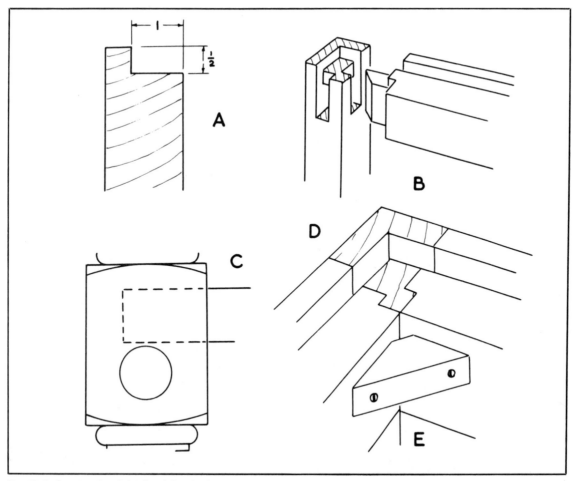

Fig. 10-9. Constructional details of the stool.

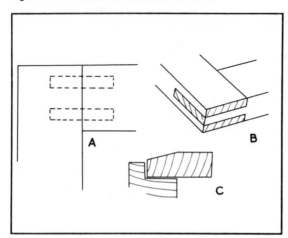

Fig. 10-10. Corner joints and section of the stool top.

removable, but it can be released if the upholstery has to be renewed because of wear, or to alter it to match new surroundings.

All the rails are shown with shaped edges. The curves on the undersides of the top rails are the same as those on the bottom rails. Lack of symmetry is very apparent to a viewer, so use a template to mark the curves. A half length will do (Fig. 10-15A), and it can be turned over. Clean off saw marks with a Surform tool or spokeshave followed by sanding. Take off sharpness so the corners of the sections are rounded (Fig. 10-15B). A spindle molding cutter will do this uniformly, or you can shape by hand carefully. Finish by sanding. At the ends leave the section with square corners, running off to rounding a short distance along.

Mark out the legs with the rails' positions (Fig. 10-15C). Shaping can be done at the bottoms, but leave

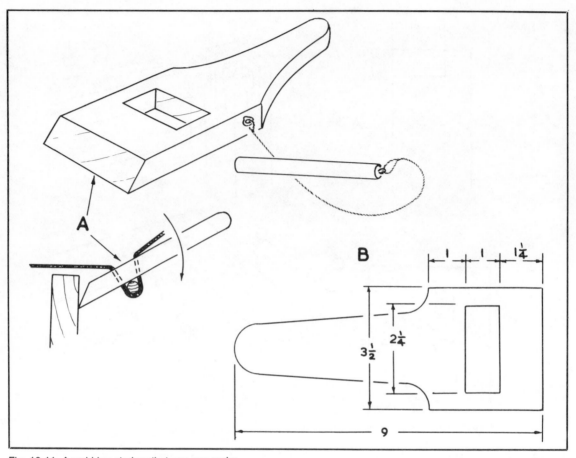

Fig. 10-11. A webbing strainer that you can make.

some excess wood at the other end to be trimmed to the curve of the top rail after that has been joined.

For doweled joints, it is important that the ends are cut squarely. Mark the lengths of matching rails together. Cut all round with a knife against a square and saw on the waste side of the lines. Use a plane to bring the ends exactly to the lines. Do all the shaping of edges. The tops of the ends are curved, but an elliptical curve looks better than one that is part of a circle. You can draw half a curve freehand on a template that can be turned over.

Dowels can be arranged with three in wide rails and two in the narrow ones. Stagger the holes as much as possible. Because of the small available space, slight overlapping cannot be avoided. Do not get the holes in line. Suggested spacings are shown (Fig. 10-16A). Make up the end frames first, clamping tightly and checking squareness (Fig. 10-16B). When the glue has set, shape the tops of the legs to continue the curve of the rails. If

you have to plane any uneven joints level, do it at this stage. Getting the surfaces to a good finish is easier now than after making up into the stool.

Stiffness is provided by gussets in the corners under the top (Fig. 10-16C). They can be screwed and glued in place, but they will be stronger with dowels one way. They can then be attached to the rails before further assembly and checked square before the stool is made up.

If there are to be lifting handles on the ends, make them and fit them before joining in the side rails. They curve down to the surface at the ends and should be given a curved section (Fig. 10-16D). Screw from inside.

Dowel holes in the end frames should be taken as deeply as possible, without the point of the drill breaking through. If you have a *Forstner bit*, that will go deeper as it does not have a projecting center point. Go about 1 inch into the end grain of the rails (Fig. 10-16E). Assemble the rails to the end frames with clamps if possible. Check

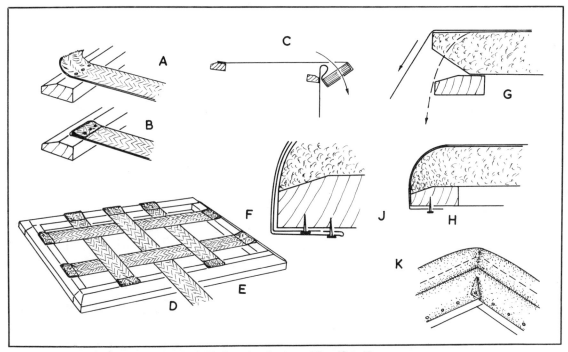

Fig. 10-12. How the webbing is fitted (A to F). Covering the foam filling (G to K).

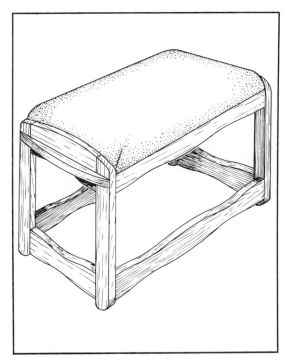

Fig. 10-13. A dresser stool with a padded seat.

squareness in all directions. Screw the gussets into the end frames.

The top is a piece of plywood—upholstered in a similar way to that described for other stools. It will be screwed down, and the ends of the upholstery will not show. You can put gimp along the exposed edges and carry it a short distance on to the ends. Trim the plywood to a size that will allow the finished top to fit tightly between the ends and with the long edges level. Put a few holes in the plywood to allow air movement, as the padding expands and contracts in use.

It should be sufficient to arrange for screwing upward through the gussets (Fig. 10-16F). Make a trial assembly, then remove the seat while the woodwork is finally sanded, stained, and polished or varnished.

Materials List for Dresser Stool

4 legs	1¾×19×⅞
2 top rails	4½×12×⅞
2 bottom rails	3½×12×⅞
12 top side rails	2½×20×⅞
2 bottom side rails	2½×20×⅞
4 gussets	2×3×⅞
2 handles	⅞×15×⅞
1 top	14×20×½ plywood

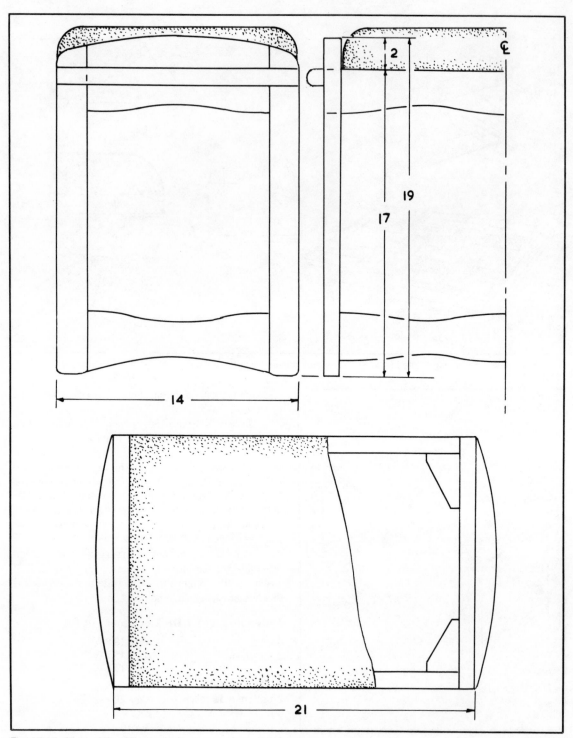

Fig. 10-14. Sizes of the dresser stool.

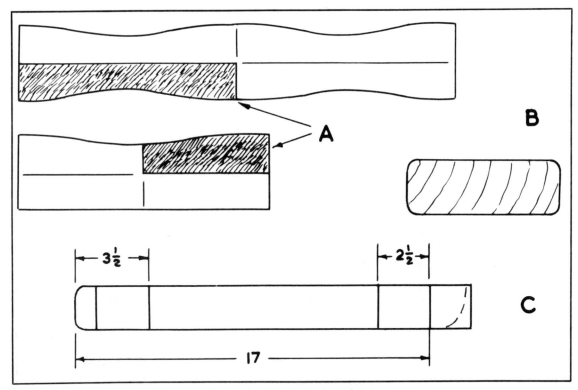

Fig. 10-15. The shaped parts of the stool frame showing the use of templates.

BUTTON-TOPPED STOOL

At one time buttoning was necessary to keep the many particles of material used as filling from moving about. With foam there is little fear of movement, but buttoned upholstery has become accepted as representative of good quality. Anything with a buttoned surface may be considered superior to a similar thing without one. A decorative pattern of buttons also breaks up a large expanse of plain material.

This attractive stool will provide the craftsman with an opportunity to deal with buttons on work of simple construction. The stool has an upholstered top with six buttons supported by splayed legs (Fig. 10-17). The top is made as one unit, complete with its upholstery, and then it is attached to the underpart of legs and rails (Fig. 10-18).

The amount of flare on the legs is the same both ways. Draw a half side view (Fig. 10-19A) and mark on it half the end view. This will give you the angles. Mark the legs from this and give them a taper on the inner surfaces from below the rails (Fig. 10-19B). Also, mark the rails for tenons or dowels (Fig. 10-19C). Bevel the top edges

of the rails, but leave beveling the tops of the legs until after the parts are assembled. Make up in the usual way by first gluing up opposite sides as a pair, then join the rails the other way. Because of the flare, make some slight adjustment to the angles of the shoulders to get close joints.

It is possible to attach the top with pocket screws driven upward from inside the rails. One screw near each corner is enough. As shown (Fig. 10-19D), the insides of the top framing are made level with the insides of the rails, so small plywood gussets can be used near each corner (Fig. 10-19E).

Frame a piece of plywood for the top, but adjust the size so the insides of the top framing can be beveled to match the rails of the lower part. There is no need to use halving joints at the corners. The top frame can be mitered, and the plywood can be glued and nailed on (Fig. 10-19F).

The covering can be any cloth to match other furniture. If there is no special selection, the stool looks well if covered with simulated leather. It has to be made in three parts, if folds at the corners are to be avoided. In any case,

233

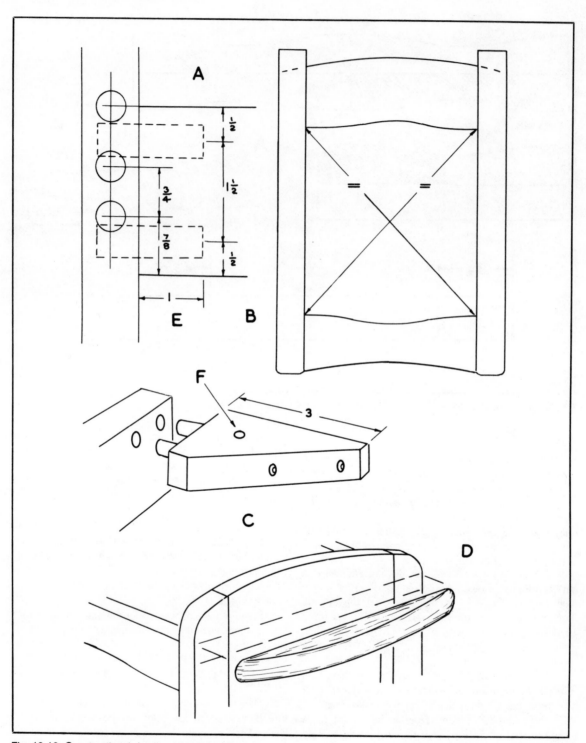

Fig. 10-16. Constructional details of the stool frame.

Fig. 10-17. A button-topped upholstered stool.

the more boxlike appearance suits a buttoned appearance better.

Cut one piece of cloth long enough to wrap across the stool over a block of foam about 2 inches thick. When you cut the foam, make it about ¼ inch too big all round, so it will compress as the cloth is tightened. Otherwise, it is liable to finish with a hard line at the edge of the plywood. Cut more cloth for the ends and allow about ½ inch around the seams (Fig. 10-20A) for sewing. Put these pieces together inside out (Fig. 10-20B), so that after making the seams you can turn the cloth the right way and show a close joint (Fig. 10-20C).

Drill ¼-inch holes through the plywood for the six button positions (Fig. 10-20D). Put the plywood on the inverted cover and mark through. Prick through at these positions, so you can see where the buttons have to come on the top. This is safer than pushing through the foam after the top has been fitted. You may not get the holes exactly in line on the top surface, where an error is obvious.

Put the top on over the foam filling and tack underneath in the usual way (Fig. 10-20E). Make sure the button holes on top form a symmetrical pattern.

Use a mattress needle about 6 inches long that is threaded with stout twine. The buttons should be of a color that either matches the covering or makes a pleasing contrast with it. It is possible to get buttons covered with the same material. For the underside you can use similar buttons, but ordinary two-hole buttons (Fig. 10-

21A), pieces of dowel rod, or square-section strips (Fig. 10-21B) drilled across will do.

Use a needle to thread the twine through, so you take up the button on top and have the thread hanging below. You can probably take the double twine through in one pass (Fig. 10-21C).

You have to tie the twine, so there is sufficient tension on each button and the same amount of tension on all of them. You need a knot that can be adjusted and then locked. An upholsterer favors a type of figure eight slip knot. Hold one end straight, then take the other around it (Fig. 10-21D). Go behind both parts, across the front (Fig. 10-21E), and under the twist (Fig. 10-21F). You can adjust the tension by sliding the knot, but there will be enough friction to keep it where you leave it. Tighten so each button is sunk below the surface (Fig. 10-21G). When you are satisfied, knot the two ends together. Work the wide knot up through the plywood, so it is out of sight in the foam.

Mount the seat on its support. There is no need to fit plywood gussets all round. A piece about 2 inches wide into the long side near each corner should be sufficient (Figs. 10-19D and 10-19E).

Materials List for Button-Topped Stool

4 legs	2×12×2
2 rails	3×17×⅞
2 rails	3×9×⅞
1 top	12×20×¼ plywood
2 top frames	2½×21×¾
2 top frames	2½×13×¾

DINING CHAIR WITH PADDED SEAT

Table chairs vary from very austere angular ones, with little concession to comfort, to those which are shaped and upholstered to fit the human form closely and let a person sit there for a while without needing to change his posture. The latter chairs are obviously intended for more leisurely meals, while the other type is best when you are expected to eat and be away quickly. Most of us need chairs that come somewhere between the two. The chair in Fig. 10-22 is of that type.

The front legs are upright. The seat is level, but it narrows toward the back and has crosswise rails which are slightly hollowed. The back leg flares outward for wider support on the floor. The upper part leans back slightly, with a hollowed top rail and a straight central splat. The seat lifts out and is padded, but not fully upholstered (Fig. 10-23). Construction is straightforward, and a craftsman with limited shop equipment

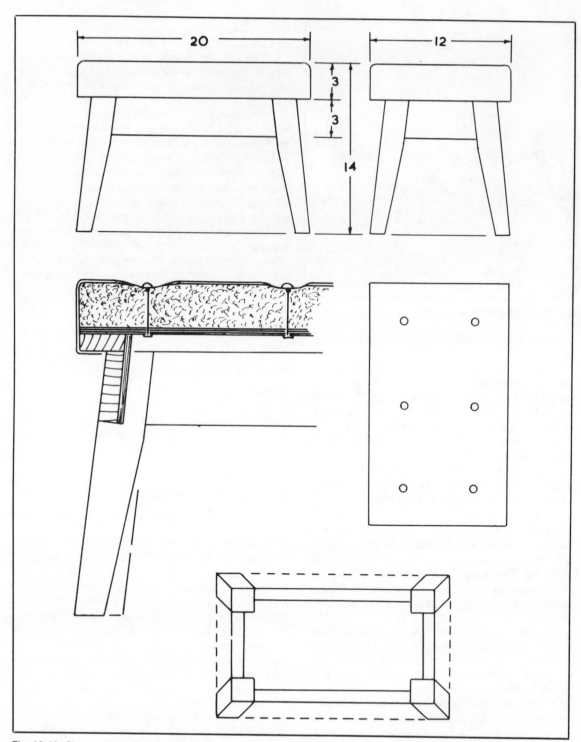

Fig. 10-18. Sizes and section of the button-topped stool.

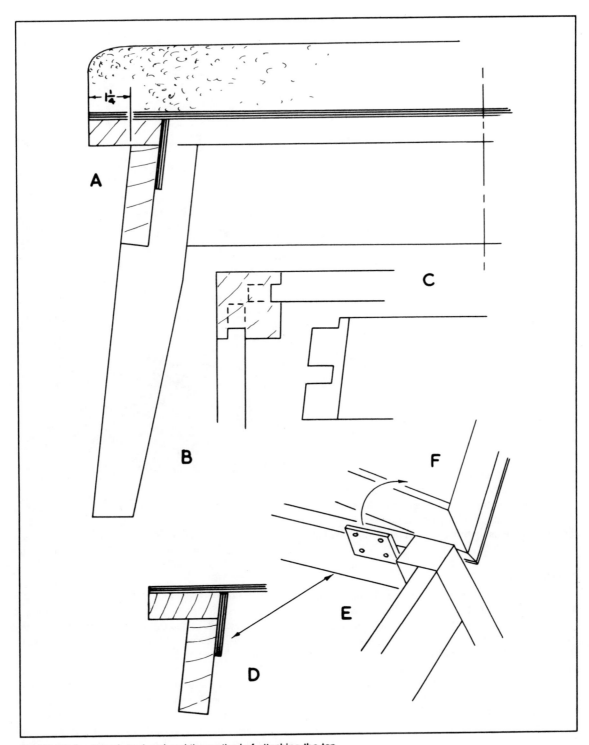

Fig. 10-19. Section of stool end and the method of attaching the top.

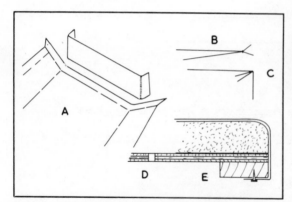

Fig. 10-20. Making up the upholstered top of the stool.

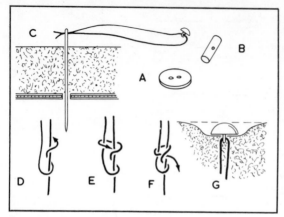

Fig. 10-21. Steps in buttoning and the knot to use.

should be able to make a set of four or six chairs without too much difficulty. If more than one chair is to be made, it is better to do everything to all chairs at the same time than to make one chair before starting on the others. They are more likely to match, and the overall working time should be less.

Making the Legs

Start with the legs. The rear leg shape fits on a 4-inch piece of wood (Fig. 10-24A). Mark the position of the seat rail joint. Keep that edge straight for 1½ or 2 inches above and below the rail, then draw straight tapers to the top and bottom. Blend the lines into the edge with curves. For the back edge, allow for a width of 1½ inches or a little more at the seat level. Taper to 1¼ inches wide at top and bottom. The cut can follow a flowing curve, without a flat comparable to the front at the seat level.

The front legs (Fig. 10-24B) come a short distance above the seat level and will be rounded after the joints

Fig. 10-22. A dining chair with a lift-out seat.

have been cut. In the simplest chair the front legs are square for their full length, but they look attractive if turned. Details are given later.

Preparing the Rails and Back Splat

Prepare the wood for all other parts. The bottom rails, seat side rails, and the splat are flat. You have to allow for cutting curves with all other pieces. A band saw is useful for these cuts, but they can be shaped with hand tools.

Start with the front seat rail. It starts 2½ inches deep, but finishes 2 inches deep, with a ½-inch curve at the center (Fig. 10-24C). Allow for straight tenons at the ends, or you can cut level and use dowels. Curves of this sort are most simply drawn by springing a steel rule or a

238

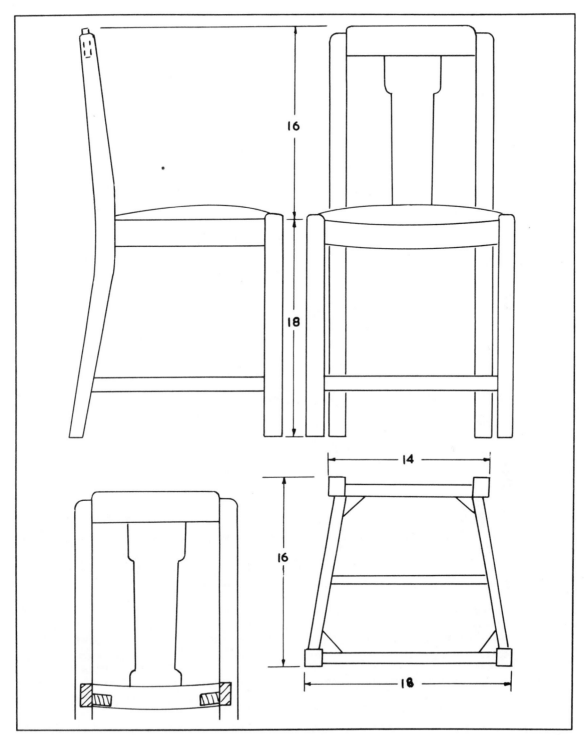

Fig. 10-23. Sizes of a dining chair with a lift-out seat.

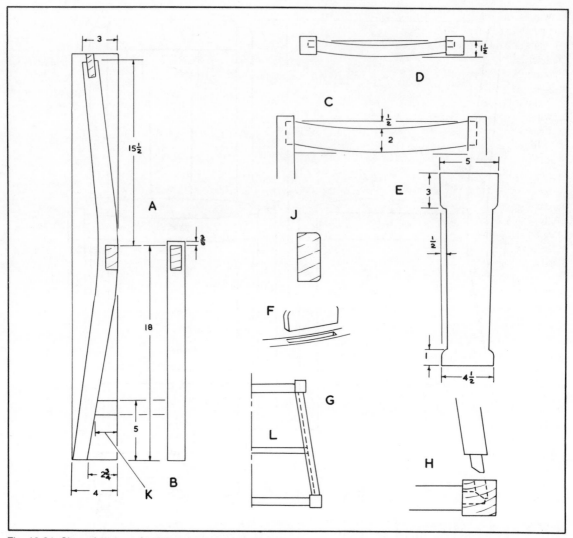

Fig. 10-24. Shaped parts and constructional details of the chair.

thin wood lath through the ends and a center point, then pencil around it.

The back seat rail is similar but shorter. Mark its length and an allowance for tenons. Use the front rail as a template, arranged symmetrically about centerlines, to mark the curves.

The top back rail also has a ½-inch deep curve, but cut the thicker way (Fig. 10-24D). Mark that out with a tenon allowance, then draw and cut the curves.

Clean up the curved cut surfaces. If the saw cuts are close to the line, there will not be much further work, but you must completely remove the saw marks. A curved

plane is useful. You can use chisels and scrapers as well as abrasive paper, working through from coarse to fine grits.

Use your own ideas about the shape of the back splat, but a simple outline is shown (Fig. 10-24E). You can fret decorative holes in it—either geometric, floral, or badges. The outline can have curves. You can carve the surface. As the wood is only ⅜ inch thick, it cannot be further thinned to make tenons. The rails can be given shallow full-size mortises for the splat ends (Fig. 10-24F).

The amount of taper in the seat is enough to make it necessary to cut the side joints at an angle. Make a half drawing of the seat plan full-size (Fig. 10-24G). Use this as a guide to the angle you will cut the shoulders on the rail ends and chop the mortises (Fig. 10-24H). Note that the back and side rails have their inner edges level with the corners of the rear legs, but at the front corners the rails are central in the leg section.

Make the side seat rails to the sizes on your full-size drawing. These rails and the other seat rails are square in section, but you can round their outer corners (Fig. 10-24J). Treat the bottom rails in a similar way, but you have to get their lengths to allow for the slope of the back legs. You can note how much longer they are from the side view of the leg (Fig. 10-24K), or you may prefer to make a full-size drawing of the chair's side view. There is a single crosswise rail between these bottom rails, and you can get its length by drawing the rails on the half drawing of the seat. This will also show you the angle to cut the mortise and tenon joints between the rails (Fig. 10-24L).

Assembling the Chair Frame Parts

The chair frame parts are now all ready for assembly, but the lift-out seat frame has to be given matching curves at back and front. Mark these curves from the adjoining seat rails before assembling the chair frame (Fig. 10-25A). Lengths of the seat parts are better left to mark from the assembled chair.

There are brackets at the corners of the chair frame which serve to strengthen the chair and act as supports for the seat. The brackets are simple triangles at the rear (Fig. 10-25B), but they have to be notched around the legs at the front (Fig. 10-25C), although the notches need not fit closely to the legs. Additionally, you have to slope the brackets in a crosswise direction to follow the curve across the seat (Fig. 10-25D). Make these brackets from your drawing, but there must be final fitting by planing edges as you assemble the chair.

Start by assembling the back and front. At the front the only joints are at the top, yet it is important that the corners are square to get the legs upright. Round the tops of the legs before assembly. They will be very obvious in the finished chair, so get the curves smooth and matching. It will help in keeping shape to put a temporary piece of the right length between the lower parts of the legs (Fig. 10-25E) while clamping. That may be advisable at the bottoms of the rear legs, but the other parts should keep the legs parallel.

Let the glue in these joints set, then add the other rails. Check the shape by measuring diagonals on the seat level (Fig. 10-25F). Fit the brackets with glue and screws. Make sure their top surfaces are a suitable dis-tance down from the rail edges to suit the seat. If you follow the sizes in the materials list, this will be ⅞ inch. Check your actual pieces of wood and plywood.

Make the back and front parts of the seat frame curved and the side parts straight. The corners can be lapped, but a bridle joint is better (Fig. 10-26A). You have to judge the size of the frame to make a close fit in the chair when the upholstery material is wrapped around. If you use woven cloth, that may have another piece of plain cloth underneath. If you use plastic-coated fabric, such as simulated leather cloth, that will not need another thickness. Notch the front corners to fit around the tops of legs (Fig. 10-26B). Spring the plywood to the curve and glue and nail it on (Fig. 10-26C).

Padding the Seat

For padding the seat, cut a piece of plastic or rubber foam slightly too large. For normal use, it need not be much thicker than 1 inch. Bevel beneath the outer edges, so they will curve down smoothly. If the seat is to be woven cloth, first cover with a thin piece of plain material. Otherwise, the cover goes on in one thickness.

Pull the material over and tack underneath (Fig. 10-26D). Start near the centers of opposite sides and work toward the corners. Space the tacks to suit the material, but about 1-inch intervals should give the top a smooth appearance. At the rear corners, cut and fold so one part overlaps the other (Fig. 10-26E). At the notched front corners, a flexible material may be pulled extra hard into the hollow sufficiently to fit into the chair. Otherwise, cut partly through the thickness, so there is something left to pull the shape without the cuts showing above. Lap the parts (Fig. 10-26F). Be careful not to build up too great a thickness that will not rest level on the brackets.

Turning the Front Legs

Appearance is improved if the front legs are turned (Fig. 10-27A). You may wish to give them a pattern that matches a table or other furniture. Making the turned part slender within the size limits of the square ends tends to make the leg look rather weak. A round section always looks thinner than a square section of the same size. Thus, it is better to have the turned parts thicker. This means either gluing pieces around a square strip (Fig. 10-27B) or reducing the ends of a thicker piece (Fig. 10-27C). With the small difference of size in these chair legs, it is probably better to reduce the ends.

If you have a jointer or power planer, you can make the reduction by lowering the front table, so you can feed

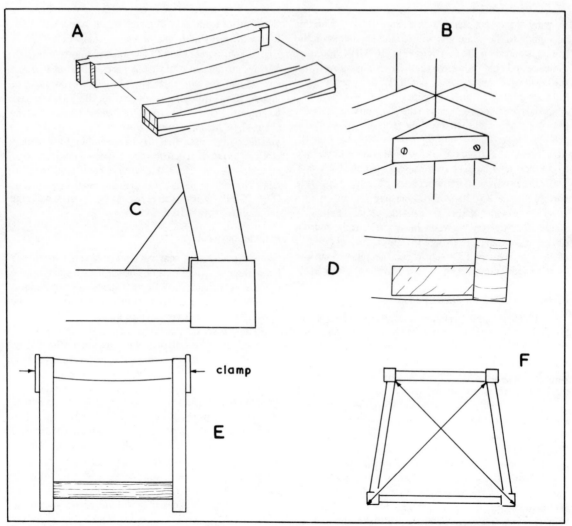

Fig. 10-25. Assembly details of the dining chair.

the wood in as far as you need on all four faces of both ends. You can use a band saw to remove the surplus wood, but you will have to follow by planing the square ends. As it is only the bulbous center that is oversize, you can carry the squares over what will be the end beads.

There are many patterns that the legs can be turned. See Fig. 10-27D. Carefully center the square ends in the lathe, so the turned parts will be true in relation to them. Allow some excess length for trimming later. You can turn a ball or other foot. Use one leg as a guide when turning the other leg. Be certain the turned lengths and greater diameters match. Slight differences in beads and hollows will not be so noticeable.

Materials List for Dining Chair with Padded Seat

2 front legs	1½×19×1½
2 rear legs	4×35×1½
2 side rails	2×16×1
1 front rail	2½×18×1
1 rear rail	2½×14×1
3 bottom rails	1¼×17×⅝
1 top back rail	1½×14×1½
1 back splat	5×16×⅜
2 seat frames	1½×16×⅝
2 seat frames	1½×16×1¼
1 seat	16×16×⅛ plywood

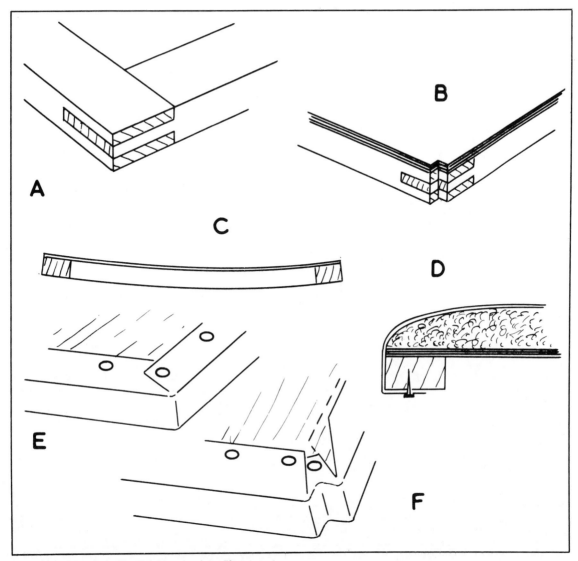

Fig. 10-26. Construction and assembly of the lift-out seat.

OPEN ARM LOUNGE CHAIR

This is a fairly compact comfortable lounging chair, with a built-in upholstered back and a lift-out cushion seat, supported on springs stretched across the sides (Fig. 10-28). Most of the woodwork is visible in the finished chair, so it should be a good quality hardwood with planed and sanded surfaces. The parts inside the back upholstery need not be as highly finished, but they should be a good hardwood for strength.

As with many of the more attractive chairs, there are not many parallel pieces or square corners, so the way to make the first layout is not very obvious. Some of the sizes of parts can only be obtained from a full-size drawing, so draw a side view of the chair (Fig. 10-29) full-size. The dimensions and the scale will help, but the best way is to start with the seat. Make it 21 inches long, 11 inches high at the front, and 10 inches high at the back. The front legs cross it at right angles and the leg drawing (Fig. 10-30A) gives its other sizes. From that drawing, draw in the back and the arm. Notice that the back comes down on top of the seat side, but the rear leg goes up to overlap the back.

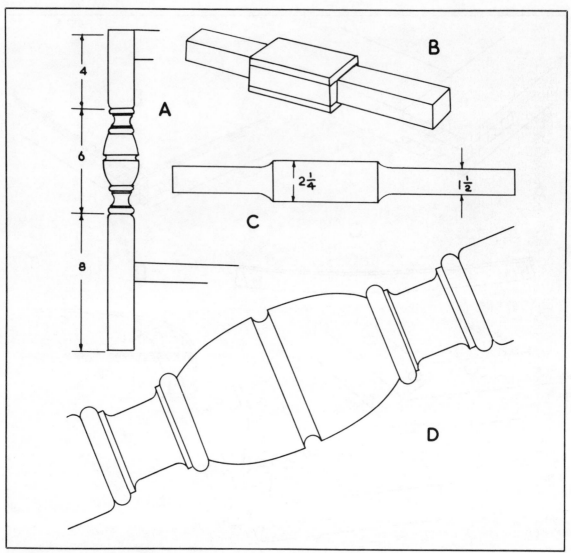

Fig. 10-27. Front leg with enlarged turned center.

Start by making a pair of front legs (Fig. 10-30A). Mark the positions of joints, then cut to curve out below them and finish with a section 1½ inches square. The seat side will be screwed and glued to the legs, but to locate it, make a shallow notch about 3/16 inch deep (Fig. 10-30B). The rail between the legs (Fig. 10-30C) comes below the seat sides, but it is also curved to give clearance and improve appearance. Its ends are shown with tenons into the legs, but it can be doweled.

The exact length of the seat sides must be obtained from your full-size drawing, but prepare strips overlong

at first (Fig. 10-30D). They are shown grooved, so the tension springs can be held with nails through (Fig. 10-30E). Some tension springs are supplied with metal strips to screw on the sides. The sides have to tenon into the legs at the rear of the chair (Fig. 10-30F), and they will also be mortised for the back.

The arms can also be cut (Fig. 10-30G). The arms are straight and parallel the 2½ inch way, but they will be cut to a parallel curve 1 inch thick the other way. Leave them overlong so they can be made the exact length as the chair is assembled. Round the outer edges and inner

Fig. 10-28. A lounge chair with open sides and cushion seat.

edges except for the rear part, which will come against the back and in the vicinity of the front leg joint. Round the front ends both when viewed from above (Fig. 10-31A) and in section. The arms are the most prominent wood parts of the chair. Make sure the finished surfaces do not have any saw marks showing through the sanding or other blemishes. Mark and cut the mortises to take the tenons on the tops of the front legs (Fig. 10-31B).

The back is a rectangular frame (Fig. 10-31C). It depends on the strength of the corner joints to keep it in shape. Barefaced tenons are suggested, but the crossbars can be doweled into the sides. All of the back frame will be enclosed by upholstery, so round edges before assembly to avoid hard lines showing through the cloth. In particular, round the top edges of the top crossbar to a semicircular section and round the top ends of the sides.

The bottoms of the sides tenon into the seat sides (Fig. 10-31D), but cut the tenons and mortises back to miss the nearby tenons on the seat sides (Fig. 10-31E).

The rear legs should first be cut too long, then the mortises for the joints to the seat sides are made (Fig. 10-31F). Trim the bottoms so they will rest flat on the floor. Cut the tops to come against the sides of the back and drill them for screws; two should be enough.

Assembly

When assembling the framework, check symmetry at every stage and make subassemblies first. Put the back together. Measure diagonals and see that it is without twist, then let the glue set. Join the front legs to the seat sides. Glue and one large screw from inside should be sufficient. Put one side over the other so you have a pair. Let that glue set. Put the front rail between the seat sides and join the sides to the back. See that the seat is square and that when you sight from the front, the top parts of the legs are parallel with the sides of the back. Add the rear legs, pulling the joints tight and screwing into the back. The screwheads will be covered by upholstery.

Finally, add the arms. Hold an arm against the top of its front leg and the marked position on the side to get its length. Make it about ¼ inch too long, round its exposed corner, and drill for a dowel (Fig. 10-31G). There may have to be a little adjustment of the mortise, as the front leg does not meet the arm exactly square. Add the arms to complete the framework.

Finish the framework by cleaning off surplus glue, sanding, and staining. There will be some handling of the woodwork during upholstery, and it may be advisable to leave the final coat of polish or varnish until after covering. There is then a risk of marking the cloth. The whole of the arms will be exposed, but there is no need to apply a finish to the back framing down as far as the seat rails.

Covering

Seven tension springs will support the seat (Fig. 10-32). Have one fairly near the front, and the others will come at about 2½-inch intervals. They can be bought in many lengths. Choose a length that will require a moderate amount of tension to fit. Drill for nails across the grooves (Fig. 10-33A). If the springs are bought with a plate, the wood should have been beveled during construction (Fig. 10-33B).

The seat cushion should be fairly thick for maximum comfort. Five inches of foam is ideal, but you may have to settle for less. Cut the foam slightly too wide, so the cushion has to compress between the front legs. That will prevent it moving about, although it can still be lifted out. Locate a manufactured edge of the foam at the front, so there is no doubt about that being straight.

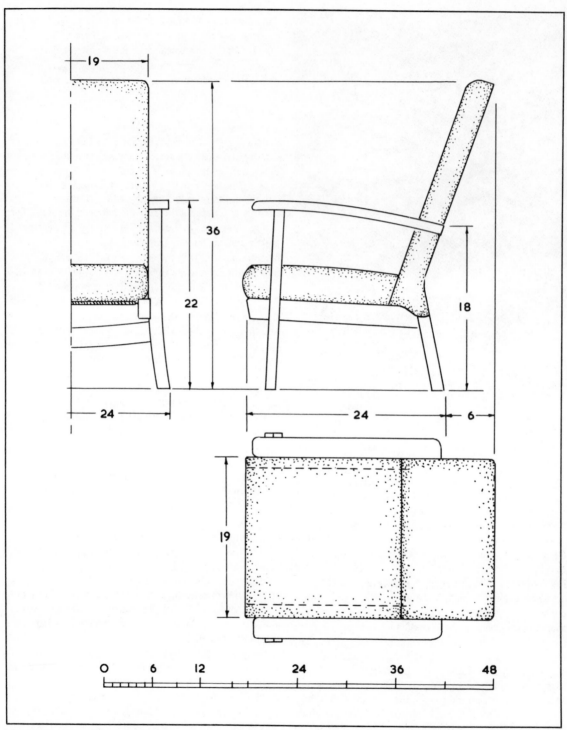

Fig. 10-29. Sizes of the lounge chair.

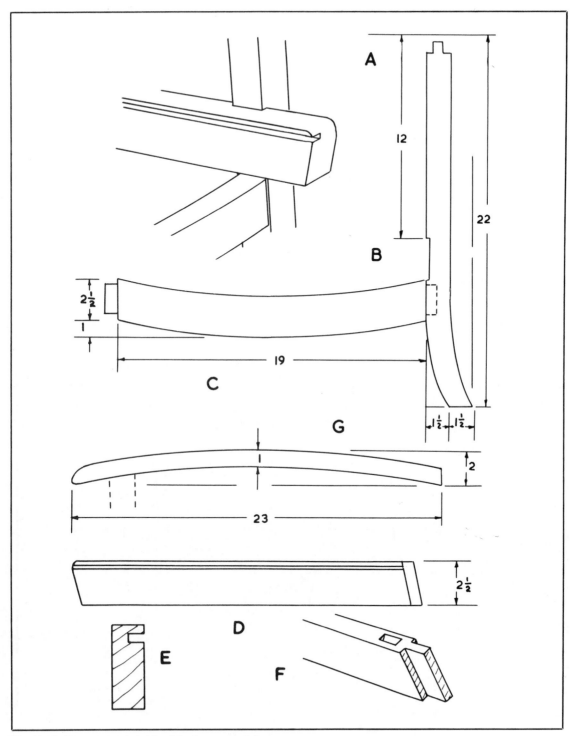

Fig. 10-30. Constructional details of the lounge chair frame.

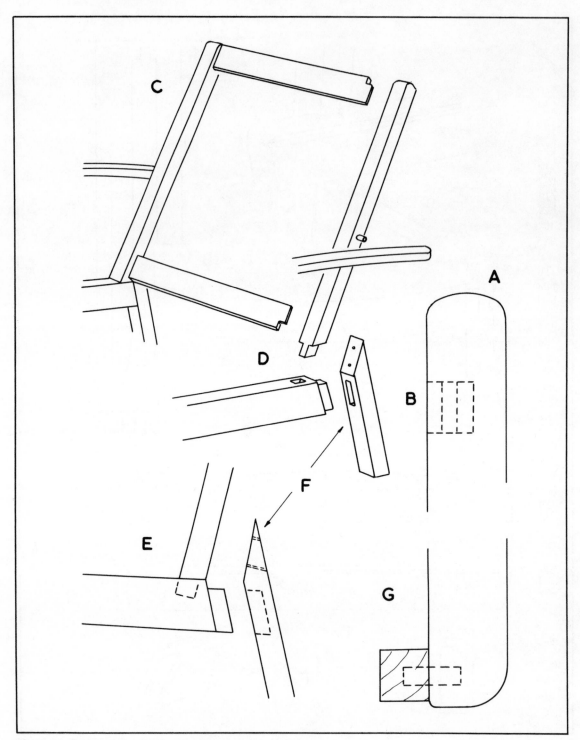

Fig. 10-31. Constructional details of the lounge chair back and arms.

Fig. 10-32. The springs that support the cushion seat in the lounge chair.

The cover forms a *wall-edged cushion*, which can be machine sewed almost all round, except for an opening at the back for putting in the foam block. That may be hand sewed, or you can fit a zip so the filling can be removed and the cover washed or dry cleaned.

Cut pieces of covering material for top and bottom. Allow about ½ inch all round for the seam, but choose a size that will compress the foam slightly. The *walling* should be a strip that is continuous across the front and along the sides, but there can be seams at one or both rear corners where they will not show. Mark the lines of the seams on the undersides of the material. It may help to pin the cloth to the foam. Also, cut darts in the edges that will eventually come inside to act as register marks when you bring the seams together at the sewing machine (Fig. 10-34A).

With the material inside out, sew the top panel to the walling all round. Sew the bottom on similarly, except for

the seam across the back, as this is where the foam will be pushed in. You may be able to sew a short way along the back seam each side and still be able to compress the foam to go through the remaining space. The more machine sewing you can do, the less hand sewing there will have to be.

When you have the covering the right way and the foam put in, the best stitch to close the remaining seam is called *slip stitching* or *blind stitching*. It is a method of hand sewing where very little of each stitch shows outside. Another advantage is that the stitches can be cut easily and picked out when the cover has to be removed.

For light cloth you can manage with a domestic sewing needle, but for heavier materials it is better to have an upholsterer's curved needle. Turn the edges in. Rub along the creases so you can see the folds you have to sew. Take the needle along a fold. Have a knot in the end of the doubled thread. Bring the needle out and into the other fold directly opposite (Fig. 10-34B). Go a short distance along that fold and out again to cross into the first fold (Fig. 10-34C). Continue in this way along the seam (Fig. 10-34D). Pull tight and the seam comes close, with only a small amount of thread showing (Fig. 10-34E). The length to make each additional stitch depends on the material, but going ¼ inch along each seam is a reasonable distance.

If a zipper is preferred, it is most easily put into the walling before that is sewed to the top and bottom panels. Make a cut along what will be the back part of the walling, near the center or just below it, and long enough to admit the compressed foam. Turn under the edges and sew in a zipper (Fig. 10-34F). The walling can then be sewed all round to the top and bottom panels. Remember that the seams are sewed inside out, but the zipper has to have the correct side out in the finished cushion. After sewing, you

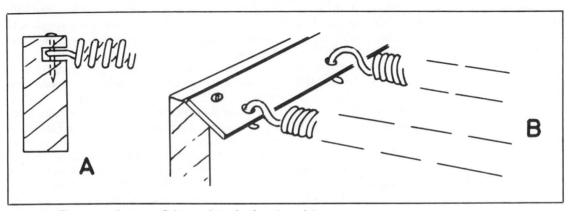

Fig. 10-33. The seat springs may fit into a slot or hook on to a plate.

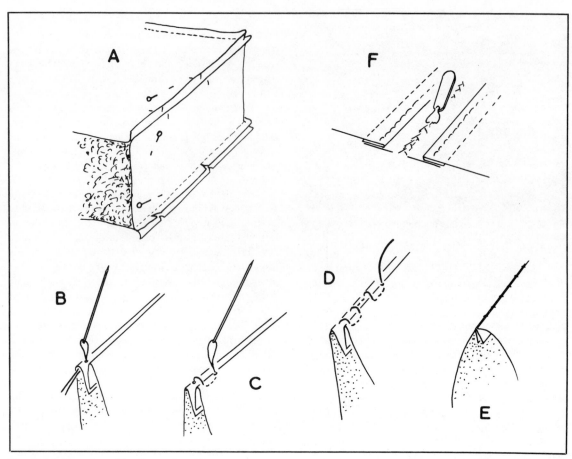

Fig. 10-34. Steps in making the seat cushion.

can turn the cushion the right way by passing all of it through the zip opening.

The chair back has a pattern of webbing and a layer of foam under the covering, which is attached to the woodwork. This is a place where rubber webbing will add to comfort, although plain webbing can be used. Most of the load is taken by crosswise strips, but there can be three upright ones (Fig. 10-35A). Tack to the fronts of the framing, but do not go to the outsides where the edges may show through.

Over this goes a piece of foam about 1½ or 2 inches thick. Make it rather full in the width, so it can be compressed to the wood edges.

It can be stopped at the top edge, but if it is rolled over and a piece is put underneath, there will be a padded headrest (Fig. 10-35B). The covering is sewed up and slipped over, but the foam has to be retained while that is done. It may be sufficient to put a few tacks through the

foam where it goes over the top rail, or it can be held with adhesive. In any case, a piece of foam used as a packing to form a headrest should be retained with a few spots of adhesive. The alternative is to cover the foam first with cloth, which can be cheap open-weave material held around the edges with tacks into the back of the frame (Fig. 10-35C).

Cut the cover in two parts. There are a flat back piece and a front piece brought around to a sewed seam within the width of the frame's back (Fig. 10-35D). You can continue the front over the top and down the back, but it is more economical to use separate pieces. That allows easier shaping around the top corners. Sew the seams inside out and allow some excess cloth at the bottom.

With the cover the right way, pull it down over the back. Check that the filling is in position, and the seams are symmetrical at the back. At the bottom pull the front piece under the rail, turn it in, and tack there (Fig.

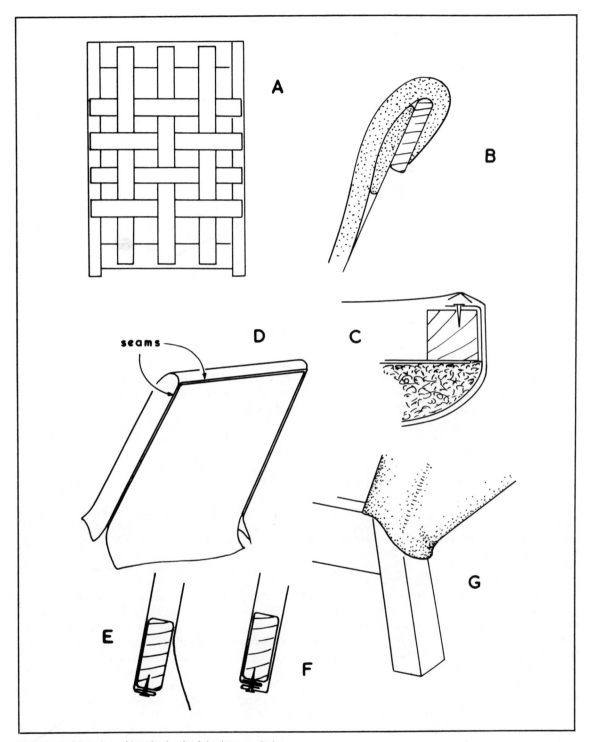

seams

A

B

C

D

E

F

G

Fig. 10-35. Steps in making the back of the lounge chair.

10-35E). The back piece also has to be pulled down and tacked over it (Fig. 10-35F), but allow for the side parts to go around the tops of the rear legs (Fig. 10-35G). Turn the cut edges under and secure these parts with a few tacks. To prevent the cover from moving, also tack down the two sides at about 3-inch intervals to keep the seams straight and parallel.

The seat cushion bears against the back. For a perfect fit there, it can be made with a matching slope. If the cushion is cut square, it can be turned over to even wear on the covering and prevent it from going out of shape.

Materials List for Open Arm Lounge Chair

2 front legs	3×23×1½
2 back legs	1½×15×1½
2 seat sides	2½×23×1
2 arms	2½×24×2
1 front rail	3½×22×1
2 rear sides	1½×32×1½
2 rear rails	3×19×1

CLUB CHAIR

Fully upholstered chairs are in many shapes and sizes. Usually the only parts of the frame that are exposed are the feet. The arms, seat, and back, as well as the front, are covered in cloth or leather. It is difficult to detect the framework through the covering at any point, as there is padding almost everywhere. The seat may be further softened by a fitted cushion that can be lifted out. There is only room here, for one example but chairs of other shapes can be dealt with in a very similar way.

As the frame is not in view, there is no need to give it much of a finish, nor to use complicated joints when simpler ones will do. Failure of the frame is serious after it has been covered, so be sure that it will stand up to normal use. If an antique chair is stripped, you may find that the frame is constructed and finished as if it is to be visible. Such care is unnecessary, providing the chosen construction is sound. Sometimes softwood is used for some parts, but generally it is better to use hardwood with reasonably straight grain. This is a place to use hardwoods that are not sufficiently decorative for furniture when they will show. Do not select wood that has been rejected for other purposes because of large knots or other flaws that will weaken it.

This chair (Fig. 10-36) has a framework that is almost completely straight lines (Fig. 10-37). There is some softening of the lines in the covering, but the shape is a popular modern one. The back of the frame is straight across, but padding will give it shape. The arms widen

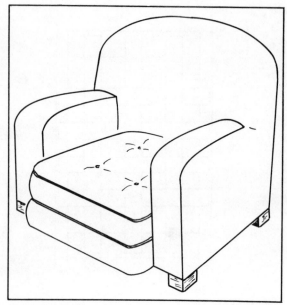

Fig. 10-36. A club chair has nearly all the woodwork hidden by upholstery.

toward the front. The seat projects forward of the arms. The narrower rails around the sides and back are called *gut rails* and are necessary for fitting the seat and the back and arm coverings.

Make a full-size drawing of the side view (Fig. 10-38A). When viewed from above, the seat is slightly wider at the front than at the back (Fig. 10-38B), but that need not be set out full-size. The feet will be blocks put on after the frame has been covered, so there is no need to include them in your drawing.

Start by making the back assembly (Fig. 10-38C). Joints can be mortise and tenon, but it is simpler to use dowels. Take care to get the curve of the top symmetrical, as that sets the curve of the covering and unevenness would be obvious. Take the sharpness off edges, but do not round the parts.

Prepare the arm tops and fronts. The front joints can be doweled or nailed, with stiffening blocks inside (Fig. 10-38D). Round the top of the arm and continue the rounding over the joint and a short distance down the front edges. The gut rails must come at the same height as those in the back. Join these and the arms to the back with dowels, but include stiffening blocks at the arm joints. Keep any stiffening blocks back from the edges, so there is no risk of them showing through the covering.

The two platform pieces that form the front of the seat go behind the fronts of the arms (Fig. 10-38E).

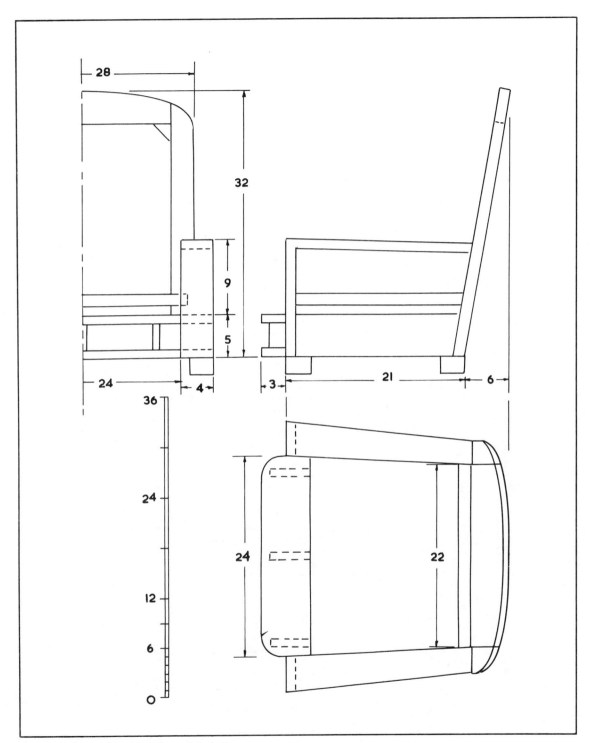

Fig. 10-37. Sizes of the frame for a club chair.

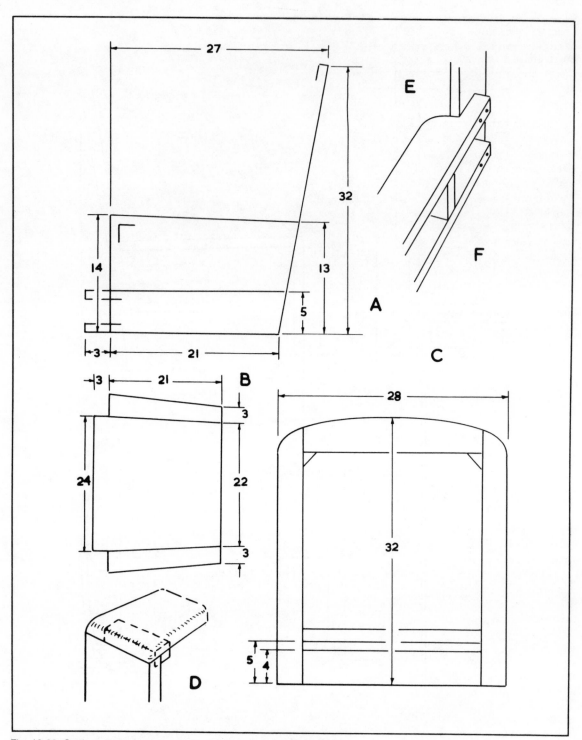

Fig. 10-38. Setting out the chair frame and some constructional details.

Counterbored screws through the laps and a spacing piece between should make strong joints (Fig. 10-38F). Be careful that the two arm assemblies match when sighted across and that the seat is symmetrical.

Seat

In traditional upholstery there is a fairly complex arrangement of coil springs, and this is followed by a sequence of cloths and materials to produce a comfortable seat. Some chairs are quite comfortable with a hard support, such as a piece of plywood, and plenty of foam. There is still some advantage in springing, and that is used here.

Below the bottom edges, put on a pattern of interwoven ordinary webbing—not rubber webbing. Tack securely, as described for a stool, with each end doubled back over the first tacks and tacked again. Choose coil springs that stand about half as high again as the depth of the rails. The weight of a sitter comes more at the front, so one row of springs should come close to the front, but the back row can be further from the edge (Fig. 10-39A).

Use stout twine to sew the springs to the webbing. It may help to chalk around the spring ends on the webbing as a guide to positioning and stitching. Stitch diagonally to the weave (Fig. 10-39B) and knot each stitch, so it is independent, even if you continue to another position without cutting the twine.

Tie across the tops of the springs. Knot at each spring and take the ends down to tie to tacks (Fig. 10-39C). Across the width of the chair, the twine can pull the springs to give a slightly domed top. From back to front, it adds to comfort if you allow the front springs more play, so the twine can be taken through each spring (Fig. 10-39D). Put a piece of burlap or canvas over the springs and tack it down all round. If you have done the tying correctly, this will finish with a domed shape and an even curve down to the edges all round.

Cut a strip of foam to a section to go on the front platform ahead of the springs (Fig. 10-39E). It can be slightly too large to allow for compressing. Cut another piece of foam to go all over the seat. This foam should be 3 inches thick. Let it come up to 1 inch too wide at the front to allow for compressing. The foam can be left full thickness at the back and sides, but the underside at the front may be trimmed at an angle so it will pull to a curve (Fig. 10-39F).

Shaping can be helped with a layer of cotton batting or some thin foam that is not very elastic and less than 1 inch thick. At the front this goes over the padding and on to the top platform piece (Fig. 10-39G). Use muslin or other light cloth to stretch over the seat and hold the padding position with the right shape (Fig. 10-39H). Turn this in and tack all round.

The outer covering will be best left until the arms and back are covered. The method of fitting is described now to complete the sequence of work on the seat.

The outer covering of this chair has the front edge seam piped. Piping is a piece of cord or string enclosed in fabric and sewed into the seam. In some simulated leather work the piping is in a contrasting color, but for cloth covering it is more common to have the piping covered with the same material or a plain material of similar color.

Piping for this purpose can be made around cord about ⅛ inch in diameter. Ready-made piping can be bought, as can special cords, but cotton or other cord of the right size may be used. Sufficient piping should be made up for one piece to go across the front and far enough back at the sides to be hidden by the arms. The cord is sewed into a strip of cloth with about ½ inch left to sew into the seam (Fig. 10-40A). Ideally the cloth is cut diagonally—*on the bias*. This may not produce very long pieces (Fig. 10-40B), but they can be joined. Two pieces overlapped on the diagonal cut and sewed (Fig. 10-40C) will open out, so the joint is inconspicuous. Sew the cord in with a line of stitches as close in as possible. Where the piping has to be taken around the curves, cut a few darts in it (Fig. 10-40D).

You can sew in piping at one pass of the sewing machine, but it is safer at first to sew the piping to one cloth (Fig. 10-40E). Add the second cloth (Fig. 10-40F), using two lines of stitches if you wish. When the seam is brought the right way, only the round part of the piping projects (Fig. 10-40G).

The cover has a walling around the front made deep enough to fasten to the lower platform (Fig. 10-39J), where it may be covered with a strip of gimp. Get the front right while there is still some excess cloth around the other edges. When you are satisfied with the front, stretch the cloth and tack the other edges down. There will have to be some trimming around the uprights. Do not cut the openings to these sizes, but leave some extra cloth that can be folded under in the angles, so there are no raw edges exposed.

Arms

Some chairs have hard arms, but comfort is increased if there is softening of the inner and upper surfaces. Start with the inner surface. Prepare it with some webbing between the top and gut rail (Fig. 10-41A). This

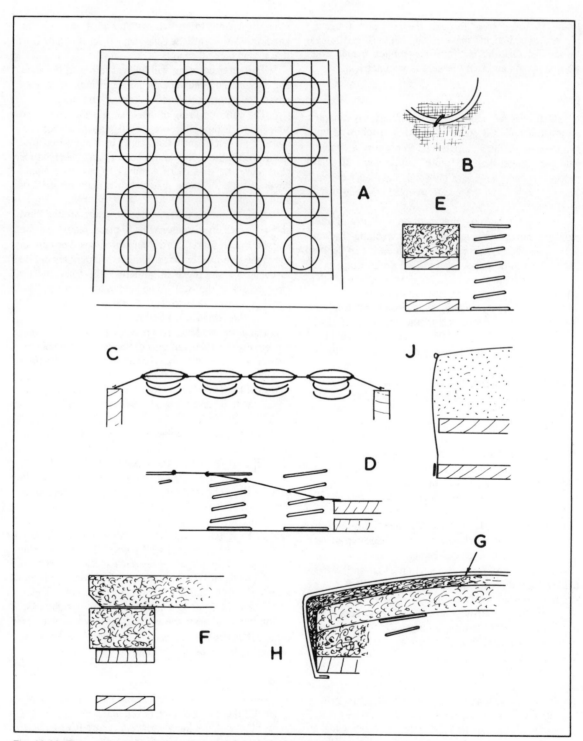

Fig. 10-39. The arrangement of coil springs and steps in padding and covering.

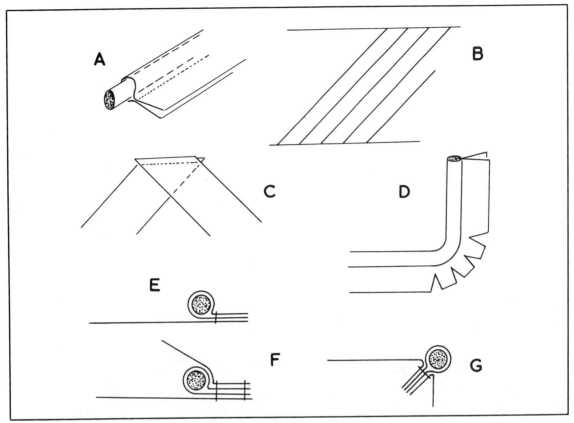

Fig. 10-40. Making and attaching piping for a cushion edge.

will resist sideways pressure, but cover it with burlap or canvas to make a base for padding. Turn the edges in and tack all round (Fig. 10-41B).

It is easier to get a good shape by building up with 1-inch foam. Put a layer on top, then wrap over the width and down to the gut rail inside (Fig. 10-41C). Cut another piece to go against the front (Fig. 10-41D). A few spots of adhesive can be used to position the foam. In traditional upholstery there is cotton batting over the padding materials, but this is not essential over foam. There should be muslin or other light cloth covering before the outer covering goes on.

This cloth can be cut as a sort of bag sewed to fit over the arm. Make two side pieces and one shaped to the top and long enough to wrap over the front (Fig. 10-41E). Sew these parts inside out. Make the cloth tight rather than loose, so it compresses the foam and settles without creases. Stretch the cloth over each arm (Fig. 10-41F). Tack inside to the gut rail. The outside can go down to the bottom rail eventually, but do not tack there until after

the seat has been covered, or you will not be able to get at the seat tacks.

Do not cover the arms with the outer material until you are ready to cover the other parts of the chair. The method is described here. The outer covering can be made up with sewed seams in a similar way to that described for the muslin inner cover. Allow enough to reach the bottom of the bottom rail, where the edge may be covered with gimp in line with the gimp in the front. Tack to the gut rail. Allow some surplus material at the back to tack over the covering of the back.

Back

For the most luxurious back, the frame can be dealt with in a similar way to the seat, with a pattern of webbing and coil springs. The method shown uses zigzag springs (Fig. 10-42A). They are stiffer than tension springs and are made so they take up a slightly curved manner, which helps to push the center of the back forward, aiding in the domed appearance. The springs have plates at the ends

257

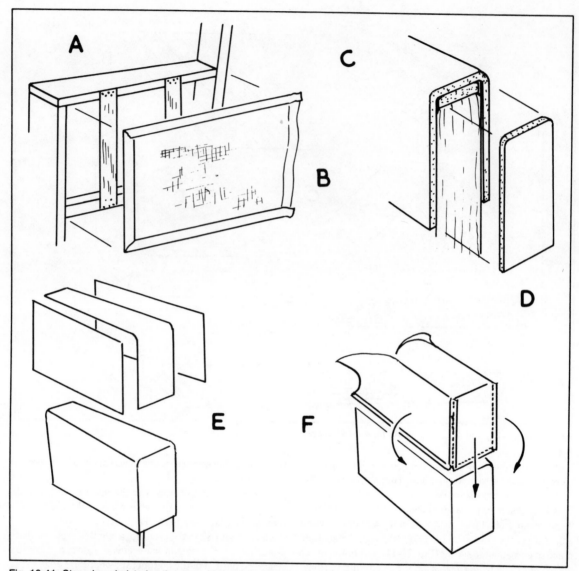

Fig. 10-41. Steps in upholstering the arms of the club chair.

for screwing to the front of the frame. Arrange them vertically between the top and gut rails (Fig. 10-42B). Tack burlap or canvas over the springs.

Foam has to be arranged to provide padding. You can use one piece 3 inches thick or more all over, but something has to be done to soften the top edge. The alternative is to use thinner foam and arrange it in pieces that pace out one overall panel that also wraps over the top edge (Fig. 10-42C). You can include an extra strip at the top as a headrest. Make sure the wood at the top has

ample padding so there is no hard line, particularly toward the front.

Secure everything with muslin. It will have to be cut around the arms and taken over the edges of the back and far enough down the rear of the top rail to compress the foam there. At the bottom, pull the muslin under the gut rail for tacking at the back.

The outer covering of the back is arranged very similarly to the muslin on the front surface. Wrap the covering material around the edges, having cut back at

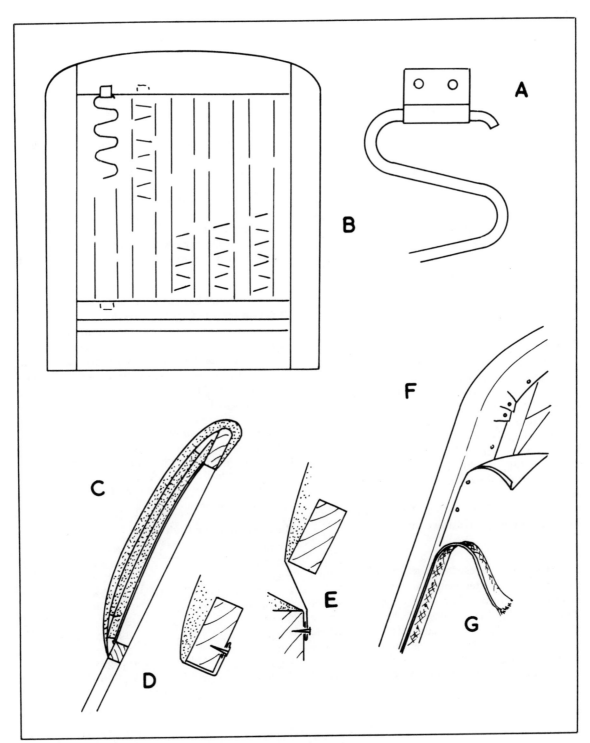

Fig. 10-42. Springing, padding, and covering the back of the club chair.

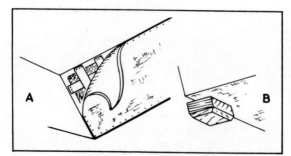

Fig. 10-43. Covering underneath and adding a foot.

the arms, and tack to the back surfaces. Do this at the top and either on to the gut rail (Fig. 10-42D) or down onto the back of the seat rail (Fig. 10-42E).

Cut a piece of the same material to go over the rear surface. Turn it in to make an even border all round as you tack it over the edges coming from the front (Fig. 10-42F). Temporarily tack it on at a few key places to avoid creases, then tack fairly closely all round. The edges can be covered with gimp (Fig. 10-42G).

Bottom

Underneath the chair it is unusual to leave the webbing exposed, although it is not normally in view. There can be a piece of burlap with its edges turned in and tacked on (Fig. 10-43A). The burlap prevents dust blowing up into the springs and webbing.

The simplest feet are rectangular blocks, finished with stain and varnish, and then screwed into the framework (Fig. 10-43B). They can be turned on a lathe or carved to any shape you wish, but they are not very noticeable.

There can be casters fitted. Make sure the bottoms have no sharp edges to damage carpets.

Cushion

This chair can be used without a cushion, but a fitted cushion gives a better height for most people. The method of construction is the same as that described for the lounge chair, except this one has to be shaped. Make a paper pattern of the seat area and use it for setting out the top and bottom panels of the cushion. Foam 4 inches thick should be enough. Cut the strip of walling to suit it.

If the front of the seat has been made with a piped edge, the top edge of the cushion should be piped. If it is intended to turn over, both edge seams should be piped. Although only the front of the cushion is normally visible, it is common to carry the piping all round. If the back of the cushion has a zipper, the addition of piping makes no difference to assembly. If slip stitching is to be used, sew the piping to one cloth across the back. Make the slip stitching through it.

The cushion does not have to be buttoned, but a pattern of four buttons in a square improves appearance. If the cushion is to be used one way only, the bottom part can have strips of wood or plain buttons. If it is to turn over, there will have to be similar buttons, top and bottom, adjusted to pull into the material and give the same appearance both ways.

Some upholstery covering material is very expensive. Before covering a chair, it helps to make drawings of the various pieces you have to cut. Put them together like a jigsaw puzzle to see how to cut them economically. You will have to watch how the weave and pattern will come. Do not cut any part diagonal to the weave. You may have to cut wastefully to get a symmetrical pattern, particularly on the back. Even the arms should look like a pair. Any difference may not matter with a small pattern, but you should try to get the tops of the arms to look alike.

You may be able to avoid waste if you use other cloth in some places. The underside of the cushion can be in a different cloth, preferably plain. It may be acceptable to use a plain cloth on the rear surface of the back, particularly if the chair is expected to be kept against a wall. As the chair is to be used with a cushion, the center area of the seat is normally hidden. You can use plain cloth, but you will have to sew on *flies* for the front and any other part that will be seen.

Materials List for Club Chair

2 arm fronts	4 ×15×1
2 arm tops	4 ×24×1
2 sides	5 ×22×1
2 platforms	6 ×32×1
3 platform spacers	4 ×4 ×1
2 sides	3 ×32×1¼
1 top	4 ×26×1¼
1 bottom	5 ×26×1¼
2 gut rails	1½×24×1
1 gut rail	1½×26×1

Chapter 11

Windsor Chairs

The name *Windsor* as applied to chairs has become mis-used. Variations have come from the original, and chairs that some people call Windsor chairs bear little re-semblance to what the name first meant—and still does to some makers and users of the chairs. The design is English, but it came to America with immigrant craftsmen. Developments of the design have gone much further in the New England states than it ever did in the Old Country.

Windsor is a town about 40 miles west of London. Windsor Castle is famous as one of the homes of the king or queen. There has been a castle there since Norman times—something like 1000 years. The town of High Wycombe is about 10 miles away. Surrounding it were extensive forests of good furniture hardwoods, particu-larly beech. There are still many of these trees around, and they are still felled and used. For many centuries craftsmen used the wood to make furniture. Factories became centered in High Wycombe. This is one of the main centers of furniture making in England.

There is a story that King George III, on a hunting trip from Windsor Castle paused to rest at a farmhouse. King George III liked a chair that he used there very much and ordered some chairs for use in the castle. The

name Windsor was given for that style of chair. There is evidence that many chairs were made about 50 years before King George III was born. This puts the origin of Windsor chairs toward the end of the seventeenth cen-tury.

Surprisingly, for most of their life Windsor chairs have not been considered high quality or sophisticated furniture. They were more the chairs of smaller homes and farmhouses. Today, there is an appreciation of what the Windsor chair can offer—both in appearance and comfort.

What is a Windsor chair? None of the variations include upholstery. Instead, the seat is a fairly thick, solid piece of wood with its top hollowed to something like an average person's posterior. There are four legs, nearly always turned, but they can be square or even cabriole-shaped. A Windsor chair also has a back and arms. A chair without arms is not really a Windsor chair. The arms are usually in one length and are curved around the back, which is also curved in a bow above it. These parts are joined to the seat with rods described as sticks. A design feature is sometimes a central vertical splat, which is a flat piece of wood decorated by shaping externally and with fretted patterns. In traditional chairs the patterns of the splats may indicate particular makers or regions (Fig. 11-1). There does not have to be a splat to make it a Windsor chair. Figures 11-2 and 11-3 show the general features.

It is unusual to find an English Windsor chair in any but a natural finish, with the wood grain showing through a wax or similar coat. Some chairs were stained, but much of the beauty was considered to be in the appearance of the grain. In contrast, most of the early American Windsor chairs were painted to obliterate the grain, possibly because of the differences in the woods used in one chair. Another particularly American feature was the making of wider chairs to accommodate two or more people, with extra legs to provide support. This *settee* pattern is never seen in England.

If you want to make a Windsor chair, you must use a lathe. It does not have to be a large one, as none of the turned parts are very big. They are all turned between centers.

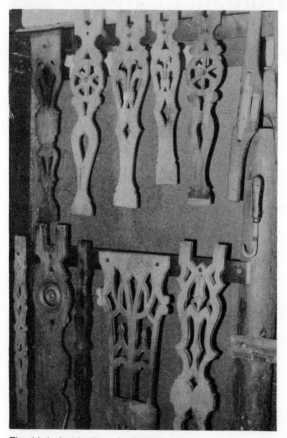

Fig. 11-1. A selection of splat templates.

BENDING

You also have to be prepared to bend wood for the arms and backs. In the original chairs the wood is bent solid, and this involves steaming. With modern glues, it is possible to laminate these parts and bend without steaming. If you want to work in the original way, there has to be a steam box. This is an arrangement of four boards long enough to enclose whatever you want to steam. If you are making more than one chair, it will save time and trouble if you do all the steaming and bending at one time. Support the box at an angle (steam rises) and arrange an outlet at the upper end. Steam has to be produced in some way. It can be an oil drum, or something similar, containing water and with a pipe leading into the box, which can be stuffed with rags (Fig. 11-4). Heat in any convenient manner, but you have to produce a plentiful supply of steam for a sustained time—maybe 15 minutes for thinner wood and much longer for thicker wood. Arrange strips of wood across inside the box to keep the wood you are working on away from the sides, so steam gets to all surfaces.

Bending is done around a former. For solid wood this needs to be fairly substantial, or you will pull it out of shape. In production work the base is an iron plate, but you can use thick plywood framed underneath with solid wood. On this goes the actual pattern. When solid wood is bent and left to cool and dry, it will spring back slightly after releasing. Allow for this in making the former. It need not be in one piece, but it can be built up and fastened down to the base (Fig. 11-5A). To hold the wood to the former, provide plenty of pegs to fit holes in the base, so you can drive wedges quickly (Fig. 11-5B). There can be blocks screwed down (Fig. 11-5C) instead of pegs, but too many of them interfere with pulling the steamed wood round quickly. A block at the top of the curve and others at the lower sides can be supplemented with pegs elsewhere. Allow for bending a slightly greater length than the finished part has to be, as the extremities do not always hold their curves so well.

If you laminate, the former is the same, but you will not be putting as great a strain on it. The thickness of laminations depends on the wood. Thin pieces are always easier to bend, but there is no need to cut wood thinner than necessary. With most hardwoods, you should be able to make up a thickness of 1 inch with three laminations (Fig. 11-5D). To prevent laminated work becoming stuck to any part of the former, put newspaper under the edges and around the curve (Fig. 11-5E). Apply plenty of glue to all meeting surfaces. You then have to pull around and clamp with wedges, so the parts meet closely. There may

Fig. 11-2. A group of Windsor chairs of traditional design.

Fig. 11-3. A group of Windsor children's chairs.

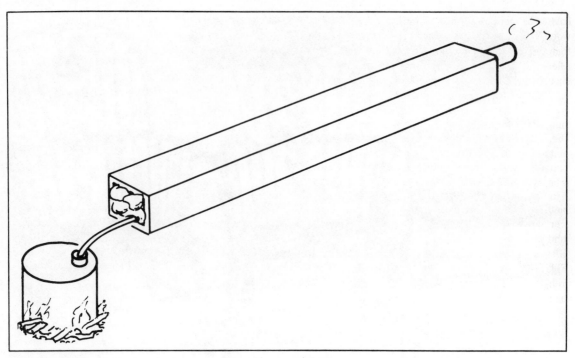

Fig. 11-4. If solid wood is to be bent, it has to be softened and made flexible in a steam box or chest.

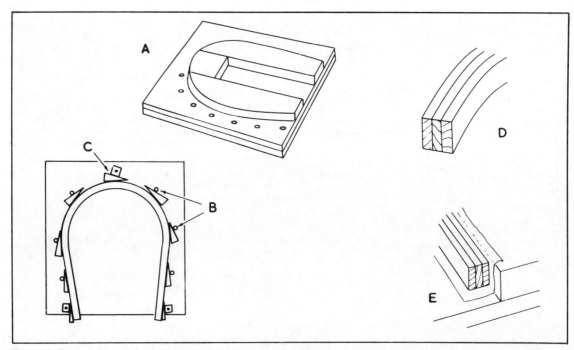

Fig. 11-5. For bending solid or laminated wood, there has to be a former to which the wood can be clamped with wedges or other means.

have to be more pegs and wedges than you need for solid wood to remove air gaps. Try to get the parts right and tight the first time. If you pull a glued joint tight, and then release it to make an adjustment, there may not be enough glue left for the second time to unite the surfaces.

Another way of building up a curve, which is found on the arms of some chairs, is called layering. It is something like laminating, but the joints are the other way. There should be at least three layers in any assembly, so joints in the layers are staggered and the parts provide mutual support. Cut pieces so the grain follows the curve as far as possible. Put together enough pieces in one layer to follow the pattern, and go on to more layers, with their joints in different places (Fig. 11-6A). Make the parts oversize, so you can cut the final shape as if working on a solid piece of wood. This method also allows for using differences in thickness, as at the curled end of an arm (Fig. 11-6B) or the raised center of a back on a captain's or firehouse chair (Fig. 11-6C). The latter is not a Windsor chair feature.

SEATS FOR WINDSOR CHAIRS

Some simple chairs are made with flat, solid wood seats. They still have to be fairly thick to allow for the holes that provide the only strength in leg and back attachment, so they can look clumsy. Appearance can be improved by beveling all round underneath, outside of the part where holes come. Such a seat may have a cushion made to the shape of the seat and tied back with tapes.

The usual shaping of a Windsor chair seat has the border at back and the sides flat. The front and the central area are shaped, working inwards from the border. Sections show the shaping required (Fig. 11-7). The depth of shaping varies between makers. Just a token hollowing is not much more comfortable than a flat seat, but a very deep shape requires more effort and skill to make.

Hollowing was traditionally done with an *adze*. This is something like an ax with the blade crosswise. For chairs, the blade is curved in its width and length and sharpened only on its top surface. Even if you can find an adze, this tool is not for beginners.

It is safer to have the wood secured to the bench top and to work around with a large gouge pointed toward the deeper parts of the hollows. Get the front edge to your liking, then work back each side until the central ridge blends into the deeper large hollow at the back. You can remove the largest of the gouge marks with further cuts across them, followed by a curved scraper and plenty of sanding.

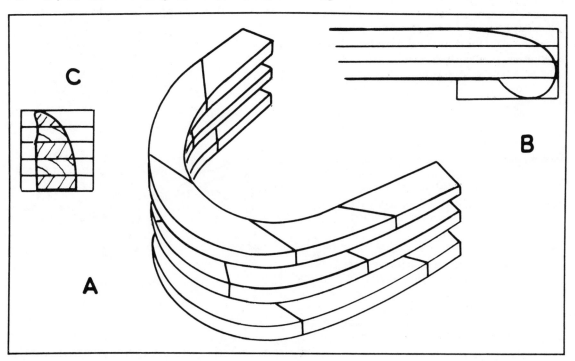

Fig. 11-6. Shaped parts can be built up from flat section by layering.

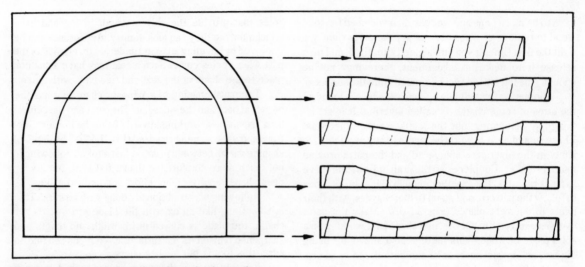

Fig. 11-7. Seats are hollowed as shown by the sections.

SPINDLED SIDE CHAIR

This is not really a Windsor chair (Fig. 11-8), but it is a chair without arms that has several constructional features similar to a Windsor chair. For anyone new to making this type of chair, it is a suitable introduction. A set of four or six of these chairs (Fig. 11-9), with one or two full Windsor chairs, makes a very good dining suite with a suitable table.

A problem is the almost total absence of straight and square lines, particularly when it comes to drilling the many holes needed. Much work has to be done by eye and estimation. It helps to work about a centerline. If you slope a part at one angle at one side, try to slope at the same angle at the other side. When you drill a hole, have an adjustable bevel standing on the wood. Set it to what you judge to be the correct angle, obtained from the drawing, but you are usually dealing with a compound angle—a slope in two directions. As you drill the hole, alter the adjustable bevel to match the angle you are actually drilling, so it can serve as a guide when you drill for the part that should be a pair to the first.

Seat

The seat is the feature to which the other parts are related. Make it first (Fig. 11-10). Have the grain running from back to front. Mark and cut the straight outline. Mark the leg positions underneath (Fig. 11-10A) and the back hole positions on top (Fig. 11-10B). Round the front corners and shape the back, as shown dotted. If you intend to hollow the top (Fig. 11-7), that can be marked out. Shaping may be left until after drilling.

Fig. 11-8. A side chair with many of the features of a Windsor chair.

266

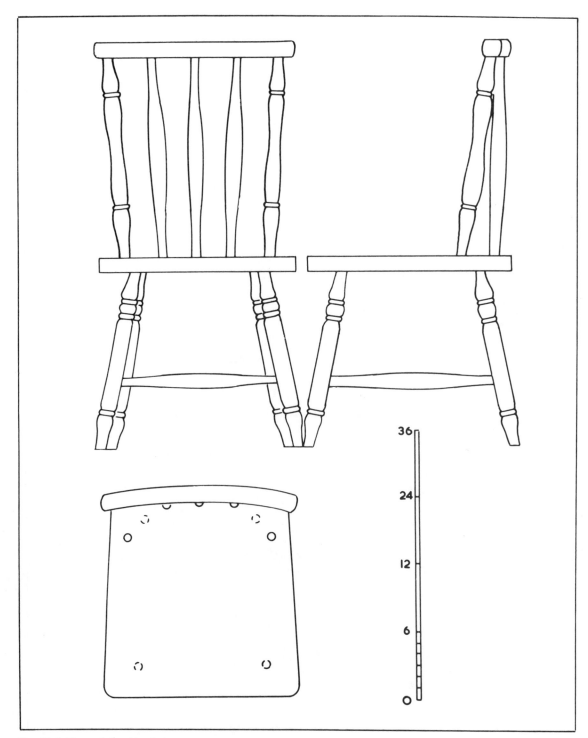

Fig. 11-9. Sizes of the side chair.

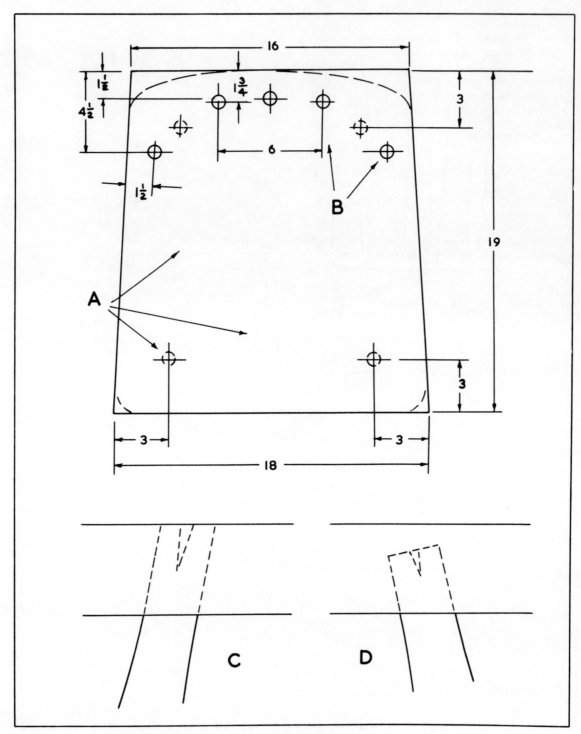

Fig. 11-10. The layout of a chair seat and two ways of attaching the legs.

All of the holes are ¾ inch in diameter. In these chairs the legs are often taken right through and wedged (Fig. 11-10C). That idea dates from the days when glues were not trustworthy, and security depended on the mechanical tightness obtained by wedging. In some old chairs the legs have loosened and come further through to disfigure the top as well as make it uncomfortable. With modern glues, it should be satifactory and neater to stop the holes (Fig. 11-10D). If a turned part does not fit as tight as you wish, there can be a foxtail wedge inside the hole. Do any wedging at right angles to the grain of the seat.

Drill for the legs first. The legs start 3 inches in, but slope out so their feet come under the corners of the seat. Hold your brace to give this angle. If you do not get exactly this angle, it does not matter providing both front legs splay outward the same, along with the back ones.

Rigidity is given to the back by having the outside back posts sloping at a greater angle than the three sticks. From the general drawing (Fig. 11-9), you can see the differences in slope. The center stick is almost upright. The two adjoining ones slope back and outward only slightly, then the posts have more slope in both directions. You will have to estimate these slopes, but make sure opposite sides are paired to similar angles.

Whether you hollow the top or not, the seat can be made to look lighter by beveling underneath, if only to reduce the edge thickness by ¼ inch or so.

Turned Parts

The turned parts (Fig. 11-11) are all shown slightly too long, so they can be trimmed as you fit them. It is impossible to get exact lengths from a drawing, so this extra allowance gives some tolerance. There is one problem where parts have to fit holes. Turn the ends parallel to the hole size for perhaps 2 inches before you start to spread out the pattern. If you have to cut off as much as an inch, the wood should still be the same as the hole diameter. If you use close-grained hardwood for the seat, it should withstand considerable hammering during assembly. There is always a limit when splitting may start. All of the ends should go to the bottoms of the holes to obtain maximum strength.

The four legs have 1½-inch maximum diameters over the beads and along the central cylindrical parts (Fig. 11-11A). Mark where the bottom rails will come. They are assembled in an H-pattern, so the rails between the legs only go from back to front. The other rail fits between them.

The bottom rails are shown with smooth curves, from 1¼-inch diameter at the center to ¾-inch diameter ends (Fig. 11-11B). Drill the two side rails centrally to take the ends of the crosswise rail. You cannot cut the rails to their final lengths until you assemble. This underframing can be put together now before making the back parts.

Try a dry assembly of the four legs. Adjust their angles as far as possible to get a symmetrical appearance. Measure between the holes in the legs and allow for their depth to get the lengths of the side bottom rails. Obviously, both side rails must be the same length to obtain symmetry, even if the first trial shows them different. From the side rail arrangement, get the length of the crosswise rail and cut it. Remember to cut equal amounts from opposite ends of these rails, rather than all from one end, which will put the thicker part out of center.

Glue all the joints of the underframing and fit the parts together. It will help to use a bar clamp to force parts fully into their holes, but pad the wood surfaces with scrap wood to prevent damage. Stand the chair on a level surface. Check that it stands symmetrically when you look at it from all directions. You can do a limited amount of pulling into shape before the glue begins to set, but be careful not to pull any spindle back from its hole.

Back

The two back posts have maximum diameters of 1¼ inch, and the ends fit ¾-inch holes (Fig. 11-11C). The three sticks can be parallel pieces of dowel rod in a simple chair, but they look better turned with the thicker centers 1¼-inch diameter (Fig. 11-11D). These parts have to be trimmed as you assemble the back.

The top of the back (Fig. 11-11E) has a 1½-inch curved shape and is cut from wood 2½ inches wide. Take off the sharpness of the angles and round the outer corners. Mark the positions of the holes and drill them, using the general drawing as a guide to angles. Take the drill about 1 inch deep.

Make a trial assembly of the back. Use the posts as guides. With them in place, you can measure the lengths of sticks. Glue and clamp these parts in a similar way to the underframing. Check that the back finishes parallel to the seat when viewed from the front end and that it is symmetrical with the back of the seat when viewed from above, before the glue has started to set. Any twist in the back will be rather obvious to a viewer.

Leave everything to set. Remove any excess glue. Ideally, the bottoms of the legs should be cut parallel with the floor. The turned ends should be satisfactory, unless you have to trim if the chair wobbles.

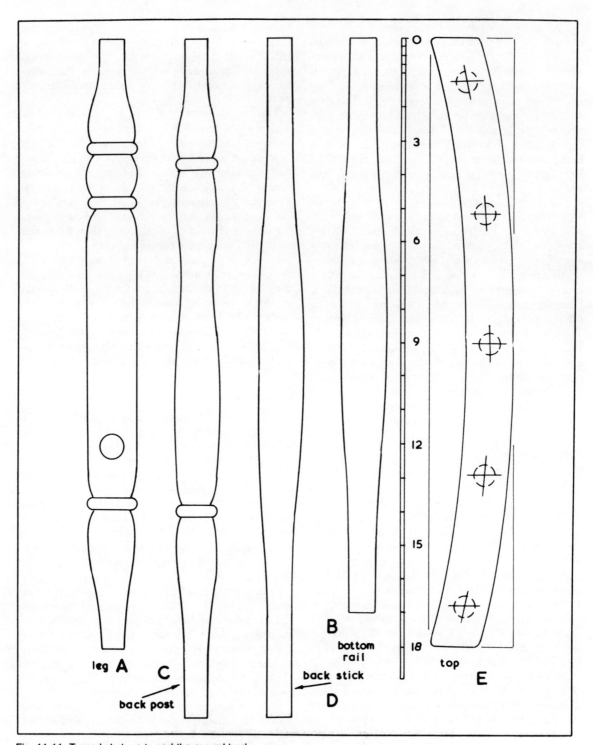

Fig. 11-11. Turned chair parts and the curved back.

Materials List for Spindled Side Chair

1 seat	18×20×1½
4 legs	1⅝×18×1⅝
3 rails	1⅜×18×1⅜
1 top	2½×19×1½
2 back posts	1⅜×21×1⅜
3 back sticks	1⅜×21×1⅜

LOOP BACK CHAIR

The characteristic that mostly makes a chair into a Windsor pattern is the bent wood back in the form of a hoop or loop. Although there are some chairs without this characteristic, they are nevertheless all part of the Windsor family. In some chairs the bent wood piece goes to the seat, and in others it stops at the back bow, which makes the arms. If taken to the seat, it is usually called a *loop back*. If it only comes down to the back bow, it is a *hoop back*. Side chairs without arms are often made with loop backs. This form is attractive and can be quite strong. A set made in this way will match one or more full armed Windsor chairs.

The chair described here (Fig. 11-12) uses the same seat and legs as the previous chair (Figs. 11-8 and 11-9), except for the extension of the seat at the back to take two spindles or sticks that form struts (Fig. 11-13A). It is possible to make a chair with a loop that is strong enough without the struts, but they are there to resist the effects of heavy and long use. They are commonly used and may be regarded as a design feature that gives a chair character and a traditional appearance.

Set out the seat (Fig. 11-13B). The loop will be tenoned into it, but the sticks go about three-fourths of the way through into ⅝-inch diameter holes. Make the loop, either laminated or solid wood. Note that the top is part of a circle, and the sides come down straight to a narrower base (Fig. 11-13C). Leave an inch or so extra at each end to allow for trimming.

Loop

The loop has to slope back, so the struts are near upright (Fig. 11-13D). Draw this side view and set an adjustable bevel to the angle. Use this when marking and cutting the joints to the seat (Fig. 11-13E). Take the tenons through and wedge them from below when you finally assemble the parts.

Put the loop in place and stand the rods in the seat holes, so they overlap the loop. These can be turned sticks similar to those in the previous chair, but they are shown as plain dowel rods, which are common in this type

of chair. Move the tops of the sticks about to get them fanning into an even pattern when viewed from the front. From these positions, pencil inside the loop where the holes have to come. Marking the center of the loop will help you to get the arrangement symmetrical. The struts will come up parallel at the back, so their holes can be marked at the same width on the loop as on the seat.

To get the holes drilled at the correct angles, which are quite acute to the surface for the outer ones, mark the centers with a deep dent made with an awl you can use a small drill (less than ⅛ inch) in the position and at what you judge to be the correct angle to guide the larger drill. It is safer to use an Irwin or similar bit in a brace than to use an electric drill, as it is then easier to control the angle and depth that you make the hole. Allow for the tops of the sticks going about halfway into the loop (Fig. 11-14A).

With the loop attached to the seat again and the rods in their holes in the seat, you can mark the lengths of them by estimating the depth they will go into the loop. In use, loads on the chair back tend to compress the two struts. Try to cut them so they touch the bottoms of their holes. If the other sticks do not quite go the full depth into a hole, it is not so important.

Molding

When all the parts are ready, clean up the loop, so it is smooth all round in section. Take the sharpness off the angles equally all round. Many traditional chairs of this type have a bead worked round the loop (Fig. 11-14B). This is often a clue to the fact that the chair was individually made and not the product of a factory. Such a bead can be made round the front outer edge with a *scratch stock*, which is an easy tool to make. There are scratch stocks that look something like marking gauges which can be adjusted for varying distances from an edge. It is possible to manage with something much simpler (Fig. 11-14C).

Cut an L-shaped piece of wood and make a saw cut in the narrow arm. Grind the end of a piece of steel to the reverse of the profile you want. A scrapped hacksaw blade is ideal for this (Fig. 11-14D). Put this cutter through the saw cut in the wood and secure it with a screw driven close by (Fig. 11-14E). A wood screw should hold well enough, but for considerable use it is better to put a small bolt through with washers each side. To use the tool, tilt it toward the way you are pushing, so the scraper begins to remove tiny shavings. You can work both ways round the loop and finish with the tool upright to get an even bead. You can put a bead on the inside curve in the same way, but outside only is more common.

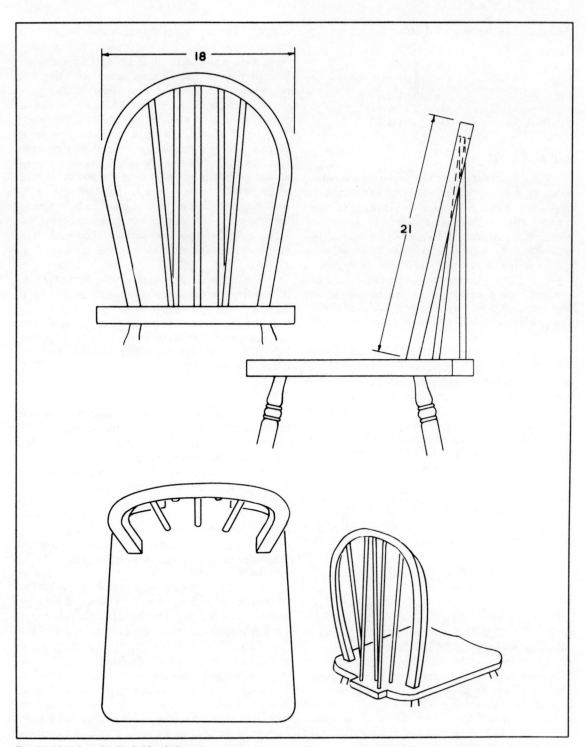

Fig. 11-12. A loop-backed side chair.

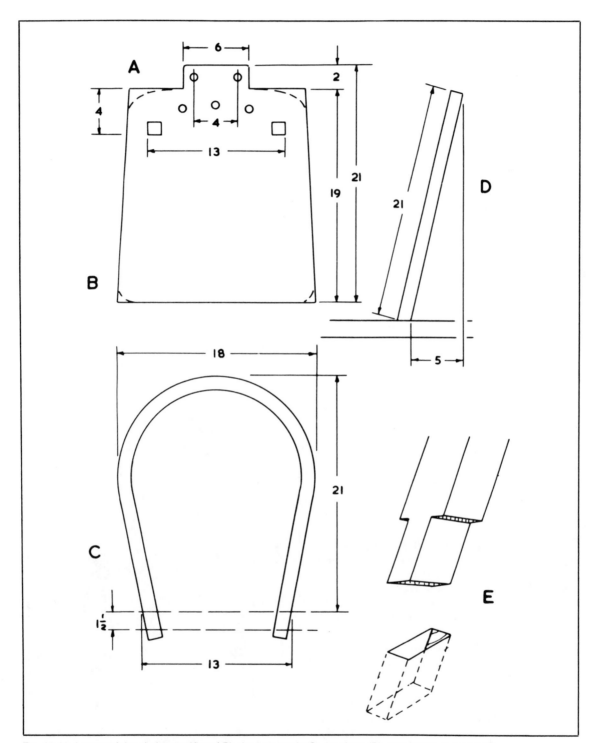

Fig. 11-13. Layout of the chair seat (A and B), the loop back (C), its slope (D), and joint to the seat (E).

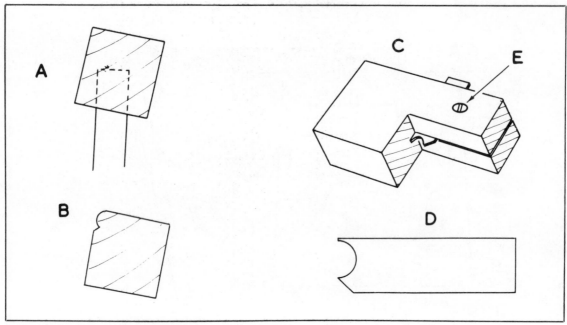

Fig. 11-14. Stick joint to the loop (A) and a bead (B) made with a scratch stock (C, D, and E).

Materials List for Loop Back Chair

1 seat	18×23×1½
4 legs	1⅝×18×1⅝
3 rails	1⅜×18×1⅜
1 loop	1⅛×50×1⅛
or 3 strips	1⅛×50×⅜
5 sticks	½×24 round rods

LOOP BACK ARMCHAIR

Windsor chairs developed while other furniture was going through what we now call Queen Anne, Chippendale, and Hepplewhite periods. Those chairs which were influenced by Hepplewhite had loops to the seat and arms brought in to them. Such a chair is a development of the last example. An armchair tends to be wider than a side chair. The back may be made up of spindles only, but a central pierced splat was common, and that is shown here (Fig. 11-15). The general drawing (Fig. 11-16) shows sizes and layout, but much of the work has to be done by trial and error. The finished chair may not have all the parts exactly as drawn. With no straight lines or square corners to work to, the main consideration has to be to fit parts at one side, so they match similar parts on the other side.

Fig. 11-15. A loop back Windsor armchair.

274

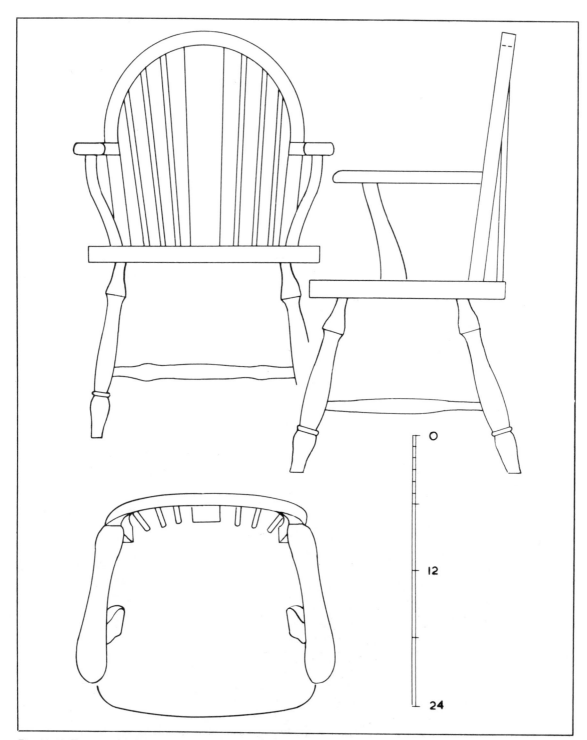

Fig. 11-16. The general shape of a loop back Windsor armchair.

This chair has a seat slightly flared to the front, with the hollowing brought to the full width forward of the arm supports. The underframing is the usual arrangement of splayed legs with rails arranged in an H-formation. The back is made like the previous chair, except for the splat and greater number of sticks. Both the arms and their supports are given shaping to make them comfortable for the user. The arms and back are braced together and should provide ample strength, but some of these chairs are made with a pair of struts at the back.

Seat

Start by making the seat (Fig. 11-17A). As it is wider than it is deep, the grain can be across it, instead of the usual back to front way of smaller chairs. Much depends on the available material. If the seat has to be made by gluing narrower pieces, it probably looks better to have many narrow pieces than only one joint. If pieces 1½ inch square are made up, there is a butcher block effect. The risk of warping is minimized.

An expert will do the shaping of the seat top before drilling, but you may prefer to drill first. When the hollowing is done, pencil the outline. Come out to the full width at the front, but keep about 1 inch inside the other parts. Round the front edge and bevel around the under edges to lighten the appearance.

The legs and rails are made in the usual way. You can use your own ideas for turning these parts, but traditional chairs had fairly simple designs. An example of a leg is shown in Fig. 11-18A. The back to front rails have a simple swelling at the center (Fig. 11-18B), but the stretcher between them can have further shaping (Fig. 11-18C). Make these parts too long, but turn the ends parallel for a short distance, so they will still fit the holes after cutting to length. The holes may be ¾ inch or ⅞ inch in diameter.

Drill for the legs so they splay outward diagonally to about 1 inch outside the size of the seat. Mark and drill for the rails between back and front legs, then drill the rails for the stretchers. Let all the holes go about three-fourths of the way through the wood in order to give ample area for glue.

Loop

Make the loop (Fig. 11-19A). Allow enough length for tenoning into the seat. The form should have a top curve as part of a circle. It should allow the sides to come in slightly too narrow to allow for them springing out when released.

Mark the mortise positions on the seat. Cut the tenons on the ends of the loop and chop the mortises. There is a slope in both directions through the joints. You can get guidance on the angles from the drawing, but it is better to hold the loop in position and set two adjustable bevels to the angles you get—for use in marking out (Fig. 11-19B). Keep the tenons fairly thick, ¾ inch on a 1¼-inch thickness will do.

The splat is a flat, thin piece of wood. It can be no more than just a parallel strip, or cut with a shaped outline, but traditional chairs had the wood pierced in patterns of varying complexity.

A wheel pattern was common (Fig. 11-18D), but some other designs are suggested (Fig. 11-20). Cutting has to be done with a fairly fine saw. It is difficult to get inside many parts with other tools, or even sandpaper, to clean the edges. For the harder woods, you may have to use a coping saw or jigsaw. A fretsaw will leave the best edge. A powered fretsaw, in which the wood is fed to a moving blade, is best, but the work can be done by hand.

Drill the seat for the sticks, which are parallel pieces of dowel rod. They will have to fan out to the loop. It is simplest to drill at the intended angle, so the sticks will be straight. If you examine some old chairs, note that the holes in the seat have been drilled more upright. The sticks are sprung to a slight curve to meet the loop. Doing this may increase comfort and improve appearance.

Splat

The splat is cut back like a barefaced tenon to fit into a slot in the seat (Fig. 11-19C). Put the loop into its mortise and have the splat and sticks in their holes in the seat, so they rest against the loop. Mark the center of the loop and put the splat central over it, so you can pencil underneath the position for its joint. Also, mark on the splat the curve of the loop, which will be the shoulder to follow when you cut the tenon to go into the loop. Arrange the tops of the sticks so they make an even pattern each side of the splat, when viewed from the front. Mark their positions inside the loop for holes. Mark the sticks so you can cut them to length to go into the holes. Take this assembly apart and drill for the sticks in the loop. Carefully cut the mortise for the splat, going about halfway through the loop.

Arms

The arms will be tenoned into the sides of the loop, then extend outward for the supports to be tenoned into them and into the seat. Some arms have double curvature, but these arms are flat on top. Shaping is only the other way (Fig. 11-17B). Set out the shapes on the two

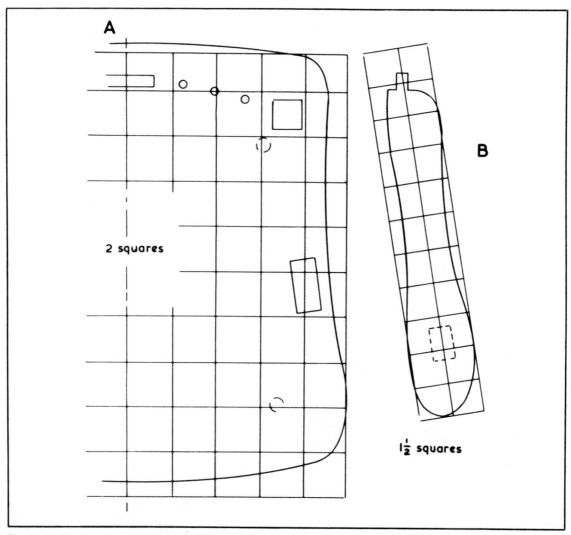

A

2 squares

B

1½ squares

Fig. 11-17. The sizes of the seat and arm of a Windsor armchair.

pieces of wood, then cut the tenons to go into the loop. They have to slope to match the angle of the loop in both directions (Fig. 11-21A). Also, mark and cut the mortises for the supports before shaping the outlines. These can be made squarely to take stub tenons (Fig. 11-21B). Cut the outlines, but do not round the edges until after making the supports.

The supports are curved in two directions, so they have to be cut from thicker wood. Mark the curves on two surfaces (Fig. 11-21C). This will give you the positions of the tenons at each end (Fig. 11-21D). Mark and cut them before doing the other shaping. As with the arms, the

supports have to be a pair. Use card or other templates, which can be turned over to mark the shapes in opposite directions. Cut the outlines one way. If you use a band saw, keep the offcuts to put back in place to guide the cuts the other way. If you cut in a way that does not remove the waste in one piece, you will have to mark again on the curved surface.

Try the arms, supports, and the loop in position to see that opposite sides match and if any adjustment is needed to the joints. If that is satisfactory, separate the parts and round them. The bottom of each support should be left with almost square corners, and it should be

277

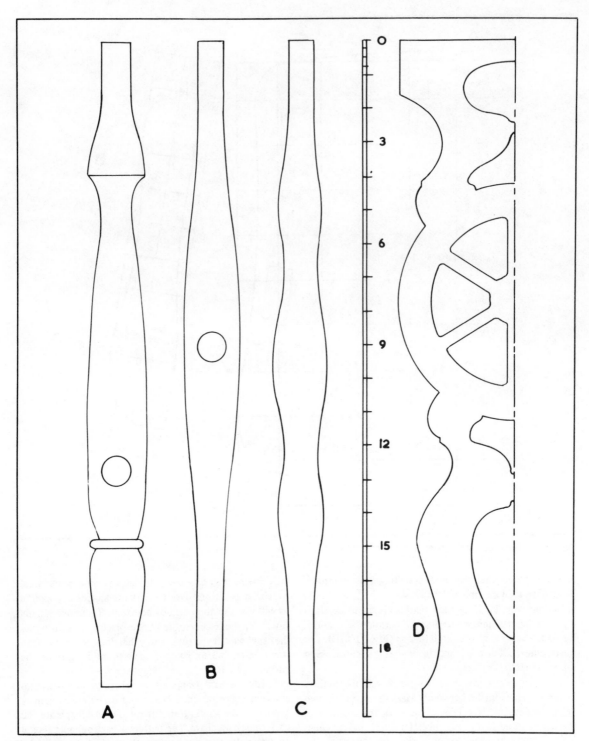

Fig. 11-18. The turned parts and a splat design.

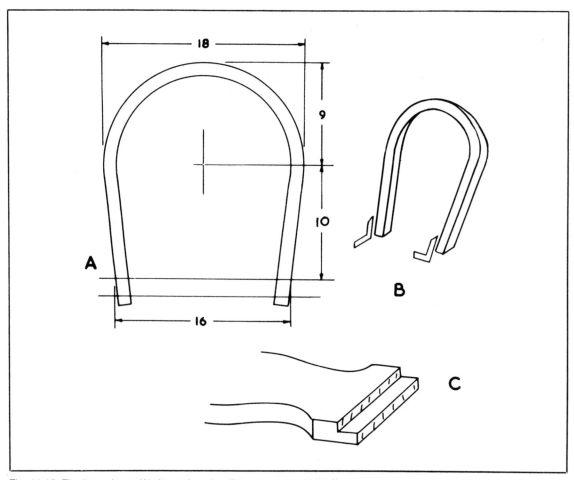

Fig. 11-19. The loop shape (A), its end angles (B), and a splat joint (C).

similar where it goes into the arm. Between those positions it should be well rounded, so sections are elliptical and no flats are left.

Let the arms remain with nearly square corners where they meet the loop, but elsewhere they should be very rounded on top. Underneath the rounding need not be as great, except that toward the front the section through an edge should be near semicircular. The tops of the arms are very prominent in use, and they should be given a good shape.

Assembly

Assemble in stages after all individual parts have been scraped and sanded. First, add the legs and rails to the seat. Pull all the glued joints tight and check that the amount of splay on the legs is uniform. See that the seat

stands parallel to the floor. The legs should stand firm on a level surface, but slight errors can be corrected by trimming later.

When that part has set, make up the back. Glue in the loop, sticks, and splat. When the parts are together, push the loop down with a bar clamp, while you drive wedges into the loop tenons underneath to lock them and get the other joints as tight as possible. Keep the clamp on until the glue has set, then trim off the tenons and wedges underneath.

Add the arms and their supports. If the joints to the seat or loop are not as tight as you wish, use foxtail wedging and glue. Before the glue has started setting, sight across the two arms to see that they are level and parallel in side view. Look at them from the front and see that they flare outward by equal amounts.

279

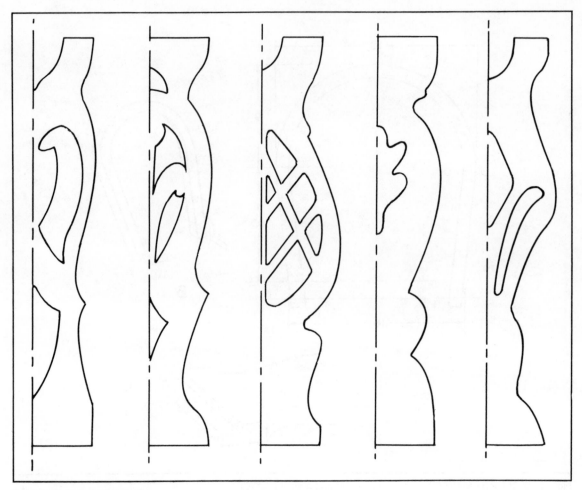

Fig. 11-20. Some splat designs.

Materials List for Loop Back Armchair

1 seat	20×24×1½
4 legs	1¾×18×1¾
2 lower rails	1½×19×1½
1 lower rail	1½×20×1½
1 loop	1¼×50×1¼
1 splat	3½×20×½
6 sticks	½×20
	round rods
2 arms	3×16×1¼
2 arm supports	5×11×3

HOOP BACK ARMCHAIR

The majority of Windsor chairs, as made by traditional craftsmen, had an arm bow which swept around the back and formed the arms. Sticks or spindles went through it and upward into a hoop that might have been taken through to the seat, but more usually was stopped above the bow. If there was a splat, and that was common, it might have gone through the bow, but was more likely to be let into its front. Along with sticks going through to the hoop and forming the back, there were other shorter ones under the arms. To distinguish this form from the Windsor chairs of the Hepplewhite period, These chairs may be called Queen Anne or Chippendale, but that indicated the period, rather than much association with other furniture of those types. Some Queen Anne period Windsor chairs were made with cabriole front legs.

This example (Fig. 11-22) is typical of the general type with an arm bow and a splat. It can be adapted to other variations. Most of these chairs have the common

280

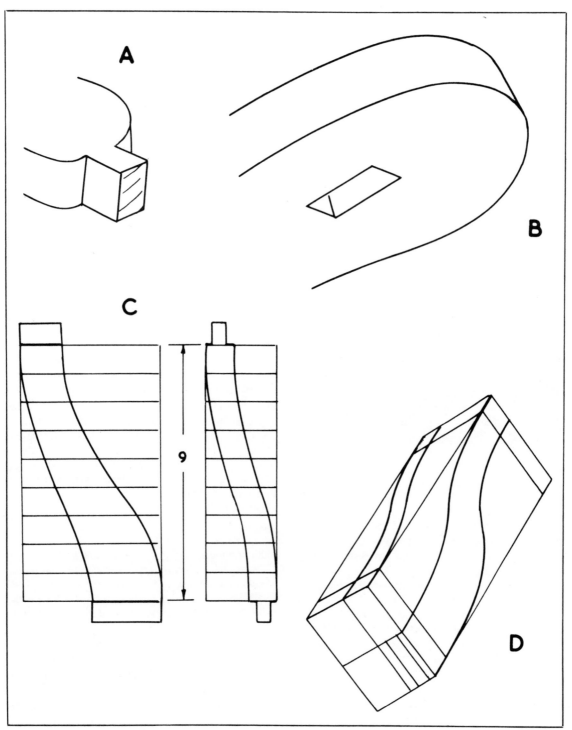

Fig. 11-21. The arm and its support.

Fig. 11-22. A hoop back Windsor armchair.

through to the hoop fairly straight. If there is a slight curve in their length, that should improve comfort.

Traditional arm bows were bent solid, but that means making a former which is justified if several bows are to be bent. It may be considered too much extra work for one. A bow can be laminated. That will require a former, but it need not be as substantial as for solid bending. The alternative is to layer the arm bow. Make it with at least three thicknesses and stagger the joints. Make the arm bow too long at first. Leave it a square section until after drilling and notching for the splat.

The hoop is made in the usual way by bending or laminating around a former, but it is not as long as in previous chairs. It will fit into holes in the arm bow, but make it first with a few inches extra on each end (Fig. 11-24D). A bead worked around its forward outer edge will follow the usual traditional treatment.

Splat

The splat is tenoned into the seat. At the top its two arms are tenoned into the hoop (Fig. 11-25A). At the bow it is notched into the front. The depth this notch is made and the angle it is cut to allow for the slope of the splat are best left to check during a trial assembly. The splat may be let in for its full thickness, or it may follow the line to the hoop better if not let in quite as deeply.

You can design the splat to your own ideas, but unlike the splats for the other chairs, you have to allow for a parallel part at the bow. You can use a wheel motif, as in so many of these chairs, or a different pattern is shown (Fig. 11-25B). If you design your own splat, avoid any very slender parts, particularly cross-grained pieces. Prepare the splat with a little excess length at the top for trimming later.

The two arm supports curve outward, but not forward, so they can be cut from a solid piece of the correct width or laminated (Fig. 11-25C). Allow for tenons into the seat and the arms. Try the supports in position, mounted on the seat and with the arm bow supported level with packings at the back. See that the flare is the same each side and that the center of the arm is directly above the center of the seat, when viewed from the front.

Drill the holes for the sticks in the seat. Allow for a similar slope backward to the splat and a slight flare out as they project upward. With all of the work done on the seat, you can put together the underframing. Join in the legs and rails, so you have the seat at a convenient height for further work.

Mark where the hoop will joint the bow. Make

H-arrangement of lower rails between the legs. The general drawing (Fig. 11-23) gives the main sizes, but as with other chairs with few straight lines, sizes of some parts have to be settled as construction progresses. It is more important to be symmetrical than to get all dimensions exactly as first drawn.

The seat, legs, and rails are generally similar to the loop back chair, except for the different layout of the holes for sticks, arm supports, and splat (Fig. 11-24A). A different design for the legs is shown (Fig. 11-24B), but this is a feature where you can use your own ideas. Make the seat and the parts of the underframing.

Arm Bow

The arm bow (Fig. 11-24C) is nearer elliptical than circular, with the curve flatter across the back than where it turns out to form the arms. This allows the sticks to go

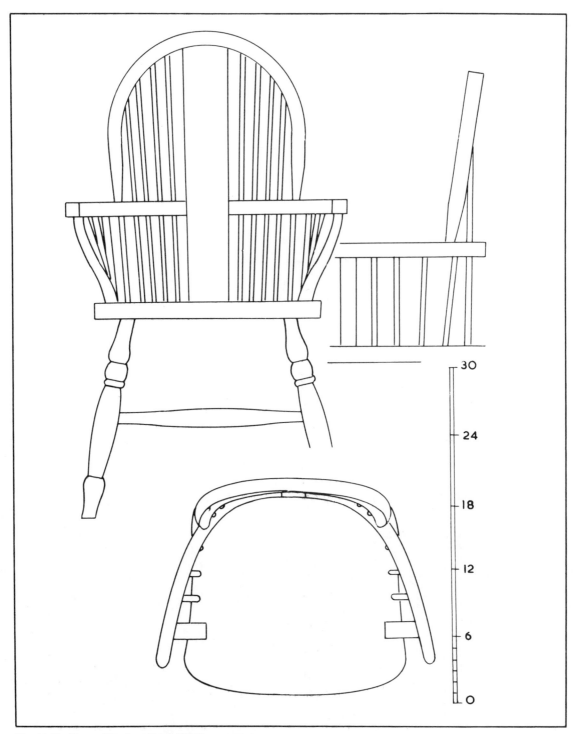

30

24

18

12

6

0

Fig. 11-23. Sizes of the hoop back Windsor armchair.

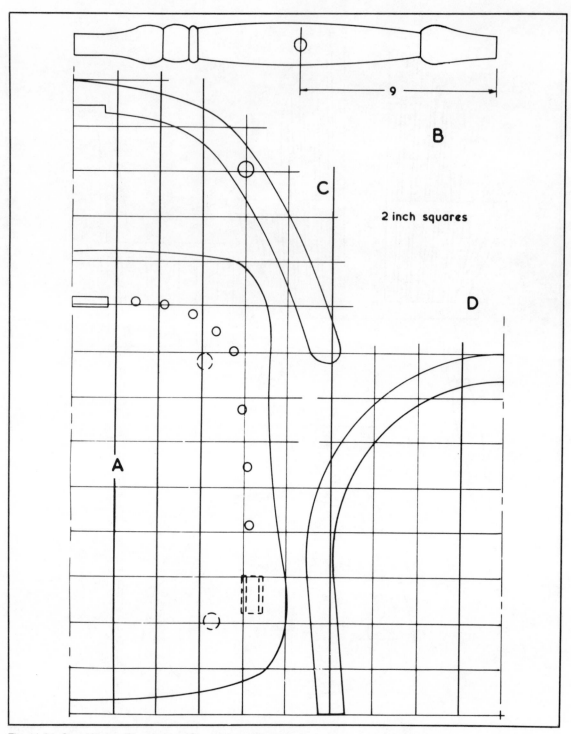

Fig. 11-24. Seat (A), leg (B), arm bow (C), and hoop (D) shapes.

9

B

C

2 inch squares

D

A

284

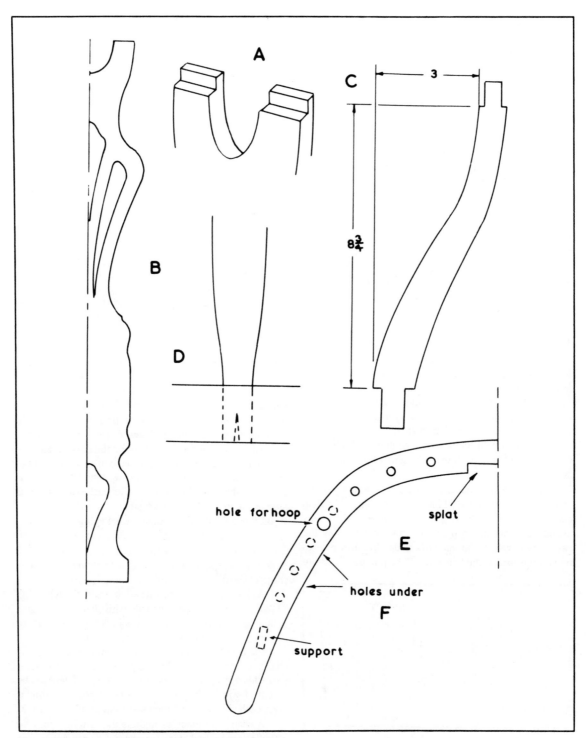

Fig. 11-25. Shapes of splat, arm support, and arm bow.

¾-inch holes in the bow, going about three-fourths through. The angle should slope back at the same angle as the splat and outward to suit the slope of the hoop. Cut the ends of the hoop to length, then taper to round by careful chisel work. It will help to draw a circle of the right size on each end. Aim to get a drive fit that will take the end through or to the bottom of the hole (Fig. 11-25D). If necessary, you can wedge the ends during final assembly.

Between the holes for the loop and the splat come equally spaced holes for the sticks (Fig. 11-25E). For the short sticks under the arms, drill upward at a spacing the same as on the seat or very slightly fanned out (Fig. 11-25F). Go about three-fourths of the way into the arms.

Make a trial assembly with the hoop in place, the arm supports in position, and sticks through the arm bow into the seat. See that the bow is supported level. A temporary packing under the bend will help. Let the sticks overlap the hoop. Mark inside the bend where the holes have to come. Check that the spacing is symmetrical about the centerline. Mark the lengths for the sticks. Check the lengths needed for the sticks under the arms.

Assembly

If everything is satisfactory, separate the parts. Round the edges of the arm bow, particularly toward the front. Cut the arms to equal lengths and round their ends.

Sand the individual parts. Glue the arm supports into the seat. Glue and fit the arm bow onto the supports. Fit the sticks that go under and through it. Make sure the arm bow is parallel with the seat and symmetrical to it. It is best to not add the hoop until the glue at this stage has set.

Put the loop in place, with glue at all joints. Fit the ends of the sticks and splat into it, as you direct the loop ends into their holes in the arm bow. Tighten by hammering the top, but use a piece of scrap wood under the hammer or mallet. Put supports under the arm bow to resist the shock at the holes. It will help to pencil on the

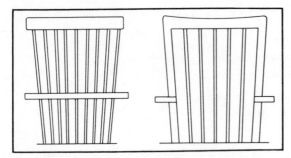

Fig. 11-26. Alternative Windsor chair back details.

loop to show where the surface of the arms should be when the ends are fully in the holes. Getting these two joints tight is important.

Materials List for Hoop Back Armchair

1 seat	20×20×1½
4 legs	1¾×21×1¾
3 rails	1½×20×1½
1 hoop	1¼×46×1¼
1 arm bow	1¼×46×1¼
2 arm supports	4×12×1½
8 sticks	½×24× round rods
8 sticks	½×12×round rods

OTHER WINDSOR CHAIR FEATURES

Although the hoop or loop back is characteristic of most Windsor chairs, it may still be given that name if the spindles go up to a shaped top (Fig. 11-26). The outer supports may be round or square and notched into the arm bow. There can be spindles all round or spindles with a central flat splat.

This type with cabriole front legs is a Queen Anne Windsor chair. The rear legs may be plain cylindrical ones, and the bottom rails are as described next.

An arrangement of rails with a curved front one joined to the back legs with short pieces (Fig. 11-27A) is peculiar to Windsor chairs. The rails are *crinoline rails,* presumably because of the clearance for a crinoline skirt. A problem in construction is making the curved rail. The curved rail should be solid and round in section, so it can be turned first and steamed to bend round a former (Fig. 11-27B). Make it with a near parallel part extending each side of the joints to the short pieces, so there is enough wood there for drilling without weakening the wood.

A comb back chair is made with a raised headrest. There can be a loop back or a shaped top, arranged so the middle set of spindles go through it to another top above (Fig. 11-28A).

Arm supports may be turned to match the legs (Fig. 11-28B). Some of these are made with elaborate designs, including bulbous parts. That should not be overdone, or the support may press into the sides of the user.

Plain spindles or sticks are common in Windsor chairs, but there can be turned pieces. There are examples where splats are substituted for sticks. There can be a central wide splat, other narrower ones of a similar style each side of it, and then short ones under the arms.

A chair only made as high as the arm bow may be called a low-backed Windsor chair. Chairs of this type

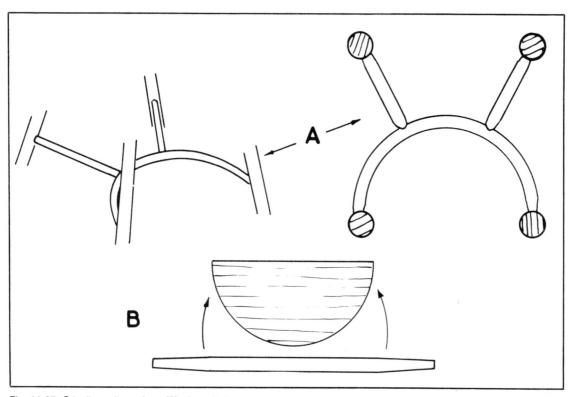

Fig. 11-27. Crinoline rails under a Windsor chair.

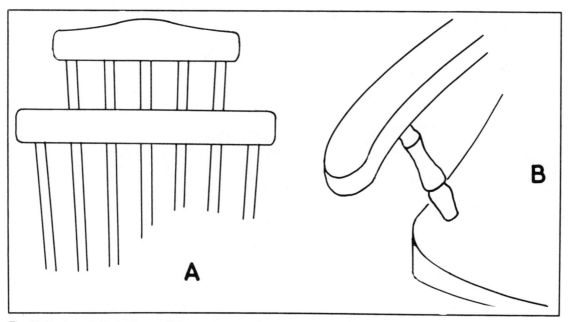

Fig. 11-28. A comb back (A) extends above the main back. Arm supports (B) may be turned.

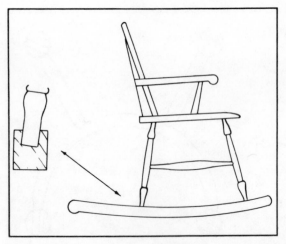

Fig. 11-29. Rocking versions of Windsor chairs are uncommon, but they can be made.

were made by early immigrants. Some of these chairs had a central group of sticks carried up to a narrow top to form a version of a comb back.

Chairs have also been made without the arm bow, but with the back loop brought down to bend outward and form arms. This involves bending in two directions and may be regarded as a test of skill, but there are construc-tional strength problems in the way this assembly is supported. Chairs of this sort were made in New England.

Side chairs were made in a similar way to the first one described in this chapter, but with higher backs, more spindles, and struts behind. Armchairs to match were made in the same way, but with thicker outside spindles into which they were tenoned.

Although most chairs have parallel sticks, and these are certainly most convenient for making with prepared dowel rods, some old chairs have tapered rods that are smaller at the top. With an arm bow, the rods are parallel to above the bow, then they taper to the loop. This is aesthetically pleasing, but involves more work and should not be taken too far or the back will be weakened.

Almost any chair can be made into a rocker. There is no evidence of this being done with Windsor chairs in England, although some New England versions are rockers. If you want to make a Windsor rocking chair, do not flare the legs to the side quite as much as normal. There can still be some slope. Make the rockers so they project forward of the front legs slightly, but carry the curve some way behind the rear legs. A projecting knob at the back will limit movement (Fig. 11-29). Drill for the legs into the rockers, so these pieces will be upright in use. Glue and wedge the joints.

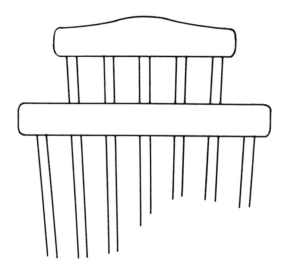

Glossary

The language of furniture includes an extremely large number of words. Not all the terms are currently in use, but you may encounter them when reading about furniture made by the great cabinetmakers. The words listed here are related to tables and chairs and may be found in the descriptions of these pieces of furniture. Nearly all words are in use today. The explanations give the interpretations that apply to modern furniture, although some of the funiture may be reproductions of earlier styles.

alburnum—The botanical name of sapwood.

anchor block—Wooden block screwed to the inside of a table rail or skirting. The top is then screwed to the block.

annular rings—The concentric rings which form the grain of a tree. One ring is added each year.

annulet—A turned raised bead around a cylindrical part.

apron—A piece of wood below a drawer, which may be carved or have its lower edge decorated by shaping.

arbor—In lathework, a turned rod for holding hollow work.

arch back—An armchair where the arms continue at the back to make an arch, as in some Windsor chairs.

arm bow—Continuous arm of a Windsor chair, where one piece goes around the back and forms both arms.

arris—The line or sharp edge between two flat or plane surfaces.

astragal—A raised molding or bead on a flat surface.

auger—A long drill with its own handle for deep drilling.

autumn growth—Part of an annual ring in a tree. It is formed by descending sap.

back flap hinge—A hinge designed to swing further back than a normal hinge. Its particular use is under a drop leaf on a table.

bail—A swinging loop handle.

ball and claw—Furniture foot carved to represent the claw of a bird or animal holding a ball.

ball foot—A round or elliptical ball on the bottom of a leg.

bamboo—Cane that is sometimes used for furniture. Bamboo differs from ordinary wood in that as it grows, new wood is formed on the inside of a tube.

banding—A strip of inlay laid around and usually parallel to the edge of a panel, such as a drawer front or tabletop.

barefaced tenon—A tenon shouldered on one side only.

baroque—Highly ornamented furniture style of the seventeenth century. Patterns were exaggerated.

base—The foundation of anything or the main bottom portion of an assembly.

batten—Any narrow strip of wood or a strip fitted across boards to join them, cover a gap, or prevent warping.

batten board—Material similar to thick plywood, but with broad pieces of solid wood forming the core. It is also called blockboard.

batting—A cotton padding material for upholstery.

bead—Ring of curved cross section on turned work.

beaumontage—A stopping for covering sunk nailheads or filling small cracks.

bench stop—A wood or metal stop on a bench top. Wood can be pressed against it to prevent sliding when planing.

bevel—An angle or chamfer planed on an edge. Also, it is the name of an adjustable tool for marking and testing angles.

bias—Cloth cut diagonally to the weave.

blind—Not right through. It is a stopped hole for a dowel or a mortise for a short tenon.

blind nailing or screwing—Driving a nail or screw in a rabbet or elsewhere so that its head will be covered by another part.

blockboard—Alternative name for batten board.

block foot—The square end of a furniture leg without a shaped foot.

bobtail—A tongue projecting from the rear of some Windsor chair seats to take the ends of two supporting spindles.

Boston rocker—A version of a rocking Windsor chair. The rear of the seat is raised where it is bored for the spindles.

bottom band—Lower part of upholstery across front of seat. It is also called a bottom border.

bow back—A chair back with a curved bow and spindles enclosed in it, but not necessarily an arched back.

bow saw—A small frame saw for cutting curves.

box ottoman—Padded seat arranged as the lid of a storage box.

bracket—An angular piece used particularly to support a shelf or flap.

bullnose plane— A plane with its cutting edge very close to the front of the body. Usually the edge is the full width of the body for getting close into the end of a stopped rabbet.

bun foot—A ball foot on a leg, flattened at top and bottom.

burlap—Coarse-weave jute cloth used in upholstery. It is also called hessian.

button—Round or shaped disc used on twine through upholstery for appearance and for retaining stuffing.

buttoning—Securing upholstery with buttons and twine. Deep buttoning draws the buttons into the upholstery to create a pattern.

cabriole hammer—An upholsterer's hammer with a small diameter face to its head for getting into confined spaces.

cabriole leg—Leg given a flourish so that it curves out from a corner in a stylized manner, like an animal's leg. It usually is given a ball foot.

calipers—Tools for measuring or comparing diameters. They may be for inside or outside curves.

cast—Twisting of a surface that should be flat.

caul—A press for holding veneer to its backing while the glue sets.

chaise lounge—Long low chair with leg supports.

chamfer—An angle or bevel planed on an edge.

channel-back chair—Chair with back padding arranged in upright tubes.

check—A lengthwise separation of the grain in a piece of wood.

chipboard—Board made of wood particles embedded in a plastic resin. It is also called particle board.

chuck—Device for holding work, particularly round things that may be turned in a lathe, or drill bits.

clamp—A device for drawing things together used especially to pull glued joints together. Also, it is a piece of wood across a wide board to prevent warping.

cleat—A small piece joining other parts together; alternative name for a clamp across wood.

club foot—Leg with an enlarged end.

column—In furniture, a pillar or post which may be turned and fluted or reeded.

comb—An undulating edge found particularly on a chair back.

comb back—Style of Windsor chair in which some spindles extend above the main back to form a headrest.

comb joint—A corner joint between boards, with parallel fingers on each part fitting between those of the other part. It is also called a finger joint.

contact adhesive—An impact adhesive that adheres as soon as parts are brought together, so movement for adjustment is impossible.

corner block—Triangular block set into the angle of a joint for support. It is sometimes called a bracket.

cotton—Natural material woven in many ways for upholstery covering and loosely compounded for stuffing.

cotton batting—Upholstery padding material.

couch—Alternative name for a sofa.

counterbore—Set the head of a screw below the surface of the wood. The hole is then closed with a glued plug.

countersink—Bevel the top of a hole so the screwhead can be driven level with the surface.

cross-lap joint—Two pieces cut to fit into each other where they cross.

crow's nest—In a tilt-top table, the assembly that connects the top to the pedestal, usually consisting of two squares connected by four pillars, and allows the top to tilt and turn. It is also called a squirrel cage.

dado—A groove in wood cut across the surface to support the end of a shelf or receive an inlay or molding.

dead pin—A wedge.

deal—Trade name for some softwoods, such as pine or fir, but now less commonly used. It may also mean a plank or board.

deciduous—Leaf-shedding tree and the source of most hardwoods.

divan—Sofa for use as a bed, or a bed upholstered in the same way as a seat.

dovetail—The fan-shaped piece that projects between pins in the other part of a dovetail joint. It is cut to resist pulling out.

dowel—A cylindrical piece of wood that is particularly used as a peg when making joints.

down—Feathers from the breast of a duck that are used in cushions.

draw bore or draw pin—A peg or dowel across a mortise and tenon joint to draw the parts together.

draw-leaf table—Extension table in which the leaves stow under the main top and may be pulled out on extending arms.

drop leaf—A flap to swing down at the edge of a tabletop and which can be supported when raised to increase the top area.

Dutch foot—A turned tapered leg finishing in a foot extending outward.

eiderdown—The best upholstery feather filling. It is from the breast of the eider duck.

ellipse—The inclined transverse section of a cylinder or cone.

face marks—Pencil marks put on the first planed side and edge of wood to indicate that further measuring and marking should be made from them.

faceplate—Circular plate to screw on the mandrel nose of a lathe to hold work of large diameter.

facet—Narrow band between the flutes of a column.

facing—In upholstery, a flat surface, usually wood, covered with fabric.

fastenings (fasteners)—Collective names for anything used for joining, such as nails and screws.

featheredge—A wide smooth bevel taking the edge of a board to a very thin line.

felt—Loose strands made into a pad for upholstery.

ferrule—A metal tube around a tool handle to prevent splitting when the tang of a tool is driven in.

fiber rush—Manufactured alternative to natural rush for seating.

fillet—A narrow strip of wood used to fill or support a part.

fillister—A rabbet plane with fences to control depth and width of cut. It is sometimes confused with a plow, which may have a similar appearance, but is used for cutting grooves.

finger joint—Joint between two boards made by cutting alternate parallel projections that fit into cutouts on the other piece. It may be used to make wood hinges for table supports and similar purposes. It is also called a comb joint.

fireside chair—Alternative name for a lounge chair, usually with upholstered back and seat, but wood arms.

firmer chisel—A strong general-purpose chisel with square or bevel edges.

flock—Reused wool from rags and used as upholstery stuffing.

flounce—Hanging cloth border below the edge of a chair.

fluting—Rounding grooves that are the reverse of beads.

fly—Piece of cloth sewed to another, usually as an extension of upholstery covering, and usually in place where it will not show.

foam—General name for plastic and rubber spongelike upholstery filling.

folding leaf—Table leaf finished on both sides so it will lie flat on the main top to provide a different surface, as in some card tables.

folding wedges—Two similar wedges that are used overlapping each other so they provide pressure when driven.

fox edging—Roll of stuffing material used at the edge of an upholstered seat.

foxtail wedges—Wedges in the end of a tenon so that it is spread when driven into a blind mortise.

frame construction—Building furniture with strips of wood to form the carcass with spaces filled by panels.

frame saw—A narrow saw blade tensioned in a frame.

French polish—Shellac finish for wood.

fretwork—Pierced work cut with a very fine fretsaw.

gateleg table—A table with drop flaps or leaves that can be held up by swinging legs that open like gates.

gauge—A marking tool or means of testing. Also, it is the thickness of sheet metal or the diameters of wires and screws by number according to recognized systems.

gimp—Prepared decorative strip to cover cloth edges in upholstery.

gimp pins—Thin, usually black nails intended for attaching gimp.

gouge—A chisel curved in cross section.

grain—The striped marking seen in wood due to the annual rings.

groove—Any slot in wood, such as a dado. It is less commonly a rabbet.

groundwork—The base surface to which veneer is applied.

haft—The handle of a tool, particularly a long one.

halving joint—Two crossing pieces notched to fit into each other, usually to make their surfaces level.

handed—Made in pairs.

hand screw—A wooden clamp, usually with the screw made of wood.

haunch—A short part of a tenon where it goes into another part at its end.

headstock—The driving end of a lathe.

heart back—Heart-shaped chair back, also called a shield back, and used by Hepplewhite.

heartwood—The mature wood near the center of a tree.

hessian—Alternative name for burlap.

hide—Leather from cow.

hoop back—A Windsor chair back where there is an upper rail of bent wood with its ends connected to the back bow.

housing joint—A joint for a shelf or similar thing where the shelf fits into a groove cut across the other part. It is also called a dado joint.

impact adhesive—Alternative name for contact adhesive.

inlaying—Setting one piece of wood in another. It can either be solid wood or veneer.

jigsaw—Small power saw with a projecting slim blade to thread through a hole and cut interior shapes.

jointing—The making of any joint, but particularly planing edges straight to make close-glued joints to build up a width.

kapok—Vegetable fiber stuffing material that is buoyant and has been used for upholstery, particularly on boats but superseded by close-cell plastic foam.

kerf—The slot made by a saw.

knot—A flaw in wood due to where a branch left the trunk. The method of joining cords.

knuckle—The pivot part of a hinge.

knuckle end—A carved end to an arm of a chair with an appearance like clenched fingers.

lacquer—A transparent varnish. Traditionally, it was a brushed finish on gilded work, but now it is more often a sprayed finish.

ladder-back—A chair back with several cross members between uprights.

laminate—Construct in layers with several pieces of wood glued together—used particularly to make curved parts.

laminboard—Material something like thick plywood, but with narrow strips of wood forming the core.

lap joint—The general name for several types of joint in which one piece of wood overlaps and fits into another.

latex—Foam rubber.

laying out—Setting out the details of design and construction, usually full-size.

leaf—Part of a tabletop that may be hinged to swing down or be arranged to slide out.

lock knot—Upholstery twine knot that can be adjusted and locked.

loop back—Windsor chair back with continuous side and top rail, joined into the seat at both ends.

lounge chair—Lightly upholstered chair, usually with padded seat and back, but plain wooden arms. Also, it is a fireside chair.

love seat—Chair for two.

mallet—Wood, hide, or plastic hammerlike hitting tool.

mandrel—The headstock or tailstock spindle of a lathe. It is also a turned rod, also called arbor, for holding hollow work being turned.

marking out—Marking cuts and positions on wood before cutting, shaping, and drilling.

marquetry—A system of inlaying that uses many woods to produce a pattern or picture. It may be solid wood or veneer.

medullary rays—Radiating lines from the center of a log, which can be seen in some woods radially cut. They are invisible in others. The markings are most prominent in figured oak.

melon foot—Large bulbous turned foot.

miter—A joint where the meeting angle of the surfaces is divided or bisected, as in the corner of a picture frame.

miter box or board—Guide for the saw when cutting miters.

miter square—A testing tool similar to a try square, but with the blade at 45°.

molding—Decorative edge or border which may be a simple rounding or an intricate section of curves and quirks. Many moldings are used in architecture as well as cabinetwork.

morocco—Leather from goat skin.

mortise—The rectangular socket cut to take a tenon.

mortise and tenon joint—A method of joining the end of one piece of wood into the side of another, with the tenon projecting like a tongue on the end to fit into the mortise cut in the other piece.

muslin—Open-weave cotton cloth used to cover the stuffing in upholstery.

Naughahyde—Trade name for a vinyl material used in upholstery.

necking—Turned bead on the upper part of a pillar, pedestal, or finial.

needle-leaf tree—Alternative name for cone-bearing trees that produce softwoods.

nosing—Semicircular molding.

ogee molding—A molding with a convex curve above a concave one. It is named from the likeness of its section to a combination of the letters O and G.

oil polish—A finishing treatment usually based on linseed oil.

oil slip—A shaped oilstone to use on the inside curves of gouges and carving tools.

oil stain—Wood coloring with the pigment dissolved in oil.

oilstone—A sharpening stone for edge tools that is used with thin oil. It may be called a whetstone.

onion foot—A squat version of a ball foot.

orbital sander—A power sander in which a flat sanding pad makes small orbital movements very rapidly. It is used for finish sanding.

ottoman—Padded long seat without back or sides.

ovalo—Classic quarter circle or ellipse molding.

overstuffing—Older name for upholstery.

padding—The covering material used above stuffing in upholstery to provide softening between it and the outside fabric.

parquetry—Wood block flooring laid in geometric designs. It is not to be confused with marquetry.

particle board—Board made of wood chips in plastic resin. It is also called chipboard.

patina—Surface texture that is particularly due to old age.

pedestal—A supporting post. Also, it is a central support for a table or a support at each of its ends.

pedestal table—A table with a central support and spreading feet.

pegging—Dowels or wooden pegs through joints.

period style—A design from earlier days without being specific.

picking—Adjusting upholstery stuffing.

piercing—Decoration made by cutting through the wood, as in the splat of a chair back. It is similar to fretwork, but more robust.

pilaster—A part column.

pillowback chair—Chair with the main upholstery of the back in the form of a cushion.

pilot hole—A small hole drilled as a guide for the drill point before making a larger hole.

pintle—A dowel or peg on which a part pivots. The name is taken from the pivot of a boat rudder.

piping—Cord in cloth sewed into a seam of upholstery covering.

platform—In upholstery, the center area of a seat.

pleat—Folded and creased fabric over an edge.

plow (plough)—A plane for cutting grooves, with guides to control depth and distance from an edge. The traditional type has a general appearance similar to a fillister, with which it may be confused.

plywood—Board made with veneers glued in laminations with the grain of each layer at right angles to the next. Normally, there are an odd number of veneers, so outside grains are the same way.

polyester—Plastic used as foam padding filling.

PVC—Polyvinyl chloride.

quartered (quarter-sawed)—Boards cut radially from a log to minimize warping and shrinking or to show the medullary rays in oak and some other woods.

Queen Anne legs—Period style of cabriole legs.

quirk—A narrow or V-shaped groove beside a bead, or the whole bead when worked to form part of a cover or disguise for a joint. Also, it is a raised or flat part between patterns in turned work.

rabbet—Angular cutout section as in the back of a picture frame.

rail—A horizontal member in framing.

rake—Incline to horizontal.

rawhide mallet—Mallet made with rolled leather head.

rayon—Synthetic fiber made from cellulose.

ripping chisel—An upholsterer's tool for removing tacks.

rod—Strip of wood with distances marked on it to use for comparing parts instead of measuring with a rule.

rod back—Type of Windsor chair with many spindles and the arms joined to back spindles.

rolled arm—The arm of a chair shaped for comfort and the front finished in a scroll.

roll edging—Alternative name for fox edging.

router—Power or hand tool for leveling the bottom of a groove or recessed surface.

rule—Measuring rod.

rule joint—Molded joint used between a tabletop and its drop flap and used with a backflap hinge. It is named from its similarity in section to the joint of a twofold rule.

run—In a long length. Lumber can be quoted as so many feet run.

rush—Marsh plant that is dried and used to weave seating.

saddling—Scooping a wooden chair seat to a comfortable shape.

sapwood—The wood nearer the outside of a tree. It is not as strong or durable as the heartwood in most trees.

sawbuck—Crossed sawing trestle. The name can be applied to table legs crossed in a similar way.

scrim—Open-weave cloth used to cover chair stuffing.

seagrass—Rope made of grass and woven into chair seating.

secret dovetail joint—Joint in which the dovetails are hidden by mitered parts cut outside them.

segments—Curved pieces of wood used to build up table rails and similar things in round work.

set—To punch a nail below the surface; the tool for doing that work. Also, it is the bending of saw teeth in opposite directions to produce a kerf wider than the thickness of the saw metal.

settee—Alternative name for sofa.

setting out—Laying out details of a piece of furniture or part of it.

shake—A defect or crack that occurs in the growing tree, but may not be found until it is cut into boards.

shield back—A chair back in the shape of a shield with a large openwork central design.

shooting board—A holding device for wood while having its edge planed.

shot joint—Planed edges glued together.

shoulder piece—An extra bracket at the top of a leg extending under a rail or framing. It is also called a wing.

side chair—A small chair without arms; a dining chair.

skew chisel—A chisel with its cutting edge not square to its sides. It is used for turning.

skewer—Large pin with an eye end used for temporarily holding cloth during upholstery.

slat—Narrow thin wood, usually horizontal, as across the back of a ladder-back chair.

slip—A shaped small oilstone for sharpening inside the curve of a gouge or similar tool.

slip seat—Loose seat, upholstered separately from the chair into which it fits.

sofa—Seat with back and arms to accommodate three or more people.

Spanish windlass—A method of twisting rope with a lever to give a clamping action.

spindle—Rounded slender part, usually vertical, as in a chair back.

spindle turning—Turning wood in a lathe between the headstock and tailstock centers to distinguish it from faceplate turning.

spirit stain—Wood coloring in which the pigment is dissolved in alcohol.

splat—Central upright in a chair back. It is usually decorated by shaping, piercing, or carving.

splay—To spread out.

spline—A narrow strip of wood fitting into grooves usually to strengthen two meeting faces that are glued.

squirrel cage—Another name for crow's nest.

staple—Two-ended nail. Also, it is a two-legged fastener driven by a special tool and used instead of tacks for attaching cloth.

stay tacking—Temporary tacking in upholstery.

stile—Vertical member in chair framing. It is a rear chair leg that continues up to form part of the back.

stopped—Not carried through, as in a stopped chamfer or rabbet.

stretcher—A lengthwise rail between the lower parts of a chair or table.

stripping—Removing old upholstery from a frame; the chemical removal of a finish from woodwork.

stuffing—The filling material in upholstery; the action of fitting it.

suite—Set of matching furniture.

tack—Tapered nail or temporary sewing stitch.

tang—The tapered end of a tool to fit into its handle.

template—Shaped pattern to draw around when marking out parts.

tenon—The projecting tongue on the end of one piece of wood to fit into a mortise in another piece of wood.

tension spring—Long coil spring used as support under cushions.

throw pillow—Individual pillow that is not intended for a particular place. It is also called a scatter cushion.

thumb plane—Any very small plane.

tote—A handle, particularly on a plane.

trestle—A strong stool to provide a lower working surface than a bench. Also, it is a cross-leg arrangement of table support or a sawbuck.

trunnel (treenail)—Peg or dowel driven through a joint.

tusk tenon—A tenon projecting through a mortise and held to it with a wedge.

twine—General name for the thin string or stout thread used in upholstery.

underbracing—Arrangement of rails and stretchers to provide stiffness between the lower parts of chair or table legs. It is also called underframing.

underslung—A drawer hung from its top edges instead of having its bottom edges on runners.

varnish—A near transparent paintlike finish once made from natural lacs, but now usually synthetic.

veneer—Thin piece of wood, usually of a decorative type and intended to be glued to a backing. Knife-cut veneer is very thin and cut with a knife from a rotating log. Saw-cut veneer is slightly thicker.

veneer hammer—Tool for pressing down veneer being glued. It is not a hammer.

veneer pin—Very fine nail with a small head.

vinyl—Plastic upholstery covering material.

wadding—Alternative name for cotton batting.

waney edge—The edge of a board that still has bark on it or is still showing the pattern of the outside of the tree.

warp—The lengthwise strands in woven cloth.

warping—Distortion of a board by twisting or curving because of unequal shrinkage as moisture dries out.

water stain—Wood coloring in which the pigment is dissolved in water.

wax polish—A finishing treatment based on beeswax and other waxes.

webbing—Straplike strip made from flax, hemp, cotton, or jute and interwoven beneath upholstery.

webbing stretcher—Tool for tensioning webbing.

web pincers—Upholstery pincers with wide jaws.

weft—The crosswise strands in woven cloth.

winding—A board or assembly is said to be in winding when it is not flat, and a twist can be seen when sighting from one end.

Windsor—General name for a style of chair with bentwood back frame and spindles, with a solid wood seat and legs socketed into it.

wing—Side headrest on a high chair back. Also, it is the shoulder piece at the top of a cabriole leg.

working drawing—The drawing showing elevations, plan, and sections from which measurements can be taken to make the furniture. It is not a pictorial view.

writing arm—Extension on the side of a chair arm to provide a surface for writing on.

Index

Edited by Robert Ostrander